AMERICAN DISRUPTOR

AMERICAN

DISRUPTOR

THE SCANDALOUS LIFE OF LELAND STANFORD

Roland De Wolk

 UNIVERSITY OF CALIFORNIA PRESS

University of California Press, one of the most distinguished
university presses in the United States, enriches lives around
the world by advancing scholarship in the humanities, social
sciences, and natural sciences. Its activities are supported by
the UC Press Foundation and by philanthropic contributions
from individuals and institutions. For more information, visit
www.ucpress.edu.

University of California Press
Oakland, California

Cataloging-in-Publication Data is on file at the Library of
Congress.

Names: De Wolk, Roland, 1953- author.
Title: American disruptor : the scandalous life of Leland
    Stanford / Roland De Wolk.
Description: Oakland, California : University of California
    Press, [2019] | Includes bibliographical references and index. |
Identifiers: LCCN 2019010307 (print) | LCCN 2019012914
    (ebook) | ISBN 9780520973565 (Epub) | ISBN
    9780520305472 (cloth : alk. paper) | ISBN 9780520973565
    (ebook)
Subjects: LCSH: Stanford, Leland, 1824–1893. | Governors—
    California—Biography. | Businesspeople—California—
    Biography. | Legislators—United States—Biography. |
    California—Politics and government—1850–1950.
Classification: LCC E664.S78 (ebook) | LCC E664.S78 D4 2019
    (print) | DDC 328.73/092 [B] —dc23
LC record available at https://lccn.loc.gov/2019010307

28   27   26   25   24   23   22   21   20   19
10   9   8   7   6   5   4   3   2   1

For Carlita, always

Such is the bitter taste of worldly power. Such are the correctives of glory.

—Winston Churchill

CONTENTS

Illustrations follow page 174.

ACKNOWLEDGMENTS

Thank you to my family, friends, and colleagues who pushed, goaded, and dared me as well as brainstormed with me, checked me, and just rolled their eyes when someone needed to:

First to my thermonuclear-powerful family: Carla Marinucci, Joseph De Wolk, and Antonio De Wolk. You guys are the central engine, fuel, and blessing of my life.

The James Brown of Bay Area journalism, Phil Matier, has been my most consistent, sharpest, and extraordinarily generous critic, fan, and counselor. And that's burying the lede: He is a true friend and solid ally, always in my corner. Thank you.

Longtime friend, author, journalist, and Teddy Kennedy imitator Jack Cheevers gets a special muchas gracias, as does brilliant, heart-of-oak friend Stefan Klocek. An extra debt of gratitude goes to stalwart bosom buddy Tony Thayer who helped sustain me with loyal friendship, cold beers, and pep talks. Garry Apgar, Adam Hochschild, Wendy Miller, Randy and Maureen Shandobil, Leonard Sellers, Teresa Drenick, Michele Kerr, and Stacy Finz all assisted me early and ably in many important ways.

A particularly wide and deep sense of gratitude goes to Professor Richard White of Stanford University's History Department who took time for me on more than one occasion, despite the constant pressures he faces from students, colleagues, and his own significant deadlines.

William Powers of the MIT Media Lab and Martha Sherrill, both noted journalists, authors, not to mention all-round quality human beings and brainiacs, took time and trouble to encourage me, warn me away from falling off the trapeze, and to find others who understood the importance of Leland Stanford and his role in the creation of Silicon Valley, as well as the significance of tech's effect on all our lives.

Noted author, reporter, and UC Berkeley comrade Don Lattin helped me connect with Reed Malcolm of the University of California Press. All he received in return was a sandwich and ginger beer. Stay cool, Don.

Reed Malcolm! deserves a very special thank you for being the consummate writer's editor who gets it, stays with it, and gets the best out his authors. He has that rare trait of being deeply informed while remaining perfectly tuned to the take-home message. In other words, he sees the forest and the trees with grace, ease, and natural ability.

A special deep bow to Julie Van Pelt, copyeditor extraordinaire. Any errors I have committed I have done on my own and despite her fastidious attention to accuracy, detail, and clarity. Eagle-eyed proofreader, Janine Baer, saved me from many embarrassments. The ones remaining are all my own.

Archna Patel, Peter Perez, Emilia Thiuri, and Tom Sullivan at UC Press are part of a mighty team that helped raise me up in so many different, crucial ways. I can only salute their talents, hard work, and integrity. Indexer Susan Storch has also been a crucial player in the completion of this work. Thank you all.

There are dozens of other professionals, coast–to–coast who have been critically important to the completion of this work.

LIBRARIES, HISTORICAL SOCIETIES, AND ARCHIVES

The Oakland Public Library circulation and reference staff; the Bancroft Library, UC Berkeley; the California State Library, with especial gratitude to the California History Room and Government Documents; California Historical Society, with especial gratitude to Frances Kaplan; Stanford Special Collections, with especial gratitude to Tim Noakes; James C. Scott, Librarian, Sacramento Public Library; Bryanna M. Ryan, curator of archives, Placer County Archive and Research Center, Placer County Museums; Michelle A. Krowl, Library of Congress; the Huntington Library, San Marino; San Francisco State University J. Paul Leonard Library; California State Railroad Museum Library; Dorothy Lazard in the Oakland Library History Room; Jacklyn Hoyt in the Special Collections Research Center, Syracuse University Libraries; Oakland Family Search Library, Oakland; Sharon Goetz and

Melissa Martin of the Mark Twain Papers, UC Berkeley; San Francisco Public Library Koshland History and Newspaper-Magazine rooms; Kelly C. Wallace, California Subject Specialist in the History and Genealogy Department of the Los Angeles Central Library; Council Bluffs Public Library; Alex Guilbert at the Center for Sacramento History; Marcia Eymann, Sacramento City Historian; Leigh Johnsen of the San Joaquin Historical Society and Center for Sacramento History; Anthony Opalka, Albany city historian; Douglas McCombs, Albany Institute; Jim Davies, reference librarian at Albany Library. Alice Kane and Rhonda R. McClure, New England Historic Genealogical Society; Oneida County Historical Society; everyone at the Port Washington Historical Society; Ozaukee County Historical Society; Ann Arbor Public Library; Doe Library, UC Berkeley; Margaret Whitehorn, Peg Brady and Shanna Dickson at the Cantor Art Center, Stanford University; U.S. Department of Treasury Public Information Office; California State Archives; California Society of Pioneers.

A note regarding virtual libraries and archives such as the HathiTrust, ArchiveGrid, Online Archives of California, Google Books, JSTOR, or the California Digital Newspaper Collection: I have used those and many more liberally, and modern scholarship would be infinitely the poorer without them. The idiosyncratic, interesting site run by the Central Pacific Railroad Photographic History Museum fits this category. All are wonderful online destinations and often excellent modern models for some of the equally wonderful, if sometimes still pleasantly mid-twentieth-century, collections listed above.

UNIVERSITY SCHOLARS

Michael Salerno, University of California Hastings College of the Law; David Carrillo, UC Berkeley School of Law and his two brilliant charges, Michael and David Belcher; Kerwin Klein, UC Berkeley (emeritus); Charles Egan, San Francisco State University; Bruce Cain, Stanford University; William Deverell, UC San Diego; Thomas Clark, Sacramento State University; Kathleen A. Cairns, Cal Poly, San Luis Obispo; Alex Filippenko, UC Berkeley; Frank Bajaras, California State University, Channel Islands; Peter Richardson, San Francisco State University; Richard Orsi, California State University, East Bay (emeritus); Timothy Greene, Cazenovia College; John Robert Greene, Cazenovia College.

INDEPENDENT SCHOLARS AND ASSORTED WISE PEOPLE

Kimberly Johnston-Dodds, independent scholar; Sarah Elizabeth Smith, MS, RPA, of Port Washington, Wisconsin; John McLaughlin, Silicon Valley Historical Association; Kevin Franklin, Town of Colonie historian; Wayne Dale Collins, scholar and lawyer; Richard E. Turley, author and Latter-day Saints public affairs manager; Peter Marschall, independent historian and all-things-Nevada aficionado.

PUBLIC OFFICIALS

Duncan Hay, National Park Service (NPS), Erie Canalway National Heritage Corridor historian; Hannah Blake, Erie Canal, NPS; Christopher Dalbeck, California State Parks senior aide; John Dingler, Army Corps of Engineers; Patrick Bernard, Colin Williams, Justin Pressfield, David John, Patrick Barnard, U.S. Geological Survey; Margaret (Peg) Reedy, agribusiness agent, Walworth County, Wisconsin; Chuck Ingels, farm and horticulture advisor, USDA Agricultural Extension, UC Davis; Alicia Clarke, National Oceanic and Atmospheric Administration; Jarrett Stedifor, custodian of records, Sacramento County Assessor's Office; David K. Ginsborg, Santa Clara County; Casey Hayden, director, Leland Stanford Mansion Historic Park and State Capitol Museum; Cathal Conneely, public information officer, California Supreme Court; Sara Schwartz Kendall, California State Parks at Coloma.

OTHER BOOK INDUSTRY FOLK

Harvey Klinger and Greg Aunapu.

EPILOGUE

A word or two of grateful acknowledgment to the past and present brilliant historians, writers, and especially those who have done both so well—abilities I reach for although they may well be beyond my grasp. As A. A. Milne wrote regarding Thomas Babington Macaulay in his introduction to my favorite edition of the great British historian's *History of England:* "He fostered that love of the great classical writers without which all study is barren and without durable impression."

PROLOGUE: FELL REDEMPTION

Spring at Leland Stanford Junior University is when the aloe, periwinkle, and rockrose begin to bloom. California buckeyes, India hawthorn, and Chinese fringe trees burst into flower. It's an extraordinarily pleasant pageant of life spread before prospective students from around the world, expecting, hoping—some praying—to be accepted for admission into the select society.

A twenty-one-year-old with a vague Russian accent was one of them in the spring of 1995. His family had fled Moscow when he was six and moved to Maryland. Having completed his undergraduate degree there, he wanted to go to graduate school at MIT but it rejected him. He would try the other end of the United States where opportunity has called millions, including the founder of Stanford University, who had also fled the East Coast when he, too, was young and discouraged.

As serendipitous history will have it, the twenty-one-year-old from Maryland via Moscow was introduced to a slightly older Stanford graduate student from Michigan. Each thinking the other obnoxious, they hit it off and eventually started talking about borrowing from the time-honored convention of academic citations—footnotes and endnotes—as a measure of relevance for the still untamed world of Web searches, which had quickly lost their way as "portals" to everything but speed and purpose. Using Stanford computers for test runs, they found it was an elegant, wicked fast way to use the Web for what they wanted: getting information.[1]

Although they argued incessantly, they finally agreed to register a domain name on September 15, 1997: Google.[2]

The birth of Google—of which Stanford University received 1.8 million shares of stock—was hardly the first time the Palo Alto school had helped issue revolution. A Stanford study in 2012 concluded that companies formed or run by Stanford entrepreneurs generate worldwide revenues of $2.7 trillion each year, and not just in the high-technology sector that has transformed the planet but also in medicine, music, finance, art, food, and clothing, among others.

The two Stanford professors heading the research project also concluded this phenomenon has been going on for generations: since the 1930s, Stanford people had created 5.4 million jobs and 39,900 companies that if gathered collectively into an independent nation creating almost $3 trillion annually, would make up the world's tenth largest economy.[3] And that's just for starters.

The origins of the Stanford campus and the Silicon Valley it has incubated, borne, and sustained could not have had a more unlikely birthplace: a frontier bar called the Bull's Head tavern in the backwoods of upper New York State.[4] The foundational person who began life there is known today as Leland Stanford, although as with so much of what is known of him, his name is only nominally and partially true.

When Facebook founder Mark Zuckerberg famously says "the biggest risk is not taking any risk. In a world that's changing really quickly, the only strategy that is guaranteed to fail is not taking risks," he is channeling Leland Stanford, who took ridiculous chance after chance and fell on his face time after time.[5] Tragedy and triumph were the staccato rhythms of his preposterous career and life.

Despite a rough beginning, a feckless youth, and a checkered manhood, Stanford became the head of the nation's biggest, most ambitious enterprise in America's young history, requiring a ferocious persistence that daunted almost everyone around him. It provided him authoritative agency, allowing him to amass multiple millions of dollars, employ thousands of workers, and create one of the first and most bitterly hated monopolies in U.S. history, outstripping America's more celebrated robber barons.

Stanford's ceaseless quest for political power met with crushing defeat time and again but finally and fortuitously allowed him to fall into high office with a critical left-handed assist from Abraham Lincoln. Leland Stanford then, in extraordinary but largely overlooked actions, fully exploited the positions of governor and, to a lesser extent, US senator to get what today would be billions of taxpayer dollars to make fortunes for himself and his notorious small band of business partners. By the time he was in his thirties, Stanford was living more ostentatiously than maharajas, building overwrought mansions, and acquiring vast tracts of land.

Not long afterward, however, the first of several government investigations commenced, prompting scandalous revelations of swindling the American people. Still, history also shows that the business Stanford pioneered was the foundation not only for Silicon Valley but for the modern corporation itself. What's more, his company incited what was among the first historic government attempts to regulate what soon became known at the combines, trusts, and monopolies, establishing precedents years before the more popularly known sanctions against Standard Oil or U.S. Steel. In fact, neither Rockefeller nor Carnegie would be household names today if not for the rail system Stanford was, in great part, responsible for. And even beyond that, Stanford's enterprise was largely what prompted a technology governing much of everyday life: the method by which almost everyone uses a clock around the world—the creation of universal time zones.

With his sybaritic life at an apex, the central calamity of his existence took place while on a grand tour of European art galleries and luxury resorts: his beloved fifteen-year-old son—an only child sired after eighteen years of barren marriage—died suddenly while Stanford and his wife sat helplessly by the boy's bedside, attended by the most expensive doctors on the Continent.

But Stanford had one last card to play. He and his underestimated wife, Jennie, created an extravagant memorial to the overwhelming heartbreak: Leland Stanford Junior University. Then the school, too, floundered, despite beginning with what appeared to be the single largest endowment of any university in American history. In fact, the entire enterprise teetered, almost failing and folding not long after its founding. When Leland Stanford Sr. died, leaving the university on the brink of closing, an examination of his personal estate found he had passed away just in time to avoid the indignity of bankruptcy.

He left his widow to fight the power of the U.S. government, which took her to the Supreme Court, charging Stanford with owing his fortune to the American public. With practical determination only a few had glimpsed beforehand, Jennie braced herself and found strength to turn the shipwreck into salvation. Then she died horrendously on a Hawaiian island. An in-depth, official medical inquest determined it was murder. A subsequent, sketchy probe paid for by the university administration did not. A modern investigation by no less than a Stanford University professor of medicine confirmed the homicide finding. Today there is clear evidence of a cover-up by the first, often revered, president of Stanford University.

Leland Stanford's singular story is that of a largely misunderstood and forgotten man, born in Jeffersonian America, when California seemed as distant as Saturn and when being able to read was less common than dying of tuberculosis or typhoid. The cotton gin was for early adopters in the primary business of America, farming. No one had yet even heard of a "tractor."

When Stanford was done with his work, his dominion had only begun. California was dressed and ready to become the leading economic, political, and cultural force of the nation. The world's economies were unknowingly headed for silicon switches the size of molecules that would serenely glide them into a postindustrial revolution. And the way virtually every man, woman, and child in the world would live would be altered permanently. All because of Leland Stanford's life.

Leland Stanford—namesake, unwitting godfather to the information economy and template to the center of the world's tech–driven economy and culture—to square the circle, is an American koan.

He was a direct descendant of iconic American origin but in essence was not much more than a country boy who made good. Indeed, toward the end of his life that was how he regarded himself.

Although throughout his years he exhibited all the characteristics of a ne'er-do-well, history also clearly demonstrates the man was made of more than just a little starch.

Although inherently a deeply conservative person in belief, deportment, and even dress, Stanford's life was one of almost unparalleled risk, failure, and reward.

Despite being a larger-than-life figure out of central casting, he was a cipher to his contemporaries and those few who later, vainly, tried to reveal his complex humanity.

Although he had many of the characteristics of an ordinary flimflam man, he headed one of the most astonishing accomplishments in American history, dwarfing those of Vanderbilt, Carnegie, and Rockefeller.

Even as Stanford projected the image of steadfast integrity he enmeshed himself in scandal after outrageous scandal.

He was a man who had it all but at the zenith of his life lost the sole something that meant everything to him.

And though he repeatedly suffered great desolation and even damnation in life, Leland Stanford—finally through his unassailable widow who had illusively appeared little more than an accessory through their more than four decades of marriage—found fell redemption as few have or will.

Best known for being the president of the enterprise that created an iron band—the transcontinental railroad—cinching together the United States just as the country stumbled broken and bleeding from its historically divisive Civil War, Stanford's legacy set the stage for the creation of a silicon chain binding not just the nation, but billions around the world. It would create a new scale of wealth and growing power unimagined just a generation past. It would put the components in motion for the center of a new global order of capitalism and culture: Stanford University and its most famous product, Silicon Valley.

Stanford University is more than this era's "it" school. It is the cynosure for today's postindustrial economy and culture, from the technology that runs the European bourse to the ubiquitous selfies on the streets of Singapore. It is the polestar for aspirational would-be leaders from Beijing to Cape Town. The ambitious in Mumbai, more than eight thousand miles from Palo Alto, or just thirty-five miles across San Francisco Bay on the torn streets of Oakland look to the barbered grounds of Stanford University as the path to all that glitters.

Although few may know it, the cultural and business genome for today's infamously disruptive, huckster, world-altering, ill-mannered, entrepreneurial technology traces directly back to this enigmatic, mythical man who very much—as a Frank Yerby poem has it about poet Percy Shelley—came clothed in common flesh.

Although there have been a handful of attempts to tell his astonishing story, they have largely relied on limited and capriciously collected bits and pieces of sometimes questionable data. *American Disruptor*, in unearthing many undiscovered primary documents as well as carefully examining hundreds of significant but ignored ones, meticulously puts together countless scattered but solid pieces of the puzzle that was Leland Stanford. The result is a sweeping portrait of this elemental American and his astonishing accomplishments and appalling failures that continue to directly and indirectly overthrow almost every aspect of our lives today.

CHAPTER I

Start-Up

At the tail end of another brutal eastern Wisconsin winter in 1852, the wind was whipping icy whitecaps off immense Lake Michigan into the frontier village of Port Washington. Brisk winds off the water are common in town, and gales can gust more than thirty miles an hour, with swells two stories high on the lake that is larger than the contiguous combination of New Hampshire, Massachusetts, and Rhode Island. Toward winter's end it seldom gets warmer than 45° Fahrenheit on that northern shore. Snow is common well into spring. In the predawn of that day it was probably closer to 25° Fahrenheit, making it difficult to stay warm in the simple plank houses clustered near the water. Many of the buildings in the settlement would have been of native white pine, a wood that is light, soft, and loves a flame.

As the little town slept, the fire broke out on the southwest corner of Canal and Franklin streets at 3:00 A.M. and "in a very few minutes," the local newspaper reported, "the flames . . . were beyond all control." In a little more than an hour the entire block was a "heap of ashes."[1] The wood frame building with a grocery store downstairs and Leland Stanford's office above burned quickly to the dirt street.

The doughty-appearing young man struggling to define himself beyond a reputation for slacking, ponderous speech, and an affinity for drink found his incipient legal practice among the cinders. Also cremated was a highly prized, costly collection of law books his father had given him for luck and fortune. Even worse, paperwork proving people owed him thousands of dollars—money he sorely needed—was destroyed. It was one of those moments when a man may be forged or sundered.

It was the capper of what might well have happened regardless of the flames. Business had fallen off steeply. The small lots of property Stanford had bought or taken in barter had depreciated so steeply he considered simply abandoning them. He was down more than a peg or two. Standing in the cold ashes along that massive northern lake, at this nadir of his young life, he followed his accustomed practice when the going got tough: he quit.[2]

His ancestors had not. For centuries they had struggled and persevered. Today the name has a brisk, clean, Anglo-Saxon sonance associated with privilege, affluence, and high station: Stanford. But six hundred to eight hundred years ago, when it likely took form, it would have signified a family at the very bottom of the social hierarchy. The clan would have belonged to a class, as historian Thomas Babington Macaulay put it, of "peasants degraded to the level of the swine and oxen which they tended."[3] From this, a strain of Stanfords emerged that would not endure the yoke imposed by the invaders and their heirs.

The soldiers from the province of Normandy who crossed the Channel in 1066 to conquer England had brought their fashion of surnames with them as they slaughtered at will and took the land wholesale. William and his victorious Plantagenets—a derivative of the Latin name for the appropriately invasive bush called French broom—were among a small but growing class of Gallic landowners beginning to take family names to help ensure their hereditary property claims. As the fashion, and later necessity, spread across England, those with French surnames marked themselves far apart from the great unwashed of the previous Saxon invaders five hundred years before them. Instead of being able to claim a name originating in Normandy, the peasantry had to adopt names referring to their occupations, kinship, place, or the topography of where they lived. *Stan* comes from the Old English/Saxon for "stone" and *Ford* from "river crossing."[4]

It was considered a "byname," and hardly able to help protect wealth, for there was likely little of that. And what little there was would have been taxed. From the thirteenth century on, the king's men began to record who paid, when they paid, and of course how much they paid. By the bloodstained reign of the Tudor dynasty, family names were required.

If the utility of a last name made harsh medieval existence a little easier for the crown to exact its due, even two hundred years later in the 1600s, everyday life for most of the then five million English remained a regular struggle to survive. Half the population died before age sixteen and few lived past sixty. Laws and cultural customs were feudal and oppressive. Civil and foreign wars and plagues were constants, especially under the notorious rule of King Charles I, who later found his head separated from his body by an executioner's axe. Getting meat on the table more than once a week was a luxury for most, and even then Britons were just starting to eat with forks and knives instead of just their hands. Toothbrushes were another emerging technology from China, with few early adopters. "In all this long, bleak intervening gap cold and dirt clung to the most fortunate and highest in the land," even Winston Churchill noted in his *Birth of Britain*.[5]

But some three thousand miles west promised a clean, sunlit shot at prosperity and property for those with pluck. It is here that Leland Stanford's first American ancestor enters the story.

Little is known of Thomas Stanford except that he crossed a forbidding ocean despite the frighteningly difficult two-month westward journey in a small, cramped wooden sailing ship. At the other end of the cold and capricious Atlantic he landed in the terrifyingly unknown vastness of North America.

Thomas Stanford arrived in Concord, Massachusetts, in 1644, just twenty-four years after the landing of the *Mayflower* and two years into the best known of England's recurrent civil wars.[6] Unlike for those pilgrims, who departed Britain largely because their religious orthodoxy conflicted with the dogmas of the then 134-year-old Church of England, the carnage of the Great Rebellion alone would have been enough to prompt Thomas's emigration.[7] The first Europeans entering the town of Concord arrived just nine years before Thomas Stanford. Those dozen English families found a land densely forested with chestnut oak, red cedar, and scrubby pitch pine. Wetlands dotted the area filled with all manner of tiny creatures feasting on human blood. The pilgrims bought some six square miles from the Native Algonquins, whom were said to be friendly.[8]

As if Thomas Stanford didn't already face astonishing odds, colonial records indicate that he was blind—there are two documented references to his sightlessness but none explaining how it came about or the suffering it must have inflicted.

Concord, of course, in 1775 would be the site of the first battle for independence and today is comfortably proud to call itself the birthplace of the American Revolution. More than one hundred years after a blind but determined Thomas Stanford lived in Concord, a great-grandson, Abner Stanford, served in the Continental Army as a corporal. His widow had to fight to get the small pension she was entitled to. Stanfords, whether by birth or by marriage, were accustomed to struggle.

Their son Lyman, still on the family quest for independence and room to grow, moved west again, to what was then the American outback seven miles north of Albany, New York. At the end of the revolutionary 1700s and the beginning of the tumultuous 1800s this new frontier, too, was choked with wild woods, abundant game, and clouds of mosquitoes during the torpid summer months. In the winter, a full yard of snow typically smothers the land, and the rivers and ponds and lakes freeze hard. Survivors would closely watch their larders, ensuring they and their surviving children would stay warm by burning the many cords of wood they had cut by hand, stacked and seasoned in the often stifling hot and humid summer months. Preserves of huckleberry, pigweed, and wild leeks known as ramp were put up for the long deep winter. Rabbit, grouse, and of course deer were hung, salted, smoked, and cured.

And there were beer and whiskey to keep a person warm and perhaps a little more fortified to face the dank, the cold, and the dark. Then, as today, true profit was made here.

Lyman Stanford—whose wife Betsey came from a family line including the surname Leland—ran the Bull's Head tavern on the Troy Road in what was then known as the village of Watervliet but would soon be absorbed by Albany. There is reason to believe he helped build the turnpike. It was sixteen miles long, one hundred feet across, with six-foot-wide footpaths on each side, all shaded by poplar trees and, most incredibly of all, said to be lit at night by silver lamps. Naturally, you had to pay a toll to use the thoroughfare. The road brought riches to those along it, although not as much as those who owned it. "It was a big thing at that time," reminisced Leland Stanford's oldest brother many years later. "That was a great event in those days."[9]

Lyman's son Josiah, in turn, inherited the inn. Before the inheritance, however, he went through a bad patch when he attempted to strike out on his own as a young man. Josiah tried starting up a farm but it failed and he lost everything. His first-born son, Josiah Jr., would never forget it, though he was very young when it happened. "I remember them taking the stock away. Then, of course, he went down in the world, and had to begin at the bottom," he recalled late in life.[10]

Josiah Sr.'s famous fifth child, not yet born, sought and found the same fate.

Albany's hardscrabble past is often marked beginning in 1624, when it established itself as a Dutch trading post. Albany's borders have changed many times during its many years as a city. Settled largely by immigrants from the Netherlands appreciating the rich farmlands of the Hudson Valley, it became the state capital in 1797.

Many found it delightful. A memoir by a French aristocrat who escaped her nation's slaughterhouse revolution of 1789 was written long after she and her family had decamped from hiding out for several years in and around Albany. Henriette Lucie, the Marquise de La Tour du Pin, found herself startled at first by passing Mohawk Indians walking "stark naked" down a road in the region. But from the start she also found herself arrested by the area's natural graces, writing sometime before her death in 1853.

> On the very day of our arrival in Albany, as we were walking in the evening down a long and lovely street, we came across some enclosed grounds, surrounded by a plain white fence. It was a well-tended park, planted with beautiful trees and flowers, and in it stood a pretty house, simple in style and with no outward pretentions to art or beauty.[11]

On the other hand, Yale University president Timothy Dwight damned the area after touring it in 1792, saying he found "the scenery remarkably dull and discouraging." He warmed to the topic, adding that "the appearances of these houses [are] ordinary, dull and disagreeable."[12] By 1804 he had visited again and although found the homes of Albany itself much improved, wrote of the region's buildings: "A great number of them were taverns; generally, however, of so wretched an appearance, as must, one would think, prevent the entrance of any traveler." Then, abandoning all pretense of charity, Dwight took a general swipe at the people of the area: "Early as it was, were gathered a number of persons from the neighbourhood; idling, and drinking away their time; rude in their appearance, and clownish in their manners."[13]

One of the local taverns was the Bull's Head, which Josiah Sr. inherited after Lyman Stanford passed away. Business began to prosper as westward movement gained momentum. As many as two thousand wagons would rumble past in a day after the trail had evolved into a hard-packed dirt and later macadam turnpike. Eventually there were thirty-five hotels along the Troy Road, one every half mile.

It was here, at the Bull's Head, the year when the White House was home to America's last founding father,[14] that on March 9, 1824, Elizabeth Phillips Stanford gave birth to a healthy baby boy she and her husband named Amasa Leland Stanford.

The choice of Amasa may seem, well into the twenty-first century, a little odd, especially since the name usually translates to hardship or burden. But it was not uncommon at the time. A cousin on his mother's side, whom his parents likely knew, was an Amasa, and the name has a tenuous biblical tie to the name Abner, Leland's great grandfather who fought in the War of Independence. One of the abundant begets of the Old Testament, Amasa was a less-than-favored nephew of the duplicitous warrior king David. The story says Amasa, in turn, joined a failed rebellion against his crafty uncle. King David, however, offered Amasa a rare second chance. But justice being what it is in the Old Book, Amasa soon fell by the sword of another treacherous rival. There is then no reason to wonder that by age twenty Amasa Stanford refused to use his given name for the rest of his life and instead took his more benign middle one, Leland, which derives from the Old English for meadowland.

He was the fifth of eight children, six of whom survived the not infrequently cruel frontier life into adulthood. Time was not measured in shifts, or days off. The work at the tavern could run deep into the night. And at the adjacent family farm it would begin at or before dawn and end at or shortly after dusk.

"We dug ditches and everything else that we were called upon to do without asking father if there was any money in sight," Leland's oldest brother Josiah Jr. recalled in 1889. There was no hired help and "no carpets on the floor." Josiah Jr. particularly remembered having to haul manure on the farm, though it smelled atrociously bad—especially the "slushy" waste. But the family considered it "so much richer." Josiah Jr. thought Leland a slacker, saying,

> I never called him a good worker as a boy. He did not take the interest in it that the rest of us did, and while we would be fixing our teams and tools, he would go around a corner . . . and when the time came to go to work we would have to call him; he did not care whether the work went on or not.[15]

Older brother Josiah added that his younger brother would, instead, rather open a book.

Although Leland liked reading more than manual labor, it also eventually became clear that his work ethic was questionable even in his studies. "He was, perhaps, a little impatient of purely scholastic methods," would be one of the kinder descriptions of Stanford many years later.[16] A late nineteenth-century San Francisco journalist, writing a flattering tribute to the by then celebrated Stanford, took a rare left turn and noted Stanford's performance in school as "rather dull."[17]

During the first half of the nineteenth century, the young nation was very much on the move. The western frontier, which had drawn the Stanfords first from England to America and then from New England to the Hudson River valley, was a powerful lure for tens of thousands. Pressure to absorb the rest of the North American continent into the United States was amplifying—the term Manifest Destiny began to be heard.

What is now called the Midwest was, until Leland Stanford's youth, difficult to reach because of the almost impassable Appalachian Mountains, running fifteen hundred miles from Alabama to Maine, one hundred to three hundred miles in breadth and up to three thousand feet in elevation. George Washington was among the first to recognize and address the concern that as the restless nation pushed over the Appalachians, it might break away from the young United States, especially with the Spanish, English, and French coveting the West. "The western settlers (I speak now from my own observations), stand, as it were, upon a pivot," Washington famously wrote in the autumn of 1784.[18]

As trails and then roads began to breach the Appalachian wilderness at gateways such as Cumberland Gap, another massive undertaking began to its north: the Erie Canal. This was a youthful, boisterous, independent nation confident it no longer had to fight its parent and instead could put its back into its own work. When Stanford was just twenty months old, when he would have been clambering to walk on his own and starting to put words together, what is still widely regarded as the greatest engineering feat of its time officially began operation. The Bull's Head was a five-minute stroll from the Erie Canal. Business was good.

Completed in 1825, the canal connected the Great Lakes to the Hudson River, and the Hudson, of course, empties its monumental payload into the Atlantic Ocean. Bolting the lakes to the Atlantic—which in effect connected the western Plains to the Eastern Seaboard—had profound, lasting consequences for the emerging nation. That such an audacious undertaking could actually take place quickened the bumptious belief that Americans were a can-do people. It was a remarkable accomplishment, especially considering the work was done with little more than shovels, axes, mules, and blasting powder through forests, swamps, shale, and limestone. The mostly male laborers, as well as some hardy females disguised as boys and men, were in large part the pariah immigrants of the day: Irish.[19] The canal effectively took Boston and Philadelphia out of the running as America's biggest city and bestowed that mixed honor on New York. The canal's effect on the Hudson River valley was particularly striking. Albany was not just growing, it was bursting. According to the U.S. Census, in 1800 there were a little more than 5,000 people living there, but by 1840 the population was more than 33,000. The canal not only opened the East to the Great Lakes and consequently the Midwest, it revolutionized commerce as it broke open the transportation chokehold that had restricted the adolescent nation that was pushing west. The pace of commerce greatly quickened, the cadence of American life briskly conforming.

For example, the opening of the canal reduced shipping time between Buffalo on Lake Erie and New York City from twenty to eight days. Freight costs plummeted from $100 to $5 a ton. And the project almost immediately started paying for itself. The Erie Canal cost some $17 million to build but soon was making $1 million annually in tolls. New York State financed the venture by selling bonds, which because of the success of the canal were paid back by 1837, well ahead of schedule. Naturally, there were some qualifications. Ice in the winter effectively shut down the canal to traffic, also freezing business.[20] Most of the traffic was commercial cargo, as passengers found the novelty of traveling the canal soon turned to monotony and returned to the stagecoaches that advanced with greater celerity.

Nevertheless, the canal's bestowal of bounty overcame most obstacles. As the jobs that came with building and running the canal created a significant new source of capital, merchants of all stripes were quick to come and exchange their goods for workers' money. Some were met with less enthusiasm than others by the good people of the region. "While a toll collector and his assistants examined a boat and its cargo," noted a canal historian, "the boat's crew and passengers visited neighboring stores and taverns."[21]

A letter written in 1843 lamented that "3 to 6 groceries, and all these for the benefit of the travelling public . . . Rum, Gin, Brandy, Wine, Beer, Cider, Bread, Milk, and Groceries meet the eye every few miles."[22] Watervliet, where

Leland Stanford's birthplace and childhood home, the Bull's Head tavern, prospered, was an epicenter of the lucre—and wantonness. The riverfront village not only had a national armory, it was also at the junction of the Champlain and Erie Canals. Furthermore, the township was the site of a handful of weigh and pay stations for canal traffic. It was also where the rowdy canal men got paid. Watervliet swiftly earned notoriety for being "a center of saloons, gambling and prostitution."[23]

Testimony before the state-created Canal Board in 1839 cemented the slander, speaking specifically to Watervliet's infamy: "The Boys who Drive the horses I think I may safely say that these boys are the most profain beings that now exist on the face of this hole erth without exception," one exasperated, if semiliterate, witness asserted.[24]

For the Stanfords, the canal changed everything. The waterway itself was no more than three hundred downhill yards from the Bull's Head tavern, which meant traffic, which meant money, which meant prosperity for the clan.

Then something never imagined roared up along the Erie just six years after the canal opened. It rolled into America signaling the most monumental change in human history since the Agricultural Revolution of 10,000 B.C.E.: the Industrial Revolution. Leland Stanford was turning eight years old. The force trundling through town profoundly disrupted how Stanford and his family conducted their lives and legacy. They could have called this primal machine Big Tech. But initially it was branded a Steam Wagon. When it screeched and squalled into already turbulent upper New York State, it jolted the entire economy, environment, and consequently, most everyone's life.

A locomotive in the early to mid-1800s typically weighed forty tons. One heavy horse weighs about one ton, or two thousand pounds. Rails were made of iron until the latter part of the century, when steel was found to have better wear and tear, was much less brittle, and pound for pound was far stronger. The first railcars could carry ten tons each of wheat, machinery, and livestock and, of course, people. The first locomotives had twelve-horsepower engines that could haul the cars four times faster than a horse's average gait of four miles per hour. And a train could run day and night, simply fed abundant timber or coal for fuel and requiring little downtime. Its metal and wood skin protected freight and passengers from ice storms, scorching heat, outlaws, or Native Americans trying to defend their ancestral homelands. If the dirt roads washed out, the rails would usually hold smooth and solid. Ice and snow were usually little worse than nuisances.

If success can be measured in part by powerful enemies, the railroad was a triumph even before the first rolling stock throttled down the brand-fresh iron tracks. Canal and steamboat forces joined with the Albany and Schenectady Turnpike Company to stop the Mohawk & Hudson Railroad, but they might as well have tried stopping the third law of thermodynamics. The M & H is widely recognized as the first chartered railroad in the nation.

And of course, there was the money—and the fight over it. The New York State Legislature at first required the railroad's stockholders and directors to be personally liable for all debts contracted by the company. It did not take long for that news to get downriver. The New York City financiers who were the majority investors in the enterprise balked, and after a two-year fight, won. Albany lawmakers amended the requirement to reduce Wall Street's liabilities, and the Mohawk & Hudson became the second railroad in America, after the Granite Railway in Massachusetts, to go into operation.

The first train soon began to roll the approximate fifteen miles between Albany and Schenectady. And, as with the Erie Canal, it almost immediately became prosperous. Records from the first year of operation reveal receipts of $16,319 and expenses of $7,477.13.[25] That left $8,842.66 in net earnings. This was a time when making $1 a day was decent money and a steak dinner at good New York City restaurants cost 25 cents. The railroad was the talk of the town.

There were engineering challenges. The train had to surmount a plateau of about three thousand feet while carrying about fourteen passengers on each car, or "coach." At first the locomotives did not always have the power for the ascent, so railroad men employed horses to haul the train up the steeper grades. Within months, however, engineers found the means to adequately harness the pitch-pine fuel energy firing the steam engines. Although that generated the necessary horsepower, there were other novel bugs in the cutting-edge technology.

There was "sufficient force to jerk the passengers who sat on seats across the top of the coaches, out from under their hats, and in stopping they came together with such force as to send them flying from their seats," recalled a passenger thirty-nine years after the train's first trip. The burning pitch pine from the locomotive sent up a "thick volume of black smoke strongly impregnated with sparks, coals and cinders," prompting passengers to shield themselves from this onslaught using their umbrellas—but the umbrellas burned to the frames. This caused a "general melee . . . each whipping his neighbor to put out the fire." When the ordeal was over, the passengers "presented a very motely appearance on arrival at the first station."[26]

The railroad drew crowds along the tracks, and not knowing the danger, people brought their horses defenselessly close. As the train approached, "the horses took fright and wheeled, upsetting buggies, carriages and wagons and leaving for parts unknown to the passenger if not their owners, and it is not now positively known if some of them have yet stopped."[27]

Who cared? To be near the train track was to be near money. To be near a railroad station was to be adjacent to prosperity. Coupled with the fortunes brought by the Erie Canal, the change wrought by the new technology can be seen in the Stanford family, as they eventually moved from above the tavern on the seamy river road into an affluent inland home framed with colonnades. Even the dullest could see that real money and power was in owning a railroad, not just being astride one. The railroad could not help but impress a young man such as Leland Stanford. He wrote to his family about the building of the railway near their land, expressing great interest in how much money they could make from being adjacent to the line.

In his teens, writing to one of his brothers, there is the first glimpse of his sharp attention to this development: "The settlement with the Rail Road Company is full as equitable as I expected; and on the whole if there is that to be made from the making it, which is stated as probably." Young Stanford's tormented prose suggests the new rail line had made a land deal that would likely affect his parents. "I think it will be no great injury; for I have an idea that there will yet be a store house built on the premises in consequence of the Rail Road; the advantages of which you will readily perceive if there is any." And then using a word reborn, if used rather too liberally, in Silicon Valley, he concluded: "Likely you will consider this as rather visionary but I am not exactly certain but that it is so myself."[28] *Visionary*, it might be noted, once denoted someone who was impractical or a woolgatherer. A flake, if you will.

The entire ecology of the Hudson River valley altered as workers began to clear-cut wide swaths of forest for fuel to drive the trains and make cheap coal, not to mention for building the flourishing number of homes, factories, and warehouses. And of course, there would be telegraph lines and railroad ties. In the not far away Catskills, the hills actually turned from dark blue to green after the indigenous hemlocks were first stripped of their bark for tanning, then the dead trees chopped down, naturally giving way to second-growth hardwoods.[29] Crucial wetlands were also often drained to provide water for the four-foot-deep Erie Canal, leaving what an early nineteenth-century visitor called "desolate confusion" and a twentieth-century historian termed "a ghostlike and disorderly cemetery."[30] In the nineteenth century this was considered the price of progress.

The abrupt realignments from an ancient agrarian way of life to an industrial-technological one had significant if unexpected ramifications for many ways of life. For example, the so-called Second Great Awakening—a religious frenzy of the first half of the 1800s—was so acute in and around Albany that the area was called the Burned-Over District, because the fury roared across the region like a wildfire.

There were the Shakers, for one, the popular name for the United Society of Believers who fled England and found themselves centered in Stanford's Watervliet by the late eighteenth century. This utopian, communal, and vegetarian group of men and women spent much of their Sundays dancing, prompting the nickname. They also called for, not incidentally, their members to remain celibate.[31]

There was also the Perfectionist Oneida movement, also utopian and communal but with at least one significant difference: it advocated "Free Love." Farther upriver, a young man named Joseph Smith said he had met an angel named Moroni, who had given—and later taken back—golden tablets that Smith said he transcribed and later called the Book of Mormon. Calling themselves Latter-day Saints, the Mormons fled west to avoid persecution. Smith was later killed by a mob in Illinois, in part because of his adherence to polygamy. The Saints then trekked farther west in search of their own Zion, where there would be new opportunities and problems, some involving Leland Stanford.[32]

And there was a preacher named William Miller, from a New England Baptist background, who held camp meetings where thousands subscribed to "Millerism," which prophesied that the second coming of Jesus would take place in 1844. Miller died greatly disappointed five years later.

There is no reason to suggest that Stanford, nominally Presbyterian, found himself much swayed by any of this. But a growing political upheaval did have some effect on the young man: a deepening unease regarding the enslavement of four million Americans in the South. New York State had outlawed slavery in 1827, when Stanford was three years old. Despite oldest son Josiah Jr.'s declaration that the family had no help, there is reason to believe that an African American couple named Freeman and Trueblood worked for the Stanfords.

The couple raised a large family during their years on the Stanford property, but they had to do so in a Stanford barn, relegated to living in a loft.[33]

The Underground Railroad, which rescued slaves from the South and brought them North, was particularly enterprising in the Hudson River valley and up into northern states and Canada. Slavery would underscore what next confronted Leland Stanford in the tumultuous environment in which he came of age. He was eighteen years old, with little or no formal education, and had no record of much accomplishment. In fact, his résumé for indolence and dubious distinction as a reader of books preceded his parents' decision to decree a drastic change in young Leland Stanford's life.

In this, however, he would struggle mightily—and fail pitifully.

CHAPTER 2

Everything Ventured

Sturdy and swarthy, full-grown Leland Stanford was an inch or so shy of six feet, weighed somewhat less than two hundred pounds, and like most men of his age before the patent application for the first official safety razor was made in 1880, would soon darken his features further with a full beard. People did not habitually pose for what was then called a daguerrean artist—a photographer—with a smile. Photography required long exposures for portraits, and holding a grin was not only unnatural and difficult, but the innovation not yet commonly called a camera was still considered far too serious to express amusement. Consequently, Leland Stanford, as did his contemporaries, appears humorless in what would become the first of his many portraits. On the other hand, there is little else to suggest he was often otherwise.

He was twenty-four when the image was taken. Several years earlier Leland Stanford's parents, likely prompted by his escapist reading or poor work habits—or both—removed their middle son from the temptations of the tavern and his failure to toil on the farm and consigned the young man to school. Unlike what they did with their other children, the Stanfords dispatched Leland to a country academy called the Oneida Institute of Science and Industry about one hundred miles northwest of home. The rules were simple and clearly drawn: in addition to daily study, the school required each student to contribute three hours of manual labor each day on the school farm.

Leland balked. He was just seventeen years old and already revealed an inconsonant cocktail of lethargy and enterprise, stubbornness and opportunism. The teenager may not have even unpacked his bags the night he arrived at the school. He wrote his father that he "saw one of the teachers and he informed me that it was a thorough abolitionist school. And he said that the whites and blacks ate at one table."[1] Leland added that the teacher also praised another school seven miles away as more worthy. It, not irrelevantly, had no requirement that students undertake any manual work, much less three hours daily. So the next morning, young Leland took off for the Clinton Liberal Institute, a place for general studies in the town of Clinton, New York. It is not clear how long he stayed there. It is free from doubt that he left no lasting mark. He may have remained for two or three years or abandoned his studies and returned between 1841 and 1843. One way or the other, he also quit that course of study and in January of 1844 enrolled at still another school, the Cazenovia Seminary, just thirty miles west. Despite being called a seminary— today it is called Cazenovia College—it was a liberal arts school and not a place to prepare for the cloth, although the Methodists who conducted the school did ensure there was an unmistakable religious aspect to the curriculum. He lasted just one year and then dropped out—or was expelled—again. Leland Stanford was done with studies for good.

There is, of course, manifest irony in the fact that the founder of what is now one of the world's great universities never graduated from any college or even secondary school. Much later in life Stanford gave Cazenovia a life-sized oil portrait of himself. Professionally restored and in an astonishingly gilded frame, today it hangs just outside the college president's office. There is no record of any other Stanford gift to any of the three institutions he briefly attended.

There are a handful of his letters home from these troubled years. Leland's teenage scribblings revolved around the prosaic, puerile preoccupations of young men away from home for the first time and at school: girls (letters to his brothers) and the need for more money (letters to his father). He also wrote about a growing interest in politics, the American political theater being as contentious and tumultuous during the 1844 presidential election as any. The Democrats were splintering, as was the rest of the nation, over slavery. Moreover, pressure to absorb the rest of the North American continent into the United States was amplifying. The term Manifest Destiny would no longer be heard just here and there; it would begin to show up as a national credo in magazines the next year.[2]

As America stepped across the threshold of the Industrial Revolution during the first half of the 1800s, the ancient definitions of hard, honest labor began to take on new meaning. Why try to navigate a three-mast sailboat up a tempestuous river when you could have horses haul a simple flat-bottomed barge up a tame canal? Why haul wagons using teams of livestock when you could get more done, faster, and at far greater profit with a locomotive and coaches on rails? Why subject yourself to hard physical work that often led to injuries, pain, and premature old age when you could work in an office? These lessons would seep and steep in young men of Leland Stanford's generation, forever changing the way Americans would regard the world.

Leland Stanford was coming of age at the same time as America. Some have called it the Age of Jackson, Andrew Jackson being president of the United States for much of the period. He has been idolized as the first original American voice in the White House and demonized as a genocidal white supremacist. He was arguably both. Regardless, his political message was to do battle against the wealthy, privileged class he warned was taking control of the young nation. Although recently emancipated from feudal Great Britain, America, he declared, was in danger of becoming what it had fought against for independence—a virtual aristocracy through plutocracy. Jackson was a self-made man, considered a war hero and the first president born in what was then the American West: the Carolinas. For many, he represented a second incarnation of Jeffersonian democracy; for others, the personification of a vulgar, hypocritical tyrant. One of his chief legacies was spending the then flush U.S. Treasury monies on major transportation projects, setting a precedent that would resemble Stanford's future. Other darker markers of his administration include a sustained effort to wipe out Native American tribes and kill any notion of a central bank. "That the modern twenty-dollar Federal Reserve Note should bear Andrew Jackson's portrait is richly ironic," noted a signature history of the time. "Not only did the Old Hero disapprove of paper money, he deliberately destroyed the national banking system of his day."[3]

The United States was finally and forever free of Great Britain after the Treaty of Ghent ended the War of 1812. The peace came just nine years before Leland Stanford was born. Then just four years after he gained his majority, the United States embarked on its own war of conquest—the Mexican-American War—sweeping up much of the western half of North America. Between those two wars, a relatively stable United States saw markets explode and a resultant new level of prosperity.

Although a young-adult United States emerged, that is not to say America was mature. Women were legally second-class citizens, superstitions remained rampant, and the entire population of the country was around thirteen million, about the same as the modern metropolitan area of Los Angeles. The nation, like Leland Stanford, had to grow up, and not at the leisurely pace of the past. Industrialism was underway, wagons crossed the Continental Divide for the first time, and the initial protection of wildlands that would become the National Park Service went into law. The first popular press or mass media outlets appeared, Samuel Morse tapped out the original message on the speed-of-light telegraph, and P. T. Barnum put on his first show.

Overshadowing it all was an ancient reality: slavery. The politics of the barbarity, of course, would fester and rend the nation bloody soon enough. During that 1844 presidential election young Stanford wrote home, sharing the great impression made on him by one of the founders of the new Republican Party: Cassius Marcellus Clay. The Kentucky newspaper publisher sparked a rather different, loftier reaction in Leland Stanford regarding the plight of African Americans than the one Stanford had at the Oneida Institute when he was disturbed by the idea of having to dine at the same table with blacks. Demonstrating a rare bit of zeal, twenty-year-old Stanford wrote to a brother about Clay that he was "known throughout the world having liberated his own slaves and having given up all political hopes on account of his humanity in ardently advocating the cause of the slave and of the extension of human liberty."[4] The tougher reality was that as with most of the new party leaders, Clay did not object to slavery because the foundation of the nation says all men are created equal but for reasons of business slavery was just plain uneconomical and he said ultimately denigrated not just all honest labor but especially white labor. "Cash" Clay, as he was known, declared that he sought "the highest welfare of the white, whatever may be the consequences of the liberation of the African."[5] This was a widely acceptable point of view at the time, a position that eventually led to the election of Abraham Lincoln.

In his still impressionable youth, Leland Stanford, swept along with the national upheavals, was anxious about his future and especially about making money. In a letter to another brother, he wrote, "That ambition which the whole family of us have naturally I am in hopes will prevent me from being contented with a mediocrity or rather from not striving after something higher."[6] The next month, writing again to a brother, the young man expressed some pique about a family land sale: "I am astonished at the low price at which Papa offered his farm and am equally rejoiced that Perry did not take him up on his offer." And then, taking a step back to reveal greater thought, he added, "I have entertained for some time that there is a tendency in the whole family to undervalue that which is their own and rather magnify the worth of which they do not possess."[7]

Young Leland Stanford was forming his own character that would address all three anxieties.

By 1845, when he turned twenty-one, Stanford's future still did not appear bright. There were few indications that he was either terribly hardworking or terrifically bright. Rather, he could be regarded as a sometimes scheming, chronic school dropout who was experiencing a tepid political awakening. The pressing question at hand was how the young man would make a living. His parents would not support him forever. His next move, then, was getting a job, trade, or profession.

And so, enjoying books and disdaining manual labor, fond of talking and not overly enthusiastic of studying, Stanford said he joined an Albany law firm as a clerk, a common way to apprentice for a career as a lawyer. It has been a convention of Stanford's publicists—and subsequent memes—to declare that he apprenticed for three years and then passed the New York State bar in 1848. The claim does not bear the burden of proof.

The available evidence suggests the only New York bar exam Leland Stanford ever passed was the sort that tested his ability to drink. Absent any reasonably solid evidence that Stanford read law and was admitted to practice in New York State, it is, at best, unwise to assert this accomplishment. It is certainly true that many documents dating back to 1848 have been lost, destroyed by fire and neglect, or in some cases were simply never recorded. On the other hand, Stanford's history for his first twenty-two years is not one of accomplishment. Key members of his family, more than a few friends, and extant documents demonstrate a consistent pattern of unfinished business. Shirking work, a bit of flimflam, and failing to finish school after school were his marks. Then suddenly most records of his life disappear for the three years he has been said to be an apprentice at the Albany law firm of Wheaton, Doolittle and Hadley at 83 State Street. No record of anyone who knew him those years has been found that confirms the assertion.

If, in fact, he did turn his life around at this time and completed his instruction in the law and then passed the bar, why would Stanford then immediately forsake what he had finally constructed? Why would he abandon his connections, his family, his hometown, and instead travel well more than eight hundred arduous miles to a remote frontier hamlet where he knew no one— and no one knew him—and would have to start again from scratch for two years before passing that state's bar exam?[8]

However, that is precisely what he did.

Forswearing the not quite 30,000-population city of Chicago, then the 20,000-population Milwaukee, he continued north to a pioneer village of 1,600 on the western shores of Lake Michigan: Port Washington, Wisconsin. It was the kind of small water town he was accustomed to and there appeared to be the prospect of getting in on the ground floor of a new boomtown.

The primary industry was timber. There was a lot of it. The wood would be needed for everything Chicago and other ascendant midwestern cities couldn't get enough of. Lumber barons systematically felled the forests for homes, offices, barns, and other buildings as well as simple, smaller inventories such as barrels, which were used for everything from grain, to fish, to beer. The cleared lands were then plowed and planted with wheat, barley, and tobacco, among many other crops before pests such as chinch bugs wiped out many grains and the dairy industry began its domination in Wisconsin. Soon the beige clays in the Port Washington bluffs of Sauk Creek draining into Lake Michigan where the town started in 1835 would become a source of what are still called cream bricks, seen today across much of the Midwest.[9]

The first town pier for shipping went in around the time Leland Stanford arrived, meaning people would no longer have to wade ashore. But when he walked around town itself, the transportation infrastructure remained limited to dirt roads with wooden sidewalks. To get past the village you would take the remnants of Indian trails, all but the last of the Menomonee, Potawatomi, and Sauk tribes having been pushed out by the 1840s. As in the outer reaches of Albany, a Euro-American might glimpse a Native American about town, but more likely when out hunting in the Wisconsin wilderness.[10]

"The old Pottawatomie village had developed into a bustling little commercial center," a midwestern scholar wrote.

> Teamsters drove sweating horses down Canal Street to unload their produce on the busy wharves of the lake front. Sailors, dock hands, merchants, travelers, settlers and curious citizens of the town itself walked between the merchandise stacked on the wharves while they waited for the ships that came in daily or watched those same ships sail away from their harbor laden with the rich produce of Port Washington's fields and industries.[11]

Small as it was, Port Washington saw 414 ships call in 1849 and almost double that by 1851. The docks were stacked with cargos of cordwood, racked hoops, barrels of wheat, rye, potash, potatoes, bricks, fish, lumber, and hides. It all looked comfortably familiar to young Leland Stanford. He also found a familiar place to stay when he first arrived: above the bar at a tavern called Powers House, down by the water.

"He was a large and rather clumsy young fellow, with a gray eye, and was decidedly phlegmatic and dull," according to one Port Washington reminiscence three years after Stanford's death. The writer then made a still snarkier reference to Stanford's drinking. "In one thing, however, he could take all the tricks of that day of hardy pioneers. He could stand up at the village bar, put all the other fellows to sleep and then walk off with a clear head. There were very many opportunities for him to show his superiority in this regard."[12] The young Leland Stanford had fretted about his future because of this situation. "From what I have observed of myself I do not wonder that one scarcely if ever hears of a person rising to eminence who has once been a barkeeper," he anxiously wrote to a brother. Then Stanford rued that he would be more studious "if I had never been around a barroom."[13]

An 1848 ad in the local paper shows Stanford started working that year with an attorney who had been admitted to the Wisconsin bar.[14] When Stanford himself was finally certified to practice in the state, a full two years later, he broke out on his own. He tried to make the best of it, but as in New York, he met disappointment and ultimately defeat. Rather than find a fresh beginning in the state whose year-old motto was "Forward," Leland Stanford stumbled backward into disaster and ended in the basement pivot point of his professional life.

The decline started when he, as have countless others hoping to highlight their commercial prospects, began the first of many runs for office. The voters then bluntly quashed young Leland Stanford's attempt to become district attorney. Stanford had run as a Whig, the progressive political party of the day split off from the conservative Democrats over the policies of President Jackson, Old Hickory's many critics considering him despotic, ill-bred, and a betrayer of the democratic spirit of the Revolution. It was arguably the commencement of the most turbulent era in American electoral politics. "The decade of the 1850s witnessed one of the few fundamental reorganizations of the American political system," noted a distinguished political historian.[15]

Port Washington was, and remains, the county seat of Washington County, not a bad place for an aspiring lawyer to establish a practice. But even before he arrived there was political turmoil regarding the location, with the nearby towns of Grafton—formerly Hamburg—and Cedarburg vying for the honor. Indeed, some county functions were held in one town and others in another. Lawmakers eventually settled on the Solomonic solution of cutting the county in half, but that didn't happen in time for young Stanford's struggling situation.

Among the complicated obstacles were the demographics of the region. Many, if not most, of the people moving to the area spoke German. Many others spoke Dutch or French. The culture wars of that era will sound familiar to Americans of all generations: "German and English were spoken on the street, in the business houses, on the school playground,—in fact, both languages were taught in the classrooms," a midwestern historian found.

> The use of German by the teachers became so prevalent that the English-speaking settlers refused to send their children to schools where most of the teaching was done in a foreign tongue. A law of 1854 making "all teaching in any other (than English) language illegal" was merely ignored and harassed school superintendents usually were compelled to yield, for the Germans would have no one but German teachers and the German teachers of that day generally spoke a labored English or none at all.[16]

Bratwurst and beer traditions, towns named Belgium, and counties such as Fond du Lac tell the story of Wisconsin's heterogeneous European origins. "It was difficult to carry on business here with more than half the population speaking only German," wrote a local historian who moved to Port Washington as a child during the Great Depression many years later. "I can vouch for it that even in the 1930s there was such a foreign atmosphere in the north half of town that a Michigander felt quite lost. It is only in the last 30 years that the north side women have mingled with the rest of the town to a great extent."[17]

Leland Stanford had no other language but English.

Then there was the locally infamous Judge Hopewell Coxe incident. According to that Port Washington story, police arrested a fellow named Nicholas Langers. Stanford reportedly represented the prosecution, arguing that the suspect was guilty of assault and battery. A "tedious address of the young Stanford" followed. "He dragged out the case and after about forty minutes of harangue closed with instructions to the Judge as to what he should do." The judge rebuked Stanford, whom was later called a "coxcomb," and threw out the case. Stanford, vexed, hurled back, "I'll be damned if I ever will appear again before such a Judge and certainly not in Washington County!"[18]

Leland Stanford's personal life also had some roil.

One of his few surviving intimate letters is a clanky billet-doux to a Hannah Clark, who visited Port Washington and then left after getting under his twenty-six-year-old skin. He prodded her regarding reports of being engaged to another, which prompted no small amount of anxiety in young Stanford:

> By the way Hannah let me ask how is Dr Bryant [and] I have heard a considerable amount about him since you bid us good bye, one has assured me that he knew you were to be married to him certainly by the fall, I have found it impossible to make him believe otherwise. How is it Hannah? Do take compassion on your friends here and let them know the truth.

A few sentences later he plaintively wrote, "Are we never again to have one of those pleasant walks. Are we to have naught of them but what memory has fondly retained?"[19] Nothing but memory was, in fact, all he was left with.

It was then that Leland Stanford made one of the most significant decisions of his life: he briefly returned to Albany in 1850 to woo and marry Jane Elizabeth—or Eliza—Lathrop, the third of seven children born to a local merchant family. A fire that consumed Albany City Hall in 1880 also destroyed her birth certificate. Since that time, there has been confusion about whether her middle name was Eliza or Elizabeth.[20] It is certain her given first name was Jane, which Stanford disregarded, much as he had his own birth name, instead conferring on his betrothed the nickname Jennie, as seen in the surviving letters he wrote her during their long marriage. They had known each other for three years and had much in common. They were both relatively big people, she five-foot-eight in height. They were both from very middle-class families and shared a decided ambition for a more opulent way of life. Neither had much formal education. Their wedding portrait is a study in mid-nineteenth-century severe and somber attitude, hardly the sort of wedding announcement photo of today. Marriage, the message was clear, is a serious business. Stanford's gaze is plainly intense, hers rather more uncertain. He had shaved his beard, revealing some more of the vulnerability of his youth, an innocence that remains strikingly immutable in both their faces, especially in contrast to the imperiousness of their later images. He was twenty-six; the new Mrs. Stanford had just turned twenty-two.

They returned to Port Washington, where they lived in a drafty log cabin at the northwest corner of the village, the Powers House having burned to the ground in 1851. The next year's predawn fire that destroyed Stanford's small law office over a grocery store, his books, and his immediate future was the final affront.

A flattering sketch of Jennie by a family confidant noted that "the climate was bleak and bitter in the extreme, there was practically no society" for the young wife from a distant, different part of the country. Jennie found "her early experience a hard one indeed."[21] Another early admirer wrote that Leland had "never indeed cared" for Wisconsin "with its harsh winters and population composed mostly of Germans."[22]

Neither would suffer it long.

CHAPTER 3

Crossing

He abandoned her. That's what the Albany grapevine whispered. Jennie Stanford seethed under the churlish glare and small-town talk that disgraced her. Many years later a family confidant wrote that Leland Stanford "was obliged to submit to the humiliation of sending his wife home to her parents." He added, "This experience had never been forgotten by Stanford. It was so painful to them both that neither of them cared to discuss it."[1] Jennie's personal secretary—besmirched herself by gossip after the decidedly troubling circumstances surrounding Mrs. Stanford's death at the beginning of the next century—also later recalled young Jennie "had suffered keenly because many people in Albany had considered her a deserted wife, circulating rumors of which she was well aware. She wished to live elsewhere, and never recovered from her dislike of Albany and its people."[2]

But there her new husband placed her, there in her family home, there to tend her invalid father, there to brook her cross while the groom set off for adventure Out West. When he would return was not clear. Leland Stanford, collaborating with Jennie's dad, declared the voyage to the goldfields too rough, too menacing, and too risky for a woman. It was 1852 and the bride, furious but acquiescent, did as instructed by her husband and father. And yet, from a mid-nineteenth-century perspective, there was some substance to their resolve. There simply was no proper way to get from the East to the West Coast, which paradoxically, was precisely the situation that would create Leland Stanford's fortune, fame, and infamy.

"In those days California seemed as remote from the East as the heart of Central Africa," a nineteenth-century writer recalled.[3] The cheapest way to get there was to sail around Cape Horn, at the very bottom of South America. But there were other costs any prudent person would have to consider: the voyage from New York to San Francisco was thirteen thousand miles long. The average trip took some six months. These were the benign factors. Mother Nature, baring her jagged teeth with preternatural malice, was not so mild. "Below 40 South there is no law," goes the sailor's adage. "Below 50 South there is no God."

Rounding the Horn was and remains one of the most perilous adventures known to human history, waves ninety feet tall moving at forty miles per hour not being unusual, for example. Unrelenting blasts of wind could drive back sailing ships so that after days of making what was considered great speed in the nineteenth century—say twelve miles per hour, or a little more than ten knots—the ships might be thrown back huge distances, sometimes causing the toughest two-hundred- to three-hundred-mile portion of the journey to take an extra six weeks. Those passengers and crew were among the fortunate. Many were less so and capsized in the storms, lost forever in the freezing salt waters.

Shooting up and down the nine-story waves would be more terrifying than riding an unsecured roller coaster, which instead of being on rails would float on liquid shrieking at immense speeds in constantly different directions. "The waves rolled up into immense billows covered with foam and dashed against the sides of the ship and over the bulwarks, deluging every person and setting afloat every loose thing upon the decks," wrote Joseph Lamson, who took the journey the same year—1852—Leland Stanford set out for California.

> Borne about by the raging waters, the ship often staggered for a moment upon the crest of a great wave, as if fearful of the plunge she was about to take, but quickly sinking down into the moving chasm, as if she were attempting to dive to the bottom of the sea, until overtaken by another billow, she rose to its crest, though only to be sunk into another then another gulf.[4]

Storms being common in the Southern Ocean, nineteenth-century celestial navigation found itself frequently hampered day and night by Antarctic thunderstorms. Ferocious winds and waves could toss the wooden ships into the unforgiving rocks scattered across the waters much like a minefield. And then there were the moving icebergs, thousands of them in places and some a mile in length, although a jagged block of ice no larger than a cooler colliding with a boat could rip off the rudder in seconds. The captain and crew—and not infrequently the terrified passengers—encased by snow and sleet, would grip the rails and strain over the gunwales scanning for the hazards, whether the icy storms serrated the foggy days or dark nights. If hazards were seen, yelling at the top of one's voice might scarcely be heard over the howls of the raging weather and waters.

"I listened anxiously to every sound on deck. Presently I heard the wind with its well-known roar approaching, and with it came over me a feeling of such terror I had not felt before, and as such few can conceive," wrote twenty-four-year-old Lucy Kendall Herrick, also sailing to San Francisco around the Horn in 1852. "I should like the Cape and its cold snows, storms, and 'South-Westers' to be blotted off the map and become annihilated on the Earth. *Never come to California around the Cape.*"[5]

Still thousands did—or tried to. Now and again a ship's captain might attempt to pilot the shortcut, a passage known as the Strait of Magellan, winding between the Horn and southern tip of Chile. Dotted with myriad channels bordered by rocky reefs, shores, and shoals, the strait—actually a labyrinth—is infamous for waters as shallow as twenty feet, high winds, swirling flows, and among the most disturbing facts of all, gales that sometimes roar in one direction while vicious currents run in another. Many ships have been lost, then pounded to paste in the narrow, complicated passages. The longer route seemed a safer bet. If ships were able to round the malevolent Horn—a fourteen-hundred-foot rock at the southern apogee of the Americas—the passengers and crew would often collapse in relief when entering the relatively pacific waters of the Pacific Ocean, although the remaining journey north to California was certainly no pleasure cruise, as many would find out.

The overland route to California was not much more promising, often being a death trek of disease, guerrilla war, and starvation.

It usually started off well enough. "The camp tonight looks very pretty. The 5 wagons with white drilling covers (double thickness over the top) are looking very much dressed up as they stand in a semicircle in the waving green grass," wrote a woman who crossed from the Midwest in 1857 and recalled the day they started west. "The cattle and horses 100 or more in all, are off to one side grazing and the camp fires within the circle are burning brightly."[6]

"Horses, picketed tents, with the star-spangled banners flying, wagons standing around, while lying by the side of logs and trees are brawny, sun-burnt men, sunning themselves, and taking their ease," wrote a man of his 1850 crossing. He estimated the "army" of people camped at six thousand.[7] During the first weeks of the expedition there were wry observations: "It was really amusing to see the men stand in the river to wash. They all acted so awkward," wrote another woman in 1852.[8]

Some of the earlier encounters with Native Americans are worthy of the same note: "When they got near the top they whopped and tried to irritate the whites by turning up their sterns and slapping them in an insulting manner."[9]

By the time the pioneers reached the Nebraska Territory, the pretty and bright and amusing had altered considerably. Hunger began to be a common site as the westward bound encountered people who had turned back. "There seemed to be twice as many women as men and twice as many children as women," wrote a pioneer of Mormons disheartened by their failed pilgrimage to the Zion of Salt Lake City.[10] "All were in rags and tatters and, I must say, scabs. They very worst lot I ever saw. All who were large enough . . . were out of the wagons holding out rusty kettles and pans begging for milk."[11]

The Platte River Route, by far the most traveled road west, became rougher by the mile. By the time people had crossed the Rocky Mountains and entered the desert of the Great Basin, the stories in the more than seven hundred overland diaries available become commonly, numbingly horrific. "Parties in advance of us found the body of a nude woman on the bank of the slough that we passed yesterday," a woman recounted, adding that the victim had been dragged back and forth though the slough. "A piece of hair rope was around her neck and one foot was an India rubber overshoe."[12]

Suffering began to take on new meaning.

"The destitution has reached its height now," a diary states. "Hundreds are entirely out of provisions, and there are none who have any to spare, and but very few who have enough to carry to the mines. Often, almost daily, will some poor starved fellow come up to the wagon and pray us in God's name to give or sell him a crust of bread."[13]

The land provided little mercy. One report described "a man and his wife about 11 miles back who were on foot, toiling through the hot sand, the man carrying the blanket and other necessities, and his wife carrying their only child in her arms, having lost all their team." Every day presented a new horror.

> Morning comes, and the light of day presents a scene more horrid than the route of a defeated army; dead stock line the roads, wagons, rifles, tents, clothes, everything but food may be found scattered along the road; here an ox, who standing famished against a wagon bed until nature could do no more, settled back into it

and dies; and there a horse kicking out his last gasp in the burning sand, men scattered among the plain and stretched out among the dead like corpses.

The writer concluded it was "a long road to obtain a narrow home."[14]

One traveler was overcome by the death of the livestock the gold rushers had driven halfway across the continent. "Dead animals all the way up, the stench intolerable. We have had the road strewed with putrid carcasses ever since we left the Platte. As soon as an ox dies he bloats full as the skin will hold (and sometimes bursts), and his legs stick straight out and soon smells horribly."[15] The Vermonter found himself lost one night while looking for his party's scattered stock, which often ran off for miles after sudden thunderclaps and lightning storms the likes of which none of the East Coasters had ever witnessed. Debilitated from what he thought dysentery made it all the more intolerable.

> I had a time of it last night. I was more faint than sick and I came to wagons. . . . They had a fire that I had seen for miles back or I should have laid out, for as soon as Clark left me I could not keep my course by the stars. Here I found a man and woman standing guard by the fire. I begged for a biscuit of them which strengthened me or I am sure I could have got in. When I laid down in the sage I dare not go to sleep on account of the wolves. It seemed as if there were 50 all around me. I was unarmed and I did not know but that they might make a supper of me. At any rate they discoursed most hideous music. Though to tell the truth I felt so bad when I first laid down that I cared little whether I ever got up or not, and when I attempted to walk I staggered like a drunken man over the sage and frequently fell my length over some obstruction. I must have walked 8 miles out and back, besides its being dark made it far more tiresome. I was right glad when I found our tent.

It was commonly said, "Cholera for breakfast, a shallow grave by lunch."[16]

The diaries are replete with accounts of the pioneers at first astonished to see how Native Americans hoisted their dead onto platforms held up by four poles, much as the Mongols had done in Central Asia. But then the settlers had a revelation when they saw the bones of dead fellow emigrants scattered across the plains and desert floors after wolves had dug up the graves and ripped apart the corpses.

As the 1850s progressed, Indian attacks began to escalate in retribution for the slaughter of the First Peoples by the U.S. Army and violent gold rushers. Scalping on both sides of the savagery was increasingly common as the decade trudged on. It was easy to blame the Native Americans for the violence, real or imagined.

"An American had swapped horses with an Indian, and the next day a part of the same company, being behind, met this Indian with their comrade's horse and accused him of stealing it," an account of a 1850 trek to the goldfields states. "This alarmed the Indian, not knowing what they would do with him. He told them as well as he could how he came by the horse, and putting spurs this horse tried to make his escape. This was taken as evidence of his guilt, so they fired after him and killed the poor fellow."[17]

There is no question that grotesque terrors were wrought by both Native people and settlers. Innumerable entries through the many diaries tell of Indians lying in ambush, usually not attacking the settlers themselves when they traveled in groups, but shooting arrows into their livestock, making them unfit to continue west. Then the attackers would butcher the abandoned cattle for food. Horses they would typically leave unharmed and steal. "None can know the horror of it who has not been similarly situated," wrote a woman headed from the Midwest to the Far West.[18]

The middle course, literally and figuratively, was sailing to Central America, crossing the isthmus, and getting another ship on the Pacific side and sailing up the relatively benign coast to California. This line of least resistance, although most expensive, was the route Leland Stanford chose, once again with the financial help of his parents. Whether he was cutting and running from failure, or was dexterous and bold in search of success, depended on the outcome of his keystone gamble. Regardless, much like his distant British ancestor Thomas, he set across the ocean west, heeding the call of his brothers' bullish letters from Sacramento, which like his childhood Albany was then a small river town. But what would soon become the state capital was the heart of the first California Gold Rush, unsuspectingly creating the paradigm for today's gold rush and the Stanford brand. In June of 1852 Leland Stanford sailed from New York Harbor.

The first established routes of 1848 crossed at what is today Panama. But three years later East Coast shipping tycoon Cornelius Vanderbilt started a rival line through Nicaragua, to the north. Neither route was absent affliction, disaster, and death. Yellow fever, malaria, and more were common for those crossing the swamps on pole boats and mules to the Pacific. Filthy accommodations, thievery, and interminable delays were not uncommon. The Nicaragua route was longer across the isthmus but had the advantages of using more navigable waterways and being closer to North America.

North Americans were typically astounded by the tropical wildlife, such as raucous, kaleidoscopic parrots and audacious monkeys. But the travelers were not so delighted by the crocodiles and snakes. Spectacular, centuries-old Spanish forts resembling castles caused wonderment as the settlers crossed sometimes placid, sometimes turbulent, immense Lake Nicaragua in canoes guided by indigenous people the North Americans considered exotic. But when the skies erupted in tropical tempests the trek suddenly became less wondrous. There was little solace on the ground. A series of rapids requiring rugged portage and marches through mud so deep walkers were up to their hips and mule trains up to their bellies were truly exhausting. The mosquitos, chiggers, and an entire insect family of what is called the assassin bug made the trip still less pleasant.

Once on the other side of the isthmus, Stanford boarded Vanderbilt's wooden two-deck *Independence* for California that summer of 1852, a trip without incident. But seven months later the same ship, on the same route, encountered a problem early one morning along the Baja California coast.

Passenger accounts declared that although rocks were clearly ahead in the early morning light and a reef was also marked on the charts, the captain piloted the steamer aground and the boiler room began to flood. The crew attempted to maintain the boiler fires in order for the steamer to pull away, but instead the flames spread. Panic broke open. Some lifeboats lowered with a portion of the five hundred passengers but did not return for others. Many more began to jump overboard. Witnesses who successfully escaped the inferno could do nothing but watch.

"The scene beggars descriptions," a letter signed by 150 surviving passengers lamented.

> Females could be seen clambering down the sides of the ships, clinging with death-like tenacity to the ropes, rigging and larboard wheel. Some were hanging by their skirts, which, unfortunately, in their efforts to jump overboard, had caught, and thus swung, piteously and horridly, until the flames relieved them of their awful position by disengaging their clothes, causing them to drop and sink into the briny deep. Mothers, going to meet their fond husbands, threw their tender offspring into the waves, rather than see them devoured by the fury of the flames and trusted to fortunes and chance to take their bodies to the shore. O! but the shrieks and cries.

On the nearby beach of a small rocky island, some survivors began the "pillaging and plundering of the dead—old and young men stripping the bodies of clothing, securing the contents of their pockets, and actually quarrelling, yea fighting over a corpse for plunder!"[19]

Some two hundred people died.

Leland Stanford, however, arrived whole in the debauchery that was Barbary Coast San Francisco. He had left behind a long account of flops, lucklessness, and even his bride. He was twenty-eight years old and dead broke.

Someone would have first spotted his ship from the lookout atop the city's Telegraph Hill, where they would have fired off a loud gun to signal the arrival of people, merchandise, and often the most eagerly awaited commodity—mail. Oscar Wilde famously wrote, "It is an odd thing, but everyone who disappears is said to be seen at San Francisco. It must be a delightful city, and possess all the attractions of the next world."[20]

The reality was less transcendental. The devil had already arrived in California and was particularly busy in the city of Saint Francis. It was a raw, rude, raunchy frontier boomtown that made young Stanford's childhood Watervliet look like a microphone check. "They were a wild and perverse race, the San Franciscans in those days," wrote a triumvirate of gold rush chroniclers in a classic 1855 compilation, *The Annals of San Francisco* There was "an almost appalling sense of the exuberant life, energy and enterprise of the place," they recorded. "Gambling saloons, glittering like fairy palaces, like them suddenly sprang into existence, studding all sides of the plaza, and every street in its neighborhood." The entire city "was mad, feverish mirth, where fortunes were lost and won, upon the green cloth, in the twinkling of an eye."[21]

Amid the smoke, the noise, and furor a player "entered the hall as he would go to war, with a knife in his pocket and a pistol in his belt," noted a young Swiss visitor who arrived in San Francisco in the fall of 1849.[22] "There were hundreds of gambling saloons in the town," sporting what would have been exotic-sounding European names such as *roulette, lansquenet,* and *trente et quarante.* "Tables piled with heaps of gold and silver coin, with bags of gold dust, and lumps of the pure metal." The atmosphere was one of "heat, drink, greed and deviltry." And this was not restricted to just one social or economic class. "Judges and clergymen, physicians and advocates, merchants and clerks, contractors, shopkeepers, tradesmen, mechanics, and laborers, miners and farmers, all adventurers in their kind—every one elbowed his way to the gaming table." And, of course, there were "lewd girls freed from the necessity of all moral restraint."[23]

A fast-growing number of indentured workers from South China, mostly men, were also arriving in search of what they called Gold Mountain. They would find some gold, much suffering, and eventually a keystone role in Leland Stanford's life and legend. For many of the Chinese women, however, especial horrors awaited. "Chinese prostitutes who remained in the city were openly sold on the docks, with bidding being carried out in full view of spectators, who frequently included police officers," noted a Hong Kong historian.[24] Many of the madams, it should be added, were also Chinese.

Prostitution, though defiantly common, was hardly the only type of lawlessness. Large gangs, especially the notorious Hounds and later Ducks, "invaded the stores, taverns, and houses of Americans themselves, and rudely demanded whatever they desired. They could not be refused, for their numbers were so great, while they were well armed, that nobody durst resist them." Dystopian San Francisco "was paralyzed with terror."[25]

Vigilante groups formed, hunted down whomever they judged guilty, and hung them from any convenient, improvised gallows. "Let each man be his own executioner," read a handbill from the time.[26] The outlaws were often blamed for setting many of the half-dozen fires that ravaged the town between 1848 when gold was first found and the population was about 850, and 1852 when Stanford came ashore along with 66,988 arrivals that year, double the newcomers of 1851.[27]

When execution was not in order, the first jails were created on abandoned boats in San Francisco Bay. But escapes were common and the rule of law was often in the hands of what was called Judge Lynch. It was every man for himself. "The practice of wearing deadly weapons became still more common. These were often used—though not so much against the robber and assassin, as upon the old friend and acquaintance, or the stranger, when drink and scandal, time and circumstance had converted them into the supposed enemies."[28]

Other amusements included bringing captured grizzly bears to fight ferocious bulls to an almost inconceivably horrendous death. Some of these contests took place at Mission Dolores, the original settlement of the Franciscan friars.[29]

Much of San Francisco consisted of deep pools of mud and hundreds of pop-up shelters of wooden poles and canvas tents made from the hundreds of abandoned ships and their sails. Many advertised themselves as hotels. Illumination was often provided by candles and oil lanterns, which also ignited frequent fires. There were reports that in metal buildings inhabitants were roasted alive as the doors melted and trapped them inside.

Gold rush poet Charles Warren Stoddard was eleven in 1854 when his parents brought him to San Francisco from Rochester, New York. His new home, he recalled, had four foreign quarters: Spanish, French, Italian, and Chinese. Stoddard's lambently lit, sentimental childhood memories included knowing he had entered the Spanish quarter by the

> balconies like hanging gardens, clamorous with parrots; and by the dark-eyed senoritas, with lace mantillas drawn over their blue-black hair; by the shop windows filled with Mexican pottery; the long strings of cardinal-red peppers that swung under the awnings over the doors of the sellers of spicy things; and also by the delicious odors that were wafted to us from the tables.

He had been there just a day or two. "Everywhere we saw the people of the quarter lounging in doorways or windows or on galleries, dressed as if they were about to appear in a rendition of the opera of 'The Barber of Seville.'" And then "a magnificent Caballero dashed by on a half-tamed bronco. He rode in the shade of a sombrero a yard wide, crusted with silver embroidery. His Mexican saddle was embossed with huge Mexican dollars." Close by "ran the Barbary Coast. There were the dives beneath the pavement, where it was not wise to enter; blood was on those thresholds."[30]

It wasn't all so fantastic. Amid San Francisco's frequent dust and sandstorms, garbage of every description flew about and landed in the swampy plank streets. "Filth, mud and stagnant water" were common. "Nobody troubled himself to remove any rubbish from the way." That attracted another sort of vermin: "Rats—huge, fat, lazy things, prowled about at pleasure." It was particularly bad when the sun set over the Pacific. "The pedestrian at night, stumbling along the uneven pavements, and through streets that were only a series of quagmires, would occasionally tread on the loathsome, bloated, squeaking creatures."[31]

And there were the poor. "In San Francisco, it is a melancholy fact that there was much destitution, sickness and even death by want and exposure to the place," an author lamented. "They probably lived in miserable habitations, sleeping often upon the bare earth. Around them were bustle and lucrative pursuits, while they alone seemed neglected."[32]

Not everyone was happy with the depictions of saturnalian San Francisco. Eminent nineteenth-century philosopher and man of letters Josiah Royce, who was born to forty-niner parents in the Gold Country, was one—and one who took exception to *The Annals:*

> Just as one cannot easily remember who the men were that did not gamble in those days, so one fails to recall in looking back on the early years the women who were respectable. Doubtless, such existed; but then they had the curious quality of respectable women—namely, they were somehow not conspicuous, especially in the public crowds. Hence, the authors of the *Annals* seem, for some probably sufficient reason, to have been personally unable, in the early days, to secure the honor of their acquaintance.

Royce, who often referred to his mother who had braved the overland passage to San Francisco, also defended the timber of men who did not achieve notoriety. He, in fact, declared that the malevolent actors in gold rush San Francisco were a "comparatively small fraction of the American inhabitants," suggesting the riffraff were not of European heritage. "The cool-headed man who did not make a fool of himself with absurd dissipations, nor destroy his health with continuous overstrain in making haste to be rich, can indeed give you helpful information about the early life."[33] He may have been referring to himself.

In the winter of 1852, the year Stanford arrived, floods across the state led to disaster, noted an early pioneer: "The miners are nearly starving, owing to the speculators buying all the provisions made them so enormously high that the up-country people thinking it might come down; neglected to lay in their winter provisions, and now it is utterly impossible to get it at all, and they are getting desperate taking provisions wherever they can find them."[34] That led to some of the first horrors by gold rushers against the Native Californians. "The flood of gold seekers into the state, and in their wake farmers who preempted land, had the immediate effect of reducing, and at time wholly eliminating, the food supply of the Indians," an eminent historian has written. The Native Californians "were prohibited from possessing guns—a restraint aimed at retaliatory effectiveness, but also making it difficult to kill game which was becoming more scarce and shy because it was source of food for the gold miners. Starving natives might steal food or kill a cow, and such acts led to punitive reactions by the whites."[35]

The Native tribes of California simply had no rights as American citizens although the Treaty of Guadalupe Hidalgo signed at the end of the Mexican-American War had explicitly given those guarantees. In fact, Indians could not vote, and they were barred from testifying in court. It was illegal to try an

American for killing an Indian. There was little outrage, even by the more liberal-minded of the day. "The fate of the Indian is fixed," read an article in one of the mainstream media outlets, the *Sacramento Daily Union*. Although at first sympathetic to the plight of the first Native Californians, it noted "he must be annihilated by the advance of the white man; by the diseases, and, to them, the evils of civilization. But the work should not have been commenced at so early a day by the deadly rifle."[36]

The newly arrived Leland Stanford, still thirty years old and far from the restraints of hearth and home, was getting an immersion education rather different than what he may have absorbed during his failed school studies back home and career failure in Wisconsin. It was time for still another plan, which promptly went into play.

CHAPTER 4

The Gold under the Mountain

It was all new. As late as 1847 San Francisco wasn't even San Francisco. It was a settlement of a few hundred called Yerba Buena, Spanish for "good herb." Something like the tip of a thumb poking out of the then remote western edge of the continent, the land was not a little uncomfortable. It was an often cold, windswept, mostly hilly sand and dirt outpost at the end of a long, heavily wooded peninsula. Frequently hooded in overcast and fog and isolated from California's luxurious sun saturating the land around it, the pueblo was, on many days, a dusty, scrubby, outskirt more or less surrounded by a sea of just-out-of-reach, glorious sunshine.

For the first half of the 1800s the village was ostensibly protected by a Spanish, then Mexican, military garrison called the Presidio that had been there since 1776. Franciscan missionaries had rounded up and subjugated the Native Californians starting around the same time British soldiers skirmished with American colonists in Concord, Massachusetts. The friars used their Mission Dolores as base of operations. There had been minimal resistance by the peaceful Ohlone who had lived around San Francisco Bay for more than ten thousand years. Subsequent to the Mexican government taking secular control of all the California missions in 1835, there was little left to the system by 1848. Moreover, it was clear by then that California was becoming increasingly populated by Americans, many of whom were agitating for a violent overthrow of the Mexican government in favor of the United States.

Initially, there was little commotion or serious knowledge regarding the rare mineral that would define California: gold. Geologists designate the "noble" earth metal by its symbol on the periodic table of elements, Au. When California began forming some 1,700 million years ago, continental plates began to fold and crush into what is now North America, eventually pushing up mountain ranges such as the Sierra Nevada. That enormous geologic pressure also released liquidized rock, ash, and gas in what is called a pyroclastic flow. Gold came up with it from beneath the ancient Earth's mantle through magma chambers and volcanic vents, making its way into the Sierras. Then, as the mountains began to slowly wash away into streams and rivers, some gold accompanied the debris.

How the gold arrived at all on the planet is a still more astonishing story. That precious metal, ingratiating to the eye and heavy in the hand, obedient to the hammer and refusing to rust, is simply not of this Earth. Gold is forged only in the foundry of deep space, the result of one of the most colossal cosmic phenomena known to science: a supernova. And not just the catastrophic destruction of one massive star but the collision of two dead cores of stars exploding as supernovas. Even then, much more must occur. The resulting neutron stars left over from the previous supernova, called a kilonova, is where gold is formed. Meteors infused with the metal, crash-landing on our forming planet about 4.5 billion years ago, carried gold to us. Because the weight of gold is unusually heavy, geologists have determined that most of it on Earth has sunk toward the molten core, although some has disgorged back to the surface. A later period of heavy bombardment of asteroids on Earth about 4 billion years ago brought another set of metals to the Earth's crust.[1]

And that is where is was first found in what is officially called the Golden State. Discoveries had been reported in the Spanish province of California as early as 1816 but were largely discounted as legend. In 1842 a rancher named Francisco Lopez, digging for wild onions in what is now Placerita Canyon State Park, forty miles north of today's downtown Los Angeles, found flecks of gold clinging to the roots, the first confirmed finding. No one made a big deal of it.

Then, on a brisk Monday in early 1848, a historic frenzy taught to every California school child began. Some forty miles up the South Fork of the American River from Sacramento and into the foothills of the monumental Sierra Nevada, an itinerant carpenter and wheelwright named James Wilson Marshall, building a sawmill for an affable adventurer and alcoholic, a Swiss émigré named John Augustus Sutter, was diverting water around the construction of a small dam. Although the Industrial Revolution had become evident with the first locomotives several decades before, in frontier California the rushing waters were still used to turn the mill, which turned the gears, which propelled the saws to slice through the then plentiful ponderosa pine Sutter wanted for construction downriver.[2]

One of Sutter's semiliterate workers wrote in his diary on January 24, "This day some kind of mettle was found in the tail race that looks like goald, first discovered by James Martial, the Boss of the Mill."[3] He brought his discovery down to his employer in Sacramento who had constructed an eponymous redoubt called Sutter's Fort, a sprawling adobe "feudal enclave" resembling a cross between an army post in the western territories and caravansary on the Silk Road.[4] Still two months later the significance of the discovery seems to have eluded even Sutter, who seemed more interested in liquor. "I have received your favor of January 21 wishing to know if I could sell the stills," he wrote to then governor Mariano Vallejo, a Mexican military commander and for some time effectively the most powerful man in Northern California. "My saw mill is now being finished and promises well; all my other projects go rapidly," and then, as a third thought Sutter offhandedly—and somewhat incorrectly—noted, "and I have made a discovery, of a gold mine which, according to our tests, is extraordinarily rich."[5]

The lucky strike could not have been timed more advantageously for the United States—and less so for Mexico. The Mexican government had signed the Treaty of Guadalupe Hidalgo, giving up California to the United States almost exactly a week after the discovery of gold. Congress voted to ratify in March, before word from Sutter's mill had traveled far. But that same month, Sutter's workers began deserting, the same month the first newspaper accounts in San Francisco appeared. Ironically, by the end of May, the *San Francisco Californian* and then the *California Star* newspapers ceased publication because their employees had abandoned the city for the goldfields.[6] On December 5, 1848, President James Polk declared the astonishing discoveries legitimate and in "abundance." On September 9, 1850, California officially, if hurriedly, became the thirty-first state in the Union.

From 1851 to 1855 the United States went from an inconsequential producer of gold to providing "nearly 45 percent" of the world's commodity.[7] The average gold worker was making $300–500 a day, some hauling in $5,000 daily, in a time when a dozen eggs cost less than 20 cents in Boston and a new home in New York some $2,500. The California Gold Rush, the largest mass movement in the history of the Western Hemisphere, was on.

Stony-broke Leland Stanford did not linger in louche San Francisco. "He did not come here with ready money," his older brother Josiah Jr., noted, who had arrived three years earlier and had done well. No ready money meant little means for food or shelter, much less the ability to enjoy the city's sordid pleasures. Instead, Leland quickly continued to follow his brothers upriver one hundred miles north by northeast to Sacramento, not yet the state capital. Led by first-born Josiah, the brothers had been among the original forty-niners but soon found that prospecting for gold was hardly as agreeable as some imagined. Louise Amelia Knapp Smith, better known to Californians as the gold rush diarist writing under the pen name Dame Shirley, captured the situation brightly:

> I myself thought (now don't laugh), that one had to but saunter gracefully along romantic streamlets, on sunny afternoons, with a parasol and white gloves, perhaps, and to stop now and then to admire the scenery, and carelessly rinse out a small panful of yellow sand (without detriment to the white kids, however so easy did I fancy the whole process to be), in order to fill one's workbag with the most beautiful and rare specimens of the precious mineral. Since I have been here, I have discovered my mistake.[8]

As with some others who saved a little money, knew how to keep ledgers, and bided their time, the Stanford brothers found a far more pleasant, reliable, and lucrative life in town, in a well-stocked store with a roof and strong door. Led by Josiah, four of the five Stanford brood of brothers had established a foothold there. Only Leland, bringing up the rear, had initially stayed behind back East. Knowing he had suffered a long string of defeats, they offered him a safe place and another fresh start if he wished. By the time he did show up in the typically scorching-hot Sacramento July of 1852, there was a two-story Stanford Brothers store made of white brick. It was about as far from the mighty Sacramento River as the Bull's Head had been from the formidable Hudson—a few hundred yards at most.

The brothers called themselves importers and wholesale dealers in grain, produce, and mining equipment. And, naturally, they sold "wines, liquors, cigars."[9] In the long game, the "provisions" became less profitable for young Leland than being next door to two particular neighbors. The store on Sacramento's K Street was adjacent to a pair of partners with not insignificant business sense: Collis Potter Huntington and Mark Hopkins, who ran a hardware shop catering to miners needing shovels, pickaxes, and of course gold pans, among other tools prospectors hoped would enable them to unearth riches.

A few blocks away was another fellow who had exchanged his dreams of finding gold in the hills, mountains, and rivers for a more dependably lucrative life behind a store counter: Charles F. Crocker. Also born in upstate New York, in Troy, he came from a large family, the oldest of which was his brother Edwin, who would play a major if largely brief and largely uncelebrated role in Stanford's fortunes in years to come. The paterfamilias of the Crocker clan was a liquor wholesaler who went from boom to bust and moved the family to Indiana. Shortly after his mother died, Crocker recalled years later, a "difficulty occurred with my father," who essentially booted him out.[10] "My early days were a struggle with poverty," he said when he was in late middle age and a man of great wealth.[11] Charles followed his brother Edwin—who would, in the fashion of the day, go by E. B.—to the gold rush, taking the rough road overland to California in 1850. He was twenty-eight years old. He soon gave up prospecting and started selling carpets, clothing, and shoes in Sacramento. He was demanding of his workers: "Charles Crocker has no desire to employ any more clerks that smoke cigars," wrote an associate to someone in Indiana looking for a job.[12] No discussion of Charles Crocker seems to go without noting he said he was five-foot-ten and weighed around 250 pounds, take or give 20 pounds here and there in his travels. He described himself as a "bull." One notable historian, in his brief description of Crocker some forty years after his death, stated, "First and last, his strong point was the handling of men."[13]

Mark Hopkins Jr. was the oldest of the forming alliance, thirty-eight. From Michigan, though born in New York to a prosperous family, he had been among the original forty-niners coming by boat and across Panama. He traveled with a friend who later chanced upon him on a trail just outside the gold rush enclave then called Hangtown, later less violently renamed Placerville. Trained as a bookkeeper, Hopkins would also find more reliable income in cash registers than in the mountains. In their serendipitous mountain meeting the two friends agreed to go into the wholesale grocery business together in Sacramento. They made "enormous profits," which they reinvested in the business and in real estate.[14]

Hopkins presented an austere image. At five-foot-ten and 160 pounds he was relatively angular and lean compared to many fellow merchants of the day

who displayed their commercial success not only by what they owned but by
haven't-missed-a-meal physiques. It was said he was a vegetarian and grew his
own produce. "Hopkins was the balance wheel of the company," recalled the
old friend, who would become one of Stanford's executives.

> He was a very careful business man and if there were matters under discussion in
> the Board of Directors as to the policy to be pursued or what they would do—he
> never took an active part in the discussion, but if they came to any knotty points
> in deciding anything, he was always prepared in some way to smooth it all over
> and cut the knots. He was a very deep thinker.[15]

Summing it up, an early biographer wrote that Hopkins "possessed in a
remarkable degree the gift of silence." Unlike his partners, he "was an attentive
listener, seldom expressing his own views until he had ascertained those of
his colleagues."[16] When he did speak, it was with a slight lisp and understated
authority.

Soon, the fastidious Hopkins found a symbiotic business partnership with
a hard-charging hardware store owner next door: Collis Huntington was a
thirty-year-old upstart from Connecticut via upstate New York. In contrast
to Hopkins, a Victorian-age historian who took Huntington's dictated reminiscences around 1889 noted in a personal postscript, "Mr. Huntington is a
storyteller and upon intimate acquaintance indulges in those which are outré
in mixed society and the humor of which runs to the forbidden." Huntington,
for example in one of his more mild jests, seemingly boasted that his family's
ancient roots were with the Normans who conquered Great Britain in the
twelfth century. Then, as the listener might imagine Huntington was embla-
zoning a pedigree, C. P., as he was known to friends, would add with a wink,
"They came over with the barbarians."[17]

Employed as a store clerk in a small town about twenty-five miles west of
Hartford, at age fifteen he had unsettled his employer by memorizing the
wholesale and retail price of every item in a fully stocked store in a place called
Poverty Hollow. Moreover, he was able to mentally calculate the net profit to
be made from each item.[18] But Huntington let it be known he was not just a
geek: "I could whip any boy in school, young or old," he declared. His enterprise
was evident early. "From the time I was a child until the present I hardly
remember the time I was not doing something," were the first words in his
dictated memoirs. Huntington had come to California, not to grub for gold

in the dirt, but with the intention of selling whatever he could to the gold seekers. "I didn't go to California with much fever," he remarked later. He spent one day mining to see what it was like and never did it again. Seeking every advantage, he would take a "little dory" on the frequently choppy waters of San Francisco Bay to intercept incoming ships so he might strike the first bargains to buy merchandise, such as potatoes. He would then sell the goods in town at substantial profit. Even his $16 trip up the river to Sacramento was a money-making venture, in which he earned $84 by recruiting that many other passengers at a dollar-a-head commission for the ship captain. Nearly half a century after he arrived in California, he still recalled how much he had paid for breakfast in San Francisco's Portsmouth Square: "50 cents."[19]

Although not taller than six feet, Huntington was already an imposing figure at two hundred hard pounds earned by formidable physical work that started early in the day. He was deliberative in assessing those who might be useful. When Hopkins opened his grocery business next door, a natural alliance began that lasted almost a quarter of a century, ending only by Hopkins's death, which he mourned for years. "These two businessmen were especially suited to do business together," recalled an associate years later. "Mr. Huntington was by nature an off-hand business man, ever ready for a trade to buy or sell; while Mr. Hopkins was careful, painstaking, with a watchful eye upon the accounts, collections and all the details that pertain to the inside management."[20]

The two ran a tight ship. They forbade their thirty employees to gamble even away from work at the 250–300 self-styled casinos and saloons around Sacramento.[21] Drinking was disallowed. No one could leave the building after dinner or before breakfast. Huntington found the sins of the river city offensive. He wrote his brother Solon, who stayed in New York buying wholesale materials to ship to Collis in California, that only six hundred of the approximately ten thousand Sacramentans were women, and four-fifths of them were "harlots."[22]

Keeping the workers away from wickedness, and instead working productively for the store, had employee incentives. Huntington and Hopkins provided their workers housing, food, and what would be a marker for a future development of some note: a lending library. Huntington bought three hundred to four hundred books for $29 from a desperate boatman on the docks. It was not for his own edification. Huntington could barely spell the simplest words. He wanted only to keep his employees busy and under his control.

The neighboring Stanford Brothers store did not offer those sorts of employee inducements. But in 1852, the biggest year of immigration for the California Gold Rush, it did acquire what Huntington and Hopkins would, with gimlet eyes, soon recognize as an unusual asset: young Leland Stanford.

A bowed if not broken Stanford had arrived just four months before a massive fire decimated much of Sacramento. It was time for the family to branch out. Josiah had started his retail trade up-country in a notorious mining town called Mormon Island. The brothers knew there was money to be made up and down the Gold Country, so they quickly dispatched Leland to a remote mountain mining settlement called Cold Spring, about fifty miles east of Sacramento and a little south of where James Marshall spotted gold on that January day four years earlier. At Cold Spring, Leland Stanford set up a Stanford Brothers branch. His family to the rescue once again, the brothers supplied him with all the materials he would need. They sold the inventory to him at a discount and allowed him to pay them back with his profits. When it looked as if Cold Spring prospecting had gone cold indeed, and that there was more money to be made some thirty miles north as the crow flies, at a mining outpost called Michigan City, Leland picked up and moved there in the summer of 1853. Settled by prospectors from the wolverine state, Michigan City was deep in the piney mountains rising at first gently but then with increasing drama above the vast Central Valley floor. What roads existed throughout the immense region were narrow, rough, and mercurial.

The largely unspoiled California the gold rushers found was a California they would begin altering almost immediately. The first significant geologic metamorphosis happening right under the fortune hunters' feet commenced just as Stanford was setting up shop in the mountains, where he would have been eyewitness to one of the first cataclysmic changes of the land.

Within three years of gold's discovery at Sutter's Mill, it had become apparent there was a great deal more gold *in* the mountains than in the existing rivers and streams coursing *over* them. What the gold rushers didn't know at first was they were inadvertently finding the bigger deposits in dry, ancient riverbeds ribboning through the Sierras that had run wet and wild tens of millions of years ago. During the ensuing millennia, those rivers had annealed into gravel and sedimentary rock, uplifted, and were sometimes evident as veins of gold in the canyon walls. By the advent of the 1850s, enterprising miners were using picks and shovels to dig out those deposits. The next step was to divert water from the mountains to wash over and dislodge the prehistoric gravel, mimicking a technology described by Pliny the Elder in Rome about the time Jesus lived. By sometime in 1852 or 1853 a radical new technology emerged: hydraulic mining.

The credit—or blame—remains in question. The consequences are not. Two men came to light as the major entrepreneurs, Anthony (or Antoine) Chabot and Edward Matteson. They independently engineered the elegantly brutal notion of pumping the Sierra waters at full charge at the ancient channels and then curating the debris as it washed down a series of troughs called sluice boxes. The heavy gold tended to sink and get trapped by the wooden waterways' perpendicular slats, as the water and detritus of the mountain washed down the flumes.

At first, it was party time. Gold strikes, which has been waning overall, rebounded sharply. The farmers and ranchers of the Central Valley reveled in the profits for their products rapidly consumed by the prospectors. The riverboat businessmen gushed over the boom in the transportation trade. Stores such as Stanford Brothers were doing what had become known as land-office business. But the day of reckoning was not yet on the calendar. "Little by little, however, the debris was creeping down the steep water courses of the mountains and coming to rest in the main river channels," noted a signature study by the U.S. Army Corps of Engineers many years later.[23] As a twentieth-century geology scholar put it, "Never before had man engineered in so short a period so massive a transfer of earth. Hills were reduced to yawning amphitheaters, ancient river channels were exhumed and the spoil was dumped into the rising beds of the modern stream system."[24] In time, it would be equivalent to filling the 363-mile Erie Canal.

Sacramento and other river and farm towns that had become accustomed to some flooding during wet years, not missing stride, gleefully enjoyed the prosperity with renewed vigor for a decade. Then came the winter of 1861–62. That season's epic deluge dropped just short of fifty inches of rain on San Francisco, thirty whopping inches more than the annual twenty-inch average, where scientific measurements had been gathered for years. It rained like that across the state. It "transformed the Sacramento and San Joaquin Valleys into an inland sea, 250 to 300 miles long and 20 to 60 miles wide," the Corps study notes. "Rivers everywhere overflowed their banks, spreading ruin, devastation and sometimes death, over wide areas. The dry creeks and arroyos became raging watercourses which converted the lowlands into shoreless lakes. Until the floodwaters subsided, transportation, business and farming were at a standstill. Thousands of head of livestock perished, and possibly a fourth of the state's taxable wealth was destroyed."[25]

Even normally arid Los Angeles, still a remote outpost with more cattle than people, went under water with fifty inches of rain, three times what it normally enjoyed.[26] Telegraph lines were down in places because "*the tops of the poles are underwater!*" exclaimed a seminal work surveying California during the period.[27] "Cries of protest were heard by the agriculturalists as their fields became covered by sand, gravel, and mud. At the same time the navigation interests and the businessmen they supplied protested long and loud because they could not get their steamboats up river as in times past."[28] The tailings from the hydraulic mining were so immense and had traveled so far that the very bed of the Sacramento River along the town where the state capitol had found a permanent home in 1860 had risen a full ten feet. The city was underwater for three months. Almost everyone suffered. The disaster was so profound the city voters agreed to tax themselves enough extra money to actually move the confluence of the American and Sacramento Rivers north by about a quarter of a mile. City streets were also raised by ten to fifteen feet, while somehow keeping the buildings intact and working. An immense levee went up along the riverfront. All this was done by men with shovels and wagons and horses.

It had finally become obvious to almost anyone that geologic change was taking place. And it was caused by humans.

There were other notable consequences. The revival of the gold-prospecting industry brought by hydraulic mining also had the immediate effect of ending its brief, rugged individual character. Instead of hardy, lone entrepreneurs using preindustrial tools such as pans, picks, and shovels they had bought at stores such as Stanford Brothers and Huntington-Hopkins, teams of workers were needed to operate the steam-powered water cannons sold directly by factories. The once sole owner-operators of one-man fortune-seeking enterprises began to work in organized groups for start-up companies in return for a daily wage. The conflicting economic and political interests representing the lucrative, if already struggling, mining interests and the young but ascendant farming and ranching industries began quarrelling, then battling, and eventually going to court over what was to be done. A new fight for California's future was on. Dumping the detritus of hydraulic mining into the rivers finally became illegal in 1884.

Outside the new state, the epoch's struggle for the future of the United States of America was also taking final form. The Sierra Nevada on California's eastern frontier had initially served as a bulwark against the war at the other end of the nation. It was insufficient. Blue-Gray battle lines were also under construction across California, with most backing the admittance of the thirty-first state as free, but many still agitating for slavery. It was a poorly kept secret that slaves already existed in the Golden State. It fell heaviest on Native California Indians, especially children.

"It has been for years a regular business to steal Indian children and bring them down to civilized parts of the state, even to San Francisco and sell them," wrote the early government surveyor, who then qualified the practice saying the children were not slaves but "servants." However, he then added, "Mendocino County has been the scene of many of these stealings, and it is said that some of the kidnappers would often get the consent of the parents by shooting them to prevent opposition."[29]

A leading historian of Native tribes noted that "about 10,000 Indians may have been indentured or sold between 1850 and 1863."[30] Even normally complacent government officials had trouble looking the other way: "I am compelled to state that a band of scoundrels, generally fugitive Americans and Spaniards, are in the habit of not only carrying off Indian children, but also committing outrages upon their women, and I have not yet the power to suppress it," wrote a federal official to the superintendent of Indian affairs in San Francisco in 1854.[31] Those Native California Indians who had survived the plagues of disease that had begun to decimate them with the arrival of the Spanish and took on pandemic proportions with the forty-niners saw just about everything else stripped from them.

For the small but not invisible African American gold rush population of California, it wasn't much better. Shortly before the discovery of gold at Sutter's Mill there was just a handful of people of African descent in California. By 1850 there were 962, according to the U.S. Census.[32] Although there is no documented number of blacks held slave in the free state of California in those antebellum years, it is certain the condition took place. "The lack of law enforcement made it possible for slavery to exist in many parts of the state," noted a history of African Americans of the era.[33] Notorious cases such as the one involving Archy Lee, a black man brought to California as a slave by his Mississippi owner, Charles Stovall, is one infamous, documented example.

Police arrested Lee in Sacramento for refusing to return to Mississippi with his putative owner, leading to legal rulings that affirmed a fugitive slave law valid in California in 1858.

Passions ran high, as illustrated by the illegal 1859 duel between antislavery California's U.S. senator David Broderick and pro-Confederacy, former California Supreme Court chief justice David Terry, who skirmished over the issue and ensuing name-calling. Terry shot Broderick in the chest at the duel just south of the San Francisco city limit. He died three days later.[34]

The consequences of not being an American citizen—especially one of northern European ancestry—were everywhere. In the mining settlement of Los Pinos, near Stanford's store in Cold Spring, notices appeared "that anyone who was not an American citizen must abandon the place within twenty-four hours and that he who did not comply would be obliged by force."[35] Force included shooting and hanging. For thirty-year-old Leland Stanford it was a completely new world of disorder, semi-anarchy, and almost anything goes. How could it not affect him?

Stanford, as with the vast majority of other Gold Country fortune hunters, was largely emancipated from the constraints of East Coast and midwestern prudence. Wives and daughters were rare, churchmen seldom at hand, moral codes from the time one arrived in San Francisco to gold digging in the mountains subverted. Stanford, with his Wisconsin law background and his enterprising brothers nearby, retained some rectitude. Seeing his chance for advancement and not having to stand election for the post, in the fall of 1854 Stanford was appointed justice of the peace for the Michigan City township by the local board of supervisors. He heard and ruled on workaday cases such as mining claims and property deed disputes. At almost the same time, Stanford, then showing his colors, bought a local bar for $575: the Empire Saloon, naturally calling to mind the Bull's Head tavern in his native Empire State.[36] A nineteenth-century newspaper, printing a reminiscence of an old-timer, described the tavern as a "building in which men gambled with short cards and long cards day and night and openly, women paying out the money at the banking games."[37] Stanford went into business marketing whiskey, playing cards, and other essentials to the notoriously improvident forty-niners. Having returned to the family's legacy saloon business but at last with some official legal authority, Leland Stanford literally held court in his newly purchased bar, where for the next six months, he dispensed liquor and frontier justice. Business was good.

Then, in April of 1855, Jennie's father died. After waiting three long, unhappy years in upstate New York, slandered but resolute, she finally saw Lady Luck appear as deus ex machina. Her betrothed had come to fetch her.

CHAPTER 5

Ditching and Hitching

Leland and Jennie Stanford were on their own, at last together again, on the eve of the most turbulent period of American history.

Leland's luck—as it is often observed in life, accompanied by working harder—was improving. His brothers had departed Sacramento for new enterprises in San Francisco, New York, and Australia, leaving him to essentially inherit the store, well set up and still prospering down by the Sacramento River port. Many years later, well into middle age, he conveniently forgot his brothers had established his beachhead, instead telling a gullible reporter in New York he had carried one hundred pounds of gold, accompanied by two armed guards, from the mining camps all the way to San Francisco, and with the commission had earned enough money to open a "large store" in Sacramento.[1] But still a young man, he had not yet fully embraced his ability to deceive.

Leland had fortuitously avoided the disaster that had afflicted his fortunes in Wisconsin by leaving his saloon, branch store, and justice of the peace business in the Sierra mining region in order to retrieve Jennie. Two years after he left Michigan City, a fire ripped through the mountain town, destroying all the buildings—including the Empire Saloon, of course—in about one hour. With forty-niner gumption and greed, the prospectors rebuilt the town and started washing away the hillsides with hydraulic mining. Just a year later, the entire settlement, built on "tolerably flat ground," began to slough off the steep mountainside, eventually washing down the steep canyon wall into the river system. Michigan City was no more.[2]

To reclaim his bride, Leland boarded a ship back to Nicaragua, traveled overland to the Atlantic, then steamed up to New York. It was July of 1855. After he made his way upstate to gather Jennie, the couple then took three months to get back down to New York Harbor and board another barque for the West. The trip more routine than it had been at first, they crossed over to the Pacific in three days and boarded another steamer bound for California, arriving in mid-November.

With his brothers gone to start new ventures, Leland had the store to himself. He and Jennie set up house a few blocks away and lived modestly, as young couples will, using boxes and boards for furniture. Leland chopped kindling and brought in water. "They spent a very happy season in their life together in that little house, and it was fondly remembered and very often referred to," declared Jennie's personal secretary years later. "There was one colored woman who helped ladies of Mrs. Stanford's acquaintance, and when it was learned she had Saturdays free Mr. Stanford engaged her for that."[3]

Boomtown Sacramento would have appeared startlingly rude compared to the still young but already somewhat ordered New York state capital Leland and Jennie had traded for California's. An unregulated livestock market took place in the middle of what was then downtown Sacramento along the riverfront. Horses being the prime transport engine of the day, manure was everywhere until someone got fed up and pushed it into huge piles on the sides and corners of the dirt streets that turned into muddy septic bogs in the winter and dung-beetle-infested stench mounds in the summer, baking in the Central Valley heat. A dead horse left in the street would not be uncommon. There were no proper sewers yet.[4]

"Three-fourths of the people who settle in Sacramento City are visited by agues, diarrheas and other reducing complaints," a *New York Tribune* reporter wrote of his Sacramento sojourn during the first years of the gold rush. "In the summer the place is a furnace, in winter little better than a swamp."[5] A Sacramento-area historian quipped that "personal hygiene was not always the most fastidious—and the odors could be horrendous."[6]

At night the never-ending influx of fortune hunters would throw down their blankets under the magnificent native oaks of the valley, not uncommonly six feet in diameter, roots deep in the ancient topsoils. But then many would build campfires beneath the stands, killing the trees and leaving their charred, mute skeletons to rot. The waterfront itself was a chaotic scene of trade, often violence such as hangings, and men hurriedly abandoning their boats for the

Gold Country, anxious they were too late to cash in on the frenzy. As in San Francisco, one of the ships was used as a jail—locals called it the Old Prison Brig—but since that was insufficient to administer the raw justice of the day, chain gangs were soon deployed. In the river itself, dead animals could commonly be seen floating downstream.

Toward the end of 1856, Stanford moved the business his brothers had built to a new location a few blocks away, although he kept the Stanford Brothers brand. He made it a wholesale grocery store and soon felt the need to take on a new partnership with another local retailer. It wouldn't last long: Collis Huntington, Mark Hopkins, and Charles Crocker had other plans for him.

It was Crocker who started it. In April of 1855 the clothes and carpet shopkeeper ran for and won a seat on the city council, a position then called alderman.[7] He ran under the banner of a new national political party surging coast to coast: the American Party, which started out calling itself the Order of the Star Spangled Banner but remains better known to history as the Know-Nothings. The name came from its origins at the beginning of the 1850s as a secret society in which members used code to communicate and vowed to tell outsiders they knew nothing about the organization. But by the end of 1855 they were a bona fide national movement, out from the political closet, with governors in eight states, more than one hundred men in Congress, and thousands in local offices.[8] Indeed, the party swept California, winning the governor's seat and both houses of the state legislature.[9] The party's primary national platform was fairly simple. They wanted immigrants, especially those of a certain "foreign" religion, banned or severely regulated: Roman Catholics.

Historians, political scientists, and anthropologists have long recognized the pattern, not uncommon after big waves of immigration, if seemingly paradoxical to founding precepts of the United States, and call it nativism.[10] The Know-Nothings said only "native" Americans should have the rights of citizens. But those natives did not include Native Indians, African Americans, or people of Mexican ancestry, even if citizens, and even if born in the United States. It did include most people from northern and western Europe. Not all, however, because at the top of the list of Americans the so-called American Party wanted out were the Irish if they were adherents of the ancient church of Rome. The Know-Nothings regarded them subject to a foreign potentate—the Pope.

For most of the party members, the Know-Nothing creed took little issue with the fact that their own adherents, too, were either immigrants or descendants of those from other countries. In fact, they valued some immigration, which was clearly building the nation. But explicitly only white, Protestant immigrants.

The Know-Nothings were decidedly antislavery in the North, but largely for the same stated reasons as early abolitionists, such as those who had impressed young Stanford in New York: "Our native-born citizens hate to work by the side of an Irishman," stated one, because it "dishonored" white labor. And it provided "the same feeling in which makes it impossible for a respectable white man to labor by the side of slaves in the South."[11] Immigrants lowered wages, they argued, hurting white, Protestant workingmen. Many scholars have suggested one of the massive appeals to adherents of the movement was fear of losing their status in the fast-changing American hierarchy. "It allowed them to blame outsiders for their declining position in society."[12] The Know-Nothings' slogan that "Americans Must Rule America" also meant fighting what they called voter fraud, which they said was encouraged by opposition party politicians cynically exploiting immigrants solely to get elected.[13]

The movement, as with most large groups, was not entirely uniform. As in the South but unlike in the North, California Know-Nothings recruited Catholics.[14] California, long settled by people from around the world, found a pariah immigrant of its own: Chinese workers who came along with tens of thousands of others also seeking the bountiful opportunities of the gold rush. That Know-Nothing alderman Crocker's coming fame and fortune would soon be completely dependent on the Herculean diligence of Asian men and women would stand a tart irony for his legacy and that of Hopkins, Huntington, and then most notably, Leland Stanford.

Since the Know-Nothings were also largely antiliquor, it stood to reason that Stanford remained a member of one of the other two main political parties of antebellum America, the Whigs. It was under that banner he had indulged his earlier desire for office in Wisconsin. Now established in California, Stanford, with the encouragement of Huntington and Hopkins, would soon follow fellow merchant Crocker in his enduring quest for political power. How to navigate the maelstrom tossing American politics inside out and upside down was another matter.

The antislavery movement had been growing steadily across the North and into the West for much of the 1800s, but there were so many factions and factions within factions that a mass antislavery political party never jelled. Then came a series of earthshaking events.

"In a very real sense, it was the discovery of gold in California that initiated the collapse of the Whig organization," notes a political historian of the era.[15] Gold hurried the entrance of California into the Union and it was clear California's leaders would not suffer slavery, despite that demand by slaveowner interests. Sen. John C. Calhoun of South Carolina and legendary defender of slavery declared that if Congress admitted California as a free state, the South must secede.[16] To placate proslavery political power in another futile attempt to prevent secession, Congress then passed a series of acts known collectively as the 1850 Compromise, essentially opening the door to future expansion of slavery beyond the South. At least as infuriating to many Northerners, it included the Fugitive Slave Act, requiring free states to turn over runaway slaves. Next was the Kansas-Nebraska Act of 1854 that repealed the Missouri Compromise of 1820 and sanctioned slavery to expand north. In 1857, the U.S. Supreme Court's notorious *Dred Scott* ruling that slaves were not citizens and Congress could not ban the expansion of slavery helped tip the balance. The Whigs were held largely responsible for capitulating to what was called slave power, which was not a reference to the slaves themselves but to the Southern slave owners, who had earned the hatred of the free North.

By then, what had once seemed like an enduring political party was dead. In California, the Whigs had all but disappeared by 1855.[17] The Know-Nothings, a hothouse product, then also collapsed. After one year in power, Californians threw them out of office, even impeaching some statewide officials.[18] The United States of America was anything but united, as symbolized by the bitter, intractable differences among the political parties that were failing at the prime mission of governing.

A new party, formally created in the summer of 1854, was coalescing out of the many antislavery movements, including the Know-Nothings. As diverse alliances often must, it survived by managing a series of awkward deals among competing political players. At its pivotal 1856 national convention, on one hand, the new party called for banning the extension of the "twin relics of barbarism—Polygamy, and Slavery," bearing in mind the Mormon movement into the newly formed Utah Territory—but stopped short of calling for abolition of slavery in states where it existed, as the so-called radicals of the movement demanded. It was, in the words of two scholars of the situation, a "theretofore unimaginable" coalition.[19] It called itself the Republican Party.

Its members nominated John Charles Frémont as their first standard-bearer, which drew many Californians as he had won some acclaim for his five difficult expeditions across the continent into the state and had briefly been one of California's first two U.S. senators. He had also participated in the Bear Flag Revolt of 1846, which provided him with some California credibility. But as the compromise candidate for the fledgling Republicans he also brought the new party a great deal of grief. Frémont had been court-martialed, drummed out of the army, and although portrayed as a dashing, romantic conqueror of the West, the reality was less attractive. "If his successful crossings of the mountains testified to his remarkable tenacity of spirit his career also provided disturbing evidence of shortcomings in his character," noted a historian of the Republican Party. "His reserved manner in conversation betrayed none of his well-documented penchant for rash and impulsive action. Perhaps because of his illegitimate birth and poverty as a child, he was extremely sensitive to actual or imagined personal slights."[20]

During the election "he spent his days fencing, riding and exercising while others directed affairs."[21] Frémont lost to Democrat James Buchanan, in no small part because the remaining Know-Nothings split Republican strength.

A thoughtful, articulate, and pragmatic thirty-seven-year-old country lawyer from Illinois, noted for his laconic sense of humor, who had served just one two-year term in Congress as a Whig, was paying apt attention. He had already joined the Republicans. And since he had made good money representing railroads, the lanky, if homely, midwesterner would have also been comfortable with one other part of the new party platform: "Resolved, That a railroad to the Pacific Ocean by the most central and practicable route is imperatively demanded by the interests of the whole country, and that the Federal Government ought to render immediate and efficient aid in its construction, and as an auxiliary thereto to the immediate construction of an emigrant road on the line of the railroad."[22]

Seeing what was what, Hopkins and Crocker got on board with the up-and-coming Republicans. Huntington, for the first time demonstrating substantial interest in what political power might do, joined them. Then the three task-oriented men experimented with some safe, beta community organizing of their own.

Attempts by forward-thinking citizens to create a library for the general population of Sacramento had failed as early as 1850, their 300-plus volumes destroyed by the great fire that consumed much of the town in 1852. Huntington and Hopkins, seeing the utility of their own bargain-priced 300–400 collection of books for their employees, joined with Crocker and some others in 1857 to form what would become the seeds of the Sacramento Public Library. The ecumenical effort had clear crossover appeal, evidenced by the local Sons of Temperance society contributing to the successful enterprise.[23] Stanford, who, as his older brother had noted had weak work ethic but stronger interest in reading, was also brought in. With the relatively small but victorious audition the library represented, the fresh new band of four players began to prepare for a far more ambitious performance, one with long-term, immense financial potential. Each man would have a specialized chair, complimenting one another. Little could they foresee how significantly this would also alter politics, culture, and the future of the nation.

In April of 1856 Crocker's older brother E. B. called for a Saturday-night meeting of the Sacramento Republicans at a downtown hotel. The rollicking newspaper account of the event lists the few stalwart supporters there, but there is no mention of Leland Stanford. The meeting of moderates caused a notorious uproar, with angry anti-Republicans rushing the stage and overthrowing the speaker's stand.[24] A subsequent attempt for a two-day state convention held during a Tuesday and Wednesday afternoon at a local church attracted less risk. Newspaper accounts declared it "dull" and businesslike. Hopkins and the elder Crocker showed up, as did Huntington, who was then appointed a member of the state central committee. Once again, Stanford's name appears not.[25]

In late summer, the newly formed Republicans had another sedate meeting in Sacramento. Charles Crocker appeared as did Huntington and this time, Leland Stanford, who emerged publicly for the first time as a member of what would soon be first marketed as the Gallant Old Party. The top officials gave Stanford a position on a low-rank committee—but it was a start.[26]

The mien of his character would appear attractive to the voters and political bosses who chose candidates. By the time he was in his early thirties, tending a wholesale grocery store in town and going home to eat home-cooked meals with his wife, instead of running drinks and a makeshift courtroom alone in a frontier mining camp, Leland Stanford had filled out his five-foot-eleven frame, weighing in at over two hundred pounds. His full but relatively trim dark beard and his solemn bearing provided a somewhat imposing impression. There is at least one reference to his "basso-profundo" voice. With his brothers gone and the large wholesale store with his name on it, there was also the appearance of business success, which would also be a political positive. He was a lawyer and had justice of the peace on his résumé. At least as important to backroom power brokers, he had clearly demonstrated political ambition.

In April of 1857 Stanford entered his name for office, ditching the Whigs, instead hitching himself, again, to a new ride, the California Republican Party. With little prospect of getting appointed to a responsible government post, as he had in the Mother Lode, Stanford ran for alderman from Sacramento's First Ward—the seat that Hopkins had barely lost two years before despite renouncing his name placed on the ballot by others and refusing to campaign. The voters crushed Stanford's hopes, giving him 87 votes of the 3,068 counted.[27]

Failure by now a comfortably familiar chaperone that did not alter his stride, Stanford remained undeterred. Something was seasoning in him. The actions of his new associates showed they sensed it. Charles Crocker, at the newborn California state Republicans meeting just three months later, pushed Stanford as the party's nominee for statewide office, lieutenant governor. After a series of bloviated speeches meant to demonstrate modesty, practicality, and other common political bombasts, the convention turned down the rather too ambitious, too rapidly attempted ascent, and instead voted to put Stanford in the considerably lesser role as its nominee for state treasurer.[28] But the result was the same: on election day the waning Know-Nothings and the still reasonably sturdy, if a little shaky, Democrats stomped him.[29]

That Stanford was severely beaten twice in California alone were just rehearsals for Huntington, Hopkins, and Crocker. They were grooming him for the Big Show.

Calls for a transcontinental railroad can be documented back at least to the early 1830s, as seen in an article in an Ann Arbor, Michigan, weekly newspaper called *The Emigrant*. "We are perfectly aware that many will laugh at this and display their wisdom by condemning it without examination," the article noted, while giving a respectful nod to Lewis and Clark's celebrated 1804–6 expedition to the Northwest.

> It is in our power to build up an immense city at the mouth of the Oregon, to make it the depot for our East India trade and perhaps for that of Europe—*in fact to unite New York and the Oregon by a rail way* by which the traveler leaving the City of New York shall at the moderate rate of 10 miles an hour, place himself on the shores of the Pacific.

The author then estimated the trip "might occupy about a fortnight."[30] Beyond its goal of "binding the East and West together," it was one of nation's first published calls for what would one day be called globalization, a concept business people always searching for expanding markets would easily grasp. Businessmen such as Collis Huntington, Mark Hopkins, Charles Crocker, and of course, Leland Stanford.

As the idea of Manifest Destiny—that infamous nineteenth-century ideology declaring that the United States of America should, and inevitably would, expand its borders to embrace the continent—gained popularity, the notion of an iron highway safely, economically, and efficiently gliding people and freight across prairies, rivers, and deserts, and even surmounting mountain ranges, provoked less condemnation and more possibilities. A powerful political imperative also arose. The escalating rancor between the North and South regarding slavery led to two different schemes for the imagined railroad's route. Northerners preferred the prospect of rails linking the Atlantic and Pacific Oceans through the geographic middle of the nation. That would mean through free states. Southern forces scoffed at this. Aside from King Cotton being the nation's number-one export but with still no ready Pacific port to exploit Asian trade, they cited basic geographic realities: crossing the Rockies would be one tremendous engineering obstacle, but overcoming the Sierra Nevada would be ridiculously improbable.[31] It would be far wiser to run the railroad across the relatively flat southern deserts and, not incidentally, give the Southern oligarchy commercial and political access to Pacific ports and California gold.

That, of course, was precisely what Northerners sought to prevent. Jefferson Davis personified the situation. Because of the discovery of gold and the subsequent admission of California to the Union, the need for finding a suitable railroad route to the shores of the Pacific became urgent for both Blue and Gray. A government survey of possible routes was called for. Although commerce, politics, and "destiny" were reasons enough, anxieties about defending the newly won West against enemy incursions meant the survey went into the hands of 1853 secretary of war—Jefferson Davis, who, of course, would become the president of the Confederacy fewer than ten years later. And so Congress directed him. "Davis relished the assignment," noted his biographer.[32] In his report that year to President Franklin Pierce, Davis loftily stated that although "its commercial and agricultural advantage, its political and military necessity, have attracted the attention and excited the interest of our whole country," he would avoid making a route recommendation based on "preconceived opinion or prejudice, and sectional rivalry." Antislavery critics immediately condemned Davis, the former colonel, congressman, and senator from Mississippi, as conniving, at best.

The agents Davis chose for the surveys found that "no railway pass could be found north" of Southern California.[33] There was one tiny glitch in the southern stretch they did recommend: a segment of the Davis-sponsored route ran through northern Mexico. Secretary of War Davis persuaded President Pierce to dispatch U.S. minister to Mexico James Gadsden to approach Mexican president Antonio de Santa Anna, with whom he negotiated a treaty to buy a strip of land for $10 million that would demark the conterminous border between the two countries in what is now southern New Mexico and Arizona. The true purpose of the purchase, of course, was to use it for a transcontinental railroad. Northern congressmen were aghast.[34]

"It takes a grand national school like West Point," bellowed Missouri senator Thomas Hart Benton, making a pointed stab at Jefferson Davis's military pedigree, "to put national roads outside of a country and leave the interior without one."[35] Pierce and Davis won that congressional fight after substantial compromises. However, the fast-approaching Civil War would render the victory Pyrrhic.

How to cross the Sierra Nevada into central California where its capital city and leading port were located, however, was an epic stumper. Its peaks are the highest in the contiguous United States, topping out at literally breathtaking 14,505 feet. Even the legendary passes of the 400-mile-long range require an ascent of some 7,000 feet, which for months are commonly suffocated in 15 feet of snow.[36] Sheer cliffs of granite are among the mountains' chief characteristics, initially formed by a crescent of volcanoes during the Mesozoic era, roughly 250–200 million years ago. Mother Nature began the finish work toward the end of the last ice age, or Pleistocene epoch, that began about 2.6 million years past and ended roughly only 20,000 years ago. As the immense sheets of ice began to melt and move, glaciers scoured and scraped valleys, creating wonders such as Yosemite.

The Sierra Nevada has a relatively gradual western slope but a boldly abrupt incline on its eastern face, which so daunted the early pioneers coming on foot across the vast plains and then desert from the East to California. How on earth a railroad could vanquish those magisterial mountains was, without qualification, a supreme challenge in the 1800s. Then a low-key engineer, all of twenty-eight years old, not of intimidating bearing but of no mean intellectual and emotional fire, got off a ferry boat on the Sacramento River docks in the spring of 1854. He and his twenty-six-year-old wife gathered their baggage, scanned their tumultuous new home, and set off to tame it.

If ever a human being fit the description by classic California writer Wallace Stegner of a poignant fate—"he met trains that had not yet arrived'—it was Theodore Dehone Judah.[37]

Born in Connecticut just two years after Stanford, Judah soon moved with his family to Troy, New York, Crocker's hometown and just fifteen miles north of the Bull's Head tavern in Albany at the north end of the Troy Road. After graduating from a local technical school, Judah went to work for the Troy and Schenectady Railroad, building a segment of the line. After that he went on to a series of jobs at a variety of other railroad companies. He was assembling a strong résumé and top-shelf professional reputation.

The Erie Canal would also be a lodestone in his brief, often exultant, but ultimately bitter life. He had just completed working on part of that epic project's connection between the Hudson River and Lake Erie near Niagara Falls and started a new railroad job in Buffalo when an early western railroad entrepreneur asked to meet Judah in New York City. Judah's wife, Anna, recalled in a letter years later that three days after he left for the meeting she received a telegram: "Be home to-night; we sail for California, April 2nd."[38] They took a steamer to Nicaragua, following the same route as Stanford, arriving on the West Coast to build a railroad line from Sacramento to the Gold Country.

The few daguerreotypes left of Judah's image show an unassuming man of medium stature and build. In almost every reminiscence of those who knew him, he was very much a person of great energy and focus. And he was a man, in the language of his time, of parts. Citing his "great love for music,' Anna wrote in a long letter to a Sacramento magazine memorializing her husband, "There was hardly a musical instrument upon which he could not play."[39] His greatest enthusiasm was for railroading, but as is not uncommon in matters of business, it was an ardor unrequited. The railroad start-up bringing trains from Sacramento to the Sierra foothills failed, leaving Judah unemployed, but a revelator: he had discovered a route over the seemingly insurmountable Sierra Nevada. It was a signal breakthrough, arguably on the order of finding a Northwest Passage.[40] But few in his own land would listen to whom some people started calling Crazy Judah.

When the idealistic young railroad man published his findings, his few remaining financial backers bolted, angry that he had given away one of the great proprietary secrets of the age. Judah, ever the ingenue engineer and never the cunning capitalist, returned their furor in kind. And he persisted in chasing his dream, arranging a meeting with a group of financiers in San Francisco who told him they liked his business plan but for one caveat: it would not make money for twenty years—too long to wait for the spoils it might bring. Judah returned to Sacramento for another meeting with a group of capitalists who might underwrite the venture. And again, he saw the faces remain immobile and heard the skepticism regarding a slow return on investment for the unheard-of capital outlay. The exposure was simply too great.

Here the story becomes more portentous and not inconsequently disputatious. One man at the meeting who gave a detailed account of the Sacramento gathering where Judah made his floundering pitch was well known to the business interests in town despite having no experience in major money ventures. Rather, he was known as a "sharp trader," who ran just a hardware store down along the riverfront and had helped start the public library. No one to worry about. After the suits shook Judah's hand, thanked him for his presentation, and left their rueful regrets, the merchant took the young engineer aside and asked him to come to his shop the next night to have a chat. His associates would be there. On the other hand was the wholesale grocer who had fallen into company with the hardware shopkeeper and was becoming a serial, if failed, political candidate. He told an early stenographer of his life he "had a conversation" with the merchant, alerting him to Judah's potential. After some discussion, he said, they agreed to meet the young engineer away from the rest of the Sacramento business leaders.

Regardless of who initiated the action, Theodore Judah, barren of devices and hardly a match for Collis Huntington and Leland Stanford, took the meeting.

CHAPTER 6

"The Road Must Be Built"

Collis Huntington, Mark Hopkins, Charles Crocker—and Leland Stanford—now informally but certainly bound together, had not been idle. They had begun to sometimes refer to themselves as the Associates, a name their acolytes would insist on employing for a century. But soon, the four men would be better and forever known by a far grander name.

Some deep tincture was altering, darkening, in Stanford. Displaying more tenacity than talent, at age thirty-five he nevertheless no longer appeared to be the ne'er-do-well of his youth. Rather, he was now a man who seemed to have no quit in him. Had the Wisconsin fire tempered something in him? The rough-and-ready Sierra Nevada years? Just a late coming of age?

Few have called Leland Stanford a quick study, but many have underestimated his late-blooming but stolid ability to keep at it. He was discovering not only the singular importance of timing but that fortune does truly favor the bold—and not infrequently the boldly duplicitous. His next history-changing lessons took place during the following, consequential twenty-four months. He and his sponsors were ready to up the stakes. The nation was on the threshold of civil war, a movement to separate Southern and Northern California had become serious, and political alignments coast-to-coast were in historic tumult.

In June of 1859, some 150 California Republicans held another convention. On the first day, Crocker insisted on forgoing all the procedural formalities in which political wonks find comfort and instead doubled down on his group's candidate. This time the new band of associates were wired deep in the still tiny party's backroom decision-making and would nominate Leland Stanford for the top office: governor of California. Initially, Stanford had four rivals for the nomination, but by the end of the night, all had dropped out, leaving the failed four-time office seeker to accept a fifth go with some astonishing words: "Were I an aspiring man, seeking political station, I might hesitate about allowing myself to be placed in this position," he declared. "But I have no political aspirations; I am content to be a humble citizen."[1]

Then came his remarks on the issue of the day and arguably, the century: slavery.

> The cause in which we are engaged is one of the greatest in which any one can labor, it is the cause of the white man—the cause of free labor, of justice and of equal rights. I am in favor of free white American citizens. I prefer free white citizens to any other class or race. I prefer the white man to the negro as an inhabitant of our country. I believe its greatest good has been derived by having all of the country settled by free white men.[2]

It was as far as his political philosophy would grow.

The party platform remained committed solely to stopping the expansion of slavery, not abolishing it; the latter position many pragmatists such as Lincoln considered political suicide. Abolition could wait until Republicans achieved political power, adhering to the time-tested maxim that politics is art of the possible. The party, and Stanford, also underscored their preoccupation with a transcontinental railroad through the middle of the nation, a platform finding greater and greater popularity among the majority Northern voters.

"We are in favor of the railroad by that natural route which the emigrant in coming to this country has pointed out to us," Stanford said. "I am in favor of a railroad, and it is the policy of this state to favor that party which is likely to advance their interests."[3] And yet, California voters once again threw down on Stanford's candidacy, awarding him less than 10 percent of the vote.[4] On the other hand, when all was said and done, as the 1850s receded and the 1860s emerged, Stanford was the nominal head of the California Republican Party. All the cards were now in play.

The meeting with Theodore Judah took place upstairs at the Huntington-Hopkins hardware store, 54 K Street, Sacramento. There are some tangential disputes regarding exactly when it was held and how many attended but little doubt Leland Stanford was there. Judah unfolded his maps and opened his

technical specifications for grades going up and over the Sierras and for baro-
metric pressures as the elevations soared. He had calculated that the locomotives of the time could chug up the canyons at 7.5 miles per hour. For the
handful of men there to listen, the most interesting part of his presentation
had also been prepared: "An estimate can scarcely be made of the profitableness of such a road, for no instance of a road with a similar business exists,"
he stated. "It is believed that the profitableness will exceed that of any known
road in the world."[5]

Judah had already undertaken several trips to Washington, DC, hoping
to push his vision of a transcontinental railroad, and although hardly successful in advancing his plan, had returned home to California with a decent
handicapping of the District of Columbia players. The four Sacramento
shopkeepers, knowing they could not possibly finance what would likely be
the biggest capital-outlay project in American history, considered this. They
had been aware of other strong factors for some time, such as the growing call
for the government to invest in the project. In fact, major legislation sponsored
by an influential Iowa congressman would have done just that, although the
bill had stalled.[6] Two more cards were in play that if the foursome could get
in their hands, might just mean a full house, or better.

One card was the increasing likelihood that the next Republican presidential nominee would be the first of his party to win the office, that gangly, brainy,
homespun, and pragmatic railroad attorney and lobbyist from Illinois: Abraham Lincoln. His unequivocal advocacy for rails across the center of the Union
was known, although his famous remark, "The road must be built," would not
become the mission's battle cry until some years later.[7] The final ace in this
hand was the long preparation of the group's own key player in California:
Leland Stanford. Even Judah knew this on some level. "A good deal depends
on the election of Stanford, for the prestige of electing a Republican ticket
will go a great way toward getting us what we want," Judah wrote to an early
ally in September of 1861. Two years later he would add, "Stanford, who I
told you is all right, is as much under their influence as ever."[8] If they—
Huntington, Crocker, and Hopkins—could finally place Stanford in power,
Judah's declaration that "profitableness will exceed that of any known road in
the world" might materialize. The play was on, but the group would again go
forward one hand at a time.

Their initial personal investment could have been anything from $50 each,
if Judah's widow is right, to $15,000 per man, if a later analysis is correct.[9] It

is most likely the men initially put in no more than $1,500 each. The four Sacramentans often said they had invested millions of their own monies, and they may have in following years. But in a much later, scouring federal investigation into their affairs, Stanford was unable to provide any documentation of those claims for reasons virtually everyone would find, literally, incredible.[10]

But at the end of 1860, for the first time in Stanford's life, everything seemed to be going his way. The next year would be extraordinary.

The 1860 presidential election turned out as the Republicans had hoped, with Lincoln president. In the custom of the person holding that high office to shower political favors in the form of federal jobs to supporters, Lincoln relied on party leaders from around the country to give advice, if not consent. And so, the head of the California Republican Party, Leland Stanford, traveled to the White House with a delegation to meet and confer with the president largely to discuss patronage, the pleasant term for the more grating word: graft. Up the road on Capitol Hill, the victorious Republicans were able to salt their fresh power widely as they also took control of the House of Representatives. The Senate would remain in Democratic hands for the time being.

Stanford remained in the East for about five months, although when he returned to the West he brought no gain for his group's railroad aspirations. He could argue it didn't matter; he had Judah now in his back pocket. The extended absence was the first of many instances when Leland and Jennie would leave business behind and all but disappear for long periods. Sometime in this hurly-burly part of his life, Stanford sold the Stanford Brothers store, which helps explain how he was able to enjoy his holiday languor for so long.[11] In 1860 he was, at last, with some means. Another factor in his having accomplished this bears some succinct scrutiny.

The old mining town of Sutter Creek is about fifty miles east of Sacramento in the foothills of the Sierras and almost exactly halfway between Cold Spring and Michigan Bluff, where Stanford first set up shop for his brothers. A gold extraction operation at Sutter Creek called the Union Mine went bankrupt in 1859, a result of "extravagant management," noted the son of one of the owner-partners in 1929.[12] One of the big debtors was the store where they had squandered much of their earnings: Stanford Brothers, which at that time under Leland's management, sometimes took IOU notes instead of money. Consequently, Leland found himself with the largest number of shares in the mine. A senior partner of the operation told Stanford he was sure he could make a go of the operation if he managed it correctly. Stanford had nothing to lose—he was holding worthless paper and was due a substantial sum. The mine partner and Stanford cut a deal: if the partner could get the mine into the black, Stanford would pay him a salary and give him one-third ownership in the operation. Hoping for a fresh start, they changed the name to the Lincoln Mine and the partner began the dirty, difficult work. He almost immediately started making Stanford thousands of dollars.

Some seventy years later the mine partner's son, W. E. Downs, recalled that the roles then reversed. What happened next would further illuminate Stanford traits that would characterize him to the end.

Stanford's "struggle for cash resources at that time was severe. He borrowed heavily from my father [the mine partner] and at one time owed him $90,000," which Stanford agreed to pay back with shares in the mine. Some thirteen years later, when Stanford was living very high, "the time came to fulfill his promise, [and] Stanford foresaw that to give him (the shares) would leave him with less than a majority of the stock and therefore without absolute control." Downs "voluntarily" waived his claim for two shares, enabling Stanford to much later sell the mine, which profited him a trouble-free $300,000.[13] It would not be the last time Stanford would wade into the mining business as an angel investor, but it would be the only such known venture that did well.[14]

The temptation to get in on the mining business exploded exponentially in 1859. It started early that year when a small group of prospectors, one reputed to be a loudmouth, was scratching around the head of a canyon not far from the California line near the Nevada mining settlement that would later become the tawdry tourist trap Virginia City. Some scant bits of gold had been scraped together in these desiccated desert hills for the better part of a decade. This band of prospectors instead found a good deal of what they described as "black sand" but that to more discerning eyes was a dense indigo. "They cursed and threw aside the heavy bluish sand," according to a study by the Nevada Bureau of Mines and Geology. When the assay office back in the California mining town of Grass Valley curated the material for gold the following July, the assayer looked up and announced that the "blue stuff" in fact also had more than a little value. It was, in fact, silver. One of the miners, the one best known until then for his braggadocio, was named Henry Comstock; the men had stumbled into one of the richest strikes in history, forever to be known as the Comstock Lode.[15]

Some Californians, notably a hardy, poorly educated, early middle-aged man originally from Missouri then working claims around Grass Valley, invested heavily in the Comstock. George Hearst's obsession with mining was said to originate in his youth. Legend has it the Native Americans in Missouri's Franklin County called him Boy-That-Earth-Talked-To. His Bonanza King fortune from the silver and gold mines would pave the way for his only child, William Randolph Hearst, to spend freely on a newspaper in San Francisco called the *Examiner*. The son's genuine infamy, however, arrived when the young Californian later bought the *New York Morning Journal* and started the yellow journalism wars with Joseph Pulitzer, who had made his grubstake by infamous means, ironically, in Missouri. The tobacco-stained, rough-and-ready father, George Hearst, and increasingly redoubtable Leland Stanford would one day cross paths.[16]

Rather than rend their frock coats about not being in on the mammoth lucky strike, Huntington, Hopkins, and Crocker—and once again Stanford bringing up the rear—agreed they could best profit from the bounty by staying away from the mines themselves but rather, as they had long been doing with financial success, servicing them. The Comstock Lode became still another face card in the group's growing gambit to build the transcontinental railroad. The East Coast power elite, already worried about the abundance of California gold not being tied securely to the Union, argued that a cross-continental railway would bind the new state to the rest of the nation. The four California associates reinforced this fear by noting the same was true of the Comstock. It proved to be a powerful play.

While Leland and Jennie Stanford were on extended holiday in the East, Leland's associates were doing the grunt work of formally organizing a railway corporation and preparing their next move. They selected a name for the enterprise: the Central Pacific Rail Road Company. They chose a board of directors. When Stanford returned to California in the summer of 1860, everything was ready.

Two weeks later the state Republican Convention took place, and this time Stanford wasn't quite as coy as he had been before. With a Republican in the White House and the party controlling the House of Representatives, as well as having a good measure of success in local elections, it was time to take advantage of the momentum and go all out. Stanford's supporters, the *Sacramento Daily Union* reported the day before the convention nominated its candidates, had been "working like beavers. The friends of Stanford yesterday were anxious to go ahead with the nomination for Governor, as they were confident of succeeding."[17]

They did. He won his third state party nomination with some ease, giving a speech in which he flayed the "aristocracy" of the South versus the virtues of democracy in the Union. Nevertheless, he also could not resist trying to sound tractable and douse the scent of his growing conceit. First, he let the 250 delegates know he had disappeared for almost half a year in order to magnanimously allow someone else a chance to take up the burden of political and press huzzahs.

"This is the first time I have really and willingly consented that my name go before the Convention, and even now, gentlemen, permit me to say it is not altogether voluntary on my part," he remarked with more than a little condescension. "My friends insisted that my name should come before the people, and so I have consented. To-day, for the first time, I appear before you, desiring a nomination."[18]

And yet, there was some significant truth in his remarks that only a handful of the delegates would have fully appreciated. While Stanford had been away from California on a little business and good deal of pleasure, his friends had been busy indeed in their Sacramento back shop preparing him for the limelight. It wasn't as if they didn't have reservations, but they also saw potential. The two views were not incongruous; they were, instead, balanced counterweights. Even his friend and personal physician, in a private letter to his son, had written of Stanford, "He is not a man of talent (distinguished) but was our choice from Sacramento because we know him, he has got just the right Albany Dutch enough in him."[19]

In other words, the foursome (and entourage) saw in their serial nominee just enough grit to stand up to wear and tear, although not so much as to cause them concern about a lack of pliancy. Now came the next play. Almost exactly one week after the nomination, the newly formed Central Pacific Rail Road Company of California, with Huntington, Hopkins, and Crocker in the respective positions of vice president, treasurer, and director, named Leland Stanford company president. He would hold the post for the next twenty-nine years.

Stanford wasted no time initiating his own priority: he bought his first mansion. Fewer than two weeks after Stanford got the job and just shy of three weeks after his receiving the Republican nomination for governor, Leland and Jennie forever abandoned their modest dwelling on Second Street near the waterfront they had furnished with crates and homemade curtains and moved a half mile uptown to one of the finest homes in the city. Initially, Stanford spent $8,000 on the Renaissance Revival–styled house at Eighth and N Streets. This was at a time when the average home price in Sacramento was reportedly around $600. And then he set about greatly expanding the already four-thousand-square-foot building, a process that would go on for years before his real estate cravings became too great for Sacramento.[20]

The gubernatorial election took place September 4, 1861. It wasn't as if Californians were different from other Americans in lowered aspirations for their leaders and were unwilling to send undistinguished men to the state capitol. During a dozen years of statehood they had run through a fast series of seven governors, at least two notorious for having a deep thirst. There was J. Neely Johnson, number four, who earned the lasting sobriquet of "a poor, miserable drunkard," and it was said of the second man to hold the high office, John McDougal, that "there was not much in him outside whiskey."[21] Stanford, despite his elbow-bending past, seemed to have, by that time, become somewhat temperate with adult beverages, in part because Jennie, at least then, frowned on drink.

Sober, infamous, or distinguished, the Democrats were divided between two candidates and the Republicans, riding the coattails of the Lincoln and congressional victories, united behind Stanford. He won with 46 percent of the vote, as his two opponents, appearing somewhat ambivalent about the South's secession from the North earlier that year, won a combined 53 percent. Because they split the ticket, Leland Stanford, in his half a dozen attempts to win office, became the eighth governor of California. He was thirty-seven years old.

The outcome was "almost surprising," one contemporary commentator wrote. "Was it for Leland Stanford as a man they cast their ballots, or was it not for the great principal he represented?" That principal, of course, was to preserve the Union, "and that treason can find no foothold upon California soil." In the end, the writer pronounced "the victory no partisan success, but a victory for the Union over secession."[22]

Regardless, Stanford's ascension was remarkable by almost any objective measure. He had come a very long way. He had struggled through fiasco and failure. He had left his secure if checkered life back East for a desperate gamble in the West. He had slept many nights on the ground in the mountains, relied regularly and heavily on his family and business associates, and endured his fellow citizens' repeatedly and unceremoniously crushing his desire for political recognition. Less than a decade after disembarking from a boat, broke in feral San Francisco, he was no longer simply another ambitious transplant.

In the fall of 1861 Leland Stanford, with a stately home and his own money in the bank, was suddenly president of a promising start-up calling itself the Central Pacific and was governor of the new state of California. He had no intention of relinquishing any of his hard-won gains. Rather, his position hardened.

The official portrait of Governor Leland Stanford is the rare picture in which he is almost grinning, or at the very minimum has a hint of happiness. It was, however, painted a dozen years after his inauguration, when the whisper of a smile had long since died on his lips. His inaugural address was largely the sort of sour speech he was becoming known for. He began by noting that settlers had a right to settle California—excepting for some:

> To my mind it is clear, that the settlement among us of an inferior race is to be discouraged, by every legitimate means. Asia, with her numberless millions, sends to our shores the dregs of her population. Large numbers of this class are already here; and, unless we do something early to check their immigration, the question, which of the two tides of immigration, meeting upon the shores of the Pacific, shall be turned back, will be forced upon our consideration, when far more difficult than now of disposal. There can be no doubt but that the presence of numbers among us of a degraded and distinct people must exercise a deleterious influence upon the superior race, and, to a certain extent, repel desirable immigration.[23]

It is often said, and rightly so, that it is difficult, sometimes impossible, to judge the past according to the present, much as one culture cannot easily, or rarely with any adequacy, judge another culture. This being just, it is then also worthy of noting that hardly every American of European ancestry in the mid-nineteenth century considered their fellow immigrants from other lands such as Africa or Asia anything but equal before God and man. Even fellow Republican Judge F. P. Tracy, dispatched by the party to accompany Stanford on his failed 1859 campaign tour of California in order to have at least one accomplished speaker draw and hold a crowd, made that clear in speeches heard by hundreds and read in news stories by thousands: "We have said to exiles of every land, here is a home for you. On these fair acres you may earn your daily bread, and, free from the tyranny of the old world, found for yourselves homes, where rights are equal, and where every man will be protected in the exercise of his rights."[24]

And in a campaign address made in front of Stanford and a hostile crowd of racists, Tracy had this to say about another ethnic group earlier disparaged by the party nominee: "The black man is our neighbor. Liberty is God's best gift to man—liberty of thought, liberty of conscience, liberty of body, of physical action. It is a sacred trust, for the maintenance of which men fight and die, and for our use or abuse of which we are responsible to almighty God."[25]

Then there was fellow Republican Frederick Low, the next governor after Stanford's brief tenure. "We must learn to treat the Chinese who come to live among us decently, and not oppress them by unfriendly legislation, nor allow them to be abused, robbed, and murdered, without extending to them any adequate remedy," he remarked, despite the howling of the mob.[26]

Making matters worse, in very short order Stanford would make his fortune on the backs these "dregs," because so many of his "superior race" could not handle the work, fell into drink, and simply could not tolerate the ballyhooed American ideology of competition when they lost. That Stanford's wife, child, and property would be cared for by these "inferior" and "degraded" people was still another expedient hypocrisy that set him apart from many of his peers.

Even Leland's older brother Josiah shook his head at the situation. "Politicians have strange ways," he reminisced many years later. "When he was first elected Governor he was opposed to the Chinese; I was in favor of them and I used to argue with him, contending that they were useful to the country. Afterwards, when he got to building the railroad, he was in favor of the Chinamen."[27]

The first real business at hand for Huntington, Hopkins, and Crocker had nothing to do with buying grand homes or excluding any arbitrary group of immigrants. It had to do with making money. The four associates used whatever capital they had cobbled together and immediately returned Judah, now also a stockholder and company chief engineer, to Washington, DC, where he undertook one of the more openly astounding acts of political bravado in American history.

His official mission was to "further the interests of this company there, in obtaining Congressional grants, appropriations, etc."[28] He was, in this instance, hugely successful, if not just plain lucky, commencing with being on the same ship east with rising Republican star and newly elected Rep. Aaron Augustus Sargent, who would play a key role in Stanford's distant, dark future. Upon his arrival in the nation's capital, Sargent got a seat on the House Pacific Railway Committee. During their days at sea he and Judah formed a close alliance that would have enormous consequences. Then, in the nation's capital, California senator James McDougall asked Judah to prepare a bill similar to

Rep. Samuel Curtis's failed Iowa proposal but tailor-made for California. McDougall, not to be confused with former governor John McDougal, then chaired the U.S. Senate committee controlling the bill. Judah, almost giddily, wrote back to California,

> I may here mention I have been appointed Secretary of the Senate Pacific Railroad Committee, having charge of all their papers, etc. being present at their meetings, and having the privilege of the floor of the Senate, while upon motion of Mr. Sargent, I was appointed Clerk of the House subcommittee, who held their meetings in our committee room, and had the privilege of the floor of the House, and I afterwards acted as the as Clerk of the main House committee.[29]

In other words, Judah had gone to Capitol Hill as a paid lobbyist, executive, and part owner of the Central Pacific Rail Road Company. Yet at the same time he had become the chief staff member in both houses of Congress, designing the legislation that would enable the company to obtain that exclusive franchise from the federal government. It would be facile to say more than 150 years later, in a different world, that Judah was guilty of political chicanery. But neither was he, as some would have it, a gentleman of stainless virtue.

The timing for Judah—at least for one more year of his life—was advantageous. The nation was ready to embrace technological revolution. And it was at war.

California was distant from the Blue-Gray bloodletting, separated by two mountain ranges and a vast desert. Nevertheless and naturally, the war was a constant topic in West Coast news. Although the economic might of the South, based largely on cotton exports, had been waning, "Southern leaders thought," observed a business historian, "in a war between the states, they would be an easy victor."[30] Anxieties were understandably at an all-time high. In a lively account of early Los Angeles, an East Coast historian has drawn a vivid and violent appraisal of the secessionist forces in Southern California, suggesting they were not inconsiderable.[31] On the other hand, a pair of West Coast historians have argued that in 1860 less than 7 percent of Californians had come from seceded states: "There was never any genuine danger that California would desert the Union cause."[32]

To a far lesser extent, but very much on the mind of westerners, were ongoing problems between the Latter-day Saints (LDS), better known as Mormons, and much of the rest of the American public. Some two hundred miles west of Stanford's hometown, when he was just five, the Mormons had settled in Utah after a series of provocations and persecutions across the East and Midwest. The president just before Lincoln, James Buchanan, had sent U.S. troops commanded by a cruel and genocidal general to quell what the federal government feared was another traitorous rebellion forming against the sovereignty of the Union.[33] The result was the Mormon, or Utah, War, culminating in the Mountain Meadow Massacre of 1857.

The benefits of a cross-continental railroad, able to rush U.S. troops to Utah and beyond before further threats of dissolution of the United States could take place, binding the regions in trade and culture, were the constant themes behind advocacy for a transcontinental railroad, with an urgency only the stick of war and the carrot of profit could instill. Following the horrific Mountain Meadow carnage, in which a phalanx of Mormons ambushed and slaughtered a wagon train of more than one hundred non-Mormon men, women, and children simply trying to get from Arkansas to California, LDS leader Brigham Young brought further discipline to his Saints, which would help make a path for a later business alliance with Leland Stanford and his railroad.

In Washington, DC—on the edge of the Confederate insurgency, preoccupied with the volley of bad news from the battlefronts—the long-winded debates regarding the cross-continental rails ceased and action was taken. With Judah's vital backroom guiding hand, a final Pacific Railway Act was hurriedly put together in both the House and Senate and sent to President Lincoln. On July 1, 1862, he signed it. Leland Stanford, Collis Huntington, Mark Hopkins, and Charles Crocker would no longer be known as just some Sacramento associates. They were now destined to be called the Big Four—and Leland Stanford was Number One.[34]

CHAPTER 7

"Egyptian Kings and Dynasties Shall Be Forgotten"

At age thirty-seven Leland Stanford was not only governor of the already legendary state of California, a state destined to be a world leader in industry, finance, education, and culture. If that might somehow be regarded as insufficient, he was now also president of the Central Pacific Rail Road, an epic enterprise that arguably would help alter the nation more profoundly than any other single venture until then in America. He could not know, naturally, that he was on a course that would also encode his actions on the next century's most significant change in world technology, economy, politics, and culture.

Stanford had trashed repeated opportunities for an education, he had abandoned his origins, and he had witnessed his first solid initiative incinerated to the ground. That past alone would have been sufficient to provide any ordinary man ample reason to simply remain behind a comfortable store counter selling groceries and at the end of the workday go home to his thirty-three-year-old wife, read the evening paper, and look forward to a pot roast dinner on Sunday.

But there was something else slow-cooking deep in this private, stoic, but intensely and unrelentingly ambitious Leland Stanford of Sacramento. It was something only a few could truly see when he was alive and fewer still long after he was entombed in a vainglorious mausoleum on a remote edge of a university campus. As 1862 dawned, he was about to embark on an enterprise without precedent in American history.

Stanford had already discovered the alchemy of dominion and dollars by alloying authority with business when running a Gold Country courtroom out of his saloon a decade earlier. That he was now governor of the state and contemporaneously president of a corporation that would quickly come to hold the whip hand over California had been orchestrated initially without concealment or reproach. In time, largely because Stanford deeply infected one responsibility with the other, it would become universally understood for more than a century by people not bedazzled by power and profit that the combination made for bad government. As one young scholar, who wrote a typical early twentieth-century tribute to Stanford, conceded with galactic understatement, "It was this mixing in politics that made the officers of the company so unpopular in later years."[1]

Being governor was a grand designation, but governing was another matter. Being president of the railroad was a fine title, while the work of building the line would be one of the greatest challenges of the age. Having both jobs at the same time was an unmatched conflict and could mean only the most enormous opportunity for Stanford equaled by the greatest risk to the public. Fearless or foolish, Stanford began.

Almost from the get-go, railroads were enormously powerful, stupendously expensive, and altogether revolutionary. In a word: political. Before the first rails such as the ones that ran alongside Stanford's childhood home, waterways were the nation's main thoroughfares, and although to a lesser extent, turnpikes were also significant routes. Transportation methods were, as one of America's most notable economic historians pointed out, "as they had been since the days of Greece and Rome."[2] This was all to radically change and change everything in one generation. A prime agent of this transformation would be Leland Stanford.

That the railroad would succeed was almost a matter of faith—the faith in that enduring American relish and reverence for invention, innovation, and technology, in believing that they, like virtue, are their own reward. The railroad encompassed all that and more in the nineteenth-century United States and continued to well into the next hundred years. A decade before the Civil War and the Pacific Railway Act, a pioneer, in the purple prose of his time, imagined a "belt of iron from ocean to ocean, with the iron horse with the sinew of steel and breath of fire for a messenger."[3] Some seventy years later the same sentiment was common. Take, for example, a 1919 book written by the founder of Moody's Investors Service, who was as besotted as any by technology in general and the transcontinental railway in particular. Without it, he wrote, "in a thousand years or so the United States might have conceivably have become a far-reaching straggling, loosely jointed Roman Empire, depending entirely upon its oceans, internal watercourses, and imperial highways for such economic and political integrity as it might achieve."[4]

The explosive growth of wealth and the potential for more of it in the West prompted a further urgency to fully integrate America's modern circuitry. On the east side of the Continental Divide countless waterways and connecting canals had long been the older part of the nation's central nervous system.[5] But in the country's newer, arid lands west of the Rockies, only a handful of significant riverways exist, making the rails particularly crucial. The Big Four were eager to assume mastery of the situation and every advantage they could muster, despite—or because of—their inexperience. A telling marker of how green Leland Stanford, Collis Huntington, Mark Hopkins, and Charles Crocker were when they found themselves getting what they had wished for was that the four never had a formal, written agreement about their partnership, something one business historian found to be "a unique venture in financial history."[6] Each simply knew his role and promptly went about it hammer and tongs. Huntington would initially raise private capital and buy materials, Hopkins would keep the books, and Crocker would run the road gangs. Stanford would be responsible for exploiting the agency he suddenly had as governor to obtain as much taxpayer money as he could from the federal government, state, California counties, and towns while being the public face—the front man, if you will—of their collective ambitions.

There were plenty of skeptics. Even before Congress and the president approved the Railway Act, many fought any attempt to subsidize the venture, citing their ideal versions of free enterprise and a pay-as-you-go credo. Still later, Nobel Prize–winning economic historian Robert W. Fogel, and more recently Stanford University historian Richard White, argued there was no authentic economic justification for Washington to help finance the railroad. Only "the promise of fabulous commercial gain for the nation," Fogel asserted, adding it "spurred the incessant drive for a transcontinental road."[7] Moreover, there was "a Sorcerer's Apprentice quality to them," White said of the Big Four. "They laid hands on technology they did not understand, initiated sweeping changes, and saw these changes often take on purposes they did not intend."[8]

Regardless, Congress stood by its 1862 Pacific Railway Act, even beefing it up just two years later, with Lincoln once again signing. There was a baked-in belief that railroads were a business with a special mission for the common-weal. Fogel noted that other major driving forces included fears of a monopoly if private money controlled the enterprise and anxieties that financial specu-lators would be more interested in making a killing than in augmenting the national interest. As it turned out, despite American taxpayers loaning unprec-edented sums for the enterprise in expectation of avoiding those disasters, both unpleasant outcomes afflicted the United States for decades.

The grand railroad venture can be said to have begun in earnest with Theodore Judah's fast work in Congress in fashioning the Railway Act, giving the exclu-sive western franchise to the Central Pacific. He returned to California with a spectacular victory, but it is the subsequent ending of his elegiac story that has fascinated railroad buffs since.[9] The agreement he returned with was everything the Big Four could have hoped. What was demanded in return from the Big Four would be a point of contention into the twentieth century. The most conciliatory, scholarly assessment has been, "It is evident that these demands were very moderate indeed."[10] The might and majesty of the United States of America, backed by the full faith and credit of its taxpaying citizens, agreed to issue bonds as major seed money to pay for the road, as well for an adjacent telegraph line, making the United States among the first truly wired nations.[11] Government bonds, of course, are merely a way to borrow money that must be paid back with interest, using taxpayer dollars.[12] Those kinds of bonds, to put it in plain, unvarnished terms, are tax increases.

In the case of the transcontinental railroad, the U.S. government agreed to issue bonds and give them to the railroad companies. The companies, in turn, were legally empowered to go into the financial marketplace and sell the bonds, using the proceeds to build the road. The Big Four signed a contract agreeing that their railroad would pay everything back to the taxpayers—principal and 6 percent interest—in thirty years. In other words, unlike most government bonds, the money was a loan. And in that, the seeds were sown for a series of historic troubles.

The government's 1862 terms were fairly straightforward if unusually gen-erous: the Central Pacific would get $16,000 for laying down every flat mile of rail on the California side of the Sierra Nevada, $48,000 per mile for sur-mounting the mountain range, and $32,000 a mile for crossing the barren stretch east of the Sierras and west of the Rocky Mountains. The arrangement also applied to the Union Pacific, starting on the plains, overcoming the

Rockies, and crossing the desert toward California. The money would not come in advance. The companies would get paid after completing each forty-mile segment.

After building less than half of the first rail section across the flat Central Valley floor, the Big Four went back to lobby Washington, petitioning for additional corporate welfare. Just two years later they would enjoy additional success at getting still more government assistance.[13]

In addition, from the start, federal officials agreed to give the railroad companies land, land that did not truly belong to the government but was where the First Peoples had settled for more than ten thousand years. The legislation in fact read, "U.S. to extinguish Indian titles as rapidly as possible."[14] This was a complete departure from convention. Until 1862, the U.S. government had deeded land rights to states but never to corporations.[15] The real estate formula would also become notorious. In addition to an ample ribbon of property for the rails, stations, and other facilities, a so-called checkerboard of land grants ten miles wide on each side of the line was gifted—one square remaining public, the next one for the railroad. This would lead to a variety of epic confrontations. In addition, the government allowed important exemptions from existing federal restrictions on lands that might yield valuable minerals. The government agreed to cede to the two corporations iron, stone, coal, and the forests along the way so they might be used with impunity for the railroad's construction needs, which of course, would be considerable.

In the end, most experts agree that an authentic estimate of what taxpayers invested in the railroad is unlikely, as is any verifiable estimation of what financial gain Americans realized from the extraordinary venture. Even well more than a century after the Pacific Railway Act, subjective assessments, politics, and not infrequently human emotion color the ceaseless debate. The totals certainly go into the tens of millions, likely hundreds of millions, in nineteenth-century dollars. It can be stated with confidence that the privately owned cross-continental railroad was, for its day, the nation's first unicorn, courtesy of the American people.

Failing to designate a point where the two lines would meet, the federal government looked for a race across the continent from each direction: the Union Pacific from the East and the Central Pacific from the West. Technically, the railroad would not be a single contiguous line running sea to shining sea. The Union Pacific would start at the Missouri River where it divides Council Bluffs, Iowa, on the eastern bank from Omaha, Nebraska, on the other. The rails would head west for the California border. The Central Pacific would start "at or near" the Sacramento River in the capital city and head toward the Missouri. The lines would meet somewhere in between. The president of the United States was designated to decide exactly where. But in fact, a backroom deal would be responsible for that fateful engagement. An existing and growing network of rails in the Midwest and East would join the Union Pacific, linking the national road to the Eastern Seaboard. From Sacramento, there were equal expectations that a railroad would make up the last ninety to one hundred miles to the West Coast. While the Union Pacific would have to cross the Rockies, that was not regarded as nearly an inconvenience as overcoming the Sierras. In addition, the Union Pacific would have hundreds of miles of relatively flat plains and desert ahead, making its assignment speedier to complete.

As it turned out, although the Union Pacific laid more track than the Central Pacific, it was beset by abundant management problems while the Central Pacific had its small, tightly bound board of directors, one of whom at the beginning was Theodore Judah.

But he was never to become really one of the main group. Almost from the start the young engineer found himself vexed by the Big Four, who were equally determined to be in the same mood. Judah unwisely mixed it up, particularly with Crocker, whose assignment was inherently if unofficially understood to be in charge of managing day-to-day construction. Judah argued with Crocker over where to grade and then, still more foolishly, over the exact geologic location they would declare the beginning of the Sierra Nevada. It was a potentially critical issue because the government had agreed to finance three times as much money for traversing mountain terrain as flatlands.

That was when the brand-new railroad foursome immediately launched another probe of Washington's mettle. If the California side of the Sierras officially started twelve miles sooner than commonly considered, that would mean at least an extra $192,000 to Stanford and company, no mean sum in Civil War America. Road boss Crocker chose a small arroyo fewer than ten miles east of Sacramento as the commencement of the Sierra Nevada. Judah was aghast. Anyone standing at Arcade Creek on a clear day could see the flat expanse that went on for miles before the distinct bump into the foothills and then up to the jagged peaks. But the Stanford group needed the money.

"We were very hard up, and we wanted to get the base down as near the river as we could," Crocker said almost twenty-five years later. So he brought the California state geologist "on a little ride," a scientist with strong credentials, Josiah Dwight Whitney. Crocker recalled, "'Well,' he says, 'the true base is the river, but,' said he, 'for the purpose of this bill, Arcade Creek is as far a place as any.'" The state geologist's boss, Governor Leland Stanford, sent word to President Lincoln, the designated decider, twenty-seven hundred miles and a world away, who made a quip about Abraham moving mountains and approved the ploy. Judah stormed.[16]

"Oh! how he struggled," wrote his wife, Anna, many years later. 'He had brought them a franchise and laid it at their door; rightly used, giving them unlimited credit throughout the world, and they would beggar it. Oh! Some of those days were terrible to us. He felt they were ungrateful to their trust and to him."[17]

It was an opening the Big Four jumped into. They offered to cashier the young engineer, who impetuously agreed and took a not insignificant buyout of $100,000 in stock, although it had no more than paper value at the time. Believing that his experience and credibility, not to mention the expectation of great wealth, would stand him well on Wall Street, he vowed to return east and turn the tables on the quartet. Toward the end of 1863 Theodore and Anna huffed back out of Sacramento, boarded a ship in San Francisco bound for New York via Central America, intending to raise enough money to instead "buy out the men," Stanford, Huntington, Hopkins, and Crocker. The rest of the story was brief. Judah contracted a fever in Panama just before the second leg of the journey across the Atlantic.[18] "That night he had a terrible headache and from that time grew worse and worse," Anna recalled. "He lived just one week after we arrived in New York at the Metropolitan Hotel."[19]

Theodore Dehone Judah was thirty-seven years old.[20]

The jeremiad of Theodore Judah does have one champion besides his wife, Anna: Leland Stanford. Judah's widow stated explicitly, "Governor Stanford was a 'Judah man,' and so long as he lived he was loyal to him."[21] Although Stanford obviously did not carry the day for the young engineer's cause, it is a rare crack of light from Stanford's otherwise often monolithic image. The young governor displayed little else to soften his otherwise stony countenance. In contrast, the not infrequently combative Collis Huntington would later condemn Judah for what he called his "low, thieving cunning" and "cheap dignity," among other ill talk of the dead engineer who charted the Big Four's road to wealth and power.[22] Much later in life Huntington would take an action that would provoke a rather different, surprising perspective on his hard-chiseled character.

Thinking the Railway Act would be sufficient to arouse the interest of California's leading financiers awash in gold and silver money and seeking bonds to invest in, Stanford and Huntington opened the equivalent of an initial public offering by first approaching well-heeled friends in Sacramento. They found only a few takers. They then traveled to San Francisco to raise some serious venture capital for what was then the largest public works project in U.S. history. It was their turn to be brazenly naive. Stanford reminisced many years later, "We thought that when we went down to San Francisco, the stock would be gobbled up, and we concluded to give the people of Sacramento the first chance." When they found few takers in the state capital, they changed plans. "We went down to San Francisco, but when we opened the books nobody came in. We were surprised and concluded there must be some mistake as to the date. On the next day the same thing occurred. I concluded to go out among them, and see what was the matter."

That's when the reality of the investment world became hard and clear to Stanford, governor or not. "They could get 2 1/2–3% every month on their money then and our enterprise, if successful, did not promise to give any returns under ten years, did not give any assurance that it would. And that was a poor out look for men then. We soon ascertained that we could not sell any stock in San Francisco."[23] What had happened to Judah was happening to Stanford.

Anyone could have bought into the enterprise if they had the money, but what was an IPO quickly turned out to be an initial public dud. The inflexibility of the capitalists would have to be revisited when the Big Four were more influential, but at least the relative pliancy of the politicians had been established. Consequently, in the political realm was where Stanford would be the foursome's best gambit. He would prove a sound a one.

In choosing between his obligations to the people of California in his job as governor or to his handful of fellow shareholders as president of the Central Pacific, Leland Stanford's priority was explicit enough to anyone paying attention. As early as six months into his term, he made it clear at a Sacramento social event that "he deemed it still a higher honor to be President of the Central Pacific Railroad Company, a position in which he believed he could render the state much more important service than any other."[24] No voice of dissent or concern was heard at the dinner nor printed in the pages of the pro-Stanford paper reporting the remarks. As one of the consequences, there was no reason for Stanford to alter his established formula of what could be generously called a conflict of interest.

In his first annual address as governor, he noted that despite lavish wealth from the mines, the twelve-year-old State of California was in debt, a situation the head of the state's Republican Party vowed to correct. Evoking his inaugural call for a "retrenchment" in spending, Stanford once again declared his preference for a "pay as you go" state budget.[25] Then he promptly set about aggressively pushing legislation to further tax Californians for his railroad. Following the Big Four's successful playbook of warming the kettle before turning up the heat to a rolling boil, Governor Stanford proposed a law allowing his company to change its route inside Sacramento as it saw fit, a move vetoed by Sacramento's president of the board of supervisors, who worried it would put the capital city "entirely at the mercy of the railroad company."[26] The overwhelmingly pro-railroad board overruled his dissent and gave license to the hometown company, a hometown that would be the first all-important terminus of the line.

Victory in hand, the governor then moved to do more or less the same thing statewide, pushing legislation that would allow his company to change its route at will, or in the words of the pro-railroad *Sacramento Daily Union,* "authorizing them to change the line of route wherever they may deem it expedient."[27] On the heels of that proposal, the new governor backed a bill giving Placer County voters a chance to borrow $250,000 in bonds to help finance Stanford's road. Placer's assemblyman Charles Dudley objected, saying "the effect would be to leave the location open as long as they pleased." What's more, he argued, "it looked as if this bill was designed to coerce the people of Placer to subscribe for the road by the threat that the road would run around them."[28]

This, too, was a preview of what Californians would increasingly witness as a successful Stanford and company business-model tactic. The bill "granted unlimited power to the corporation," the assemblyman argued, adding not only that "such an advantage was unheard of," but that "corporations were soulless, and it was wisdom on the part of the State to carefully restrict them."[29] Dudley lost that fight.

Stanford extended his winning streak by asking the state legislature to allow the City of Sacramento to issue $300,000 in bonds so the taxpayers there could borrow money for the railroad. That met with some grumbling but ultimately success. Then Stanford traveled down to San Francisco and petitioned its board of supervisors for $600,000 in bonds, since the private equity firms there refused to invest. That infamously argumentative town stood on the brakes and told Stanford there would be no public financing until he would guarantee the money would be used to bring the train past Sacramento and into the bay city itself. The governor wrote a long public letter that both scolded and then implored San Franciscans to pony up as had Sacramento and Placer Counties. The *Sacramento Daily Union*, still advocating for Stanford, accused San Franciscans of having "the rankest envy and most extreme selfish views" as well as being "unscrupulous."[30] The voters of San Francisco were asked to make the decision.

It was then that the first outright, blatant, and difficult to dispute scandal tarnishing the Stanford name took place. Court documents claimed one Philip Stanford went to seven polling places on the day of the May 19, 1863, special election, throwing out gold pieces worth $5 to $20 each in return for a pledge to vote for the $600,000 city loan to the railroad and to persuade others to do the same. "A. Phillip Stanford," documents filed with the state Supreme Court claimed, "unlawfully, wickedly and corruptly," multiple witnesses testified, was seen "throwing out many handfuls of said money." People "scrambled among themselves" to scrape up the gold pieces that "for the most part," the testimony added, were "furnished by said Company."[31]

The "Company," of course, was the Central Pacific, whose president, of course, was the older brother of Philip: Leland Stanford, a.k.a. governor of California. The votes for the railroad subsidy won the day and the court confirmed the decision. That hardly ended the drama. A host of public officials defied the law and refused to sign papers to help finance the enterprise. Infamous arguments about the railroad's real intentions, bare-knuckle political struggles, and a series of further contentious court decisions finally ended two years later with San Franciscans settling for financing $400,000 in railroad bonds. They would not get Central Pacific trains into their city for seven years and even then, only after further significant concessions and political brawls.[32]

When, also in 1863, Governor Leland Stanford pushed for an audacious statewide subsidy that would give his railroad an extra $10,000 of taxpayer money for every mile of track it laid down in California, skepticism greatly increased. So did the consequent counterattacks by Stanford's sympathizers at the *Sacramento Daily Union*, which irrelevantly likened opponents to "those who sympathize with the rebels in the South."[33] Although the legislation passed, the next session of the state legislature was forced to rescind the bill after the courts found it illegal. Stanford's forces rallied and replaced it with a technically proper, and far grander, $2.1 million subvention to be paid by the people of California during the following twenty years. In short order, many Californians suddenly found themselves in a far less agreeable humor regarding the railroad, and their governor, than they had enjoyed just six months earlier.

The next governor of California, Frederick Low—also a staunch Republican who was then representing California in Congress—many years later reminisced of the time, "I told Stanford very frankly, I didn't think that thing would stand at all, and then he went to work and whipped it around, pulled very strongly on everybody." Low, who went on to a distinguished career as a diplomat and banker, recalled that Stanford "went into the Legislature and lobbied considerably for the Pacific Railroad, of which he was President." Low added of Stanford's methods, "He went upon the floor of the Senate and cajoled and bullyragged and got his bill through."[34]

The heart of the matter, of course, was always money. Despite the generosity of the taxpayers and government that acted on their behalf, the notion that bankers and other investors would finance the rest of the road continued to prove problematic. And that meant the Big Four also faced problems about paying themselves. But they had a solution for their personal circumstances, one utilized by the far more troubled Union Pacific coming west to meet them eventually in what was then called the Great American Desert between the Rockies and the Sierras, where so many pioneers had suffered and perished.[35]

Charles Crocker once again took the forward position. He officially resigned from his director's job at the Central Pacific, ostensibly forfeiting that seigneurial rank, and started his own company, one that coincidentally built railroads for railroad companies. The carpet salesman had absolutely no experience in the business. Nevertheless, Stanford and company awarded him a $400,000 contract to start building their line. There was little delay in the reaction of the press. The *Daily Alta California*, based in San Francisco and becoming the leading voice of dissent, was severe: "There are responsible parties that would have taken the contract for less than one-half of that sum," the paper stated. "Instead of advertising for bids, as they should have done, and thereby creating completion for the work, the Directors let the contract to one of themselves, at their own price, which is more than double what it is said it could be let for."[36]

Crocker lashed back immediately:

> I took the contract to do the grading, the masonry, trestling, bridging, piling, furnishing the ties and laying the track from the foot of I street, Sacramento, to the line of the California Central railroad, twenty miles, including side tracks and turnouts, payable, five-eighths in cash and three-eighths in bonds or stock in the Company, if there are "responsible parties would have taken the contact at one-half that sum," I am anxious to find them.[37]

Later, he and his partners would say they had hired some outsiders to build some early parts of the road, but for one reason or another they had failed. It was never clear exactly what happened or precisely under what terms Crocker took on the work, a scandal that would take years before coming to light. Meanwhile, the secret formula the Big Four had found would make them colossally rich, with Stanford the most ostentatiously displaying great wealth.

Almost exactly midway through his single two-year term in the statehouse, the governor presided over a symbolically momentous day for the nation, for California, and of course, for Leland Stanford himself: the ceremonial ground breaking for the western end of the transcontinental railroad.

It had been raining for much of the first week of 1863, but on January 8 the sun appeared and the flags unfurled. A company of politicians and railroad officials sat in comfortable chairs on a platform near the banks of the Sacramento River. Crocker took the podium and introduced the governor. Stanford's speech was the usual convoluted cant of political platitudes, although he allowed a glimpse into his youth, declaring that rails would be for California "what the Erie Canal was to New York," before preparing to shovel a few scoops of ceremonial soil hauled in on wagons. The state senator from Sacramento, Newton Booth, who would soon have a rather different perspective of the railroad, proclaimed, "Egyptian kings and dynasties shall be forgotten," but referring to Stanford declared, "You sir, to-day, have inaugurated a more glorious work."[38]

Before the governor lifted a spade with the first dirt, the Reverend Joseph Augustine Benton, said to be the first Protestant pastor to come to San Francisco but then presiding over Sacramento's Congregational assembly, consecrated the railroad: "Bless these Directors and officers," he intoned to the heavens though referring to the path of the rails. "It shall be called the way of holiness."[39]

CHAPTER 8

Dungeons and Depredations

Whether the railroad was in a state of grace or not, Leland Stanford undertook some baleful tasks as governor. Among the first events to confront him was a riot, massive escape, and ultimately slaughterhouse chain of events at the state prison, sitting on a peninsula jutting into San Francisco Bay. The area was eventually called Point San Quentin, which does not derive directly from the Christian martyr beheaded almost three hundred years after Jesus. Instead, San Quentin is named for rebellious Coast Miwok Chief Quentin, said to be captured there in 1824 by Mexican forces and imprisoned in San Francisco.[1] The land became known as Punta de Quentin, anglicized later as Point Quentin. There was nothing saintly about what would soon be known as San Quentin State Prison—it was universally agreed to be in a state of deviltry.

After chronic escapes from the abandoned gold rush ships turned jails in 1852 the state finally commissioned a permanent prison on that point about twenty miles north of San Francisco, on the other side of the Golden Gate. One remaining, but no longer used, part of the complex built by inmate labor in 1854 may be the oldest existing building constructed by the State of California: the Dungeon. It is made of four separate cells, each eleven by seven feet, with two-foot-thick granite walls, each with an iron door relieved only by a thin slit. "Cell spaces were excessively small, with little ventilation, inadequate light, no fresh water supply, and only buckets for toilets," a 2009 state-sponsored study found. "On average, four inmates were locked up in one dungeon cell. Prisoners also received substandard clothing provisions; fewer than half possessed shoes." If a prisoner broke the rules, the most common punishment was flogging with a rawhide strap. "Lashes varied: twelve for insolence, lying, and gambling; twenty for stealing, fighting, disobedience, refusing to work, and similar offenses; and 150 for escaping and inciting a riot," the study found. If a prisoner was lucky enough to escape the whip, he could find himself in a dark cell, half his head shaved and his limbs shackled with heavy chains. A medieval form of punishment, though also used by the U.S. government not too long ago, was "the use of the 'shower bath,' whereby prisoners stripped naked and were tied to a ladder and then sprayed with a stream of cold water from a large hose under high pressure."[2]

The facility holding an average of five hundred to six hundred prisoners was run under private contract to the state and the usual serious problems began: "to keep profits high they generally overworked and underfed prisoners," along with the other issues of excessive punishment and general abuse.[3] Almost all the money spent on running the prison came from subcontractors paying for prison labor. Escapes remained commonplace, speeches in the state legislature about the horrific, counterproductive conditions more so. Finally, after long battle, the lawmakers stripped the private administrators of their overseer powers and created a three-member board of state officials to take charge. The governor was one of them, as was the lieutenant governor, a John F. Chellis, who would also serve as the nominal warden. The board was expected to submit an annual report to appraise Californians of reforms.

Toward the beginning of 1863, Stanford and his two fellow board members signed the first such assessment of the prison. They "found it without even a day's supply of necessary provisions," the buildings in "dilapidated condition that rendered them almost inhabitable." What's more, there was the "humiliating fact that bills purchased as early as (a year past) have not yet been paid." And then there was this: "It has been feared that the practice of turning out prisoners by the hundreds, to work on brick contracts, and other outside labor, would result in a serious outbreak, deliberately planned and perfected by those who were thus daily permitted to leave the yard. These fears were realized in July."[4]

It was the biggest prison escape in California experience, and quite possibly remains the biggest in American history.[5] On July 22, 1862, somewhere between 90 and 150 inmates—Stanford's administration used the smaller number, most press accounts the larger—working in a brickyard in the summer heat snapped. Armed with "axes, hatchets, knives, files" from work-shops, they broke into the armory and gathered what guns and ammunition they could.[6] They stormed Chellis's office and took the lieutenant governor hostage. From there, they sallied to the gates and demanded the guard there put down his weapon and open the locks. The guard refused, prompting Chellis's cowardice: he ordered the sentry to do as the prisoners demanded, which the officer, of course, did. The escapees then beat the guard unmercifully and "whooping and yelling" cries of "liberty," swarmed to the next battlement, where a second guard had pointed a cannon at them loaded with grapeshot.[7] Once again, Chellis cravenly pleaded for his life and demanded the guard stand down, which he also did. The prisoners then threw the guard and the cannon over a thirty-foot precipice, seriously injuring the officer and destroy-ing the weapon. From there, many went to the docks and tried to launch a sloop, but lacking any seamanship they almost immediately grounded the craft in the notoriously sticky San Francisco Bay mud. A large group broke off and marched north through the countryside, ransacking homes along the way.

Meanwhile, Governor Stanford, relying on his sketchy older brother Philip, dispatched him to command a militia from San Francisco. That force gathered and then boated across the Golden Gate to the prison, arriving well after the bloody event was over. As they beat the tides across the gate, the rioters tramped on, pushing Chellis with them, who complained of the heat and kept pleading for release. When the mob met a difficult-to-surmount fence, "Chellis being rather stout" could not comply with the order to climb over it.[8] Rather than be trapped on that side of the enclosure, they freed the lieutenant gov-ernor and left him behind. Which is when a posse of some fifty well-armed civilians, accompanied by an unnumbered law enforcement force on foot and forty mounted police, opened fire on the escapees, then trapped on the other side of the barrier. The government reported thirty-two men shot, fifteen dead. The rest of the group of prisoners surrendered. Even five months later, another fifteen inmates remained at large. Other bits and pieces of the aftermath were equally discouraging. At least one of the guards who had followed the lieuten-ant governor's orders was disciplined and then resigned. The prison's contrac-tual physician, J. D. B. Stillman—personal friend and doctor to Leland Stanford who had privately expressed reservations about the governor's abilities—wrote of San Quentin, "While academies and colleges are so lightly endowed for the promotion of intelligence and virtue, they have a gigantic university supported at great expense, sending forth, almost daily, graduates educated in every crime known to the laws."[9]

More than a few of the prisoners held at San Quentin when Stanford took office were First Peoples. The records are inexact at best, but official sources refer to about sixty men—about 10 percent of the prison—who were from Native tribes.[10] At the same time, the 1860 U.S. Census categorized 4.6 percent of California's 380,000 people as "Indian." That Native Californians were victims of not only widespread child kidnapping and rape but a sustained war of extermination is graphically documented and indisputably clear. Although Governor Stanford signed legislation in April of 1863 making it illegal to bind Indians to labor contracts that fit the definition of indenture, it had little to no effect.[11] While Stanford was governor, "the practice of murdering California Indian adults in order to kidnap and sell young women and children for a profit likely reached its zenith in 1862," notes a landmark history of tribes in the state.[12]

Some survivors rose to rebel. Stanford was resolute in punishing California Indians for what he, other officeholders, and newspaper editors termed "depredations." A crime typical of those that settlers accused Native Californians of committing took place in 1863 along the wild Trinity River. A settler said on a May evening that he was standing on the stoop of his cabin when "two rifle balls passed close to my head." He said then he was attacked by forty Indians. He rushed inside, got a weapon, but then decided to abandon the home and ran into the woods, returning the next morning to see it had been burned to the ground. He was very much under the impression that the attackers first took all the food they could find inside. The next day he and more than a dozen others, well-armed, went hunting for the Native Californians but found only one other cabin, also torched. "Had we a few more men and arms," the settler told the newspaper, "I have no doubt we could have got back a good portion of the goods and number of redskins in the bargain."[13] The story made no mention of any possible provocation by the whites—no Indians were interviewed.

The following September, just to the south in Mendocino County, the local newspaper reported that "our citizens have suffered severely from a recent raid" by Native Californians "who made a descent on the valley last Friday night, and drove off fifty or sixty head of cattle." The story was not without some context. "The people are very much alarmed for the safety of themselves and property, on account of the fact that the Indians from all the country north of here have been rendered desperate by being driven from their own country down this way."[14]

In the remote northeast corner of California, near Honey Lake, settlers bitterly complained of government inaction, citing "a powerful tribe of hostile Indians east of us, who are constantly stealing from us and who occasionally murder some of our citizens." Another newspaper account commented that they felt "abandoned by California except when her officers collect taxes which they do not fail to demand."[15]

Still another source noted that the Honey Lake settlers were "to pay 25 cents for Indian scalps taken by the company."[16] As an indication of the pressure the settlers were putting on Sacramento, they sarcastically asked,

> Is it possible Governor Stanford and General Wright are all so ignorant of Indian character and their mode of warfare as to expect a military company to find bands of Indians prowling around the valley and making hostile demonstrations when we were prepared to receive them? Every one that knows anything of Indian character, knows that they attack when least expected and when we are least prepared for them, and immediately flee to the mountains, where they can find rocky cliffs to shield them and give them an advantage over an equal number of white men. Must our rulers have a view of the murdered and mutilated remains of scores of our citizens, and the remainder leaving their homes and their property and fleeing for their lives from a barbarous foe, before they will consent to give us protection? On the first day of this month a party of eleven men, returning from the Humboldt mines were attacked when within about eight miles of this valley, by a band of Indians numbering from fifty to seventy-five, and two of the whites were killed and more were severely wounded. The Indians got several of their animals, some provisions and several hundred dollars in money, with which they escaped.[17]

The California tribes would have argued, had anyone bothered to hear and tell their story, that they had no recourse. They were stalked and slaughtered across the land. Mothers and fathers were executed so kidnappers could steal and sell their children. Their hunting and gathering grounds had been largely taken by settlers. Vast numbers had fallen to disease brought to America by the Europeans. They were prevented from voting and testifying against their tormentors. They were routinely starved on the reservations where soldiers had herded them as if they were beasts. It was commonly said and written in mainstream society that they faced inevitable annihilation. This is not to minimize the thefts, retaliations, and violent insurrections they were sometimes justly accused of. The situation had been composting for years "To put it in essence," concluded a scholar of the situation, "a peaceful, sedentary highly localized group underwent conversion into a semiwarlike, seminomadic group."[18]

While Native Californians were forbidden from possessing guns, Stanford requested and received huge caches of weaponry from the Lincoln administration. Secretary of War Edwin Stanton sent him fifteen thousand of the "best Springfield muskets" and promised fifteen thousand more as well as five cannons, despite the Union's need for arms in fighting for an end to selling adults and children, raping women, and starving the African Americans of the Southern states. With the ordnance on the way, the governor issued the following orders: as "commander-in-chief of the militia, thereof, [I] do call upon the citizens of the frontier counties of Humboldt, Mendocino, Trinity, Klamath, Siskiyou, and Del Norte, of this State—as many as shall be necessary to fill up the foregoing requisition—to organize themselves."[19]

Stanford instructed the U.S. Army's commander of the Department of the Pacific, Brig. Gen. George Wright, to raise six battalions containing hundreds of men each "for special service against the Indians." They deployed military forces against Native Californians across much of the the state's far north, ranging from the northeastern corner where the state line meets Oregon and Nevada, across the ancient redwood forests, west to the rugged Northern California coast, and southerly into Mendocino County. General Wright instructed his colonel, "Every Indian you may capture, and who has been engaged in hostilities present or past, shall be hung on the spot." As one distinguished historian put it, the state had created "California's killing machine."[20]

"Our troops in their various encounters thus far have killed some 70 or 80" Indians, one of a deployment of six hundred North Coast militiamen wrote in the summer of 1862, "but have rarely succeeded in taking any prisoners, as, after exchanging a few shots, those who are not killed or very badly wounded, escape into the thickets, where it is generally impossible to overtake them." The soldier found some solace in the imprisonment of "about 350 Indian prisoners, three quarters of them squaws and children," many coming in themselves because of starvation.[21]

To help finance the apparatus, in April of 1863 Governor Stanford set aside $600,000 through legislation called An Act for the Relief of Enlisted Men of the California Volunteers in the Service of the United States. He was hardly alone in his campaign against Native Californians, not infrequently called "Red Devils" by those who wished them harm. Citizens regularly banded together in mobs, joined by vigilantes and men simply interested in kidnapping women and children they could outrage and sell. Hundreds were massacred during Stanford's time as governor alone.[22] In Sacramento, as an example of the level of official discourse on the subject, in April of 1862, Assemblyman Caleb Fay proposed an amendment to the laws of California that would allow "persons of not more than one-half Indian blood to give testimony" in courts of law. Assemblyman J. W. Griswold "said he was opposed to all these bills, first, last and all the time. They would admit to testify South American, Portuguese and Mexican negroes, who did not speak English, and were no more competent witnesses than Chinese."[23] The proposal failed and the years of sustained war against Native Californians, met by sporadic violence from the Indians long before Leland Stanford became governor, would go on long after he was eased out of office.

It must be noted that the chronic culture of violence was hardly unique to California. Not only was it continuously refreshed in the abattoirs of the Plains and Southwest, where Indian wars raged, but during just the first year of Stanford's gubernatorial reign the Civil War soaked much of the nation in the blood of Americans slaughtering their fellow Americans. At Chancellorsville, more than 30,000 died in the spring of 1863. Soon afterward, greater than 37,000 men fell at Vicksburg. And in three ruinous days at the beginning of July 1863, the dead numbered more than 50,000 at Gettysburg. The United States was anything but united, save in relentless, barbaric bloodletting from one end of the continent to the other.[24]

In the timeless strategy of squaring off one oppressed group against another, there were multiple accounts of angry Native Californians committing crimes against even more powerless Chinese immigrants. "White men are not usually hanged for killing Chinamen," the San Francisco Bulletin wrote in a story taken in part from the Gold Country's Jackson Ledger. "But Indians who commit such a crime are strung up with little ceremony." The account then described in some detail how a Native American had murdered an Asian newcomer, then had confessed and "died with courage" before "about 150 persons around the gallows." Two years later, the Bulletin sardonically wrote of the trend, "'Lo, the poor Indian,' is fast becoming civilized."[25]

The Chinese came to California for the same reason as Leland Stanford and almost everyone else: opportunity. There was very little of it in the Cantonese region's Pearl River delta, where most Chinese immigrants to

California originated. In the mid-1800s the booming population of the region was beset by famine, war, and an unrelenting state of chaos. "The unbearable situation in China during the late 1840s and early 1850s forced many Chinese to emigrate from their own country," noted a Chinese scholar documenting the immigration to gold rush California.[26]

In China an ancient feudal government remained in place, a binary caste system in which one was born into privilege or poverty. Men and women were sold, and sold themselves, into labor contracts they were obligated to fulfill for many years. For centuries, they had been shipped to other lands such as Malaysia, to toil for their freedom. When word reached China of the gold rush just on the other side of the Pacific Ocean, the very real prospect of working for a few years and returning home with enough money to free one's family from the yoke of servitude was as magnificent as it appeared to others worldwide.

They did not come as immigrants looking for a new home. The Chinese came, in the word commonly used by historians of the era, as "sojourners."[27] Almost every one intended to secure a small fortune among what they considered the "barbarians" in America and return to Asia to live a full, free life. Generally illiterate, unworldly, and saturated in a culture of submission, the Chinese peasantry had little idea of what was awaiting them. For many, the only way they would return was by a special shipping company that did a robust business sending back the bones of the Chinese, fulfilling a last wish to be interred in their native soil.

One Chinese poster from the Canton region provides a clear idea of the situation:

> The American people are the richest in the world. They welcome the Chinese. When you arrive in the United States, you will live in big houses, receive very high wages, have good food and nice clothes. You can remit your money home and our company will handle it for you. There will be no soldiers and officials to maltreat you. All people are equal; weak ones will not be harassed by strong ones. There are many Chinese in the United States; you will not feel lonely there. Please do not be afraid, our company will take good care of you. Seek your fortune now, our agencies in Canton and Hongkong will provide all the detailed information you wish to have.[28]

Because it was technically illegal to depart what many called the Middle Kingdom, the Chinese would often take a short boat ride across the Pearl River delta to Hong Kong, where brokers such as a San Francisco–based

Dutchman named Cornelius Koopmanschap would arrange to have them board a ship that would typically hold several hundred.[29] The vast majority were men. The crew would herd them belowdecks, where they were usually required to stay for the stock two-month voyage across the Pacific. The crossing was not a pleasure cruise. Aside from the stultifying conditions, poor food, and rancid drinking water, ships such as the *Bald Eagle* in the autumn of 1861 went down with all hands, lost during a typhoon on the China Sea. For the shipper, it was worth the risk. A boat with five hundred Chinese meant $37,000 in passenger fees.[30]

Upon arrival in San Francisco the newcomers were met at the docks by their Chinese masters, who quickly put them on boats up the Sacramento River and then set them on foot overland to the mountain mines. They typically worked in companies made up entirely of other Chinese, including the bosses. Inevitably, some would find their way to the towns and cities, where they might find work as farmers, ranch hands, fishermen, laundry workers, and cooks. Yet they were rarely far from the grasp of the people who controlled them. The secret societies of China known as the Triads came with the indentured workers, and tongs—what could be called gangs—formed as criminal organizations. They all fought over control of gambling, opium, and prostitution.

By the 1860s, with approximately thirty-five thousand Chinese in California, some order was brought to the situation as a consortium called the Six Companies formed to internally govern the Chinese who had arrived through the 1850s. "The companies controlled the Chinese relations with the American world, arbitrated disputes among their members, and dealt with problems involving overlapping jurisdiction or quarrels which originated on shipboard during the passage," notes a key history of the Chinese in California. "They offered rewards for apprehension and conviction of the murderers of their members."[31]

None of this pleased many of the European-Americans who ran the nation and California. The rationale of cheap labor unnaturally depressing the value of white labor, used against African Americans, was easily iterated into bigotry against Asians. To placate the white power structure, in 1852 California had imposed a monthly $3 Foreign Miners Tax that largely affected the Chinese, or Celestials as they were commonly called in the press and public. The Chinese companies not only approved of the tax per head but soon suggested it be raised to $4, knowing that the money financed 25–50 percent of many county budgets and without it the governments would go broke. In this way, the Six Companies helped make themselves indispensable.

Governor Leland Stanford and his state legislature of 1862 reacted to the growing discontent of their all-white, all-male constituency with something bearing the unwieldy title "An Act to Protect Free White Labor against Competition with Chinese Coolie Labor, and to Discourage the Immigration of Chinese into the State of California."[32] The law required "Mongolian races" eighteen years and older not already paying the miners' tax or involved in agriculture to pay $2.50 a month. People who employed the Asian workers would also have to pay. It was nicknamed the Chinese Police Tax.

Two events deserving mention subsequently took place. First, the American consul general in Hong Kong sent Stanford an unusual letter protesting the law: "The Legislation of California on the subject of Chinese emigration I cannot but regard as unjust," wrote the U.S. official. "Through this trade we possess and maintain a due degree of consideration in the East, which would not otherwise be accorded, and yet the whole efforts of certain parties in California seem directed to destroy it." Instead, the consul general suggested that labor issues "should be met in a spirit of wisdom and not prejudice."[33] The state Supreme Court struck down the legislation, ruling that immigration and foreign commerce laws were the exclusive business of the federal government, not the states.

That prompted a second event worthy of notice: Governor Stanford significantly—if briefly—softened his usually sclerotic stance. In his inaugural address of January 1862, it may be recalled, he had said, "To my mind it is clear, that the settlement among us of an inferior race is to be discouraged, by every legitimate means. Asia, with her numberless millions, sends to our shores the dregs of her population."

But one year later he addressed the state assembly and senate with a rather different attitude: the law itself, in some particulars, was probably not judicious, he said of the anti-Chinese legislation, but the true object desired was the discouragement of Chinese immigration, and not its total prohibition. Then, in saving-face fashion, he insisted he had not changed his mind about the Chinese—before not insignificantly altering much of his stance and even more of his tone:

> By our constitution the Chinese cannot become citizens—by our laws they are incapacitated from testifying in courts of justice against citizens, or those who may become such. This state of things induces oppression, of which they are the victims; and as they are entirely cut off from the right of suffrage, they are denied, among us, the benefits of freedom, and are compelled to taste, in part, the bitter

fruits of oppression and slavery It is not humane—it is not in accordance with the principles of justice and of right, that we should invite or encourage the immigration of a people regarded so unfavorably by our fundamental law.[34]

Leland Stanford's fighting facade flexed a little more human, although there was reason to suspect it was because something was in it for him. In short time it would become apparent there was.

Soon afterward, the California State Supreme Court had still another noteworthy role in the trajectory of Stanford's career.

The governor stirred not a little political turmoil for himself and his associates when Lincoln appointed California State Supreme Court chief justice Stephen Field to the U.S. Supreme Court in May of 1863. Not only had Stanford been instrumental in obtaining his friend Field's appointment, he also took the opportunity to replace him with E. B. Crocker, Charles Crocker's older brother and one of the initial directors of the Central Pacific Railroad. The ham-fisted political patronage caused an uproar, as evidenced by even the pro-Stanford *Sacramento Daily Union*, along with many others, stating that "the appointment is 'not one fit to be made' under the circumstances."[35] The term expired on January 1, 1864, shortly before some critical railroad cases were heard by the high court. Then E. B. Crocker went right back to work as legal counsel for Leland Stanford's railroad.[36]

Governor Stanford made it perfectly clear time and again that he was a Republican and would consider no identification with any other political party. But political compromise among Californians supporting the Union and opposing the "traitorous" South was very much in the air. The governor's political nose once again failed him. By the spring of 1863 it was obvious to insiders that something was afoot regarding Stanford and a second term.

"No word of politics is now heard in the press or from the stump, and on the surface all is calm and placid, but underground the politicians are at work like beavers," reported the *Daily Alta California* of San Francisco. "They are at it night and day. They are burrowing while good men sleep."[37] As a biographer of Collis Huntington put it, "Stanford should have been on his toes."[38] He was not. Too late, the governor sprang suddenly alert and hoping to update, patch, and relaunch his political station, began espousing the cause of the Union Party, or as they were sometimes called, fusionists. Later that month the *Sacramento Daily Union* reported a "rumor" that Stanford was considering withdrawing from the contest.[39] The *Alta* followed by stating, "Everybody knows that Governor Stanford is a candidate for reelection."[40]

There was, indeed, much subterranean work taking place beneath public view. Sen. John Conness, an Irish immigrant and former assemblyman who had lost to Stanford in the last gubernatorial contest, had been industrious, syncing together the coalition of Democrats and Republicans who were staunchly antislavery, antisecession, and pro-Union.[41] Whether the early stirrings of dissent regarding the railroad's method of raising money or Conness's desire for revenge was the fuel behind their labors, he and his followers had their own candidate, Republican congressman Frederick Low. The stakes were not inconsiderable. The next governor of California would serve a full four years, the two-year terms being deleted from the state constitution. If Stanford was reelected, his power would amplify considerably.

Then it all blew up in public. On June 3, the Union Party nominated Low for the governor's race. Stanford's people walked out of the convention, complaining it was "unfair."[42] Stanford's fellow Republican, Attorney General Frank Pixley, delivered a "stentoriously" passionate speech, accusing the convention's participants of lacking decency in denying Stanford another term and allowing him to eventually retire from the job "gracefully and with dignity; yet you denied him that privilege." His speech, received with cheers—and catcalls—made page one of the *Sacramento Daily Union*, which usually published pure political news deeper in the paper. "It was taken for granted that a majority of the Convention would be for Stanford, and no small degree of surprise took place when a different result was announced," the pro-Stanford editors wrote. "The Stanford men were evidently so confident in their strength that they made no extra efforts to secure a majority of the Convention before it was too late."[43]

Stanford formally withdrew his candidacy, maintaining years later he did so only because he wanted to concentrate on running the railroad.[44] Low subsequently became California's ninth governor. Leland Stanford, not quite forty, looked as if he was washed out of politics. But anyone who sensed the sand in his character knew better than that.

CHAPTER 9

Living Up to the Landscape

That January of 1864 saw William Tecumseh Sherman begin his infamous march through the South. He would burn much of Atlanta to its red clay nine months later and begin his equally notorious, incendiary March to the Sea. Abraham Lincoln would comfortably win reelection to the presidency that November. As for Leland Stanford, he received a polite thank-you two weeks before the New Year and was graciously shown the door of the governor's office, the state budget still very much in the red. Through the sponsorship of his old business associate, E. B. Crocker, whom he had appointed to the state Supreme Court, Stanford was awarded admission to the State Bar of California. Even so, he would never practice law in the state.

Although he had long made it artlessly obvious that his first priority was being president of the Central Pacific Railroad, Stanford took deep pleasure in being addressed as governor and in fact enjoyed that title above all others for the remainder of his life. He was beginning to openly, if not consciously, embrace his paradoxes. Stalwart or stubborn, foolish or daring, hero or goat, Leland Stanford's peculiar traits were beginning to present themselves on a grand scale.

Nothing was as grand in America as the building of the railroad over, through, and across its purple mountain majesties, remorselessly vast deserts, and enameled plains. Commensurately, nothing could have been more formidable. Only four impossibly ambitious and naive dry goods salesmen from Sacramento who initially didn't know a railroad Howe truss from a smokebox would

have undertaken and kept at the mission, testing, pushing, and finally breaking every limit before them. It would require a singularity of teamwork for an
unparalleled purpose.[1]

As early as January of 1861 Stanford had used his position as head of the
California Republican Party to write a letter of introduction to President
Lincoln for Collis Huntington, "who visits the National Capitol for the purpose of obtaining aid in the construction of the first and most difficult section
of that work of National Importance the 'Pacific Rail Road.'"[2] After Theodore
Judah died embittered and estranged from the Big Four, and no lobbyists yet
hired, Huntington took on the East Coast role of working the federal government. In the beginning it was not his primary mission, though it rapidly
became so. The hard-boiled Californian's well-earned reputation as a "trader"
made him the best qualified among the Big Four to rummage for potential
investors to unload the so-far difficult-to-sell bonds. In addition, he was
charged with seeking out the best deals for materials to build the railroad.
Now he would begin foraging for political allies at the executive mansion, on
Capitol Hill, and in the bar of Washington, DC's Willard's Hotel. Incredibly,
his chief job experience for those challenging tasks was having run a hardware
store.[3] Although a close negotiator when it came to merchandise such as
potatoes, books, and pickaxes, Huntington was as ignorant as he was confident
about persuading politicians to do his bidding. It was a perfect template of
how the Stanford group would conduct business for many years.

Huntington's first order of business was to get Congress to amend the 1862
Pacific Railway Act to provide the foursome with more money, once again
using the political strategy of conflating the national interest with their financial ones. In this, Huntington, an autodidactic and fast study, began to demonstrate a natural affinity for the role of persuader, although in his first major
outing he had considerable help from the slick general manager of the Union
Pacific, who was also in the capital. The newborn UP would be laying track
from the other direction to meet the Central Pacific at a still unknown nexus
somewhere in the western wilderness.[4] When the House of Representatives
and the Senate finally agreed to the 1864 amendments and sent the legislation
off to the president, it had doubled the amount of land given gratis by the
government to the railroads from 6,400 to 12,800 acres per mile. For the cash-
strapped Big Four, the retooled law was a godsend as it also significantly
expedited the turnaround for getting paid for grading and laying down track.
But that was only the beginning. The biggest takeaway had to do with the

bonds. Instead of having to try to sell the government notes guaranteeing $12,000, $24,000, and $48,000 per mile depending on terrain, those figures also doubled overnight. The best part of that gift was the government agreeing to let Stanford and company sell their own bonds, with the U.S. government guaranteeing it would pay the interest for decades. Investors found the offering far more attractive because they now would be in the first position to recover money; taxpayers were pushed to a secondary status, a reversal of the original terms. As if that wasn't enough, the U.S. Treasury also agreed pay the first year's interest free of charge, much as an auto dealer might when having trouble moving cars off the lot. President Lincoln signed the bill on July 2, 1864, and immediately got back to the work of winning reelection and the Civil War.

Getting the work done of grading the land for the railbed and laying the rails themselves into the foothills, and then through and across the forbidding valleys and peaks of the Sierra Nevada, would not succumb to persuasion, politics, or sleights of hand. It would take labor. A lot of it.

With extraordinarily generous refinancing packages soon to be in their back pockets and the California spring equally warming, the Big Four's first slow work of crossing the flat, fertile Central Valley and then inching up the Sierra foothills hammered on. By July the rails reached the mining community of Newcastle, about thirty miles east of Sacramento and just shy of one thousand feet above sea level. Passengers could take the train daily from the state capital. Grading the next stretch of road across an area called Dutch Flat that led to the Donner Pass route Judah had mapped allowed stagecoaches and freight wagons to save as much as three day's travel across the peaks and into Nevada. Stanford and company charged a toll for that. And that caused some trouble. The small but multiplying band of critics, especially in skeptical San Francisco, said the massive amounts of government loans to the Big Four were a sham and the Stanford group's only real goal was to milk the new toll road for money, then abandon the rail project. Many years later, Charles Crocker, in his reminiscences, said he had been ready to pull out around that time because he and his partners were having to put their own money and credit into the project and any real payout was still beyond the horizon. A well-regarded history of both the Union and Central Pacific, however, says the toll pike soon made the Big Four $1 million a year. The work went on.[5]

Although the first thirty miles across the valley floor and up the forgiving foothills had been slow, it had gone relatively well. The next thirty miles, however, would need to climb some twenty-seven hundred feet to a mountain settlement appropriately named Alta. In addition, the engineers were looking at traversing a three-mile U-shaped canyon wall about thirteen hundred feet above the North Fork of the American River. The idea was to cut a deep ledge or shelf into the angled mountainside so they could lay the tracks. They called it Cape Horn, likening it to the passage around the bottom of South America that many new Californians, including a new superintendent of construction, had survived. The work was, of course, all done by hand, the most sophisticated tools being carts hauled by mules. The relatively pliant rock would be pried and hammered loose, then kegs of black powder—the invention of dynamite by Alfred Nobel just around the corner—would be stuffed into the seams and blown apart. To initially get down the steepest segment of the rock face, however, would probably require that men be secured and lowered on ropes along steep but sloping cliffs well above the river canyon, not a job that appealed to everyone.[6] But first, coupled with an increasingly severe labor shortage, Crocker faced a problem of critical bearing. He had a solution in mind, but to achieve it the stout self-described "bull" of a man would have to deal with his latest hire, the extraordinary superintendent of construction.

If a call for a railroad boss went to central casting, it would send up James Harvey Strobridge. A good deal of his mystique derived from the signature black patch he reportedly wore over his right eye.[7] Beneath it was what was left after a delayed black powder blast shot a piece of the Sierras into his head. Tall, built like a locomotive, and having the personality of a martinet almost as unyielding as the stone that had crushed his eye, he was legendarily profane, fulminating, and abusive. In short, the template of the middle-management tool executives like to use as a lightning rod for their employee's wrath. Strobridge ran a crew of six hundred to eight hundred men, when he could keep that number of his workforce. The Vermonter abstained from liquor and rigidly demanded the same discipline from his workers. When, for example, Strobridge later was working another rail line for the Big Four, he usually had a U.S. marshal working for him. "If a saloon opened near the front the keeper would be arrested because his license was not ready, taken to some court a long distance away, and his stock of liquor would be destroyed by parties unknown," one of Strobridge's men reminisced years later.[8] In this way, none of the notorious "wicked cities" popularly known as "Hell on Wheels," which afflicted the Union Pacific, troubled Stanford's railroad. But not only did the largely Irish crews, initially drawn to California by the prospect of gold and who were not infrequently wildly independent characters, keep running off to the mines at the first word of a new strike, they also scurried to the bars on payday. Too often they failed to return. The Stanford group would need much more reliable workers—thousands of them.

On January 7, 1864, an advertisement appeared in the *Sacramento Daily Union*:

PACIFIC RAILROAD

WANTED,

FIVE THOUSAND LABORERS,

For Constant and Permanent Work[9]

Only two hundred applicants showed up.

Many were Irish. Some were Chinese. Although Crocker shared Stanford's deep bigotry toward Asians, his desire to make money overcame his avowed principals and in desperation he instructed Strobridge to hire several dozen "Celestials" for menial labor. Strobridge balked, saying they were too small to handle the work, along with insults about their eating rice and dried fish, their clothes, and their self-protective tribalism. But leathery as he was, Strobridge also found that his desire to keep his job overpowered his professed code of conduct. At Crocker's urging, he brought on some fifty Chinese men and gave them the most menial work at less pay than his white workers. He was soon astonished to see how tough, thorough, and dependable the new hires were. Before Stanford much later famously took the first swing at the last spike connecting the two ends of the transcontinental railway, some ten thousand to twelve thousand Chinese workers would be the main reason the road got built. They were, in a very real way, the authentic John Henrys of the steel-driving man legend. Indeed, the president of the Central Pacific Railroad Company didn't miss a beat as he expeditiously renamed the men and women he had as governor just a few years prior scourged as "dregs" and "degraded and distinct people" instead as 'quiet, peaceable, patient, industrious and economical—ready and apt to learn all the different kinds of work required in railroad building." Coming to the hard reality that he needed them to create the wealth and high station he so thirsted for, Stanford conceded that "without them it would be impossible to complete the western portion of this great national enterprise, within the time required by the Acts of Congress." But perhaps most telling was this statement, made at the same time: "More prudent and economical, they are contented with less wages."[10]

Although he zigzagged between condemning the Chinese and exploiting them, Stanford held his essential views until the end of his life. Responding to criticism by racists that he hired Asians, Stanford said, to be soothing, "They are not a prolific race, and negroes are increasing at ten times their rate yearly." He later declared that not only do "they make good domestic servants," but "they do simply the commonest kind of work, and in doing so they do not really come into competition with white labor. The white men are, as a result, promoted to a better and more paying kind of labor"—exactly the same view he had formed forty years before in his youth about African Americans and slavery.[11]

Rightly or wrongly, "more than anyone else, Leland Stanford is held responsible for the mistreatment and exploitation of thousands of Chinese workers in the United States," declared an eminent historian of the Chinese experience in California.[12]

Despite Stanford's handful of critics who have suggested his abilities were hardly sufficient to take a rather ordinary man to extraordinary eminence, his aptitude for retooling to whatever seemed to suit his plodding but insatiable ambition is worthy of some clinical, if left-handed admiration. There is no reason to suggest Leland Stanford was among that most base of all human forms, an amoral as opposed to immoral person. Rather, his bedrock morality regarding his family was sacred to him. On matters of business, however, Stanford could change his position on almost anything he had earlier declared inviolate. He could color facts without a blush, and he could downright lie without remorse. He was very much what an extravagantly forgiving person might call a practical man. If it worked, Stanford used it. If it didn't work, he tossed it in the rubbish bin. It was a code hardly restricted to the robber barons of America's Gilded Age.

The men, and women, who came to California from China worked. Resilient, collaborative, and clean—they washed and changed their clothes each evening after work and before supper, startling the considerably less sanitary non-Chinese in adjacent work camps. They also generally found little pleasure in alcohol, though a pipe bowl of opium on Saturday night was not uncommon. The Stanford group generally compensated the white, largely Irish, workers about 15 percent more than the Chinese.[13] And if one takes into account the bread, boiled beef, and potatoes the railroad fed the white workers but the Asians declined, not inconsiderably more.[14] Instead, the Chinese paid for and kept to their own food and employed their own cooks, who would augment a staple of rice with herbs, fresh produce, and game when they could find it, and with shipped-in food such as dried duck, cured hams, cabbage, dried seaweed, bamboo shoots, and garlic.[15] In addition, rather than simply drinking the water found along the route, the Chinese habitually boiled it, brewing what would cool to lukewarm tea to be drunk during the day and thereby generally avoiding intestinal ailments such as dysentery that sometimes afflicted the other laborers. Although the Chinese workers did not frequent bars and gaming dens, gambling among their own was common, as were internal conflicts they tended to settle themselves.

Strobridge expressed his revised opinion of the Chinese when he said "they learn quickly, do not fight, have no strikes that amount to anything, and are very cleanly in their habits. They will gamble and do quarrel among themselves most noisily—but harmlessly."[15] But of course there was more to the story than just decorous behavior. "The company in three years saved approximately five and half million dollars by hiring Chinese instead of white unskilled laborers," Alexander Saxton found in his signature history of the Chinese in California. "The characteristic picture appears: the face of the engineer, always white, capped and goggled at his cab window, one gloved hand raised in casual greeting to the gandy dancers along the trackside."[17]

The Chinese workers not only reported to Strobridge and his white captains—they were never given supervisorial jobs—they also answered to the Six Companies, which supplied the workforce through brokers such as Dutchman Cornelius Koopmanschap. The partnership between those who recruited and transported the workers from South China to Northern California and the Six Companies that managed them on the railroad and in Gold Country kept its power base in San Francisco. "For many years the Six Companies kept a special Chinatown contingent of San Francisco policemen on their payroll," observed Saxton. "They also retained competent lawyers who were frequently in court seeking the apprehension of runaway laborer or sing-song girls on complaints of petty theft which would later be withdrawn."[13]

The Six Companies also provided a measure of protection for their charges. While the railroad was under construction they wrote to the government—the California State Archives keeps the letter, written in Chinese, in Leland Stanford's gubernatorial file—protesting the enslavement of women, which had been winked at since the beginning of the gold rush, when they were sold in open markets on the docks of San Francisco: "In our humble opinion the sale of women into prostitution breaks the law and offends order, and we petition that Your Benevolence will not allow this practice to continue." The plea to treat all people alike notes that the

> people of Tang [China] also came here, to search for gold and to conduct business. We perceived that [the United States and China] as neighbor countries are like a single body, and that within the four seas all men are brothers. This country's public morals are pure and fine, and its rules and laws are strict but impartial. This is particularly clearly shown by the case of human slavery, which has now been completely prohibited.

The lengthy letter, which gives a sharp perspective on the conditions the Chinese encountered in late nineteenth-century California, then asks in part,

> Yet why has the abduction and sale of women into prostitution alone not been prohibited? Since (1852), when Chinese prostitutes began to arrive here, day by day the numbers have increased. Soon there will be ten thousand. Upon investigation, all were women of good families who were purchased by treacherous kidnappers and their ilk. Most were forced into prostitution.
>
> The result has been that young merchants and sojourners from every country have lingered in brothels to indulge their lust, and so lost all their money and property and destroyed their businesses. Their industriousness turns to indolence, and wealth becomes poverty. Their poverty begets shamelessness, and shamelessness brings thoughts of doing evil to their hearts. Criminality has become rampant. They rob here and snatch there; disputes arise and troubles are many. In truth, the situation has become a disaster for the whole country. Even worse are those who have been infected by the poisons of prostitution and have been stricken with insanity or developed ulcers and abscesses and other such maladies that medicine cannot remedy. Over the years many have been hurt, disabled, or even lost their lives. There are not enough words to describe the depravity caused by prostitution.[19]

The Six Companies were somewhat more passive regarding the health and welfare of the Chinese workers doing the dangerous railroad construction. That many died doing the work is unambiguous. There are no confirmed numbers of the dead, Chinese or otherwise. But since the laborers from the Orient outnumbered those of the Occident by some ten to one, and they performed almost all the singularly harsh tasks, it is more than reasonable to conclude they suffered not only the most injuries by far, but also fatalities. For example, avalanches, which were hardly uncommon during the record snowfalls of the mid- to late 1860s and were exacerbated by the incessant blasting through the Sierras as workers graded the track in preparation for the ties and rails, more than a few times trapped Chinese laborers, whose frozen bodies were sometimes found much later. "If white workers were unwilling to undertake the job, the Chinese were always sent in," noted a history of building the railroad. "This was so true that the expression 'Chinaman's chance' was coined during the Central Pacific's construction period."[20]

A conservative estimate of about fifty Chinese fatalities during the six years of heavy work is fair, if not exact, since records of construction deaths were either not kept or were destroyed.[21] Aside from the horror of witnessing so many of one's countrymen and fellow workers perish on the job, there was the added burden of a deeply imbued custom of wanting one's remains to be interred almost seven thousand miles back across the Pacific Ocean.

"It was widely believed that to be buried in a well-chosen site according to *fengshui* principals not only enabled the dead to rest in peace but, perhaps more importantly, would bring good fortune to one's descendants for generations to come," wrote a historian of the Chinese experience in California. "Nothing was more abhorred and feared than dying in a strange land, deprived of attendance from one's family and becoming a hungry, lonely ghost, unfed and unclothed, drifting into limbo."[22] The business of sending the remains of the dead back to China was therefore a prosperous one, though often mocked by non-Chinese.

Admired and scorned at the same time for being docile, in June of 1867 the Chinese had simply had enough and went on strike, demanding wages and hours equal to white workers. As the *Daily Alta California* reported a few days later from the mountain town of Cisco, "Work here and beyond is entirely suspended."[23] No one came to the Chinese workers' rescue. Instead, Stanford and Crocker kept all food away from the High Sierra camps and starved the "Celestials." In about a week, they submitted and went back to work for the same pay and hours.

As the railroad crews detonated keg after keg of black powder and later used even more dangerous nitroglycerin, ground down countless pickaxes and shovels, and often simply scraped their way to the summit day and night, finally blasting, drilling, and smashing through the last of more than a dozen solid granite tunnels, oftentimes literally inch by inch, they came upon Donner Lake, a wide valley, and the Truckee River flowing east into Nevada.

If Americans were to ask someone to show them men to match their mountains, the responders would have done well to point to the often diminutive, tidy men who spoke Cantonese and quietly went about the business of getting it done and done. This is not to disregard the labors of the workers of European descent, who more often than not supervised but not infrequently shouldered the heavy lifting side by side with those who came from Asia. And it would be unjust not to recognize Leland Stanford, Charles Crocker—and his brother E. B., who would soon pass away—Collis Huntington, and Mark Hopkins. It was this small band of major risk takers who worked night and day, year after year, raising the capital and putting together the construction team, despite all bets against them.

The mechanical means by which the railroad builders moved the impossible-to-comprehend amounts of earth, stone, and timber to surmount the Sierras is one matter. Keeping the grades gentle enough to be able to compel nine-teenth-century locomotives to haul freight and passenger trains over one of the planet's most formidable mountain ranges, hugging steep cliffs teetering hundreds of feet above river canyons, driving through granite tunnels—one as long as sixteen contiguous football fields—conquering epic snowfalls, constantly concerned about not having enough working hands and the money to pay them, were just some of the very nonvirtual barriers always before all of them.

On top of that was the still more unlikely prospect of coming to terms with the grandeur of the Sierra Nevada that has drawn and baffled countless writers, poets, and artists for generation after generation. Perhaps California's native daughter Joan Didion said it best by simply throwing up her hands and conceding "the sense of not being up to the landscape."[24]

The builders of the Central Pacific Railroad were.

CHAPTER 10

Command and Control

Remembering the time of Leland Stanford's quickening public profile, one of his lieutenants privately observed that "Stanford was looked upon by the general public as having the most authority of any of the so-called 'Big Four.'" The railroad executive and engineer described him as "a man of imposing appearance, deep chest. Large shoulders and arms, large face with whiskers and moustache usually trimmed fairly short. He was rather slow of movement and in business was disposed to procrastinate."[1]

Jennie Stanford, meantime, was leading a comfortable bourgeois life in their Sacramento mansion, hosting grand parties featuring late-night dinners for hundreds and dancing into the early morning, dressing in the elaborate brocaded haute couture of the Victorian age, and beginning to acquire a jewelry collection that would soon prompt a whispered condescension similar to what she had suffered in Albany when Leland was grubbing for position in his mountain store saloon and ersatz courtroom. They had greatly expanded their home, making the grand palace of Sacramento even more so. But more than that, noted an architectural historian, "locomotives sketched onto the gaslight fixtures, locomotive motifs on the dining room's new furniture, and pictures of the conquered American wilderness on the walls, Stanford's Sacramento mansion underscored the triumph of technology."[2]

The couple had been married for almost twenty years and had been on their own. That was about to change—and change everything.

The free states' triumph in the Civil War, the subsequent assassination of Abraham Lincoln, the impeachment of Andrew Johnson, and Reconstruction were political, economic, and cultural behemoths of the second half of America's 1860s. But they were largely just headlines, emotional rents, and distant events for the West. More of the moment up and down what was then often called the Pacific Slope was a disruption met with great revelry and can-do American pride: the railroad's ascension and overcoming of the High Sierra in the summer of 1867. The mostly Chinese workforce not only conquered what a generation of native U.S. naysayers claimed could not be done but did so much sooner than anyone imagined. Now the rail workers began to joyfully descend the Sierra Nevada's eastern flank and enter the Great Basin.

The first railroad town at the western end of the desert was a frontier outpost and mining settlement Charles Crocker decided to name after an obscure Civil War general, Jesse Lee Reno. The largely desiccated landscape from Reno east through Nevada and into the Utah Territory was not terrain many found appealing. It was the western end of the great desert that had so bedeviled the early pioneers, hardy men and women, and their children who died by the score in the alkaline stretches with little potable water, game, fodder, or even shade when the temperatures hiked into the hundreds. Now the race against the rival Union Pacific coming from the East was in earnest.

In this home-stretch adventure Leland Stanford was having his first skirmishes with the man who had been and still was his friend and partner but would become his great rival and then bitter enemy: Collis Potter Huntington. In this opening scuffle, Stanford would come out the winner and better man, although history has been far kinder to Huntington, a prodigious if semiliterate correspondent who left many hundreds of letters barking his side of the story. Stanford remained his stoic self in the well more than five hundred letters and telegrams he wrote just to Huntington alone between 1867 and 1894, most of which are concentrated in the late 1860s and 1870s. His sometimes brief but not infrequently lengthy letters deal almost exclusively with pure business matters. If he committed his personal thoughts about the relationships with his partners, they may have well been in his many letters to wife Jennie. But soon after his death many years later, the widow burned whatever correspondence from her husband she possessed.

Huntington, living then on the East Coast to be near DC politicians, New York financiers, and factories making the equipment the railroad needed, was a restless man, rarely content with reaching a goal, instead hardwired to find purpose and the contentment it supplied by relentlessly seeking and conquering his next target. Now he set his sights on two new endgames: One was beating the Union Pacific to coal deposits in the canyons east of Salt Lake City so the Central Pacific could get ownership of the mineral rights for twenty miles on each side of the tracks. Grander still was the concept of creating a brand-fresh city to the north of the lake, altogether bypassing Brigham Young and his Saints. Huntington imagined his new city would be be best positioned to exploit the coming cross-continental trade. To Huntington, pacing in his East Coast offices two thousand miles distant, the two were as achievable as the far more challenging goals the Big Four had already accomplished. To road boss Charles Crocker, lashing his twelve-thousand-man workforce to lay down as much as ten miles of railroad track in one day, Huntington's goal of beating the UP was luxurious speculation.[3] Mark Hopkins, bent over the books back in Sacramento, became chary of leveraging the company to the breaking point. As for railroad president Leland Stanford, traveling the rough road back and forth between California and Utah, the idea was madness.

As a lawyer who knew something about the law, Stanford told Huntington, who was more expert in buying officeholders and railroad ties, that trying to grade a railbed on a route obviously in the Union Pacific's domain would clearly violate their contract with the government and cause more trouble than reward. Moreover, Stanford was familiar with the actual work from spending so much time in Nevada and Utah and saw the proposal as simply impractical. Hopkins and Crocker agreed. Stanford first made his case gently, while still trying to engineer means that would satisfy his old friend and business partner. Then, finally fed up, he wrote from Salt Lake City to Huntington in Manhattan, "Your views and mine seem to be directly opposite. One or the other must certainly fail utterly to comprehend the situation." Then noting Huntington's ceaseless drumming about encroaching on the UP's right-of-way, he added, "This would seem the greatest folly."[4]

The quarrelsome Huntington swallowed defeat without remark. His attention turned to his plans for a new railroad town in northeast Utah. Stanford had been thinking the same thing, but knowing the land, argued it would have to be near fresh water in an existing Mormon settlement. "I think we had better have it [a junction] as far east as Ogden, and have a town of our own near Bear River," he wrote Huntington in the spring of 1869.[5] Huntington had been pushing for another location, which an exasperated Stanford finally quashed with facts dry as the desert itself:

> There is not a sufficient supply of suitable water for a terminal station at any point between Rosebud Creek forty miles west of Monument Point and Bear River, where it must be pumped and which at a low state is strongly alkaline. At Ogden is an abundant supply of pure water, a good elevation. Prior to the commencement of our work there was not and is not now a resident along the line between river & the western boundary of Utah excepting those brought here by railway work. Brigham Young has organized a company to build a railroad from Ogden to Salt Lake city this station.[6]

In the end, Huntington finally backed down from his dreamed-of city as well.

Stanford also had his hands full dealing with events set in motion by Congress and President Lincoln some five years before that were coming to a head, laying the groundwork for one of the more absurd episodes in American history. In the territory north of Salt Lake City where the two lines would eventually link, there was no obvious claim to the right-of-way or where they would meet. Instead, the president of the United States was to decide where the rails would join. This created an opportunity to scrape up extra money, inciting both railroad companies to ignore reason and prudence.

In its hurried generosity, Washington had agreed to help finance the competing companies for every three hundred miles each graded in advance of laying down the tracks. Although this was the least amount of money per mile, the work was less challenging and the profits were potentially significant. Consequently, the two competing railroads began to grade land parallel to each other and astonishingly, even crossed each other's railbeds in several places. Before it was all over, they had graded side by side for 250 miles, both hoping to get the taxpayers' money and the right to lay ties and rails on the ribbons of prepared desert terrain, which would earn them still more dollars. Far from the centers of bright lights of public scrutiny—muckraking reporters from San Francisco and New York rarely ventured into that desert expanse—there were rumors that the rival crews tried to sabotage each other's work as well as waving cheerfully as they ground past each other.[7]

After the Union Pacific had crossed the Rockies, it was struggling through the canyons of Utah Territory toward Salt Lake City, where Mormon leader Brigham Young eagerly awaited, as it would turn out, in vain. Meanwhile, Stanford and company were scorching across the desert from the opposite direction, ostensibly aiming for the same destination, while privately beginning to quarrel among themselves. Huntington, who had already shown signs of irritation with Stanford, began a ceaseless, not always gentlemanly campaign for Stanford to sit on Young's doorstep until the Big Four got what Huntington wanted: help getting into the coal canyons before the UP and some financial assistance building the line.

"I notice what you say about leaving Salt Lake City so soon," Huntington wrote to Stanford. "I may be mistaken, but I think it was and is very important that some one of us is willing to take *any responsibility* should have been at Salt Lake for the last year and should be there until the rails of the two roads come together, and I think it all important that you should be there."[8]

Crocker, in turn, castigated Huntington for not supplying him with sufficient matériel ranging from rail spikes to locomotives. Hopkins, in character, stayed mostly silent. As they neared the still undefined finish line, the squabbling turned more serious. Huntington's splenetic correspondence singled out Stanford most pointedly, constantly harping that the company president did not respond to his letters with sufficient speed. Stanford finally noted curtly, "I do not pretend to reply to your letters because I am often absent when they reach the office."[9] In other words, while Huntington focused on Stanford not being in Utah for what he considered adequate periods and not writing back often enough to satisfy his neediness, the very reason Stanford wasn't responding at the drop of a hat was because he was often in the territorial desert for weeks and even months, many times camping in the harsh outlands while Huntington stayed at his Manhattan apartment or the luxurious Willard's Hotel in the nation's capital.

Regardless, Huntington continued to press him: "It does seem to me that you do not realize the very great necessity there is in pushing forward the track," he condescended before adding with obnoxious emphasis, "*Now what is the matter?*"[10] And the others, not inclined to suffer criticism, turned aside reproaches targeted at them and instead joined the campaign against their company president. "Stanford will not stay long or go away willingly from his Wife," wrote Crocker to Huntington. "If it was Washington, N.Y., London or Paris, all would be right; he would go immediately & stay indefinitely. As to work he absolutely succeeds in doing nothing as near a man can. He spends an hour or two per day at the office if we send for him."[11]

While Huntington's intelligence, passion, and take-no-prisoners personality come through in his many impatient-of-restraint and often plainly pouty letters, Stanford's relative taciturnity did little to disarm the suspicion that he was guilty of the same sort of laxity that had bedeviled him since youth. Huntington's anxiety mounted: "I know nothing of what you go to California for, but suppose it of importance. It would seem to me there cannot be anything of importance enough to take you away from the east end of our line at the time."[12] He was wrong.

The often ponderous Stanford had no doubt earned suspicion among those who knew him for slacking. But what Huntington, Crocker, and Hopkins did not either know at first and what Huntington clearly had very little appreciation of until much later was the most momentous moment of a man's life: Leland Stanford's wife was pregnant and after eighteen years of barren marriage, on May 14, 1868, Jennie Stanford gave birth to a boy, Leland DeWitt Stanford Jr.[13] It would be their only child. Stanford, who was forty-four, would not leave thirty-nine-year-old Jennie's bedside in their grand Sacramento home, regardless if Huntington wrote him dozens of scathing letters or telegraphed his partners a gross of attacks against him. Huntington's ill-advised schemes, red-faced rants, and perennial one-long-emergency would wait. And Stanford, through all the surviving correspondence among the Big Four in those tense years, was consistently businesslike, often gracious, and even at times self-deprecating. He did so from a position of strength.

Leland Stanford, was, after all, the former governor of California and the firmly established president of the Central Pacific Railroad, heading a company he estimated at upward of fifteen thousand workers, which made Stanford's company the largest employer in the country, easily rivaling that of any Rockefeller, Carnegie, or Vanderbilt to come.[14] From Stanford's perspective, he regarded himself as a man with new family responsibilities, someone familiar with the politics, finance, and construction of his massive enterprise. Company vice president Collis Huntington was the childless chief lobbyist and head of purchasing thousands of miles away from what was happening on the ground where the complex, brutal desert railroad race was nearing completion.[15]

When mother and child were clearly healthy and happy, Stanford discharged his work responsibilities by once again making the difficult trip to Utah on several occasions, walking the line with James Harvey Strobridge, pouring over the maps, and negotiating with the wily Brigham Young, as well as having to deal with federal investigators who finally arrived on site to inspect every rail, tie, spike, and grade. Jennie, presenting the sweet symptoms of postpartum joy, wrote Leland a gentle, brimming-with-love letter gushing about their little boy. It is one of the very rare, intimate notes left: "I see so little of you nowadays, a letter is more dear than ever. I feel as though I had so much to tell you about your being so good to me, doing so much," she concluded.

> My heart is full of love running over with the feelings I have for you, my blessed husband. I am not half good enough. I would like to be perfect that you might think me the best of wives. I shall be glad when we can be together all the time. I feel so lonesome, even here in the Hotel. I miss you all the time.[16]

The Mormons, who just a few years before had sparked a good deal of anxiety with their separatist movement, violent encounters, and overreactions by those opposed to them, had settled into their Zion of Salt Lake City and environs, at last rendering to Caesar what Latter-day Saint leader Brigham Young conceded belonged to the government. In return, Young and his Saints expected the railroad coming at them from both directions would bring disruption, but also prosperity. "I want this railroad to come through this city," Young declared. It would not only "bring our brethren and sisters here. It opens to us the market, and we are at the door of New York, right at the threshold [of] the emporium of the United States. We can send our butter, eggs, cod fish[,] cheese, and fruits, and receive in return oysters, clams, cod fish, mackarel, oranges, and lemons."[17]

But the route over the northern end of the Great Salt Lake was shorter than that to the south where the city lay. Moreover, there was timber and water in the Promontory Mountains to the north. The railroads wanted those resources. The Union Pacific's chief engineer, Grenville Dodge, recounted in one of his many memoirs how Brigham Young became a wild card in the final months of construction:

> We found the line so superior on the north of the lake that we had to adopt that route with a view of building a branch to Salt Lake City, but Brigham Young would not have this, and appealed over my head to the board of directors, who fully sustained me. Then Brigham Young gave his allegiance to the Central Pacific, hoping to bring them around the south end of the lake and force us to connect with them there.[18]

Stanford wrote Hopkins that he initially found Young "cold and close," but as the summer of 1868 warmed so did the Mormon chief.[19] The next time Stanford described him it was to Huntington, suggesting he was the manner of man they might respect: "About Brigham Young. He is a shrewd man fully alive to his own interest," adding, "I did not think it best to offer more to Brigham as that was satisfactory."[20] In the correspondence with Hopkins,

Stanford boasted, unlike the far less duplicitous Union Pacific engineer Dodge, that the Saints still did not understand his railroad's plans to bypass Salt Lake City to the north and, he wrote, "I have not found it advisable to enlighten them."[21]

When Brigham Young finally did learn that neither railroad line would be coming to Salt Lake City, he declared before his congregation, "It is an insult to the people of this city."[22] In the end, to assuage the Mormon leader, both lines threw business to Young—or more technically correct, to one of his many sons from his many wives—giving him a lucrative contract to build the railroad through his part of the state. With that money and work experience, the pragmatic Young saw that not only would he be able to build his own connecting lines, but the Latter-day Saints would control what traveled on them.

Stanford saw that although there were challenges still ahead, he and his crew had placed the Central Pacific in a fine spot. "I think our position impregnable," he telegraphed Hopkins in March of 1869.[23] Huntington finally agreed to come to Utah to see what was what—he and Stanford spent Christmas of 1868 together in Salt Lake City, Stanford sacrificing this first big holiday with wife and infant son.

Finally, facing the reality that Stanford had slowly—too slowly for his partners—been trying to demonstrate, Huntington also met with his rival from the Union Pacific and cut a deal to stop the redundant parallel grading before the public found out and the government stepped in. The Central Pacific got the bonds money for much of the parallel work on the east side of the Great Salt Lake and paid it to the UP for land rights. Most notably, Huntington, without any government representative, hammered out a deal everyone wanted about where the two competing railroads would lay down their sledgehammers, meet, and join rails: Promontory Summit. Congress and the president were then informed. No one made a fuss.[24]

It was a practical location, not a romantic one. Albert D. Richardson of the *New York Tribune* described it that summer of 1869:

> Promontory is neither city nor solitude, neither camp nor settlement. It is bivouac without comfort, it is delay without rest. It is sun that scorches, and alkali dust that blinds. It is vile whiskey, vile cigars, petty gambling and stale newspapers at twenty-five cents apiece. It would drive a morbid mind to suicide. It is thirty tents upon the Great Sahara, sans trees, sans water, sans comfort, sans everything.[25]

The month of May in the high desert just north of the Great Salt Lake can be unkind to anyone counting on good weather. But on May 10, 1869, seven years before the congressionally mandated deadline, it was fine enough for what is not infrequently compared to the symbolic significance of the first man on the Moon almost exactly one hundred years later.

The story, told often, bears repeating: The Union Pacific's boss arrived late for the big ceremony, having been held up by angry workers who did not get their pay. Central Pacific president Stanford had to cool his well-cobbled heels in a luxurious executive railcar for two days waiting for him. The last, ceremonial spikes were made of gold and silver. Another was attached to telegraph wires that would transmit nationwide the great moment of the spikes being driven into their ordained slots, emblematically uniting the recently divided United States of America. On the big day, Stanford, who had scooped the symbolic first shovelful of western soil for the project 650 miles away in Sacramento six years earlier, took the first swing, aiming for the gold spike—and missed. He got a second chance, prompting champagne to rupture coast-to-coast. Leland Stanford sent Collis Huntington a telegram: "The Rails Connected with appropriate Ceremony."[26] That was it.

The iconic photograph of the two train lines joining, workers reaching out from each side with bottles of champagne, shows Leland Stanford's locomotive to the left: the Jupiter. It had been a last-minute substitute because the engine originally sent to the ceremony had broken down. It was almost as if a power with a salty sense of humor had intervened: Scolds had suggested the haughty Stanford was arrogantly fashioning himself after the supreme Roman god. Votaries countered he was a titan more appropriately compared to the great planet but in the firmament of American elites.[27]

That same afternoon Stanford laid down one of his most imprudent, tone-deaf, peckish bombasts. The reminiscence is in the memoirs of the Union Pacific's Grenville Dodge, a highly respected man of his time often credited with firmly convincing Lincoln to support the transcontinental rail project: "After the ceremonies were over, Mr. Stanford invited the principal men of the Union Pacific, contractors, etc. into his car where he served a lunch, had plenty of California fruit and plenty of champagne. Several speeches were made, by Stanford, Crocker and some others."

According to Dodge, Stanford then mouthed one of his most infamous orations, biting down hard on the hands that fed him even as he feasted:

Stanford in his speech, made a severe attack upon the Government. He went so far as to claim that the subsidy, instead of being a benefit, had rather been a detriment, with the conditions they had placed upon it. His statement struck everyone so unfavorably that Dan Casement, who was feeling pretty good, got up on the shoulders of his brother, Jack Casement, and said: "Mr. President of the Central Pacific: If this subsidy has been a detriment to the building of these roads, I move you sir that it be returned to the United States Government with our compliments." This, of course, brought a great cheer but put a very wet blanket over the rest of the time. Casement's apt response was spoken of for years and years afterwards.[28]

Reporter Richardson, now recovered from his wretched impressions at Promontory, was among the very first to ride all the way to California, having found a sleeping car: "At nearly every station through to Sacramento the people, attracted by the novelty, crowded up its doors and windows, eager to inspect it, and prompt to exclaim, 'isn't it gay!' 'That beats the world!' We found it smooth-running and comfortable, a vast improvement upon day coaches, but far inferior to Pullman's." Through the desert: "Nobody can realize how great a work this has been until he takes the long ride of four or five days and nights through dreary wastes and unbroken solitudes." Surmounting the mountains and into the lush Central Valley: "We glide across the broad American River, and over half a mile of trestlework; through the spreading suburbs of Sacramento."[29]

A first-class berth cost about $150, steerage about half that. What had taken months of hellish overland travel now took about a week in relative comfort and safety. But more than that, the transcontinental railroad signaled the end of America's pioneer era. Survivors of that almost inconceivably rugged age would be followed by generations of Americans facing very different challenges.

Getting the job done was momentous but only the beginning. Now the real business opportunities arose.

The Stanford group's clandestine concept was audaciously simple and among the first of its time: control as much of the traffic possible going to the Pacific Ocean. Because the Central Pacific's line terminated in Sacramento, that first and foremost meant getting rails to one of the world's great natural ports: San Francisco Bay. But there was a bug in the plan—the bay itself, 70 miles long and 4.5 miles wide at its closest connection between Oakland on the east side and San Francisco on the west. Oakland's natural shoreline is essentially a mudflat with enough water for recreational boating but sound-ings insufficient for serious shipping.[30] On the San Francisco side, however, swift currents scoured the bay floor to an average of seventy-five feet, accom-modating big ships since the Spanish had arrived one hundred years before Stanford's time. In the middle of the bay between both cities lay Yerba Buena Island—then colloquially called Goat Island—with the deep water against its western shore facing San Francisco but three miles distant from the city. The U.S. government owned the island of 160 acres, or about a quarter of a square mile in size, dedicated to military defense of the Bay Area. If the rail-road could obtain control of the isle, it would not have to deal with the cele-brated, cantankerous City by the Bay. Instead, it might build a railroad trestle across the mudflat from Oakland to Yerba Buena and completely control the Pacific terminus for the transcontinental railroad: for Stanford and company, the ideal terminus, the perfect port.

When news reached San Francisco that Huntington was in Washington, DC, trying to secure the island from the federal government, the city bellowed again in righteous wrath.[31] Did this not smell of the same scheme to construct and own a city in the desert to take a fat slice of the transcontinental traffic's bounty? Did this not prove that the new railroad barons had planned to take San Franciscans' tax money but cut them out of the action? Stanford publicly denied it all, while confidentially counseling Huntington to forego the Yerba Buena scheme and instead aim for controlling the Oakland waterfront.[32] In the end, Huntington failed in his task of attaining Yerba Buena, but the acrid taste of betrayal remained in many mouths—and spread new doubts across the West. The Big Four turned to other quietly hatched plans.

From early on, Stanford had been plotting the group's next big play. Stan-ford made no bones about it in a letter to written from Ogden: "*We must name those directors,*" he wrote with extra emphasis about a move to secretly plant their people on the board of a new rail line that could connect Sacramento with the Bay Area and then much of the rest of the state, "*and they must be ours and no ones else. There is too much at stake to do otherwise.*"[33] Stanford later referred to the new railroad company as a "very serious competitor" and said "it would become a dangerous rival." Hopkins and E. B. Crocker cautioned against the plan, concerned it would draw the attention and wrath of the growing number of railroad critics and eventually lead to serious problems such as rate regulation. Huntington, on the other hand, was gung-ho.

The name of the new company was the Southern Pacific.[34]

With that, the Big Four, under Stanford's leadership, began to quietly acquire and merge one railroad after another across the vast state of California, enabling control of all the rates and creating one of the first, most lucrative and most bitterly hated monopolies in U.S. history. Stanford even bought one of the few shipping companies that competed with the railroad to bring California's abounding agricultural products to port and finished goods from around the world to booming California. Leland Stanford called it smart business. The press called it a combine. The people of California began to call it the Octopus.

CHAPTER II

"The Machine of Steam on the Road of Iron"

When the first transcontinental train finally did reach the West Coast on September 6, 1869, it ended its run on the eastern shore of San Francisco Bay in the town of Alameda. From there, passengers boarded a ferry across the water to what was then the Davis Street wharf in San Francisco. Two months later, Alameda was abandoned and the western terminus moved a few miles to Oakland, where the ferry crossed to San Francisco. However, on that first day, in the words of a newspaper report, "the most frightful railroad accident that has ever occurred in California" took place. The eight-car passenger train collided head-on with a four-car train loaded with gravel. A switchman preoccupied with his breakfast blamed a heavy fog for not being able to see the southbound train roaring by and headed for the same track as the northbound one.

The crash happened on a November Sunday in 1869, just six months after the Promontory Summit party, in the town of San Leandro, adjacent to Oakland and Alameda. "The scene presented on our arrival beggars description," the story ran. "The wrecked trains, with their engines and cars smashed and shivered, the groans and shrieks of the wounded, the mutilated remains of the dead, the tumult and confusion of those who were endeavoring to render assistance, combined to make the picture horrible in the extreme." The collision "suddenly launched into eternity" passengers and railroad workers alike. In the end, fourteen people were dead, one of whom was a U.S. district judge. Nevertheless, a big celebration was held in Oakland welcoming the first train, even as victims of the crash were dying in local hospitals.[1]

This was an ignominious start for the western end of the transcontinental railway. Perhaps because the last connection between Sacramento and the Bay Area was not yet controlled by the Stanford group, the tragedy did not preoccupy the Big Four. Instead, Stanford and company were considering how to finance the acquisition and merger of the line and any potential competitor. Moreover, they had to keep their now growing number of shareholders happy with the prospect of dividends and still compensate themselves handsomely, while avoiding the scrutiny and criticism of the press, public, and government investigators. The Big Four had chanced on their solution in 1862 when they began assigning construction jobs solely to themselves—or to be more technically precise, to Charles Crocker—often without a written contract. But the furor that quickly followed the brazenly noncompetitive use of taxpayer money had not gone unnoticed.[2] The railroad line coming from the East to meet them at Promontory, the Union Pacific, was employing a similar money-laundering method—a company called Crédit Mobilier—but not surprisingly given the UP's chaotic affairs, the scheme had fallen into outright corruption, resultant public outcry, and finally government investigation. Ownership and management of the UP upended and radically changed. The Stanford group thought it would not be so foolish.

Consequently, in 1867 the Central Pacific stopped blatantly giving the work to Crocker and instead formed the Contract and Finance Company, providing a scrim to conceal the Big Four's names from the casual eye, although initially Crocker was named company president. The concept was elegantly simple in the days before competitive bidding for public contracts became regular and required and antitrust laws went into wide effect. The railroads' financial deceit would eventually lead to and fuel the success of reform Republicans such as Hiram Johnson in California and Theodore Roosevelt in New York in the coming years. But laissez-faire was still very much the hopeful policy of the day immediately after the Civil War.

All construction, maintenance, and operating work of the Central Pacific was undertaken by the Contract and Finance Company. If Contract and Finance bought a railroad tie from a manufacturer for 10 cents and sold it to the Central Pacific for 20 cents, so be it. The same would be true if it purchased a locomotive, undertook routine maintenance for the railroad, strung telegraph lines, or built a bridge. Any profit, whether 100 or 1 percent, went to the owners of Contract and Finance in cash and stock. The owners, of course, were Leland Stanford, Collis Huntington, Charles Crocker, and Mark Hopkins.

The only solid proof of any swindle was in their private accounting books. With that, the instruments were prepared for one of the great plunders in American history.

The conflict between Huntington and Stanford did not abate after the completion of the transcontinental railroad enterprise at Promontory Summit. It festered and began to infect what had been a robust quartet. Exactly one year and one day after the last spike secured the cross-continental railway, Huntington wrote Stanford a long letter revealing a cause for his enmity: his salary. Huntington noted that since the beginning of their work he had received $25,000 annually, but after three years was getting nothing but $6,500 a year for expenses. "I wrote to you on this subject about two years since, but up to this time have received no reply; but the time has come when I want this matter settled up," wrote an exasperated Huntington. "I want for my services in doing this business one hundred thousand dollars ($100,000) per year for the last five years." He noted he was willing to subtract the $32,500 he had received for personal expenses, but "I shall not be satisfied with anything less."[3]

Was Stanford Huntington's boss or partner? Did Huntington make the man or did Stanford triumph regardless of Huntington's early sponsorship? Either way, how could the mutating lines of authority and responsibility not cause some confusion, anxiety, and upset?

With evident anger growing as steadily as their business became increasingly complex, Huntington continued to make stealthy inside moves against Stanford. Feeling beset by one crisis after another they would or could not see was of their own making, they instead remained convinced the nation and state should have treated them as triumphant saviors. Huntington, writing to Hopkins, fingered his scapegoat: "These difficulties will always exist so long as Stanford is at the head of our affairs."[4]

A little more than a year and half later, the querulous Huntington wrote his first and favorite partner Hopkins again:

Everyone makes mistakes, I believe. I know I do, and I am not disposed to find fault with any one; but I have met several people in the last few days that were just from Cal., and they all tell the same story—viz., that Stanford acts as though he was mad at all the human race and that and as long as he is at the head of the C.P. road we will have trouble.

Then, "If we are wise men should we not look for the cause of all this trouble, and if we found it, try to remove it?" Concluding his attack, Huntington wrote that Stanford "should let it be understood he wanted rest and proposed a trip to Europe, some one else might succeed to the place of the president of the C.P. Co. to advantage." He ended the screed by modestly asserting he did not want to be company president.[5]

Outside of the executive offices the Big Four carried on. Their ravenous appetite for any rival railroad quickly became a gluttonous compulsion to absorb anything resembling a competitor. It began in the immense state of California and then oozed across the West. The precedent for the Central Pacific's methods for satiating its hunger had been on display before the first rail was spiked into place. In early 1863, when Governor Stanford was pushing Placer County taxpayers to borrow $250,000 in bonds to help finance his railroad, local officials feared if they didn't agree, the Big Four might lay tracks around and away from them. After the successful completion of the cross-continental railway, that intimidating power greatly multiplied. Now it wasn't just a small town or rural county that felt the bulking muscle of the railroad. Having secretly taken control of the small but potentially powerful Southern Pacific in the summer of 1868, the Big Four had a still stronger hand across the state.

In Northern California, Stanford played Oakland and San Francisco off each other while not so discreetly fingering the Yerba Buena Island card. In the end, he got control of much of the waterfront in Oakland and the critical Mission Bay shoreline of San Francisco—the large acreage in the southern stretch of San Francisco's Bayshore—after he regressed to his old promises of not hiring Chinese there. Yerba Buena was out of reach, so Stanford used it as a bluff.

In Southern California, which had remained largely undeveloped, old plans for a more efficient route across the bottom of the United States reemerged without the pre–Civil War baggage. Los Angeles, founded in 1781 as El Pueblo de Nuestra Señora la Reina de Los Angeles—the City of Our Lady the Queen of the Angels—had barely forty-five hundred residents when Leland Stanford was governor of California.[6] But it was quickly losing its Californio character and was increasingly infected with lowlife outlaws and traitorous Confederates.[7] One of the major obstacles holding it back was not having a deepwater port. Instead, the town was along what is today known as the Los Angeles River but was then called the Rio Porciuncula, shallow and well inland from the Pacific. Even into the 1860s, drayage between the city of Los Angeles and the Pacific Ocean was often by oxcart. The growing number of Angelenos of business, family, and education wanted more and better.[8]

In a paper-thin 1868 vote, the citizenry decided to spend almost $250,000 hammering down rails between the town and a Pacific port twenty miles west in Wilmington, adjacent to San Pedro. The signs in Spanish along the resulting route warned "Quidado por La Maquina de Vaho del Camino de Fierro" (Look Out for the Machine of Steam on the Road of Iron). One of the most successful Southern California exports was oranges, which "began a citrus frenzy that would long shape the economy and landscape of southern California," a historian of the region found.[9] The significance of the railroad can also be seen in how the short-haul tracks helped prompt excitement regarding the next, longer railroad on the way. Thomas A. Scott, by then head of the Union Pacific as well as the powerful Pennsylvania railroad, announced plans to construct a line across the Southern states—the route the North had earlier quashed to prevent the Confederacy from exporting its lucrative cotton crop and establishing a direct trade route with Asia. But that line was to end in San Diego, then regarded as a devilish rival to the City of Angels. Into the breach strode the new masters of the still mostly venerated transcontinental railroad: the Stanford group.[10]

A committee of Angelenos met with the railroad executives. The new owners of the Southern Pacific Railroad—still technically a separate company from the Central Pacific—laid down their terms: they would graciously extend their line down to Los Angeles but there would be a cost. A dear one. The good people of LA would have to pay the Southern Pacific more than $600,000 and give the company sixty-five acres for depots and workshops as well as all the land for the tracks. Moreover, the company demanded control of the line the city had just paid for to connect it with the Pacific Ocean. Scott's team, alarmed, countered with a plan almost half the cost. In contrast to the Southern Pacific's scheme, and inevitably crippling its Los Angeles sales presentation, Scott's plan would have also run the line to San Diego and its port first and LA afterward. The choice was placed on the November 1872 ballot.

"Orators and newspaper correspondents painted in roseate hues the era of prosperity that would dawn upon us when the whistle of the locomotive broke the stillness in our unpeopled valleys," wrote a Los Angeles historian in the early twentieth century.[11] Nevertheless, the contest had decidedly unpleasant aspects. Reports of widespread bribes arose, and once conciliatory citizens broke off from one another. A doctor meeting someone in the street who was a friend, business associate, and patient fell into heated argument over the issue. The physician ended the quarrel by reportedly beating his old ally with a cane.[12] In the end, Leland Stanford's forces won at the ballot box, giving the Southern Pacific years of monopoly over the rails going in and out of what would soon be one of the fastest growing cities in the nation and control of what would become one of the great ports of the world.[13]

The story, with different twists and turns, repeated itself across the Golden State. But it didn't conclude with just bullying cities and counties, squeezing out competing railroads, or controlling seaports. The lingering old-world transport of simple river boats carrying wheat along the few navigable waters of California was not too small to draw Stanford and company's wintery gaze. When the Central Valley town of Stockton, situated at a strategic junction of California's two main rivers, the Sacramento and San Joaquin, refused to bend a knee to the Southern Pacific and instead began to complain about the railroad's punishing freight rates, the rail executives eyeballed its competitor there, the shipping company moving grain down river for export out to the rest of the world. Their template solution reemerged: build a new railroad town ten miles south of Stockton to take over the market. Family-man Stanford named it after his in-laws: Lathrop.[14] Business was good.

And then there was the rumpus over much of the 17.5 million acres the government had given the railway, ostensibly for the railroad itself and to encourage independent development along the line.[15] In 1878, the Stanford group still had more than 11 million acres "unsold."[16] When this land was desert territory, there was little enough noise to ignore. But when a steady stream of settlers kept pouring into the Central Valley, that was a different matter. The rich valley floor, blessed with weather enabling two and three crops annually, particularly beckoned farmers. Just north of the town of Hanford, a village toward the southern end of the valley, dozens of families set up homesteads, started running livestock, and began tilling the fertile soils along a natural irrigation channel called Mussel Slough. The Southern Pacific called these newcomers squatters, and a judge named Lorenzo Sawyer agreed. That, in itself, set up a howl, as he was known to be an ally of the railroad and Stanford in particular. In fact, toward the end of 1870, Stanford had written to Huntington back East, asking him to pull some political levers and have Sawyer appointed to the federal bench—just as Stanford had pushed Lincoln to appoint Stephen Field to the U.S. Supreme Court—because Sawyer "has always been a good friend to the Pacific R.R.," adding, "Sawyer will understand who does it and will appreciate it."[17]

The settlers, some of whom were former Confederate soldiers hardened by war and bitter in defeat, argued the railroad had promised to sell them land for a few dollars an acre, and after all, did not the government just give the land to the railroad, which promised to make it available to the public? Dodgy, self-appointed leaders emerged. A ruinously volatile mixture arose. Even Huntington, a man with a legendary zest for combat, counseled compromise.

Enter Leland Stanford. What happened next prompted more lasting damage than can be properly measured. Men died, public perception greatly hardened against the railroad, and government investigations and subsequent regulation would soon commence in earnest. And a novel still read in California schools was later written, The Octopus, immortalizing what is still called the Mussel Slough Tragedy.

Stanford came to Hanford, met with the squatters, and according to the three-man committee that met with him, promised to broker a deal amenable to both sides. Tension eased. Briefly. As soon as Stanford departed Hanford, his railroad company moved toward evictions. The fuse was lit. Evictions began on May 11, 1880. Some of the settlers responded with weapons. A gunfight erupted. "It is impossible to say who began the firing," wrote one scholar sixty-eight years later, "or the immediate cause which precipitated the direful result."[18] Seven men died from gunshot wounds. Stanford, however, left the state, headed with Jennie and Leland Jr. for their first luxurious shopping romp through Europe.

In California, indictments of the Mussel Slough settlers took place and then court trials, again heard by Stanford's judge, and five settlers were sent to prison for eight months. Rather than incarceration in the Central Valley, the men did their time in the San Jose jail, about 175 miles north of Hanford. That Bay Area town—today the metropolitan southern capital of Silicon Valley—treated the convicts as if they were martyrs, organizing food drives from around the state, allowing them to leave lockup for mail and lodge and church meetings. Well-attended birthday parties took place in the jailhouse. The only unmarried convict married a jailer's daughter, the ceremony taking place at a local hotel. The eight months passed and the men returned to

Hanford, welcomed as heroes. For Stanford, it was, in the plain words of a historian of late nineteenth-century California, a "public relations disaster."[19]

If Mussel Slough was a tipping point in the public's perception of Stanford and the railroad he headed, it resulted in serious spillage, not breakage. Well into the nineteenth century, many retained the innocent belief that business was a self-governing force, that there was no need for regulation because raw competition would sort out bad from good, and the people would ultimately profit from the tournaments. It was a faith from an ancient world that had fueled the government's motivation to prompt the Union Pacific and Central Pacific road race for miles and money. But the Industrial Revolution that Stanford was not just witnessing but very much helping usher into America was not just a new game; it was a different way of life. No industry showed that with earlier graphic clarity than the railroad—and few governments were quicker to start responding to it than California's. Many would follow during the next three decades.[20]

The timing was suddenly not good for Leland Stanford and company. Just as the consolidation and corporatization of the mining industry had effectively closed much of that entrepreneurial opportunity, the rails connecting the East to the West, instead of bringing a new round of prosperity to all, seemed to bring great wealth to only a few. It was a huge letdown. Many of the promotional expectations for the opening of the transcontinental line were soon followed by a dreary reality: California manufacturers found themselves competing with inexpensive East Coast factory products. Laborers suddenly were competing with thousands of newly released railroad workers, most of whom were Chinese. Unemployment in San Francisco reached 20–25 percent. Nationally, the "panic" of 1873 hit the West, with consequences such as the collapse of the Bank of California in 1875, its "Gallant, Genial" president's body found floating in San Francisco Bay shortly after he was removed from his job.[21] Hundreds of homeless San Franciscans slept on the wharfs and in the back alleys, emerging at daylight to scour the city garbage dump for scraps of anything that might have value.

"Although widespread social mobility had occurred in the past, it no longer seemed likely. Economic transformation, economic depression, and the increased maldistribution of wealth—all seemed to block the road to success," noted a University of Virginia historian. "The completion of the transcontinental railroad tied San Francisco to the national market, and competition with eastern traders diminished the profits of local merchants." Instead of the railroad bringing renewed opportunities to the white working class, "in every sector of the economy, growth and change seemed to threaten opportunity."[22]

A demagogue arose in the person of Denis Kearney. A charismatic young Irishman, he had quickly become head of the Workingmen's Party—an odd alliance of violent thugs and reform-minded merchants who wanted to stop labor competition while also stepping on the brakes of Leland Stanford and his railroad. It attracted thousands of followers. "Earlier crowd historians have demonstrated that the crowd enabled people lacking access to formal political institutions to express political opinions and make political demands," the Virginia scholar found.[23] This crowd had, as do so many, a scapegoat that looked different, dressed differently, spoke a different language, and was enjoying some economic success by working hard and well. In the West's late 1800s it was the Chinese immigrant.

An almost Satanic mood had been in the air since at least the autumn of 1871, when some five hundred rioters had looted and torched the Los Angeles Chinatown, killing almost twenty. The mob left fifteen hanging in the streets. In the summer of 1877, crowds rampaged through San Francisco's Chinatown, burning businesses and demanding that Chinese residents leave the city. Later the rabble marched to the docks and tried to set fire to the shipping companies controlled by and in bed with the Big Four. The rioters accused the shippers of colluding on rates and being responsible for bringing Chinese workers to California. Four men died in the street fight. Thousands of shocked San Franciscans, reprising a chapter from their Barbary Coast past, formed a vigilante countermilitia. The U.S. secretary of war dispatched three warships from a nearby naval base to the city waterfront.[24] Stanford himself became alarmed for his personal safety and property, scribbling a fast note to San Francisco's chief of police: "I know the mob have considered the question of burning my house and the house of Mr Hopkins. Their threat may be serious. I would be glad to have you detail a proper guard."[25]

If Leland Stanford had, as governor, helped legitimize the racial hatred of Asians and then as president of the railway had been, with his three partners, largely responsible for the wrath against his road, there is no indication whatsoever that he ever understood, much less acknowledged, the consequences of his actions. He simply carried on, no regrets, heading full steam, bound for still more profound outcomes.

An uneasy citizenry, meantime, was in no temper to entertain the patrimony of four enormously wealthy, powerful men who had financed much of their own standing using public money and were now complaining of not only needing more but suggesting they did not feel compelled to pay back the taxpayers, who were essentially the last in line of stockholders. If any remark provided testimony of how public perception had altered in just a few years, it was that spoken by the man present at the ground breaking of the Central Pacific in the winter of 1863, who had stated, "Egyptian kings and dynasties shall be forgotten," referring to Stanford. "You sir, to-day, have inaugurated a more glorious work." Newton Booth, who had purchased Stanford's grocery store when Stanford finally got elected to office in 1861, was also active in Republican politics. In the summer of 1874 he was the Republican governor of California, but before an appreciative San Francisco audience he expressed his sharp about-face from mythologizing Stanford and his rail enterprise: "Every tie in the road is the grave of a small stockholder," he declared.[26]

Small stockholders would not see much, or any, return for their investments, to be sure, putting many at risk. But large institutional investors were also frequently unhappy about returns on investment. When American banks and early venture capitalists were skeptical about the potential ROI from the railroad, the Big Four aggressively shopped their stocks abroad, especially to more willing German and British concerns. This early version of globalization meant, among many potential consequences, that non-American interests were in a position to inappropriately influence what was becoming critical infrastructure inside the United States.

Before it was over, Leland Stanford was the head of some twenty railroad companies and the ferryboat line that controlled most of the shipping on California's two main rivers and San Francisco Bay. The longest railway line, of course, was the Central Pacific, with more than twelve hundred miles of track. The shortest was less than four miles long, running into Berkeley from a little south of the university town. In time, having so many names, companies, and separate operations caused more trouble than the Big Four wanted, and they began to talk a great deal about consolidation. Once they decided it was a fine idea, the discussion became how to go about it in a manner that would be most advantageous. In the early 1870s they made their first move.

Grouping several of the smaller lines under the roof of the Southern Pacific Railroad Company, the SP began to enjoy a status similar to the Central Pacific, though both were, in fact, quietly run by the same quartet. As the first serious efforts began in Sacramento to regulate the rails, the Big Four would continue to improvise means to protect themselves by continuing to reorganize their holdings. The tension continued to mount.

The first oversight bill in the state legislature would have placed limits on the fares charged by railroads such as the Central Pacific. The sponsoring assemblyman testified that "as most of the railroad and steamboat lines in this State are now consolidated into one incorporated company, I fear the people will not be protected in the present low rates, and this bill is to prevent possible higher charges."[27] Former governor Stanford lobbied heavily against the bill, testifying it would cripple the long-sought rail line. His clout was still mighty. The legislation died. Three years later another attempt was made by a different assemblyman, but it, too, failed.

It wasn't that the people of California, or their elected officials, were still acolytes of Stanford's railroad. Rather, it was that, as a detailed history of the situation found, "a maximum freight and fare bill, whatever its provisions, opened a Pandora's box of conflicting local interests, which were used by Central Pacific politicos in carrying out their strategy of divide and conquer." In the case of the second attempt, as an example, former governor Stanford cautioned the legislature that his railroad was trying to keep California connected to the rest of the nation by opening a southern route through Los Angeles, and "Stanford warned that, if the Southern Pacific did not reach the Colorado [River] first, San Francisco itself would fall to the invaders from St. Louis," which, of course, Californians had absolutely no control or influence over.[28]

What choice did they have? It appeared to many that either the government should regulate the known Stanford's railroad or abandon citizens to other, unknown predators. But in the new industrial economy and culture, who was the predator and who was the prey?

CHAPTER 12

Unmasked

Rather than dialing back on his personal and professional liabilities as he and his railroad company came under fast-mounting attack and growing threat of government regulations, Leland Stanford amped up on both.

On the personal side Stanford was already accused of sloth, and his partners began to express concern about his greed. Responding to an inquiry by Collis Huntington, who wanted to know how much cash had been withdrawn by the directors of the Central Pacific, the company financial officer answered that in the summer of 1877 Mark Hopkins had drawn $800, Charles Crocker almost $32,000, Huntington not quite $58,000, and Stanford more than a quarter million dollars—$276,242.36 to be precise.[1] The large draw was hardly an exception. Crocker wrote Huntington, still back East, that he and Hopkins had been "calling on Gov. Stanford and remonstrating with him in relation to the state of his account and his constant and large drafts for money for outside private investments while we are denying ourselves all such investments." As examples, he added, "Mr. Stanford continues to draw 50,000. and $100,000. at a time frequently."[2] This was at a time when a full meal at a New York City restaurant cost about $1, the average American daily wage was under $3, and a ten-room house in a nice part of San Francisco was going for $3,000. Displaying, as a venerable expression goes, more fuse than fireworks, Crocker then begged not to be quoted, instead imploring Huntington to step in.

Around the same time, Stanford also wrote Huntington. Having conquered much of California, Stanford's gaze turned north, south, and east. It is a remarkable letter, as it is one of the few surviving documents of Stanford describing his unvarnished ambition: "The Territory west of Ogden in great part must always be open to the U.P. Our only protection is by the control of that road, and sooner or later we shall be compelled either to buy or consolidate. It is a question only to whom it shall be done." With that stated, he then outlined a plan for "controlling" the area from the Columbia River to the Gulf of California and across to Texas—in other words, the American West. "I would like to work up to this. We can develop an empire," Stanford wrote, adding that the Big Four already commanded some $70 million in assets, which he suggested they use in the method they had become accustomed to: as collateral to borrow still more money to acquire still more assets. Those assets, of course, would be the Union Pacific, then controlled by Tom Scott and Jay Gould, the two most powerful railroad men on the other side of the continent.

Then, an elegiac lament: "Can't we brace ourselves up with our old spirit and be equal to the occasion. If we are true in ourselves I believe we can wrestle successfully with Scott and Gould both. Let us believe that we can and determine that we will, the fight will be ours."[3]

Was Leland Stanford the furtively lazy, avaricious poser or the quietly competent, aspirational leader who took simply what he had reason to believe he had earned? Was he a duplicitous schemer or a stand-up family man? Great professional and personal tests awaiting him might reveal an answer. "Fortune does not change men," French wit Suzanne Necker, née Churchod, once observed. "It unmasks them."[4]

Throughout this period a set of events brought increasing charges of villainy against Leland Stanford and the railroad company of which he was president. These began to take place in courthouse litigation and they were of no light bearing. The first of some note was brought by one of San Francisco's more celebrated, disreputable, outsized characters—a distinction not easily acquired in that city. He was an infamously rich, charismatic, and very often drunk fellow named Samuel Brannan.

Legend has it that in 1846, Latter-day Saints leader Brigham Young sent the youthful Brannan to shepherd 238 Saints around Cape Horn to San Francisco, where he was to meet with more LDS adherents coming overland and establish a Mormon Zion on the Pacific Coast. Young learned there were irregularities in Brannan's financial accounts. The church leader reportedly sent his deputies to the get the church's money back. Brannan is said to have insolently replied he would return the money if he, in return, received a receipt from the Lord. Young excommunicated him. From there out, an unfettered Brannan made a fortune selling merchandise to the forty-niners, speculating on real estate, and starting one of San Francisco's first newspapers.

At one point Brannan bought two hundred shares of railroad stock, but proving it is unwise to try to con a con man, he soon smelled a rat in the business of the Contract and Finance Company, Crocker's supposedly independent concern hired by the Central Pacific to do all its construction, maintenance, and operating work. Brannan tried dunning Stanford into buying back his securities at a greatly inflated price. Stanford righteously refused. In the summer of 1870 Brannan went to court, saying Contract and Finance was a cover for the Big Four to extract huge personal profits and deceiving shareholders. Stanford said the charges were "false, malicious and without foundation." He dismissed Brannan's motivation as "blackmail."[5] The fight was on.

Other angry railroad stockholders joined Brannan, one being the still resentful widow of Theodore Judah. Economic historians have dismissed the charges as exaggerated, but the suit nevertheless put much of the company's business in every newspaper across the country. After several minidramas, the complaint was dropped, and cosmetically it appeared the Stanford group had dodged serious mischief. Below the surface, however, the damage was like dry rot deep in the wood.

It crept back to the surface six years later. A dispute between the Big Four and a complicated on-again, off-again ally and attorney named Alfred A. Cohen found himself getting sued by Stanford and company, and he in turn filed suit against them, using much of Brannan's charges and adding his own keen abilities at public derision. It made for spectacular news copy, not only labeling Contract and Finance a "fence," but better yet for the daily front page, hurling wonderfully quotable denunciations about the company president, the best known taken from this part of Cohen's testimony: "There is Mr. Stanford, the heavy character of the plot—sullen, saturnine, remorseless, grand, gloomy and peculiar; with the ambition of an Emperor and the spite of a peanut-vendor. He stalked across this court-room and ascended the witness box; spoke his part in a basso-profundo growl and departed, while the attendant actors held their breaths in awe."[6]

Cohen, often bitterly, but laughingly sardonic, did not offer amnesty to either Crocker or Huntington.

The sight of Mr. Crocker's well-fed person would convince anyone that the first great want of his life is a cook—and a good cook—that which Huntington wants only as an adjunct in obtaining congressional votes to restrain congressional interference, Crocker desires for his own personal gratification. Both Huntington and Crocker have adopted for their motto the immortal lines:

We may live without poetry, music and art;
We may live without conscience, we may live without heart;
We may live without friends, we may live without books;
But civilized men cannot live without cooks.[7]

Cohen's theatrics were not complete without some Shakespeare:

Truly, one may say to the plaintiff:
"You have among you many a purchased slave,
Whom, like your asses and your dogs and your mules,
You use in abject and in servile parts."[8]

In the end, the court document simply declared that "immediately, on the conclusion of the arguments, Judge Daingerfield rendered Judgement for the Defendant."[9] Cohen, not sated with the victory, went on to publish a pamphlet further ridiculing Stanford. It was called *The California King* and was found across San Francisco and beyond for years. Huntington complained from New York that it had "been sent to, I think, every broker, banker, and money lender in the country that man Cohen could think of, and it has stopped me from getting $300,000 I expected to have got to-day and to-morrow."[10]

The public demeaning of the railroad chief grew worse. On June 14, 1876, the same year as Cohen's suit, San Francisco police arrested lawyer, company president, and former governor Leland Stanford after another stockholder said he had been denied his legal right to view the books of the railroad company, which the *San Francisco Chronicle* the next day called a misdemeanor and would be a preview of something much bigger ahead. Company controller and fellow board director E.H. Miller also found himself under arrest before the two posted $200 bail each and were released.[11] It was in this era that the brilliant nineteenth-century satirist Ambrose Bierce began calling the president of the railroad "$tlealin Landford."[12]

Change in press coverage had been relatively sudden. Through most of the 1860s the railroad enterprise and not yet Big Four had enjoyed mostly gushing notices. That started to change in the 1870s, when the once often absurdly forgiving *Sacramento Daily Union*, at the time the most influential news outlet in the West, made a 180-degree turn and began regular, harsh criticism. To counteract this, the Big Four resorted to the time-honored tactic of quietly buying a rival media outlet, the *Sacramento Record*. Stanford and company's attempt to control the message had little success until 1875, when they were able to buy the *Union* as well, merge it with the *Record*, and shut down at least one skeptical voice.[13] But by then Sacramento had become second on the card, the real top of the bill in the West shifting to San Francisco, where pro- and antirailroad newspapers duked it out daily.

Ironically, the technology of the transcontinental railroad and the telegraph lines that went up above it made it so much easier for newspapers to share stories coast-to-coast, with a speed never imagined before. Cohen took advantage of this and saw his remarks in everything from the *San Francisco Examiner* to the *New York Journal* in a twenty-four-hour period. Both those newspapers, not incidentally, were owned by William Randolph Hearst, only child and heir to Comstock Lode tycoon George Hearst, who would soon have more to do with Leland Stanford.

In the end, regarding the Cohen-Stanford drama, the railroad's sometimes friend and sometimes antagonist proved to be cut from the some of the same cloth as Stanford, Cohen flipping again when it suited him and becoming a high-profile defender of the man he had so colorfully libeled. It was just as well, as the coming trials would cut very sharply indeed.

In Washington, DC, Congress was also watching the railroad's troubles with keen interest. The federal government had, of course, made the American taxpayer ultimately responsible for the massive government loans that made the cross-continental railway possible. The people were owed many millions of dollars from the Big Four. Who could fail to notice that Stanford was going about saying the government should be expressing its great gratitude to him and his partners rather than requiring them to pay their contractual debt? The troubles with the scoundrel Brannan, who had similar attitudes about using other people's money, and legitimate lawyer Cohen did nothing to inspire any public sense of trust in the Central Pacific. A strong political impulse to provide extra protection for American taxpayers prompted Ohio senator Allen Thurman to introduce legislation requiring the railroad companies to put aside a percentage of earnings in a special account for eventual application to their debt. The bill glided through both houses of Congress and became law, but only after Stanford thundered against it and his company lost in court trying to have it overturned. One justice dissented in favor of the railroad: Stephen J. Field. He would later have further opportunities to help his friend Leland Stanford.

And although the railroad companies finally had to start putting some money toward the remuneration of their debt to the American people, distinguished historian Richard White has pointed out that the amount repaid included just simple, not compound interest: "The court's interpretation proved an incredible gift to the railroads," White quipped in his signature book, *Railroaded*.[14] The state government seemed to have reached its limit in limiting Stanford and company. The federal government would step in with a far bigger foot before the whole story could begin to come out.

Early in the 1870s Stanford had found a new means to satisfy his increasingly extravagant urges. The first subtle changes were visible signals that he was listening more to the comfortable whisperings of courtiers than the unpleasant cries of critics. Before the end of 1870 he had his official letterhead changed to grand fonts, prominently declaring "President's Office." Soon enough he began to display far more than that.

Much in the way a twenty-first-century person with great wealth—or great credit—might demonstrate his or her fortune by driving top-shelf Italian racing cars, German luxury sedans, or stylish high-tech automobiles, Stanford turned to racehorses. At one point, he had 775 steeds. After a few years, that would no longer suffice. Although he had little formal education, he became a member of the California Academy of Sciences and lined his shelves with weighty books bound in vellum embossed with gilt. He gave his horses names that were tributes to technological progress: Electricity, Electro Benton, and Electrician.[15] Impervious to the risk of being considered a dilettante, he began to spend time wondering if all four hoofs of the expensive beasts in his stables were ever in the air at one time. The answer would become a paradigm for hippologists and photography historians. But for Stanford, even such a peculiar and inoffensive endeavor became one of enduring acrimony, pitting his ever-inflating ego against a deeply eccentric cameraman with a flair for lethal violence.

Sometime in 1872 Stanford met Edward Muybridge—he changed his name and the spelling repeatedly to versions such as Eadweard and Muygridge—hiring him to take pictures of his ornate Sacramento mansion. Soon the railroad president, who appeared to have some time on his hands with the completion of the cross-continental road, had the photographer meet him at a local racetrack to see Stanford's prize equestrian Occident, the name a conscious or not homage to the West. He told the cameraman he wanted to see if the beast ever had all four hoofs in the air at one time as he ran. He left it to Muybridge to work out how to determine this. And he did. The technological feat made international news.

But not as much as what happened the next year. That was when the sudden celebrity photographer with the funny name, wild beard, pre–Albert Einstein hair, and odd manners walked into a cottage in the town of Napa, about fifty miles north of San Francisco, and point-blank shot dead a rake of questionable European pedigree who had seduced and impregnated Muybridge's much younger wife. At the trial he pled insanity. He was just eccentric enough to pull it off, and the jury acquitted him. Soon afterward, he was back to work for Stanford, whose stables had grown a great deal, along with several other very costly hobbies. Having photographs taken of his horses galloping remained one of them. But his musings had increased. Muybridge, pleased to be working with a man whose deep pockets paid for enormously expensive equipment, devised an intricate set of machineries able to not only capture the horses running, but actually see them in motion racing by. Many still consider this feat one of the first major advancements in the technology of motion pictures.[16]

The situation changed when Stanford incited his physician-friend J. D. B. Stillman to publish a book titled *The Horse in Motion*. It was the beginning of a lifelong feud between the railroad president and the innovative photographer. Muybridge sued, saying Stanford was taking credit for what was his accomplishment. Stanford insisted he was the brains behind the process, saying, "Muybridge was the instrument, but it was my idea."[17] The photographer lost his legal challenge and Stanford kept the glory, however tarnished.

The Big Four as a group had their own, far weightier problems. Their reputation further soiled by the bad publicity the prototypical money-laundering Contract and Finance Company attracted, the Big Four shredded the enterprise and started what they intended to be their next solution: the Western Development Company. Formed in 1874, it appropriated all the functions of Contract and Finance, but this time the Big Four would not make the foolish public relations mistake of naming Charles Crocker president, or anyone else closely associated with the railroad. However, they made a deafeningly discordant decision to use the Western Development Company to build three of the most ostentatious mansions in the United States. Stanford, not content with his flamboyant Sacramento mansion, built the first of the four. Even Huntington was initially aghast.

In 1873, Stanford and company's railroad moved its headquarters from the state's capital city of Sacramento, as many there had long feared would happen, to the increasingly glamorous and certainly by then important city of San Francisco. Because of a serious national economic downturn, it was a good time to buy property but not such good timing for an embattled president of what was swiftly becoming the dominant corporation in the West and was experiencing one volley of attack after another. "For many San Franciscans," observed one historian, "it was bad enough that the rapid onset of industrialization only provided upward social mobility to the white-collar elite; the outlandish palaces sprouting atop Nob Hill were even more outrageous emblems of the railroad oligarchy's greed and excess."[18]

The real estate Stanford started putting together was atop one of San Francisco's many hills, one at the time that had no particular cachet except being among the highest in what was then the central part of the city and commanding superb views of the bay, the Golden Gate, and out toward the blue and windy sea.

The house there took two years to build, but when it was done the manse sprawled across much of the top of the rise, complete with fifty rooms in more than forty thousand square feet. It was not inferior in ostentatious magnificence to the most vulgar nouveau-riche homes of Newport, Rhode Island. At the time, it was one of the biggest mansions in the nation. It was for three people: Stanford, Jennie, and their son, Leland Jr. As with his first extravagant mansion in Sacramento, Stanford indulged his growing infatuation with technology by furnishing the vast building not only with the baroque splendor of the Victorian age but with machines such as mechanical birds that chirped, using the same compressed air tools found in train whistles. In order to surmount the almost four-hundred-foot- hill, Stanford also backed a plan for underground steel ropes to pull coaches on rails to his front door. Naturally, they were soon called cable cars. The scheme did not sit well with the people charged with balancing the books, who nonetheless tried to put on a good show for the bosses.

"I am afraid the California St[reet] City Rail Road will cost the Governor much more than he calculated at the start, and I understand he now owns it nearly all, so he will have some very large bills to pay there, which I presume, he will draw the money for" wrote a Central Pacific finance executive to Huntington. "We will, however, hope for the best."[19]

Crocker, not to be outdone by Stanford, soon followed with his château; then the austere Hopkins, bowing to his wife's wishes, did as well. It was only some years later that Huntington also submitted to his second wife's grand tastes. Soon the neighborhood was known as the part of town where the nabobs lived, a bastardization of the Hindi word *nawab*, a person of some royal standing such as a duke or sovereign. In time it became known as Nob Hill, one of the city's most famous addresses.

Dwellings such as Stanford's were "far larger and more opulent than previous private homes in the United States[;] they were intended for the public gaze and enjoyed as much celebrity status as their occupants," an architectural historian commented.[20] Robert Louis Stevenson, recalling his visit to San Francisco, wrote that Nob Hill was a place where "millionaires are gathered together vying with each other in display."[21]

Leland Stanford's imperial impulses continued to assert themselves more forcefully during the mid-1870s, and he escalated dramatically. In that period, he commissioned distinguished California painter Thomas Hill to depict the ceremony in which the last railroad spike was driven at Promontory Summit. "With autocratic power Stanford would direct Hill to decapitate a too prominent rival and on the shoulders of the figure place the head of a man better favored by the railroad millionaire," noted a later UCLA scholar, saying that in the painting "even the Reverend Dr. Todd, in the left foreground, seems to be paying homage to Stanford."[22] When Hill asked Crocker to sit for the painting, although he was not at Promontory that day, the old road boss looked at the portrait depicting Stanford as the central, towering figure and growled, "What nonsense is that?" leaving the studio "with malice in his eye."[23] Shortly afterward, Stanford told a shocked Hill he would not pay the $25,000 the painter said was the agreed amount for the work, which the artist had labored to finish during four years and at his own expense. The 8-x-12-foot painting bounced around California and out-of-state exhibitions for decades before coming to rest at a museum in Sacramento.[24]

In that same period, but before he stiffed Hill, Stanford asked the artist's opinion of drawings a sculptor was working up as studies for statues Stanford was planning to commission. "Mr. Stanford was represented coming out of the clouds on a locomotive, and in many other godlike attitudes figurative of the life and doings of the governor," reported the *San Francisco Call*. Hill was somewhat taken aback: "I spoke in praise of their execution, but thought, as any sensible person would, that they were in bad taste."[25]

Stanford continued to nurse his grudge against the government that had loaned him the money that incubated his fortune. Even some of his allies began to look askance at the cant they were becoming wearily accustomed to hearing.

"I shall never forget an incident related to me by the late Governor Stoneman, as coming from Justice Field, of United States Supreme Court," wrote a contemporary of Stanford's in his memoirs. "Stanford gave a dinner to a select circle of friends at his palatial residence on Nob Hill." After the meal, Stanford complained

> very bitterly about the ingratitude of the Government towards the builders of the Central Pacific railroad. He claimed that the Government, for which he and his confreres had made so many and such enormous sacrifices was hounding them . . . for the pound of flesh. "Yes," said Justice Field in a low voice to those sitting near him, "one has only to look around him here to see how shamefully these gentlemen have been treated by an ungrateful and ungenerous Government," and with a sweep of his hand he took in the statutory, bric-a-brac, painting and de luxe that were worth hundreds of thousands of dollars."[26]

Real estate was never far from the mind of Leland Stanford or his partners. Much of the railroad track laid down, the Big Four's attentions were drawn to the millions of acres the taxpayers had so generously given the railroad. Then the quartet underwent a major management change. Three years after the death of Charles Crocker's brother—the moderate, hardworking E. B., a passing that had been a blow to the stability of the alliance—the most genuinely conservative member of the Big Four, Mark Hopkins, died in Arizona at age sixty-three. He had been the so-called balancing wheel in the partnership as well as the quiet bookkeeper. The other three, especially Huntington, who had been his partner from very early on, had always paid particular attention to Hopkins's counsel. His absence would leave the sometimes wobbly gyroscope increasingly off balance.

That same year, 1878, the Western Development Company had also run its course. New ambitions of the surviving three required a fresh front to put their plans in play. Western Development was deleted and the Pacific Improvement Company was launched. Its true mission was to improve the account balances of Leland Stanford, Collis Huntington, and Charles Crocker. Pacific Improvement proved to be the best iteration of the Big Four's many versions of creating an instrument for their cash-reaping business. As with the others, this new entity constantly borrowed money from the railroad company itself, helping obscure the true profits that could be used to pay back its debt to the taxpayers or pay appropriate dividends to its shareholders. The new company's scope and depth grew far greater than almost any other in the West, except for the railroad company itself. Even one of the most forgiving historians of the railroad concluded the new device "had a more profound meaning for the history of California, and indeed the Far West and Southwest."[27]

Arguably, Pacific Improvement's greatest role was exploiting the millions of acres reserved for the railroad right-of-way and the checkerboard twenty-mile swath of land to each side. Early on, Stanford and Huntington in particular realized that station locations along the routes were critical decisions, ones that could make them great sums of money. If an uncooperative town, such as a Stockton or San Francisco, didn't want to sit at the table, Stanford or one his agents could simply speak quietly with the city fathers and suggest that another town not too far away might be a better alternative for the railroad. If another town wasn't near, they could build one. The Big Four held all the cards with their ever-growing monopoly.

The rails running up and down the 450 miles of the Central Valley and along the Pacific Ocean on their way north to Oregon, east to Arizona, and south to Los Angeles opened unique business opportunities to create new towns that would add value to the free land the railroad already possessed. Anyone could get in the game. If they anted up. Cities such as Davis and Merced in the valley and Monterey on the coast were the children of Stanford's railroad. A station would be built, then streets laid out and lots subdivided. A good hotel would be constructed, and businesses would start to populate.

Stanford and his partners did not limit their holdings to California. "At the height of their operation, this group—the first large scale capitalists on the Pacific Coast—owned 24 companies, 8 large ranch properties and 49 townsites and smaller real estate holdings," noted a business historian in the 1940s. Moreover, they owned hotels in New York, Texas, Arizona, Nevada, and Louisiana. The Pacific Improvement Company was the primary instrument for these acquisitions, although "the development of new outlets for investment and their management were largely in the hands of Leland Stanford and Charles Crocker."[28]

Stanford was learning that many of the highborn, or those with aspirations to that peculiar status, not infrequently enjoyed dabbling in viticulture. In 1881 Leland, Jennie, and Leland Jr. toured the Château Lafite and Larose cellars in the Bordeaux region of France. Some of the properties had been recently purchased by one of Stanford's angel investors, Baron Rothschild. That same year a man named Nicholas T. Smith bought at least five parcels of land near a village named Vina (pronounced Vy-nah) along the upper Sacramento River, about thirty miles north of the town of Chico. Smith then promptly sold the property to Stanford. Then a fellow named Joseph S. Cone sold another three parcels to Stanford. In a few short years it became clear that Stanford was putting together an operation that would "dazzle the world with statistics."[29] What wasn't clear until quite a few years later was that the purchases were connected to another highly disreputable episode in Stanford's life. Smith was the treasurer of the Southern Pacific Railroad, and Cone was one of the three members of the scandal-stained California Railroad Commission that was supposed to put some breaks on Stanford's runaway railway company.

Stanford had grown wine grapes before—zinfandel and riesling, among others—and devoted some hundred acres to vines at a secluded fertile property in the East Bay, in a township called Warm Springs, now regarded as the northeastern end of Silicon Valley. Not long after going through the paces of wine making, Stanford effectively gave the venture over to his oldest brother, Josiah, who had started the Stanford Brothers store in Sacramento and financed his little brother when he came to California. Josiah had later turned over his successful main shop to Leland and then went to San Francisco, where he bootstrapped one of California's first petroleum companies. Tossing Josiah a hundred acres was the least Leland could do.

As for Leland, that throwaway property was hardly grand enough for the president of the railroad. He amassed fifty-five thousand acres around the village of Vina and devoted about four thousand of them to just wine grapes. It was the largest vineyard in the world.[30]

About a thousand seasonal workers augmented hundreds of imported Frenchmen in planting three million grapevines. Stanford also hired some three hundred Chinese workers, prompting criticism from the rabid racists who not only had not let go of their vitriolic bigotry, but had major successes in excluding many Chinese from America. Stanford once again tried having it both ways, saying the Chinese workers were entitled to the same "just treatment" as anyone else, but adding, "My race prejudices, however, incline me to my own people, and I am desirous of giving them, on all possible occasions, the preference."[31]

The work crews constructed one hundred miles of irrigation canals, one ten-mile stretch being ten feet deep and twenty-four feet wide.[32] The colossal spread brought forth an abundance of fruit, vegetables, and grain, the choice parts of the harvest sent swiftly by rail to Stanford's homes in the Bay Area. And there was the livestock: 800 hogs, 270 horses, and hundreds of head of cattle. But problems at "the ranch," as Stanford called Vina, became just as monumental as the harvest. At its height, the village of Vina had a population of thirteen hundred, two hotels to house visitors, and five saloons. "Vina was not an attractive town," a Stanford scholar noted. "Gambling and carousing were common."[33] Celebrated California poet and writer Joaquin Miller reported about "this dismal and primitive railroad town of Vina; in fact the less that is said about this flat and dirty Vina the better." He added that the people are "indolent, poker-playing-all-day-fighting fellows who loaf around and tramp up and down the town."[34] If this sounded a little like some descriptions of the Stanfords' hometown of Watervliet, New York, it must have been a coincidence.

Leland Stanford was cavalier about the challenges of a vintner, saying, "It is just as easy to make good wine as it is to make bad."[35] "Unfortunately," noted a viticulturist many years later, Stanford "mainly planted common varieties of grapes—Burger, Blaue Elbe, Trousseau, etc. In the hot climate of the Northern Sacramento Valley this proved disastrous for the quality of table wines." The result was that "the first two commercial vintages at Vina, those of 1885 and 1886, were disappointments."[36] Others have been considerably more blunt: "The wines were hardly drinkable," a wine writer declared in his history of California vintages.[37]

There were other problems. The original vines were not grafted on resistant rootstock, and the result was an invasion of a tiny insect called phylloxera, which can cause enormous damage. Stanford tried drowning the aphid-sized pests, but that failed, resistant rootstocks being the effective means known to eradicate the vermin. Then there were the floods. "The Stanford monster vineyard," reported the *Daily Alta California* one wet season, "known as the Vina ranch, has been ruined, and nearly half a million dollars in improvements have been swept away."[38] An arson fire in 1885 destroyed a huge barn at Vina, killing thirty-five horses and seventy-five mules.[39]

Stanford's disdained vintages soon were reason enough to fall back to distilling the failed wine into brandy, hardly to be mistaken for the spirits from Cognac, France, despite Stanford's having imported thousands of cuttings from that fabled region. This was "medicinal" brandy. In the late 1800s medicinal brandy, although certainly not the most sophisticated beverage, was conventionally regarded as a serviceable tonic for stimulating the heart or sedating a patient, however paradoxical that may seem.[40] Stanford stored the brandy in the holds of ships, where it remained for five years, "pitching and rolling" in cool temperatures and reputedly aging in a particularly beneficial fashion.[41] He had apparently forgotten his earlier condemnation of hard liquor: "It is in the countries where distilled spirits are used that you find drunkenness," he had pontificated about the advantages of wine over hard liquor. "In Ireland, Scotland, England and Norway you see those drunken, bloated faces."[42]

The Nob Hill edifice overlooking San Francisco and much of the Bay Area, as might an ancient royal castle over the king's dominion, suited Stanford's purposes in town. But a true tycoon must have a country estate in his portfolio—an authentic *château de la campagne*, where one is very much at leisure. To escape the cold, damp, perennial overcast of San Francisco, Stanford mimicked many of the town's other well-to-do and traveled just beyond the city limits to the sun-drenched outskirts of the lower San Francisco Peninsula. A little more than thirty miles south along that pleasant route, in the mid-1870s Stanford began to buy land that would become especially notable. His holdings were about two miles north of a small settlement known as Mayfield, originally a stagecoach stop between San Francisco and San Jose. The area could rightfully claim a surfeit of blissful weather, alluvial soils, and verdant creeks. The butterscotch utopia soon became a Southern Pacific railroad stop and received a lovely, historic name from Stanford himself: Palo Alto.[43]

CHAPTER 13

Gone Dark

The name Palo Alto came from a tall, if somewhat scraggly coastal redwood tree where early Spanish explorer Gaspar de Portolá had established a camp during his 1769 California journey of discovery, during which members of his party became the first Europeans to see magnificent San Francisco Bay. The redwood was, for him, El Palo Alto—literally, "the tall stick" in Spanish. For Portolá's crew, El Palo Alto was easily seen from many points and served as a navigation aid and rendezvous point. This particular *Sequoia sempervirens*, Latin for "always living," was almost one thousand years old and about one hundred feet tall when Stanford first saw it almost a century after the Portolá expedition.[1]

Finding the money to start buying property from early ranchers was not an issue. Stanford and company had dissolved the Western Development Company and formed Pacific Improvement, an instrument that immediately began creating huge new sums for the three surviving members of the original Big Four. But in the reorganization, bookkeepers found a mammoth disparity: about $1 million that should have been coming to the three partners was not there. Although Stanford in particular had been withdrawing large amounts, those sums and dates were reportedly in the ledgers. Where had the money gone?

David D. Colton was said to be a large, imposing man, crowned with angry-red hair. Born in Maine and raised in Illinois, he crossed overland in 1850, seeking his "pile" in gold. His family lore says he found no fortune waiting for him in the Sierra foothills and so went to the far north of California, where he became sheriff of Siskiyou County at age twenty. As such, he became known as someone who hunted down Native Californians for alleged crimes. He also joined the state militia in the 1850s, further pursuing Indians and getting himself appointed to the rank of general, a title he liked so much he had people address him as such for the rest of his life. Colton hobnobbed with politicians, ran for office, and practiced law. He also spent a big sum of taxpayer money on junkets back to the Midwest to court and win a bride, a sharp young lady named Ellen White.

In middle age he found himself in San Francisco, making large quantities of money from practicing law, speculating on real estate, and investing in mining. With that money he was among the first to build a mansion atop what would become Nob Hill, an impressive dwelling that caught Leland Stanford's eye, who soon followed. It could not have hurt Colton's relationship with Stanford to have gone to school in Albany, New York. Colton had also caught the attention of Charles Crocker, who befriended him, and Collis Huntington, who admired his brand of hustle. The executives hired Colton and found he fit right in. His importance to the Big Four was underscored by the fact that the railroad town of Colton, near San Bernardino in Southern California, bore his name. He was awarded a generous salary and stock option plan, and he assumed the title of financial director. A not unimportant condition of the pay package was Colton's agreement to repay a note of some $1 million by autumn of 1879.[2]

Then the accident happened. In the summer of 1878, while riding a horse on his Mount Diablo ranch in the East Bay, Colton took a spill, the steed crushing him. His initial injuries spawned more problems, and nineteenth-century medical knowledge being what it was, he died several weeks later. The next month, while the Western Development Company was transforming itself into Pacific Improvement, $1 million was discovered missing—and then traced back to the fine hand of David D. Colton.

Stanford and Crocker went to widow Ellen Colton and offered what they and Huntington considered a generous exchange: they would cancel the $1 million debt in return for her reassigning railroad securities she had inherited to the partners. At last, she acquiesced. But three years later, after reading a newspaper account of a court-ordered accounting of the Mark Hopkins estate—the fastidious bookkeeper left no will and the disputed distribution of his wealth went to probate—she had second thoughts. Seeing that Hopkins had left behind almost $21 million in securities and properties, she sought legal advice.

What happened next threw more light on Stanford and company's business than Alfred Cohen or Samuel Brannan ever could. Ellen Colton filed suit, claiming she had been swindled. If Stanford, Huntington, and Crocker did not come to terms, they were informed, her lawyers had a weapon of mass destruction: hundreds of private letters, largely between David Colton and Collis Huntington, that went far beyond the sometimes exaggerated and often impossible to prove charges Brannan and Cohen had proffered in their sensational court cases. She made it clear she was willing to barter what was left of her late husband's good name in return for a substantial sum. It might have been just the sort of transaction that sharp trader Huntington would admire. But the combatant in him, joined by Stanford and Crocker, who had less to lose, won out.

If the trio were to be victorious in this contest, they would need a very good lawyer. One with a certain amount of dash, one well-acquainted with them and their business, one with a demonstrated ability to counter the news coverage the widow Colton's charges were certain to command. They hired Alfred A. Cohen.

The task before him was immense. The letters graphically revealed a good deal of the railroad's internal business, and it wasn't handsome. Moreover, they disclosed more about company president Stanford and his standing in the eyes of Huntington that did considerable damage to both men, yet not so much as to the once revered railroad enterprise itself. The letters were read aloud in court to the jubilation of the railroad's enemies. Just a dozen excerpts provided plenty of news copy.

There was the manipulation of the press itself to undermine the Union Pacific and give advantage to the Central Pacific. Huntington to Colton:

> I would suggest you make the wires hot with dispatches to the Associated Press about the outrage of the UP Co upon the rights of the people. You can judge what is best for you to do, but keep the CP out of it.
>
> If you could get some well-written articles published in the SF papers showing up the great value of the country traversed by the SP, and the vast business that road must be doing trying to market the product of the country; in fact such articles would tend to induce people to buy SP bonds and lands.[3]

There was the strategy to monopolize the nation's railroads, hoping to hide the fact that the Central Pacific and Southern Pacific were controlled by the same small cabal. Huntington to Colton:

My only fear, then, would be the cry that the CP and the SP were all one, and would be a vast monopoly, &c. and that is what we must guard against.

It is very unfortunate, Colton, for us, that Jay Gould is in the UP. Our matters will never run smoothly until we control that road.

The Governor said—Governor S(tanford)—some good things to the Chronicle interviewer; but I think it unfortunate that he should so closely connect the CP with the SP as that is the only weapon our enemies have to fight us with in Congress.

It will be the strong point this winter with the communists that the CP wants to control everything that crosses the continent.[4]

There was the exploitation of the vast tracts of land they had already received from the taxpayers and the hunger for more. Huntington to Colton:

I am doing all I can to have the Government take 6,000,000 acres of land and give the R(ailroad) C(ompany) credit for $15,000,000 but the prospects of their doing it are not as bright as I wish it was.[5]

And then Colton to Crocker:

Crocker, what do you think of the idea of our building, say 20 or 40 miles of road on the East side of San Benito Pass, so we can get all the really good land on the old route and then, having secured this, there will be no opposition from the people of the old line. Would the land not pay for the road? Get the land, and then, next Congress apply to have our change of line bill pass.[6]

Huntington, charged with using their holdings as collateral to borrow millions of dollars to simply buy more railroads, was constantly on the edge of despair trying to raise the money. Huntington to Colton:

I am glad to learn that you are borrowing money for railroad purposes on the credit of the railroads, that is as it should be.[7]

Less than a week later, Huntington wrote Colton again:

A Mr. Jenkins, who was for several years with Blake Brothers, bankers, returned from Cal(ifornia) a few weeks since, and I think I have heard from him through sixty parties. He says no one in Cal(ifornia) has got any money except for the railroad magnates; that they are expending their money with recklessness that no set of men ever spent money before for personal expenses; and that further they are building a road through a country that has no business now or ever can have, &c., &c., and he has hurt us here very much. Three large institutions that we have been getting money of, have refused us on account of this.[8]

There was the sarcastic disparaging of Leland Stanford. Huntington to Colton:

> I saw S(tanford) to-day, so he has not left. I am told he has found some very fine diamonds at the show they had in Phil(adelphia), and that Tiffany is putting them in frames, and Mr. McLaughlin told me yesterday that he bought $40,000 worth of horses, or rather, that he bought horses that he agreed to pay $40,000 for.
>
> I was told today that Gov (Stanford) had just bought of Tiffany a diamond, something of which he to pay $80,000 for, so you will be glad to know that money is becoming more plenty.[9]

And there was the ungentlemanly bashing of Jennie Stanford. Huntington to Colton:

> Mrs. S(tanford) has certainly managed to get the ill will of most of the women of Cal(ifornia) that she has come in contact with and much of it on account of her having toating her Kar of 30 tons weight around from tea party to tea party, and she never takes any on herself and there are some that think she is the **** of all the world.[10]

In the end, after an appeal to the state Supreme Court, Ellen Colton lost her fight to the railroad barons and their attorney. Nevertheless, Huntington, who ceaselessly complained about Stanford's indiscretions, left this paper trail, introduced as evidence in a public courtroom, which did more lasting damage than anything Stanford every said or wrote.

Stanford's eulogists have insisted on calling the former governor's estate the Palo Alto Stock Farm. But what became his eight-thousand-acre country holding was hardly just a farm. Another grand home was constructed, enormous landscaping projects never ceased, and a miniature railroad was built for Leland Jr. Extensive stables for hundreds of finely bred horses went up. Some 150 men and women were employed as staff.[11]

Stanford was not the first San Francisco magnate to carve out an immense part of the area for genteel rusticating. But, it has been noted, "of all the San Francisco squires, the noblest was Leland Stanford." Stanford was the very embodiment of America's nouveau riche: "The new millionaires replicated noble settings and a rhythm of life divided among town house, country estate, and exclusive spa," noted one detailed examination of the time. "San Francisco's upstarts donned the habits of the English nobility—landscape gardening, country sports, and entertaining."[12] Thomas Hill's painting *Palo Alto*

Spring is a fine representation of this milieu. Croquet players in haute couture attire, vast lawns, and even toddlers on a wildcat rug were all engineered to speak to the conceit. Stanford himself is attired in his habitual formal wear, a Continental tie beneath the collar and a tycoon-caliber cigar casually held between fore- and middle fingers.

Although they may have been Republicans, and although Stanford had earlier condemned the Southern oligarchy as un-American because it had played the role of feudal nobility, "the new millionaires modeled themselves after, and presented themselves as, aristocrats."[13] Not to be outdone, the older San Francisco money was aghast. "One topic of discussion was the impertinent invasion of Menlo Park—a term that embraced all that part of the county," wrote socialite and author Gertrude Atherton regarding the wealthy enclave adjacent to Palo Alto where she grew up. She referred to her set as the "ancient aristocracy," as opposed to the upstart millionaires such as James Flood, who began his California work life, as did Stanford, as a saloon keeper but later found great wealth in the Comstock Lode. "For weeks," she wrote, "the topic on the veranda was whether or not the Floods should be called upon when they moved in. However, for business reasons, impressed upon them by their husbands, the women did call."

Atherton remembered that her people were scandalized by the manner of bespoke clothing the arrivistes wore outside the city. Referring to Jennie Stanford, she wrote,

> "Miss Jennie" [wore] a confection of tourquoise-green flannel trimmed with deep flounces of Valenciennes lace! We always wore the simplest thin frocks in summer—generally white batiste or cross-barred muslin—but I doubt if we, in our ostentatious simplicities, made the initiates feel out of it. I fancy they went away after that stiff and nervous call with the pleasant feeling of superiority that only multi-millions can give.[14]

Those millions were coming from far more than California by 1881. The transcontinental railroad tariffs, fees, and schedules affected businesses and individuals from one end of the nation to the other. And that brought problems as well as profits for Stanford from as far away as his native state. No less a conservative, probusiness organization than the New York State Chamber of Commerce, hearing its members express discontent with the railroad business and knowing the Empire State was considering some railroad regulation, created a committee to investigate the situation. "No body of men is less likely

to be open to the charge of attacking vested interests or the legitimate rights
of property or of capital than the Chamber of Commerce of a great commercial city," noted the *New York Times* in April of 1881. "Its objects are practical,
and it has to do with business affairs in their actual operation." The chamber
received, in response to a questionnaire, what the *Times* called "the extraordinary letter of Leland Stanford."[15]

Regulation of any type, the railroad baron stated, is "to my mind, on a par
with the principals contended for by Communists." Stanford compared it to
"the agitator, Kearney." The chamber, horrified, concluded of Stanford's
screed, "It is remarkable for a boldness of assertion of railroad claims, and a
lofty contempt for the decisions of our Courts." The chamber's investigating
committee found that Stanford "denies that railroads are public highways and
common carriers, deriving their existence from the State, and asserts that they
owe no duties to the public other than those of the merchant, the farmer or
the laborer." It found that Stanford "denies the existence of discriminations
upon the roads with which he is connected but justifies them in principal."
What's more, said the chamber, the railroad president "substantially admits
that railroad companies contribute large sums to control nominations or elections, and states that it is no better or worse than where the same is done by
individuals." Finally, lambasted the state business body, "he claims that stock-
watering is a matter which affects only individual owners, and in which the
public have no interest."[16]

After a point-by-point refutation of Stanford's assertions, the chamber
cited court documents, Congressional testimony, and financial figures and
claimed, "The corruption of our elections and legislation by great corporations
is one of the most dangerous and regretable of features in modern society."
One chamber official referred to the railroad magnates as "vampires."[17] The
Times condemned the railroads for "the ruthless tribute extracted from the
industries of the country for their enrichment."[18]

Since the Stanford group did not have any direct business in the railroad
president's home state, the real work of confronting the charges remained in
California. But with many in the Golden State fed up with failed attempts to
install not just a watchdog but a watchdog with incisors over the railroad,
regulation became a central goal in calling for a convention to overhaul the
state constitution. Stanford sneered. "To give the free use of the R Roads is a
cheap way to buy votes and a majority of the convention have no conscientious
scruples to restrain them from so doing," Stanford wrote Huntington.[19]

"There is a bad disposition there. Have done what I could to counteract it," he also wrote, with some optimism. "It is the general opinion that what the convention will submit to the people will not be adopted."[20] He was wrong. The convention created a three-member California Railroad Commission and California voters approved it the next year. Stanford had to reach deeper to fight this new antagonist, and deeper he did.

"The first line of defense for the railroad was to control the Railroad Commission," noted a California scholar. Consequently, the commission found little amiss with the railroad and published vapid reports assuring a skeptical press and public that everything was just dandy. The commissioners issued "statements that sounded as though they came directly from Southern Pacific's legal department."[21]

The legislature, angry at the commission's lack of action, investigated and found all three commissioners guilty of negligence, two of collusion, and one of outright bribery. One member—George Stoneman, who would later become governor and play another important if brief role in Stanford's story—ignored his responsibilities and instead "devoted most of his time to the management of his ranch near Los Angeles." Another, Joseph Cone, "made a large acquisition to his wealth, which was already great when he was elected Railroad Commissioner and your committee believe[d] that such acquisition of wealth was largely due to extraordinary and unusual facilities afforded by the railroad officers." He was, in fact, the same Joseph Cone who had been involved in the real estate laundering maneuvers at Vina. The investigating legislative committee found that he, "in the purchase of thirty-four thousand acres of land for twenty-nine thousand dollars was made a privileged purchaser, and received from the railroad company facilities in this regard denied to other applicants for portions of the tract." Moreover, he then turned around and sold land to the treasurer of the Southern Pacific, Nicholas Smith, for another $100,000 profit that, the investigators said, "gives rise to the suspicion that more was contemplated in the purchase and sale than appears on the face of the transaction." This was the land that ended up in the hands of Leland Stanford. The investigation found that Cone fought proposed reductions in passenger rates "through the personal solicitation of Governor Stanford." The committee also concluded that Cone "sacrificed the best interests of the State through personal friendship for Governor Stanford, and in return therefor received favors from him."[22]

As for the third railroad commissioner, an impoverished young lawyer named Charles Beerstecher, the probe found "he was without means at the time of his election, and his sudden acquisition of wealth while Commissioner was without adequate explanation." His conduct, the final report concluded, "admits no other explanation than that he was bribed."[23]

The corrupted Railroad Commission did not follow the legal mandate to require Stanford's company install a uniform system of accounting, but let it do what it wanted, making what books were available "not intelligible" to anyone but the railway company itself—a situation that would come up again soon enough in even more dire terms.[24]

Jennie Stanford had been a quiet, if somewhat ostentatious presence so far, enduring the scorn of the more established San Francisco moneyed class with the same stoicism she had mustered in the face of slander more than two decades earlier, as she waited three years in Albany while her husband relied first on his brothers then his three partners in his early California days. But Leland had done what he thought fitting to compensate her, first with properties and parties, then by bedizening her with jewels. The spectacle of Jennie's gems, noted with some derision by Huntington, caught a good deal of attention, and as with that from her husband's business partner, not all of it very pleasant. "Mrs. Stanford was a very large woman," wrote a society woman of the time. "Not particularly refined—and rather careless about her grammar but she wore magnificent jewels—such emeralds and diamonds!"[25]

In addition to gems she owned that were once the property of Empress Joséphine, first wife of Napoleon, "Mrs. Leland Stanford bought a set of the most beautiful opals surrounded with diamonds, which had belonged to the ex-empress Eugenie," noted the New York Sun.[26] It was hardly an exception. "Queen Isabella II, a hearty and apparently not quite bright nymphomaniac, who was deposed from the Spanish throne in 1868, sold Tiffany's over $1,600,000's worth of gems, which the Spanish Bourbons had been hoarding for one hundred and fifty years. Most of Isabella's jewels became the property of Mrs. Leland Stanford," noted a history of Tiffany & Co. "If America as a whole owned more diamonds than all the courts of Europe, three women—Mrs. John Jacob Astor, Mrs. Clarence Mackay and Mrs. Leland Stanford—were each were said to own more jewels than any of the crowned heads, with the exception of Victoria and the Czarina of Russia."[27]

Of course, travel to places such as Tiffany & Co. in New York was by train, and although the executive coaches were for Stanford, they would have also been available to his partners. In 1882 Jennie quietly commissioned the exclusively private "Car Stanford." It was a luxurious coach with extra-heavy steel rails along the bottom to ensure an especially smooth ride. The interior boasted velvet and hand-rubbed rosewood, heavy carpeting, and furniture of blue crushed plush. Plate-glass windows surrounded the sitting room, "affording an excellent view that Mr. Stanford could make a very thorough inspection without leaving the car. At every important station these windows were polished."[28] A five-octave organ was near the hallway, which ran down to the dining room, where the upholstery was of leather. A full-time chef was assigned to the car, and he was responsible for provisioning the coach with everything from frozen oysters, to fresh produce, to cookies that were three inches square and half an inch thick. Jennie Stanford ordered those in boxes of five hundred.

To top it off, the Stanfords started spending a considerable amount of time touring the most fashionable, expensive parts of western Europe. Their declining health was one major rationale for this; both Leland and Jennie were succumbing to the idle, gourmand, and altogether sybaritic way of life they considered the definition of success. In the late nineteenth century that included European spas.

Soon after completion of the transcontinental railroad, both Leland and Jennie Stanford began to complain of a series of illnesses that would plague them off and on to the end of their days. It is not easy to always know exactly what ailed the couple—sometimes the diagnosis was the catch-all "vapors" so commonly blamed for maladies baffling doctors of the era. It is evident today, if only by existing photographs, that Leland and Jennie gained considerable weight as they aged and prospered, and in many cases their many physicians repeatedly advised them to eat less and avoid lethargy by taking regular, brisk walks. Leland was the first to experience serious health problems. In the 1870s he was sometimes bedridden for months at a time, taking an ever-changing series of medicines that seemed to do no good. Suspect explanations were given, prescriptions taken and then discarded when no improvement came about.

One particularly appealing medical fashion of the time was "taking the waters." American physicians to the idle rich of the Gilded Age often recommended it and their patients as often gladly acceded. A good number of the great European spas of the nineteenth century were in Germany, referred to there as *kurort*. Leland Stanford and then Jennie began to visit these curative resorts in the 1870s. They soon found much more appeal in these settings than simple bathing in hot mineral pools and eating foods healthier than steak, potatoes, and cake.

"Far from being only about wellness, the grand spas in their heyday amounted to their world's equivalent of today's golf and tennis resorts, conference centers, business retreats, political summits, fashion shows, theme parks, and sexual hideaways—all rolled into one," according to a modern history of Europe's grand spas.[29] They were noted for their equally grand hotels with spectacular lobbies, wide corridors, and magnificent suites. Butlers, maids, cooks, and many more waited on the patrons day and night. The gilded dining rooms were filled with the declining aristocracy and the ascending capitalists, both intent on exchanging their value in return for the other's. The Stanfords, of course, brought their cache of great wealth, political power, and legendary American archetypes with them. Whatever sangfroid greeted them at home or abroad, they were the Stanfords, high lords of the new industrial age.

Leland and Jennie had a particular fondness for a Bavarian spa called Bad Kissingen, a luxurious resort that attracted not just royalty but also statesmen such as Otto von Bismarck. They, either together or sometimes separately, would spend months at the *kurort*. In one of the rare remaining letters from Leland to Jennie that betray any emotion, he wrote from Kissingen that when he had stayed alone briefly in Paris he had been "inexpressibly lonely."[30]

In most instances, one parent would be taking the waters while the other traveled or stayed home with Leland Jr. The boy was, by all accounts, a precocious adolescent as the 1870s ended and the 1880s commenced. "I hear my dog Toots has developed vagabond propensities in California, under the tutorship of my other dogs,"[31] he wrote home during the last year of his life, prompting one to wonder what fifteen-year-old American boy ever wrote like that? His parents, determined to raise their only son as the scion of nineteenth-century landed gentry rather than offspring of a barkeep and shop girl, dressed their beloved child in velvet suits and, until an uncle stepped in, allowed his locks to grow something resembling Thomas Gainsborough's *Blue Boy*. He was more often with his frequently ailing mother than his father, noted his tutor, who affectionately recalled that "when she was ill he took a daughter's part rather than that of a son."[32]

It was a given that Leland Jr. would take the Grand Tour with Pa-*pah* and Ma-*mah* sooner rather than later. He traveled well, along with his parents, a retinue of servants, and his tutor. He learned to speak French fluently and had a good deal of German. The child grew up with everything he could want, of course, so he began to collect things: antiques, artworks—and still a boy—pine cones, among them. The Nob Hill mansion, with its dozens of rooms, filled with artifacts, also began to fill with Leland Jr.'s adolescent accumulations. Much of what he drew, wrote, and collected clearly demonstrates a gifted child.

His upbringing was not what most of that era would call normal. When he was just nine, he had a Christmas party featuring a live band. Some 150 guests in silks and satins arrived in carriages. Party prizes included gold rings. When he was twelve, his parents gave him a gold watch and chain, which he kept in a vest pocket. Regardless of those sorts of indulgences, the boy was said to be sweet, well mannered, and devoted to his mother and father. Leland Sr. openly groomed his son to follow him into being a titan of industry. When Leland Sr. fell ill again at the beginning of 1883 and returned to Europe for still another visit to the spas, mother and father thought it wise to take advantage of the situation and take Leland Jr. on one last Grand Tour before they had him admitted to Harvard, where he was to begin his studies at age sixteen.

The little family departed the United States a dozen days after Leland Jr. turned fifteen, commencing a lengthy trek across western Europe. Although both mother and father were ill during much of this time, there is no indication that the teenager had any health problems until the end. They traveled luxuriously across England, Germany, Austria, France, and Italy and took what was then an exotic spur to Constantinople. Shortly afterward, the fifteen-year-old was not feeling well. When they returned to Italy via Greece, it became clear the boy was seriously sick. "We came here from Rome with our darling boy quite ill," Jennie wrote from Florence to friends back home in February of 1884. "He had complained while we were in Athens and again in Naples; he was sick enough to be in bed a few days." They made their stand in the Florentine city.

> We had to bring him in a saloon car, with a bed in it. A physician met me at the hotel and took charge of him immediately, and after two days he pronounced it a mild case of typhoid fever. We have been here five days, and Leland is nearly at the highest point. The doctor thinks he will be confined for four weeks, even under the most favorable circumstances.

Revealing a mother's deeper anxiety and anguish, Jennie wrote, "I have turned for comfort to the giver of both good and evil and my faith has increased, and now again I turn to Him with entreaties to save to me my darling boy."[33]

Then "the fever which has been smouldering within him broke out in all its malignancy."[34] Notable physicians from Rome and Paris were summoned to the boy's hotel bed, where he lay decimated from typhoid. One doctor required the boy be wrapped in coils of ice head to toe, exacerbating the teenager's suffering.

It was all in vain. At 7:30 in the morning of March 13, 1884, two months before he would have turned sixteen, Leland Stanford Jr. died as his parents could only watch. That day Stanford Sr. wrote to Huntington, "Our boy after an illness of these weeks left us this morning for a better world."[35] Mark Twain, writing from San Francisco afterward, noted in an unpublished letter that Stanford "at once lost all interest in life."[36] Jennie's private secretary wrote years later that "Mr. Stanford broke down completely, Mrs. Stanford fearing for his reason and his life." Stanford "sank into an unconscious state, a brokenhearted man. His life was despaired of."[37] Six years later, in an unusually poignant letter of condolence to someone who had lost both a son and daughter, Stanford wrote, "With the departure of children hopes and ambitions of our lives in great measure go out, and their places are never filled."[38]

Leland and Jennie Stanford's seemingly endless cortege home with the body of their boy took on a theatrical aspect of some mark. "Even by Victorian standards," noted an exhibit at the Stanford University museum, "the Stanfords' mourning was staggering in its public display: Leland Jr.'s body was transported home in a series of funeral processions conducted over eight months, lying in state in Paris, New York and finally in San Francisco."[39]

The memorial took place at what was then called Grace Church, and an unemployed young woman named Bertha Berner took her brother and ailing mother to the service.[40] "When we reached home my mother made the remark that she had never before seen a face so sad as Mrs. Stanford's, saying her eyes appeared wept blind, and she surely could not use them to read or write," Berner wrote in her reminiscences almost fifty years later.[41] That afternoon the enterprising woman, still in early twenties, wrote to Jennie saying she was seeking work and thought she might assist her. Within days she was hired, and having "earnestly cultivated cheerfulness in my endeavor to dispel her sadness," Berner found herself Jennie's personal and confidential secretary until the day some twenty years later when she rushed into Mrs. Stanford's Hawaiian hotel suite to find her writhing in pain and dying of poison.

When the Stanfords were back in the Bay Area still mourning the death of Leland Jr., Jennie tried séances to talk to her dead son, a ritual disdained by her husband but not uncommon in their time. Having both grown up in the Burned-over District around Albany, it would have been understandable for both to subscribe to the common superstitions of the day. Nevertheless, to escape ridicule, Jennie soon learned to disguise what even her confidential secretary called "pitiful" attempts to contact little Leland.[42] With the first of many elaborate entombments of the child, the couple presented a stoic public continence, understandably lost in a grief that allowed little respite or remedy.

They were to find solace, however, in an ultimate cenotaph that would have global consequences of unfathomable reach.

CHAPTER 14

Ingeniously Contrived Devices

By many measures, Leland Stanford, who had lost and won much in life, was at his acme that day in 1884 when he, his wife, and son checked into the Bristol Hotel in Florence, Italy. He was the head of one of the most storied enterprises in the world, he was fabulously rich, he was one of the most powerful men in a country rocketing toward the position of most powerful nation on earth. He lived not just large, but Olympian. When the porters loaded Leland Stanford's valise on a train along with the casket of his son, and he and his wife departed Italy for the arduous journey home, he was a shattered man confronted with the overwhelming feeling that he very suddenly had absolutely nothing of any real value.

Life had tried to break him many times before. There was nothing in Stanford's early years that would have suggested he could withstand those tests, and yet he did and somehow had not just overcome them but found means to outpace his losses.

The massive, technological enterprise he had been instrumental in creating would not slow for him or anyone else simply because a child had died. Stanford was still the president of his railway company and beholden to its many-tentacled entanglements. And because of how he had been a key entrepreneur in the railroad combine, he would soon encounter an extremely powerful new threat, this one from no less than the power that had incubated the cross-continental railway itself: the government of the United States of America.

That epic confrontation would define the very essence of Stanford's infamy, however much it puzzled him. Leland Stanford, like so many before and after him, never fully grasped that fame, fortune, and force are often met by accountability, sometimes revealing itself sooner, sometimes later.

For a man like Stanford, there was always more to reach for, grasp, and hoard. Then, as for many still, "the most desired office was membership in the United States Senate," a historian of the time observed. "Five San Francisco millionaires attained this lofty position." Stanford, once again, was foremost among them.[1]

Until enactment of the Seventeenth Amendment in 1913, state legislatures selected U.S. senators, and in 1885 Stanford still had a hold on the one in Sacramento. But he did not retain command of his partners' support, and this would lead to a humiliating downfall just five years later. Once again, not anticipating that, he simply took the Senate appointment as an opportunity to outfit still another grand home, this time in Washington, DC. It had another stable of fine steeds his servants would use to conduct Stanford in his elegant coach to Capitol Hill, at least when he was in town and feeling well enough to do business. Otherwise, his undistinguished service was noted for frequent and lengthy absences, since Stanford was often in Europe taking the waters at Bad Kissingen. As for his Senate duties, "Stanford found them 'irksome.'"[2]

He attempted to get a handful of bills passed, but generally failed. As with many U.S. senators, there was some scattered talk by his promoters of his running for president—some said Jennie was behind the rumor—but nothing came of it. One major piece of legislation that aroused some of his waning energy was the landmark Interstate Commerce Act, which gave Congress the authority to regulate railroad rates, among other powers. The legislation required "reasonable and just" rates and prohibited special favors to high-volume users and higher rates for short hauls. The act created the Interstate Commerce Commission, which was the first independent federal regulatory panel. It became a paradigm for others such as the Federal Trade Commission, the Securities and Exchange Commission, and the Consumer Product Safety Commission.[3] Despite Stanford's vehement opposition, the bill passed and became law in 1887. It would be a bad year for him.

A little earlier there had been a seemingly smallish court case that has escaped much historic notoriety. San Mateo County, immediately south of the city and county of San Francisco, assessed the Southern Pacific property taxes the railroad refused to pay, contending, among other issues, that the state constitution's tax provisions violated rights assigned in the U.S. Constitution. The case went to court. The county beat the railroad and the Southern

Pacific was ordered to pay a little more than $14,000. "In collusion with certain San Mateo County officers they paid, or pretended to pay, the taxes due that county," noted a historian who conducted a close examination of the litigation.[4]

Nevertheless, the railroad lawyers appealed the ruling all the way to the U.S. Supreme Court, where Associate Justice Stephen Field sat. He owed his job, in large measure, to his friend Leland Stanford, who as governor had been instrumental in getting Field appointed to the high bench, where he had already written opinions favoring the railroads.

Shortly after the San Mateo litigation, the Southern Pacific fought another similar case. The next county south, Santa Clara—which, incidentally, remains the location of Palo Alto and Stanford University—assessed a tax on the railroad, not just for its land but also for fences along its tracks. That case, too, went to the Supreme Court. While it was being tried, Justice Field was a guest at a feast hosted by Stanford at an upscale Washington, DC, restaurant, causing sharp rebuke in San Francisco newspapers.

This simply underscored earlier, far more potent anxieties about Field and his cozy relationship with the railroad corporations in general and Leland Stanford in particular. Some years before, when ruling on the Union Pacific's Crédit Mobilier scandal, Field "desperately wanted to write the opinion" that would favor the railroad, noted a later biographer of the justice. In that instance, Chief Justice Morrison Waite, who not infrequently tangled with Field, prevented him from authoring the decision. Instead, Waite told his fellow justice, he would make that assignment "to someone who would not be known as the personal friend of the parties representing the railroad interest." Then the chief justice added with a diplomatic barb, "There is no doubt of your intimate personal relations with the managers of the Central Pacific and naturally you, more than anyone else in the court, realize the vast importance of the great work that has been done."[5]

In the subsequent San Mateo and Santa Clara cases, the high court issued a mixed ruling awarding the counties some tax money from the railroad, but not for the fences.[6] Field, later free of the chief justice's constraints, would soon have an opportunity to render a far more significant service to his friend and sponsor, Leland Stanford of the Central and Southern Pacific Railroads.

Engaged in a constant state of warfare with the public, press, and government, Leland Stanford, Collis Huntington, and Charles Crocker decided in the mid-1880s to drop the pretense that the Central Pacific and Southern Pacific were two distinct railroad companies, thereby sloughing off some of that controversy. The Southern Pacific became the holding company and officially leased what was left of the old Central Pacific. Rather than file incorporation papers in troublesome California, where the railroad men were making money hand over fist, they registered the Southern Pacific in Kentucky, where it had no rails but "taxation was practically nominal." Stanford would later comment that the intent was to "allow us to lease all the roads in the country."[7]

While Stanford's insatiable thirst for acquisition and empire continued unslaked, the U.S. government was increasingly taking notice that California lawmakers were making little headway in responding to the incessant drumbeat by press and public that the new barons of industry were robbing them. In March of 1887, Congress acted. The federal government, not incidentally anxious it might be defrauded of its massive loans to the railroads, began an ambitious probe into what had happened to the people's money. It created the Pacific Railroad Commission through "an act authorizing an investigation of the books, accounts, and methods of railroads which have received aid from the United States and for other purposes."[8] What followed were months of a sweeping and granular investigation into the business of both ends of the transcontinental railroad, starting with the Stanford group.

Stanford telegraphed Huntington with the news—and some advice on hard-headed strategy: "Congress having directed an inquiry into the equities between the Government and the R.R Cos must be content to abide by them. The proof is clear and cannot be contradicted, that instead of the Co. owing the Govt. anything, the Gov't equitably is largely indebted to the Cos. I think we ought to take that position and decline to make any offers of future payment."[9]

In April of 1887, the three-member PRC commission with a generous budget held its first hearing of what would include testimony from 252 witnesses coast-to-coast during an investigation that would run for the rest of the year. Stanford, Huntington, and Crocker, not to mention their many top factotums and family members, did little to disarm suspicion, instead putting on a show akin to a mob of gangsters, so blatantly smug in their belief they have covered their tracks and would remain untouchable. If the artful dodging of accountability until that time had not convinced a reasonable person that a great crime against the American people had taken place, the testimony during the PRC cross-country investigation emitted the overwhelming stench of scandal.

The commission's first witness was Collis Huntington. "I came to Washington to get some aid from the Government, which was obtained," he testified in New York about the 1862 legislation that provided the authority and start-up financing for the transcontinental railroad that few private investors would fund. "That is," Huntington added contemptuously, "what we supposed would be some aid. It has not turned out to be of any particular benefit to the company," as if $27 million in taxpayer money in 1862 was a trifle.[10]

The commissioners, taken aback by the great sums spent by the railroad's holding companies as "legal expenses," asked Huntington if much of that money was, in fact, spent bribing government officials. First subtly shifting suspicions to his partner and rival, he said, "Governor Stanford has attended to these matters in California and I have attended to them here. They [legal expenses] were always too much, I thought."[11] But, noted Huntington, he personally had never corrupted anyone, and he was certain his chief lobbyist, lawyer, and not incidentally, childhood friend Richard Franchot never had either. But what about sums such as $63,678.13 spent in 1872 alone and annual amounts much the same and more each year afterward? Huntington said he knew nothing about this. He just gave the money time after time to Franchot and never asked questions.

Did he have receipts or remember what the money bought? No, answered Huntington, the notoriously exacting trader who could recall the price of a breakfast when he first arrived in San Francisco almost a half century before. He never asked for receipts. Did he fail to get them for everything, for example, when he bought iron and steel for the tracks? "No, certainly not. I always had them bring a bill in and very carefully looked it over," he answered blithely. "How do you distinguish your way of purchasing rails and in dealing with your solicitor?" the commission asked. "I could not explain it," was all the usually loquacious Huntington responded.[12] Perhaps they could talk to Richard Franchot? Sadly, no. Franchot was dead. So, too, was the man who followed him in the lobbyist position.

Would not all the expenses be in Huntington's ledgers? "Book-keeping is a good deal like Greek to me and I never learn either," he replied, back in form.[13] Well one hundred years later, one can almost sense Huntington smiling in the transcript. "I have always been like the Dutchman that did not keep books, who said he knew how much he owed and how much he had to pay it with. That is about all the book-keeping I have ever done," he testified. "I never look inside a ledger if I can help it, and I almost always can. Mr. Hopkins was a most excellent man for those things; he was a good bookkeeper and lawyer."[14] And what of Mark Hopkins, would he be able to explain? Sadly, Huntington testified, Hopkins, too, was dead.

When the commissioners arrived in San Francisco that summer of 1887, finished with their first round of testimony in the Midwest regarding the Union Pacific, Leland Stanford was the star witness. He arrived fists up—and chin out—saying the Central Pacific was incorporated under California laws and the federal government had no jurisdiction over it, but he would deign to cooperate, regardless. Then, following his own counsel to Huntington, he declared that American taxpayers owed him, not the other way around, asserting he and his partners had lost some $63 million because of Washington's meddling.

With the Stanfordian bombast over, the commission got down to business. What was revealed during the next many days was nothing short of astonishing. Although some of the books of the old Central Pacific and the new Southern Pacific holding companies were available, the serious financial data Congress wanted—namely, exactly how much it cost to build the transcontinental railroad and how much the Big Four profited—were not in them. Those numbers were in the books of the notorious Contract and Finance Company. When asked to produce that accounting, Leland Stanford, president of the Southern Pacific Railroad, which by then had leap-frogged over the Union Pacific and most other possible competitors to control the majority of cross-continental rail traffic in the United States, had big news: not only was the contract of the Contract and Finance Company missing, so was the financing. All the vital documents were gone. "Vanished."[15] Lamentably, no railway official seemed to know how or where to.

The railroad men said Mark Hopkins was the last person seen with the twelve to fifteen extra-big books, two to three inches thick with cloth covers and kept in a large vault. Someone had seen him packing them in boxes. They presumed the ledgers were going to be shipped from old railroad headquarters in Sacramento to the new one in San Francisco. Charles Crocker supposed Hopkins had destroyed them, thinking they were not needed. And Hopkins, of course, remained dead.

Stanford placidly testified that one of his minions "told me yesterday, or the day before, I believe."

An incredulous commissioner asked, "Did he not tell you that it [the contract] was missing before this matter came up?"

"No, sir; I supposed that the contract would be found in the files of the office. I had no reason to think otherwise. I do not think I ever heard the subject mooted before."

The commission had done its homework and knew the possibility of missing books and contracts had been mentioned during the failed suits involving Samuel Brannan and Alfred Cohen: "Do you know that it was missing as long ago as 1876?"

"No; I have no recollection of that. If I ever did know it at the time I have forgotten it."

"Were you not examined as a witness by Mr. Cohen?"

"Yes, sir."

"And did you not state in your deposition that the contract was missing?"

"It is possible that I did; but if so I have forgotten it."

Had Stanford ever seen the books? Reading from the same script as Huntington, Stanford, president of the company that was one of the biggest and most powerful in the nation, replied, "I do not know that I ever looked over a page of the books since the history of the road commenced."[16]

It wasn't just the critical accounting of Contract and Finance that had taken wing. All documents—such as the contract for the controversial company that had preceded Contract and Finance, Charles Crocker and Co.—were also gone. "They have disappeared," Stanford simply said. Clearly frustrated, a commissioner said it appeared Stanford and his cohorts had "drained" the business, adding later that it was "a matter of common notoriety in San Francisco and throughout this state, and I might say throughout the United States, that this contract and all the books and papers of the Contract and Finance Company, and the papers of the railroad company in connection with the Contract and Finance Company, are missing and cannot be found."[17]

The investigators intended to find out what had happened to the books and consequently called several other railroad executives, such as E. H. Miller, a member of the Southern Pacific's board of directors and official record keeper. Miller, it might be added, was the official arrested with Stanford years before. "I do not recall anything about it," he testified.[18]

Stanford's personal secretary was called to testify regarding the matter. He said the last person he had seen with the books was Hopkins, and Hopkins, of course, remained quite silent in his monolithic marble mausoleum.

Stanford himself testified at great length during a period of seven days, entering volumes of ponderous statements into the record, often suggesting that despite the magnificence of his accomplishments, he was a victim: "It seems that this whole matter is in the nature of an inquisition."[19]

In one of the less contentious portions of the hearings, a commissioner asked Stanford to name the public offices he had held. He replied justice of the peace and governor of California, adding the plaintive aside, "From all that I can learn, I made a pretty good justice of the peace."

"What other offices have you ever filled?"

"None other."

"Are you not a Senator of the United States?"

"Oh, yes; I did not think of that."

With that startling answer, the railroad men's testimony sometimes seemed to take on the flavor of a carnival. For example, one of Stanford's lawyers insisted on being able to turn the tables and call on a commissioner to testify at his own hearing. Indignant at the highly unusual demand, the chairman snapped, "I regard it as highly offensive."[20]

At times the commission took the opportunity to illuminate some of the dark arts by which Stanford and company had squeezed profits out of almost every venture. In 1877, for example, the Southern Pacific had ignored federal rules and built a railroad trestle across the Colorado River into Arizona, to connect the railroad with its prize terminus in Los Angeles. The object was to crush rival Tom Scott's plans for a southern route across the continent and at the same time take rail traffic away from the Union Pacific east of Promontory Summit. The Stanford group had been successful in both goals.

"Is it your opinion that the management of the Central Pacific is, in fact, diverting what would be naturally your traffic to the Southern system?" the commission asked Union Pacific lawyer John Dillon. "Yes; we believe so," he responded.[21]

In its later questioning of Stanford, the commission pointed to documents showing it had cost $50,000 to build what was essentially the illegal bridge into Yuma, and then the company had leased it back to itself for $15,000 a year, enabling the Big Four to start making an extra profit in just four years. "About the rent, I have forgotten," Stanford told the commission. "If you want to ask me about details, you will find me a very poor witness." When the commission asked Stanford about a letter from Huntington outlining some of the trestle tactics, Stanford simply answered, "I do not remember."[22]

At some point, Stanford brought his old sometimes-enemy-sometimes-friend lawyer Alfred Cohen to sit at the table as counsel with the railroad witnesses. It was a brilliantly audacious move. There was probably no one who better knew the most vulnerable attack points and the cleverest countermoves. Early in his appearance, Cohen noted with deft admiration any man who "always does the best he can for the side that employs him." When it was later pointed out that some of the matters Cohen was defending were the same he had prosecuted years back, Cohen renounced his past actions. He had been "young and green" when he had "early ebullitions of temper," adding, "What I thought then I knew, and what I have since found to be facts."[23]

Cohen was instrumental in shielding Stanford from perjuring himself. The recurrent subject of bribes prompted distinctly testy exchanges. When the commission asked the railroad president about millions of dollars listed in some ledgers as legal expenses, but completely lacking in receipts or further documentation, Stanford first answered, "I can say this, that I never corrupted a member of the legislature in my life and I do not know that any of my agents ever did."

A commissioner pointed out, "It is my right and duty, sworn to ask you."

"It is your right and duty to be a gentleman in asking your questions," Stanford shot back.

"Well, if I have not been, I will apologize," the commissioner graciously responded.

"Well, I think you have occasion to apologize for asking such questions as that over and over," Stanford snarled.

Finally, Stanford resorted to simply answering, "By advice of counsel, I decline to answer that question."[24]

That became the formula response of the railroad men, some of whom were, as in the Cosa Nostra, close family members. Charles Crocker's son, Mark Hopkins's stepson, and Collis Huntington's nephew all became top lieutenants in the organization. Two of them testified, revealing nothing but a refusal to give useful information. Executive after executive increasingly answered questions about missing documents, and evidence of bribes, and vanished books with responses such as having "no knowledge" or "I have no such recollection" or "on advice of counsel I decline to answer."

Stanford's refusal to answer many questions prompted the commission to take the extraordinary step of filing papers in federal court to compel him to respond. Though it may not have seemed likely that any further injustice could take place, it did.

The case was heard in the U.S. Circuit Court, today known as the Court of Appeals, which then issued its closely watched ruling: the majority declared that the congressionally mandated inquiry had no authority to compel Stanford to answer questions. The authors of the opinion were Justice Stephen Field and Judge Lorenzo Sawyer, two of Stanford's close, longtime allies. Field was the former California State Supreme Court justice Stanford had been key in getting promoted to the national bench and who had sided with the Southern Pacific in prior cases. Sawyer was the judge Stanford had so aggressively promoted and who had ruled for the railroad company concerning the Mussel Slough massacre.

A not unsympathetic biography of Field notes, "Certain intangible facts need to be taken into account if we are to gain a more than superficial understanding of the relations of the railroads to the political life of the state." As an example, "when Leland Stanford gave a banquet at his palatial home in San Francisco Field, if in California at the time, was apt to be there." Several others were in this circle, including Stanford's more aggressive lawyers: "The same men came together on many other occasions. Upon the death of a person of prominence it was the fashion to call on other notables to serve as pall-bearers, and it was not uncommon hat a federal judge and a prominent railroad official strode side by side."[25]

None of this halted the work of the congressional commission. "I have never seen vouchers in such a state before in my life," testified an independent expert accountant with thirty years' experience working for a multitude of railroad companies. "They are all in disorder, and nine-tenths of them are merely scraps of paper without receipts." His staff of fiduciaries concluded that "while it is the custom of all railroad companies to expend large sums of money to prevent hostile and unjust legislation by State legislators, it is unusual and exceptional to confer such unlimited powers as were given to Messrs. Stanford, Huntington, Crocker and Colton in distributing millions of dollars on their personal and non-detailed vouchers." They noted that the Big Four had spent at least $4.8 million between 1863 and 1887 for these unexplained expenses, and "such an immense sum of money expended for an account of this kind requires special attention." But, "UNFORTUNATELY, many books, papers, minutes and vouchers were missing that were of vital importance in pursuing the thorough investigation required by the United States Pacific Railway act."[26]

The Government Printing Office published almost 5,400 pages of testimony and documents. At the beginning of 1888 the Pacific Railroad Commission issued its final report. It alone ran an additional 217 pages.

Regarding the unaccountable almost $5 million: "A large portion of this money was used for the purpose of influencing legislation and preventing the passage of measures deemed to be hostile to the interests of the company, and for the purpose of influencing elections."[27] In other words, the Stanford group had used much of the government's money to fight the government.

As for the missing books and other documents, their "disappearance by accident or inadvertence is simply impossible." The Pacific Railway Commission stated, "These books were not produced, and in the opinion of the Commission, were purposefully destroyed by direction of Stanford, Huntington, Hopkins, and Crocker. The evidence on this point appears to be conclusive." Their "concealment" the commission found, "must, therefore, be assumed that the object was an illegitimate one." The commission underlined,

> All the duties and obligations above referred to have been constantly and persistently disregarded. The result is that those who have controlled and directed the construction and development of these companies have become possessed of their surplus assets through issues of bonds, stocks, and payments of dividends, voted by themselves while the great creditor, the United States, finds itself substantially without adequate security from repayment of its loans.[28]

The means by which Stanford and company used Charles Crocker's construction company and the subsequent Contract and Finance concern were "wholly indefensible." The company conducted its business in a manner that was a "violation of every duty which these directors owe to the stockholders of that company and to the Government as its chief creditor."[29]

The Big Four made an estimated $62.6 million "surplus" on transcontinental railroad construction and a similar $55.5 million from the other many railroads they controlled. Those sums didn't include other profits such as repairs and payments—for example, Wells Fargo paying the Big Four $15 million in stock in return for an exclusive contract on rail rates—not to mention company securities and the quartet's salaries. For some context of what these sums were worth in 1887, the entire annual California state budget in 1886–87 was about $6 million, the total U.S. budget about $312 million.[30]

The U.S. government couldn't sue the railroad at that time because the debt was not yet officially due, and stockholders wouldn't sue because they would likely lose their investments. The commission lamented,

> There exists a settled conviction that by application of ingeniously contrived devices in the construction and operation of these railways the bounty of the Government, intended for the support, development and insurance of the finance strength of these corporations, has been slowly but surely filtered into the pockets of a few favored officers and managers, who have not scrupled to use their powers as directors and trustees for their own personal advantages.[31]

Leland Stanford sought refuge from all that beset him by turning to his towering Nob Hill citadel, his immense vineyards at Vina, the opulent spas of Europe, the gilt corridors of the U.S. Senate, and his vast country estate in Palo Alto. It was clear to his wife, however, that he was finding authentic solace from his troubles in creating the university bearing his son's name and not incidentally, his. "Before he had resolved to found this college, I was afraid that Gov. Stanford would lose his mind or his life, so much was he afflicted by the death of our son," Jennie remarked.[32]

He could not know, of course, that the steel wheels he had set in motion would arrive at destinations far more substantial and potent than anything he had ever done, could imagine, or could possibly foresee.

CHAPTER 15

Deposed

As Leland Stanford raucously drilled his way into deeper and deeper trouble, some of the profound consequences of his role began to embed themselves into significant changes in everyday life.

From the moment human beings became conscious that something called time was streaming by and they found means to measure and, somewhat wistfully, attempt to obtain a measure of control of its passage, there was little reason to worry about different times in one place or another. Wherever you were the sun rose with consistency, reached its zenith, and then descended only to resume its journey in what was called the next day. Some of the bigger blocks of time were called moons, seasons, and years. Since it would take weeks for a person to travel any significant distance, not to mention the much later voyaging from one continent to another, time adjustments were generally accomplished with ease.

The stars provided early guidance. The constellation Orion, boasting some of the most brilliant heavenly suns, especially attracted attention by its regular movements across the night sky. An ancient ivory artifact of the stars on Orion's belt suggests the constellation was used to plot time more than thirty thousand years ago. There is also evidence that others of the same epoch were measuring time based on lunar phases. This worked well enough until the Agricultural Revolution, when hunting and gathering began to give way to planting and harvesting. As people settled, and villages became towns, and towns became the start of cities, new tools were needed. Sundials during the day, oil lamps for the dark, and hourglasses with the iconic sand running through carefully calibrated choke points came into use. With the Industrial Revolution and its attendant mechanization, clocks took their place.

Bostonians in 1850 had one loosely agreed upon set time, but the people of Albany, 170 miles away, very much another. And then again, 290 miles distant, Buffalo had still a different time. A person traveling by foot, horse, or barge between distant destinations could adjust to the unique local times with some ease, capricious as the hour might have been.

Then the railroad arrived, traversing longer distances in shorter periods than humans had ever experienced. One could take a train in Philadelphia at noon and arrive in Pittsburgh some three hundred miles away in eight to twelve hours but find oneself there at some arbitrary time. Philadelphia had one standard, but every stop along the way, not to mention Pittsburgh, may have had its own as well. In fact, points out one historian, it was not uncommon to see two clocks in a train station, one for the railroad time the other for the local hour.[1] And they might not be just on the hour. There are stories of times differing by thirty-seven minutes.

When the Stanford group and the Union Pacific came along with the transcontinental railway, especially after adding a multitude of branch lines off the main road, it tossed an already complicated situation into chaos. By 1869, when the last spike found itself finally driven into place, there were eighty different railroad lines in the United States with different timetables. By 1880 almost six hundred railroads were operating using fifty-three arbitrary times.[2] It was not just the passenger who could not rely on a solid schedule. The time discrepancies affected the all-important freight to be picked up, transferred, and delivered. One of the many great promises of the railroad was the ability to replenish inventories and fulfill orders with a measure of efficiency never seen before by shipping and drayage. How could the industry fulfill that imperative without some standardization of time? A historian points out that "around 1870, if a traveler from Washington [DC] to San Francisco set his watch in every town he passed through, he would set it over 200 times."[3]

Almost immediately after Stanford departed Promontory Summit and returned to San Francisco to start buying and building more railroads, the people who had to actually operate the trains began talking openly among themselves about establishing reliable, published times of departure and arrival that could span the continent. They found allies in other industries, especially in ocean navigation and the sciences, but none so motivated as the railroad men. A series of General Time Conventions had been held for at least a decade before the spring of 1883, when interested parties convened in Chicago and agreed on a deadline. In the autumn of that year the railroad managers unveiled their solution: slicing the United States into four different time zones, each staggered by an hour. It was called Standard Railway Time.

On Sunday, November 18, 1883, the first instant, mass software reset in history took place. "In most cities people gathered at jewelry stores and near public clocks, waiting expectantly to see what happened," a scholar noted. "Crowds of several hundred began forming in front of New York's Western Union building as early as 11:30 A.M. to await the time ball's drop."[4] Almost every railroad line in the United States froze its clocks and reset them to the appropriate hour of their newly invented time zone, whether Pacific, Mountain, Central, or Eastern. For some places, the lunch hour would come again later that same day, prompting the perplexing name associated with the event: the day of two noons.

Most American and Canadian cities followed the standard. The decisive action by the railroads prompted international diplomats, accompanied by scientists and naval authorities, to finally stop having meetings around the world to discuss the situation. In October of the next year, twenty nations met, argued—and preened—but agreed to carve a global grid of twenty-four zones staggered by consecutive hours, the starting point being the observatory at Greenwich, England, and the north-south dateline through the Pacific Ocean. The slices were called universal time zones.

There was a good deal of resistance in many quarters, as usual when change is afoot. Among the most notable were some members of the clergy who argued the multitudinous local times were "God's Time," as He had set the Earth's rotation in motion. Conversely, another not infrequently cited, if apocryphal, quip gibed, "The sun is no longer to boss the job. People must eat, sleep and work by railroad time. People will have to marry by railroad time. Ministers will be required to preach by railroad time. Banks will open and close by railroad time. Notes will be paid or protested by railroad time."[5]

When Leland Stanford was a child in 1830, there were 23 miles of railroad track in the United States. By 1890, when he was approaching the end of his life, the mileage was calculated at 166,703.

The railroads of the East, Midwest, and West upended markets, especially those for food such as grains and meat. Many retail businesses no longer needed to warehouse immense inventories, concerned about deliveries dependent on volatile weather and drayage. A precursor to on-demand logistics, the railroads obviated much of those worries as they all but ensured reasonably regular, prompt transport more or less on demand. The railroad catalyzed the creation of massive iron and then steel foundries, most famously Andrew Carnegie's in Pennsylvania. The mills opened America's coal industry, which would begin to decline only with the ascendancy of oil, which in turn made the Rockefeller fortune. Oil tankers then used the rails to fuel America. The repercussions went on and on. What's more, "the railroads were the first American business to work out the modern ways of finance, management, labor relations, competition, and government regulation," observed business historian Alfred Chandler.[6] His work also documented how the railway companies were instrumental in creating the modern investment houses, the first modern business managers, and unions, as well as the first all-important government regulatory commissions.[7]

Another scholar later demonstrated that the railroads, reminiscent of what had happened in latter stages of the gold rush, were leading forces in taking Americans "from predominantly self-employed proprietors to large corporations run by salaried managers." Adding to Chandler's work, he wrote that "the Gilded Age marked a significant increase in the influence of business in America, corresponding to the emergence of the modern corporate form of ownership," railroads being the first such industry.[8]

Leland Stanford's role in these historic, earthshaking phenomena was and remains with few rivals.

In the end, Stanford too was convulsed and crushed by the churn he had a direct hand in creating.

Fissures among the Big Four had begun to show during the intense final months and days before the snapping together of the two transcontinental lines at Promontory Summit in 1869. The testiness between Leland Stanford and Collis Huntington was how the friction presented itself then, and although it waxed and waned during the following years, the underlying causes were never fully resolved. Like a virus hiding in nerve endings or source code, it waited only for an opportunity to resurge with added malignancy. Stanford's clumsy but successful ascension to the U.S. Senate created that opening.

What happened involved the kind of sordid machinations those seeking power often fall into, whether in politics, business, or other perceived hierarchies. The dramas often play out behind the curtain, with only some noises and maybe pratfalls heard by the audience. Stanford's ambitious performance, however, required a degree of betrayal and counterbetrayal that could not be wholly contained backstage.

"I am not afraid of my enemies," East Coast shipping and railroad magnate Cornelius Vanderbilt famously remarked, "but, by God, you must look out when you get among your friends."[9]

The spectacle started simply enough: a sitting U.S. senator from California named James Farley had been seriously sick and did not seek another term in 1885.[10] The state legislature at that time was narrowly controlled by the Republicans, which was Stanford's party and not as uniformly opposed to the railroad combine as the Democrats. It seemed obvious to political observers that Republican stalwart Aaron Sargent would get the Senate appointment. He had been in the House of Representatives a long time, having been of prime importance in getting Theodore Judah his key congressional appointments in the early 1860s that, not incidentally, enabled Stanford and company to secure the initial funding for their railway. Sargent enjoyed the unqualified support of Huntington and had no reason to doubt that his friend Stanford would also endorse his bid.

He was wrong.

Sargent, like any powerful person, had rivals, and they were determined to deny him the Senate seat. They had their tool in mind. He was the same instrument Huntington, Crocker, and Hopkins had guided into the governor's job and presidency of the railroad company when they needed someone to drum up public financing for their business: Sargent's friend, Leland Stanford. This became apparent by indicators such as a writer pushing Stanford as a candidate for the seat. The scribe referred to the railroad king as an "intellectual Olympus."[11] Others close to the backstage maneuvers were hardly so kind: "It did not seem to me possible that Stanford could be false to the lieutenant who had been loyal to him," reminisced political insider Jerome Hart many years later in his memoirs. "I was young then. I know better now. The appeal to Stanford's vanity proved irresistible." Hart did not put too fine a point on the conclusion of the story: "He fell." And then, comparing Stanford to Shakespearian accounts of ancient Romans backstabbing each other in the Forum, Hart wrote, "The great man had condescended to take the toga."[12] He won the job, at the cost of deeply embittering Huntington.

Stanford insisted, as he had so many times before in his ceaseless quests for political power, that he had not desired the job himself but was instead

[FIGURE 1:] Bull's Head tavern, circa 1850

The bar where Leland Stanford was born in 1824 rarely looked this festive. Its everyday reality was painted far more graphically by testimonies of the times, describing the area as a place where workers for the brand-new, adjacent Erie Canal got paid and then subsequently drunk, among other vices. Courtesy of Albany Institute of History and Art.

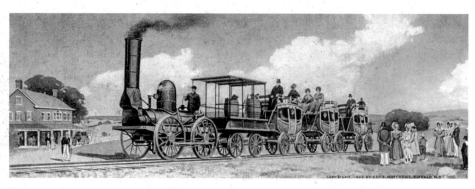

[FIGURE 2:] Mohawk & Hudson railroad

The first chartered railroad in the nation, the Mohawk & Hudson roared through Leland Stanford's hometown of Albany, New York, where his family lived in and ran a bar as well as a farm. The arrival of the railroad had a profound effect on the region—and young Stanford.

1848

Taber

ELEVATOR,
8 Montgomery Street,
Opposite the Palace and Grand Hotels.
San Francisco. (Over)

[FIGURE 3:] First photo of Leland Stanford

The first known photograph of then twenty-four-year-old Stanford. He had, until and beyond this 1848 daguerreotype, failed at most everything he put his hand to. Courtesy of the Department of Special Collections, Stanford University Libraries.

[FIGURE 4:] Leland and Jennie Stanford's wedding day

Leland and Jennie on their wedding day, September 30, 1850. They were not much more than young country bumpkins; photography was a relatively new and certainly revolutionary technology. They may look a little shell-shocked, but the innocence captured remains immutable. Courtesy of the Department of Special Collections, Stanford University Libraries.

[FIGURE 5:] Young Jennie Stanford

Jennie circa 1855, when she rejoined Leland in California after he had left his bride for three years in Albany, New York, so he could chase his fortune during the gold rush. He failed at that but later headed one of the most important—and scandalous—enterprises in American history. Courtesy of the Department of Special Collections, Stanford University Libraries.

[FIGURE 6:] The prime of Mr. Leland Stanford

Stanford in his prime, circa 1869. After one, two-year term as governor of California he enjoyed being addressed as governor for the rest of his life. In 1887, when he was under intense federal investigation, he had to be reminded he was a U.S. senator. Courtesy of the Department of Special Collections, Stanford University Libraries.

[FIGURE 7:] Collis Potter Huntington

Too often given credit for being the brains behind the western end of the transcontinental railroad, the combative Huntington was a driving force among the Big Four but also a great self-promoter. Moreover, he was willing to tear down anyone who rivaled him, including his once business partner, Leland Stanford. Courtesy Special Collections, Syracuse University Libraries.

[FIGURE 8:] Charles Crocker

A "bull of a man," Crocker was the member of the Big Four who served as road boss of the twelve thousand mostly Chinese workers who conquered the Sierra Nevada and Nevada desert to bring the transcontinental railroad across the West to meet a rail line coming from the East. Courtesy of the Department of Special Collections, Stanford University Libraries.

[FIGURE 9:] Mark Hopkins

The quiet, thoughtful member of the Big Four who watched the books,
counseled caution when he could, and lived plainly. After Hopkins died, his
all-important ledgers of company president Leland Stanford's railroad
business disappeared, bringing to bold relief one of the greatest scandals in
American history. Courtesy of the Department of Special Collections,
Stanford University Libraries.

[FIGURE 10:] Theodore Dehone Judah

Judah was the naive engineer who found the railroad pass across the Sierra Nevada and most importantly, infiltrated Congress for the Big Four, securing the exclusive railroad contract with the federal government. But Judah quarreled and broke with the Stanford group. Soon afterward he met a plaintive end. Courtesy of the Department of Special Collections, Stanford University Libraries.

[FIGURE 11:] *The Last Spike*

Leland Stanford commissioned Thomas Hill to portray the golden spike ceremony, then directed the painter to decapitate heads he did not like and insert those he did. This included Theodore Judah, whom Stanford had added although he had been dead six years at the time. After Charles Crocker called the portrait "nonsense," Stanford refused to pay Hill. Courtesy of the California Railroad Museum, Library and Archives.

[FIGURE 12:] Jennie Stanford and Leland Stanford Jr.

Leland Jr., three or four years old, with Jennie. The boy was said to be precocious and especially attentive to his mother. His father expected his heir to take over his wealth and power. When the fifteen-year-old died, Mark Twain wrote privately that Stanford "at once lost all interest in life." Courtesy of the Department of Special Collections, Stanford University Libraries.

[FIGURE 13:] Nob Hill mansion

Leland Stanford was among the first to build one of the grandest—and most ostentatious—homes on San Francisco's Nob Hill, helping create one of the most exclusive neighborhoods in America. The forty-thousand-square-foot mansion built for three people burned to the ground in the 1906 earthquake and fire. Courtesy of the Department of Special Collections, Stanford University Libraries.

[FIGURE 14:] Palo Alto hacienda

Leland Stanford's eight-thousand-acre country estate he called his "stock farm" was in Palo Alto, where he had 150 workers, many hundreds of thoroughbred horses, a miniature railroad for his son, and this grand mansion. The property is now the site of Stanford University—the birthplace, incubator, and heart of Silicon Valley. Courtesy of the Department of Special Collections, Stanford University Libraries.

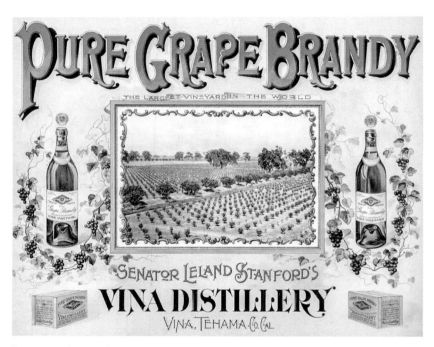

[FIGURE 15:] Vina advertisement

The largest winery in the world at the time, Vina was Leland Stanford's Northern California fiasco that he put together through scandalous maneuvers revealed in a state investigation. The wines proved "undrinkable," so Stanford distilled them into medicinal brandy. The Vina property never paid for itself and was eventually sold off after Stanford died. Courtesy of the California History Room, California State Library, Sacramento.

For Josie, from Leland
just 8 years old

[FIGURE 16:] Leland Stanford Jr.

Leland and Jennie's beloved only child at eight years old in this undated photo. The baroque
furniture, tailored sailor suit, and pose all speak of a child with extraordinary privileges.
Stanford University is a memorial to the couple's fallen son. Courtesy of the Department of
Special Collections, Stanford University Libraries.

[FIGURE 17:] Stanford University museum, before 1906 earthquake

The grandiose Stanford University museum circa 1905, shortly before the 1906 earthquake destroyed much of it. The museum was more important to Jennie Stanford than teacher salaries or classrooms, as it not only housed her and her husband's immense art collection but had special private rooms with her dead son's belongings. Courtesy of the Department of Special Collections, Stanford University Libraries.

[FIGURE 18:] David Starr Jordan

A carefully crafted portrait of Stanford University's first president toward the end of his life. Though Jordan was instrumental in keeping the university open through its turbulent early years, he sullied his reputation by being a foremost advocate of eugenics and through his cover-up of Jennie Stanford's murder. Courtesy of the Department of Special Collections, Stanford University Libraries.

[FIGURE 19:] Old Leland Stanford

Stanford shortly before he passed away in 1893. He left his widow with the very real prospect of bankruptcy, having to shutter the new university, and defending herself against prosecution by the U.S. government, which brought its case against the estate all the way to the Supreme Court. Courtesy of the Department of Special Collections, Stanford University Libraries.

[FIGURE 20:] Jennie Stanford

Jennie, appearing somewhat more softened than in earlier photos, shortly before sailing for
Honolulu in 1905. She was murdered there in her luxury hotel room and a cover-up
commenced, engineered by the president of Stanford University. Courtesy of the
Department of Special Collections, Stanford University Libraries.

[FIGURE 21:] Stanford mausoleum

Leland Stanford's 1886 will called for spending $100,000 on this mausoleum, where he, his
wife, and his son would be interred. It stands today on a northeast portion of the Stanford
University campus, not far from what is now the high-end Stanford Shopping Center
Courtesy of the Department of Special Collections, Stanford University Libraries.

[FIGURE 22:] *Palo Alto Spring*

Palo Alto Spring, by Thomas Hill, 1878. Leland Stanford Jr., at his father's left, died in 1884 at age fifteen. (The hand pointing to the right of Stanford's right shoulder belongs to the painter.) Stanford University, named after the boy, is on the eight-thousand-acre country estate where the aristocratic-styled outing is depicted. Courtesy of Iris and B. Gerald Cantor Center for Visual Arts at Stanford University, Stanford Family Collections. Conservation of this work was made possible by a generous gift from Honorable "Bill" and Jean Lane.

recruited and had accepted only in the interests of the party, state, and nation. Without conscious irony, he told a reporter in Washington, DC, "I had no idea of coming to the Senate, any more than I had of becoming Governor twenty-five years ago."[13]

Time had not tamed Huntington's temper. He was furious that Stanford had knifed Sargent so he could take the Senate seat. His baked-in desire for revenge, although briefly enflamed, then seasoned, allowing him to quietly plot while waiting for it to cool. Then he would serve his retribution with frosty relish.

In 1887 the other U.S. senator from California, John F. Miller, died. To fill that term, the Democrat in the governor's office appointed a man who had also become fabulously rich, though not through any taxpayer subventions: George Hearst, father of William Randolph Hearst, whose San Francisco Examiner was the first newspaper in what would become a highly controversial chain of news outlets.[14] Hearst Sr. had made his great fortune in the Comstock Lode and other mining interests and never lost his rough-and-ready ways, including his infamously tobacco-stained beard from spitting out chaw. Neither trophy senator accomplished much, but their situations being equal, Stanford and Hearst didn't quarrel with each other.[15]

Stanford's recurring lethargy, declining health, and time spent playing the role of U.S. senator were accompanied by unfulfilled responsibilities to the failing Vina ranch, his San Francisco and Palo Alto properties, as well as his numerous other investments. And, of course, there were the significant demands of planning the ambitious multimillion-dollar institution meant to be the memorial to his child: the incipient Leland Stanford Junior University. It was almost easy to forget the job that was the source of his wealth and fame: presidency of the railroad. Something had to give.

Charles Crocker, intent on enjoying his 25 percent share of the great railroad fortune, found his sybaritic pleasures in food, drink, travel, and real estate. He also shared Stanford's fondness for horses, especially, again like Stanford, those used in the nineteenth century's rich man's sport of harness racing. While in New York in April of 1886, Crocker had a terrific accident, reportedly the result of street racing another railroad executive. That it happened because of an inopportune crossing of a railroad track might have been darkly ironic. The morbidly obese sixty-three-year-old was thrown from his buggy, landing on his side and head. The doctors at Manhattan Hospital said he was badly injured, with cracked ribs and a concussion.

One of Crocker's more ostentatious investments was the Hotel Del Monte in Monterey, California, where—mimicking European spa protocol—he later repaired intending to further recover. He did not. In August of 1888 he died at the luxurious Del Monte. It was said he had never fully recuperated from the racing accident, although it was also noted he had a serious case of diabetes. Only Leland Stanford and Collis Huntington were left—and Huntington's last potential obstacle vanished.

He pounced.

On the last day in February of 1890, the top brass of the Southern Pacific met in Huntington's New York City office and drew up a simple document in the hand of Stanford's private secretary. They agreed that any "papers in possession of C. P. Huntington in reference to the Sargent matters be either destroyed or be delivered sealed to the undersigned to be disposed of as they shall see fit." Stanford was one of the signatories. Then, proving where the real money was, the document added that "all the parties owning or representing interests in the property of the Pacific Improvement Company shall in good faith refrain from hostile or injurious expressions concerning each other and shall in good faith co-operate for the election of Leland Stanford as Senator in the next term of the U.S. Senate." This classic smoke-filled-room bargain would keep a fellow oligarch in power. But as with all negotiations, no one got something for nothing, and Stanford had to submit something very precious: the grim cast of executives compelled him to relinquish the most important role of his life. "C. P. Huntington," the document stated, would "be elected President for the ensuing year."[16] Stanford would retain other, irrelevant titles in the railroad corporation.

The agreement was kept quiet, giving Stanford time to spin the story his own way, in his own time. Two months later, upon his return to the West Coast, he began a soft launch, telling people he wanted to resign the presidency, not that he was pushed out because the Southern Pacific executives were deeply concerned he was neglecting his duty. In a somewhat odd interview with a local reporter, he said, "While I am without any organic disease, I am troubled at times with a sort of nervous derangement, and am, consequently, desirous of greater liberty of action." The same paper on the same page noted Huntington had also arrived in town and was "looking exceedingly well and expressed himself as enjoying the best of health." He also denied knowing anything about Stanford resigning.[17]

The next day, at the annual Southern Pacific Board of Directors meeting in San Francisco, the cold news was served. Stanford was out and Huntington was in. In order to be certain every nail was driven well into the coffin, Stanford's brother-in-law was dumped from the board of directors and replaced with a Huntington ally, and two of Stanford's closest aides were forced to resign their executive positions. The new railroad company president, in remarks made available to the *San Francisco Examiner*, derided his partner of more than three decades: "In no case will I use this great corporation to advance my personal ambition at the expense of its owners, or put my hands into the treasury to defeat the people's choice, and thereby put myself in positions that should be filled by others." Then, immediately after the coup, no longer able to hoard his grievances, Huntington told a reporter what he really thought:

> We are railroad men and intend to conduct a legitimate railroad business. To do that successfully politics must be let alone. The two don't go well together. If a man wants to make a business of politics, all well and good; if he wants to manage a railroad, all well and good; but he can't do both at the same time.[18]

Huntington's remarks were enthusiastically reprinted in newspapers coast-to-coast.

Huntington's public invective was staggering in its mendaciousness. For decades he had purchased politicians, not just in state legislatures but in the very lobbies of Congress, not to mention his being instrumental in setting up Stanford to become governor and using that office to grasp essential public financing for the railroad company. "I'm not down on politics, mind you. In a free country like ours men should take an interest in politics, and it is laudable for them to have political ambitions, but it wrong to mix it with business," Huntington remarked. "This corporation shall not be used henceforth for any such purpose if its President can prevent it."[19]

A vanquished "Mr. Stanford returned from San Francisco to his country estate in Palo Alto, a sick man," Jennie's private secretary recalled of that evening in her memoirs. "He appeared to have grown years older than when he had left in the morning. Mrs. Stanford was very much alarmed." He then told her he had lost his job as railroad president, a job that "was very dear to him."[20] The price of Southern Pacific stock was more dear to Huntington, who wrote a left-handed letter of apology to Stanford five days later at the insistence of his board of directors who feared the open feud would depress the value of the company. Stanford released the barely penitent letter to the press, still trying to save face. A little more than a month after that, Leland

and Jennie once again fled for a lengthy, plush European holiday, reprising hopes of regaining their health.

While they were abroad, Huntington wrote to another California newspaper that had promoted his role in the theatrics. He declared he could "indorse all you say about the rottenness of the politics of the State as conducted by Leland Stanford, through which he used the Southern Pacific Company, very much to its own disadvantage, in order to accomplish his own selfish purposes."[21]

Huntington remained president of the Southern Pacific for the rest of his life.[22]

It has been suggested on occasion that Leland Stanford considered a memorial to his fallen son as vengeance against the University of California, which had at the time just one campus at Berkeley. A history of Stanford University's early years notes that nineteenth-century San Francisco congressman Thomas Geary "raked up the old story of how Stanford University had been conceived in spite and with the deliberative intention of injuring the State University."[23]

The notion arose because in 1882 an outgoing Republican governor of California, who became wealthy in the shipping business, appointed Stanford to the University of California Board of Regents, the body with authority over the university.[24] In 1883 Democrat George Stoneman took office, and although he had ties to Stanford dating to the corrupt state railroad commission, he rescinded the appointment. It was the first time that had happened, and the last time for another 125 years. "Mr. Stanford acted for a few days as a member of the state Board of Regents," wrote David Starr Jordan to a U.S. senator from Massachusetts.

> He was very much surprised to find that this board ignored the recommendations of the President of the University, and in general were disposed to treat the University chairs as personal "spoils." This led Mr. Stanford to doubt whether, if he should endow a University for California, it would be wise to place it in the hands of a political Board of Regents.[25]

It goes without saying that Stanford would also not have had total control of any new institution he might create under state auspices.

At first Stanford saw the school he would name after his late son as a technological academy. "I was thinking of starting a school or institution for civil and mechanical engineers on my grounds in Palo Alto," he had remarked to a churchman during his mournful return to America with his son's casket.[26] While not tossing out the notion of teaching disciplines such as history, English, and philosophy, Stanford repeatedly made it clear that his priorities were what he deemed utilitarian. His stock speech on the subject usually began with remarks about the many job applications he said he regularly received from graduates of the Ivies: "I would learn upon examination that while knowledge of Greek and Latin logic and metaphysics might be thorough, they were actually helpless, so far as practical knowledge went." These declarations, of course, were certainly colored by his own failure to earn a formal education. Stanford, never able to stop promoting his own shaky sense of worth, also, incorrectly, tried to take credit for the concept of offering a technical education alongside a more conventional curriculum: "I then conceived the idea of a university from which young men could graduate fully equipped for the battle of life in whatever direction their taste might run."[27]

Leland Stanford's taste usually ran toward money. "As far as I could see, Governor Stanford's whole conception of university building was purely material," wrote Columbia University president Nicholas Murray Butler in his memoirs. "He thought that money could buy anything and could do anything and was both chagrined and surprised when he found sometimes it could not." Butler stated that after trying to recruit the president of Cornell University and then MIT to head the new school in Palo Alto, Stanford approached him. Butler met with Leland and Jennie in New York, where he found the couple "most agreeable and most interesting." They offered him the post at an annual salary of $10,000. "My breath was taken away, since I had only recently been advanced at Columbia from an instructorship at $1200 to an adjunct professorship at $3500." Stanford raised the stakes from $10,000 to $15,000 and then $20,000. Butler declined. "My strong conviction is that he thought I was a lunatic."[28]

Butler recalled that Stanford had earlier met with Harvard University president Charles Eliot. "While crossing the Yard," Butler wrote, "Governor Stanford stopped, and with a wide sweep of his arm, said to President Eliot, 'How much would it cost to duplicate all this?'" Eliot responded that the real value of the institution was less that in its buildings and grounds—the hardware—but in its history, traditions, and achievements. Butler called Leland and Jennie "naïve." Eliot's first-person account was far more diplomatic and a testimony to Leland Stanford's steadfast commitment to family. "Mr. Stanford really had two objects in view," Eliot recalled later. "He wanted to build a monument to his dead boy; but he also wanted something which would interest his wife for the rest of her life and give her solid satisfaction."[29]

Jennie, who also had not attended any college, parroted Leland's anti-intellectual cant for years: "I think it absolutely cruel to give a young man or woman who must depend upon their own exertions a livelihood a classical education pure and simple," she told a reporter in remarks that, like her husband's, were reprinted nationwide. "There is scarcely a week that Mr. Stanford is not asked to give employment to graduates of Yale and Harvard. He has six of them as car-conductors on the Market Street line now."[30]

Although she could not resurrect her son in séances, Jennie, as did Leland, found authentic purpose and contentment, as her husband had hoped, through the undergraduates who began to walk Leland Stanford Junior University's Moorish arcades of local sandstone in the fall of 1891. Anxious about female students at her boy's cenotaph, Jennie wanted enrollees to be only boys—no girls allowed. Leland persuaded her to allow the entry of females, but the issue would not entirely go away until long after both Leland and Jennie had gone to glory, rejoining their beloved son.

The choice of top administrator for the new university would have a profound effect not just on the start-up's future but very much on Jennie's legacy. In 1891, following the recommendation of the president of Cornell University, the Stanfords settled for a young college president from the Midwest, David Starr Jordan. His mother had reportedly admired San Francisco Unitarian minister Thomas Starr King and so honored the namesake. Jordan had been a professor of natural sciences, specializing in ichthyology, and then at age thirty-five became president at Indiana University. Jordan was also from upstate New York, some 250 miles west of the Stanfords' hometown, which could not have been a disadvantage in his hopes to come to Palo Alto. He had other traits that would have seemed attractive to Leland and Jennie. He came from old New England stock but was raised in relatively modest circumstances. He had found his voice not only in education but in a deep inner drive to become a boss at Indiana. He was strongly inclined to follow the late nineteenth-century political fashion of a person's race conferring special status, which of course found preference for people of one's own ethnic background; this would cause some upset in Jordan's legacy. He also came from a religious background but not Bible-pounding orthodoxy. And shortly before he met Leland and Jennie, he had suffered great loss: his wife had died, followed by the death of one his two young daughters.

Jordan's ideas regarding education would have also had some appeal for the Stanfords. Although he was, for his time, liberal in his educational philosophy, it was in a manner that dovetailed with Leland's discomfort with formal schooling. "The oldest and best-endowed university in the world," he wrote, quoting another wag, "is Life itself."[31] Jordan's forgiving biographer, Edward McNall Burns, noted that Jordan "contended that there was much more educative value in the study of magnets than in the diacritical marks or the distinction between shall and will." Moreover, "The idea that in order to be an educated man one must be able to compose verses in Latin or read mythology in Greek he ridiculed as empty pedantry."[32]

Incongruously, he favored public education over private. But Jordan's compulsive personality was marked by paradox when it was to his advantage. He was quite flexible when the situation was strongly scented by opportunism. Beneath his placid intellectual veneer lay a scent of smoking fumes from a burning soul, not unlike that previous California immigrant zealot, Franciscan friar Junípero Serra. This would clearly present itself when, years later, Jennie was murdered in her Honolulu hotel room.

Jordan was forty years old when he came to Palo Alto, seeking a new life and a chance to head a new university many supposed would be the most generously endowed in the nation. He would have a few summer months to study fish along the Pacific before the first classes commenced. Old photos show a tall but not imposing man, with a somewhat triangular head, accented by a receding hairline, narrow chin, and face dominated by a large, bushy mustache that he cultivated as it turned snowy white in old age.

Even as Jordan was moving into his comfortable campus home and before the first class of 559 students entered the new classrooms in 1891, there was public controversy. The taint of filthy lucre once again engendered suspicion, envy, and acrimony. Huntington had famously called the university Stanford's "circus," seeing the enterprise as just further self-aggrandizement by his former friend. Many others, such as Representative Geary, were bitter that the endowment had not gone to the state university in Berkeley. The *Golden Gate Catholic* stated, "It is now well known that the Stanford University, which is just on the eve of its opening, is proving itself to be one of the great shams of the age."[33] The papers were filled with guesses about how much money the Stanfords were going to spend on the new school, many deciding on an unverified $20 million, which would have been far grander than any other university in the United States. In fact, as a history of the university's early years shows, Stanford himself "had set aside no specific sum."[34]

Instead, the very first bequeathal in Stanford's 1886 last will and testament demonstrated a different priority: $100,000 was allotted to build a mausoleum on the university campus containing three massive marble sarcophagi for his remains as well as for those of his wife and son. Those walls were up, the roof was on, and the biers were in place, ready to be filled before the end of the decade.[35]

CHAPTER 16

The Fundamental Standard

By the late 1870s it had become fairly obvious that Leland Stanford's phlegmatic character, luxurious lifestyle, and unaddressed stresses were mighty contributors to chronic illness. "A man in his condition is so liable to colds and backsets, and one thing after another," wrote Charles Crocker to Collis Huntington in 1879. The next sentence betrayed Crocker's indifference regarding his longtime friend and partner's health and keen concern for the business affairs in which they were all entangled:

> There's no telling what may occur, and in view of that I assure you I think it is best for us to *go slow, very slow*. You know the state of his finances, and in case of his death his obligations must be paid. I hope for the best and really do not feel alarmed, but, at the same time, I deem it necessary to be cautious.

Wondering if Stanford was suffering from typhoid, Crocker's anxieties mounted, and he added, "You know the large amount of indebtedness he is carrying for himself personally."[1] Stanford, after months of staying in bed in his Palo Alto mansion, recovered, but all manner of ailments afflicted him off and on for the rest of his life, despite his serial, lengthy trips to the luxury spas of Europe.

Stanford undertook his sixth voyage in 1892 to the Continent for a cure for his many maladies, accompanied by the not infrequently unwell Jennie on her fifth voyage. He was at least forty pounds overweight, suffered from gout, was going deaf, and had difficulty walking. Nevertheless, the elaborate, staged portraits we have of Leland Stanford from the time are designed to present a figure of august attainments. His massive torso and leonine head, framed by a white beard and silver hair, helped create an image that has spun lasting power over many. By the time he and his court had returned to the Palo Alto estate in the spring of 1893, he was at the threshold for what an early twentieth-century disciple called "the inevitable summons."[2] Sometime between going to bed on the evening of June 20 and at or shortly after midnight on June 21, when his valet checked on him, Stanford had a massive stroke or cerebral hemorrhage, presumably while he slept. He was sixty-nine years old.

It was front-page news coast-to-coast. Joseph Pulitzer's *New York World* published a somewhat ungracious obituary, remonstrating the deceased for failing to abide doctor's orders for a "reduction of the flesh."[3] The *Fort Wayne Sentinel* followed the traditional newspaper convention of not writing ill of the dead: "Statesman and Philanthropist is Called Home," was the headline, with a lower deck adding, "Death Comes to Him Like a Thief."[4] The death was the lead story in the *Los Angeles Times:* "Stanford. The Millionaire ex-Governor is No More."[5] The San Francisco papers, of course, gave the story big play. The rhapsodic obituary in the *Chronicle*, however, succumbed to a tart "He has lived as a king, travelled, as all know, by special car, and with a retinue of attendants that has astonished even the richest men of the world."[6]

The funeral took place three days later on the Stanford University campus. Three of the pallbearers were judges. Most of the others bearing and escorting his casket were his railroad executives. Jennie placed university president David Starr Jordan among them. The one surviving member of the Big Four—Collis Huntington—was not reported seen at any memorial. A hearse drawn by two horses brought the body to the campus quad for the service and then to what the *Sacramento Daily Union* called "the house of death"—the marble and granite mausoleum, where Stanford's son lay and wife would. Some five thousand people attended in the brilliant summer sunshine. The heavy metal doors of the white stone sepulchre lumbered to a taut close. Mrs. Leland Stanford went home to mourn and consider her situation.[7]

The situation was a skein of entanglements, commitments, and massive debt that would have daunted a team of lawyers, managers, and fiduciaries. Jennie Stanford had spent the previous many decades choosing party settings, jewelry, and Victorian fashions. She had traveled first cabin everywhere, with an entourage that took care of all her wants. She had little formal education, few friends who knew the railroad industry, and almost no sense of the unforgiving machinery of business grinding away just below her vaulted way of life. "For about twenty years before the university was founded Mrs. Stanford had literally nothing to do. She never had a hobby. She would have enjoyed reading but for many years she had trouble with her eyes and was cautioned about straining them with small print," wrote Jennie's personal and confidential secretary, Bertha Berner, in her memoirs. "She found she could not walk even a short distance without becoming completely exhausted."[8]

Caught short, Jennie was confronted by the plain fact that her husband's finances were a train wreck. He had become habituated to imprudently borrowing large sums, frequently from the robust financial laundromats of Contract and Finance, Western Development, and Pacific Improvement. The sloppy manner in which he had managed his affairs began to emerge publicly soon after his passing, with one of the first, most revealing postmortem accounts published in the *San Francisco Examiner* just four months after Stanford's lifeless body was found in his bed.

When Frank Shay, an attorney for the Southern Pacific and for some time Stanford's personal assistant, and others went to tidy up late man's railroad office, they "came across a fortune which the governor knew nothing about," Shay recounted in an interview with the *Los Angeles Herald*. "In his desk was a central drawer like that in my business desk. This was nearly full of uncashed checks, paid to the governor as dividends from the project in which he was interested. They were for large amounts in many instances, and their total aggregated hundreds of thousands of dollars. Many of them ran back for years."

Another portion of the lengthy interview revealed the shocking admission of what lawyers call spoliation—the destruction of evidence. This had taken place shortly before the Pacific Railway Commission hearings. "In 1885 we had a big bonfire down in the governor's office. We were making a sort of cleanup at the time, getting rid of old checks and worthless papers. You would have found your eyes sticking out if you had seen what went into that fire," Shay said.

Hundreds upon hundreds of thousands of dollars were represented in such notes burned that day. They ran from $100 to $25,000 each. I tell you, everybody had a slice. No one knows the politicians, newspapermen and all sorts, all kinds and conditions of people whose names were represented on those notes. The governor burned nearly all of them. The fact will console some eminent citizens and rousing some anti-monopolists who may have been expecting their notes to appear in the inventory of the governor's estate. Only a few were kept. These were generally those from politicians, and the governor thought they might be useful as reminders.

Shay estimated Stanford's estate worth to be somewhere between $50 million and $60 million. But he said this was not much more than a guess. Even Stanford "didn't know how much he was worth," Shay said. "Often he asked me to tell him, but I couldn't do it. Nobody could."[9]

Naturally, many wanted to know how much money Stanford had left behind. Estimates ranged from less than $20 million to more than $90 million. The truth, when it finally shook out, was far more complicated—and dark. Widow Jennie was now solely responsible for trying to keep the enormously expensive memorial to her dead son and husband operating. A slow fall of ten tons of brick began to descend directly on top of her grieving head. Soon enough it became clear that the author of so many calamities and triumphs had passed away in time to avoid finding himself in bankruptcy court. Leland Stanford's estate showed that he was not only deeply indebted, he had left no real endowment for his grand university.

Jennie couldn't pay even the university's heating bill. The new school trembled, teetered, and very much looked as if it would shutter its doors before graduating its first class. Jennie directed Jordan to delay paying the new faculty members their full salaries. Jennie did have seventeen servants in her own household, and in what was deemed a major sacrifice for her, the widow fired fourteen of them. One of the remaining three didn't get paid for a year. Mrs. Stanford was "emotional in temperament, impulsive in action, accustomed to wealth and the large use of it, she had seemed free to indulge her fancies at will," concluded a not unsympathetic early university history.[10] She "always felt she owed a certain style of living to her position as the widow of Leland Stanford," noted her personal secretary.[11] But now her world was once again turned upside down. "People think that Governor Stanford left me a very rich woman, I thought so myself, but now it seems that I was left a legacy of debt, trouble, and worry," she reportedly told a friend.[12] What money was left was tied up in a probate court. How Jennie would get the estimated $10,000 a month she said she needed to keep the nascent university barely operating and her minimum living standards in place was in the hands of the probate judge. Because the estate was complex, beset by multiple claims, and certainly not helped by the haphazard, semilegal structure of the university Stanford had personally created, the disposal of assets remained in probate for almost six years.[13]

Stanford's last will and testament named many family members to share in what Leland assumed would be his postmortem bounty, most getting $100,000 each. Although this was no small sum at the turn of the twentieth century—a quart of milk cost 10 cents, a dozen eggs 20 cents, and a pound of steak 25 cents—some wanted more.

Jennie was ready to make what was for her a still greater sacrifice: selling her jewels. She packed them in a valise and sailed to London, where she expected to obtain premium prices. But she returned home with most of the gems, saying she was disappointed at the offers. There was the immense vineyard and ranch at Vina, which was still a money loser. In fact, university president Jordan said Vina was draining the estate of $500 every day, money the university badly needed. Jennie took the private railcar up to the property to see what she could do. One scholar who made a study of Vina said she cut costs "with gusto."[14] Mrs. Stanford's solution to the poor management that had led to the financial losses was, once again, to fire people. She sacked 150 workers and slashed salaries for those she did not.

Jennie, though understandably portrayed in most of the day's mass news media as the heroic widow deserving sympathy and admiration, was not so very well loved by the people of Vina. A series of violent acts took place in town, culminating in 1894 when a small mob that had been drinking heavily at little Vina's surfeit of saloons marched toward Jennie's private railcar and started firing weapons. Accounts of what happened next are conflicting, and none are verifiable, except that Jennie fled unharmed. When she returned to the Bay Area from a Mount Shasta resort she often escaped to, about one hundred miles north of Vina, a railroad workers' strike stopped her eponymous Car Stanford. Jennie appealed to Eugene Debs, who had risen from a fourteen-year-old railroad-shop worker to head of the American Railway Union. The famous labor leader graciously instructed his rank and file to allow her passage home and even supplied an armed guard to keep her safe.

In 1898 she wrote about another ill-fated venture at Vina:

> I came here last Wednesday to pacify a bitter feeling existing between white employees and Chinese. The manager had leased the grape picking to a Chinese firm, and white men had to go to them for employment and were paid and discharged by them. They rebelled and, thinking I had approved this course, they threatened to burn everything in sight. They commenced, and all the vineyard tools, ploughs, and so forth were destroyed—also 300 tons of hay and the same amount of alfalfa.[15]

She had the authority to close and sell Vina, but Jennie chose to give the operation still another go. Her late husband had said it would return profits that would sustain the university, and sustaining the memorial to their boy was for the widow, now in her sixties, the core, even sole, purpose of her life.

At the same time, keeping the Stanfordian legacy of paradox alive, Jennie insisted, as had her husband, that not only would there be no alcohol on the university campus, there would be no liquor in Palo Alto. That was a problem. The settlement next to the campus's southern frontier was a small place named Mayfield whose main attractions were two breweries and some twenty saloons. "But a rule of prohibition is difficult of enforcement," was the terrifically understated assessment of an early Stanford University history.[16] The informally dubbed Mayfield Road roadhouse was particularly notorious for student drinking parties.

Naturally, Mayfield's small-business owners chafed at the imperial command from the rich newcomer and, as another local history added, "the townspeople laughed—they were skeptical of the grand plans for the emerging university, and they liked liquor."[17] Stanford's old railroad playbook called for a rival town under the Stanfords' control. As a rebuke to Mayfield and a means to cauterize the conterminous border with its dissolute neighbor, the new town of Palo Alto—initially called University Park and largely a real estate speculation of Mark Hopkins's adopted son, Timothy—decreed it illegal to manufacture or sell alcohol inside its city limits.[18] Meanwhile, Mrs. Leland Stanford insisted that Vina's brandy would pay the bills. Never mind Vina's mounting losses. Never mind providing VIP guests on campus with alcoholic beverages. Never mind that university president David Starr Jordan preached abstinence. The situation provoked everything from scorn to sport.[19]

Trying to take the high road, Jennie and her agent, Jordan, did not see this as a double standard. Instead, they wrapped the discrepancy in a lofty commandment they called the Fundamental Standard: "Students are expected to show both within and without the University such respect for order, morality, personal honor, and the rights of others as is demanded by good citizens. Failure to do this will be sufficient cause for removal from the University."[20]

Then came a nine-pound hammer blow. The U.S. government, understandably fearing it would not recoup the money it had invested in the railroad and was coming due, took legal action against Stanford's estate.

The premise was fairly straightforward: in the railroad acts of the early 1860s, Congress and President Lincoln had agreed to advance seed money to the transcontinental railroad companies. That money and interest was contractually due back to the taxpayers thirty years later. Aside from Stanford's astonishing assertions that the Southern Pacific was owed money from the government instead, and that there was no provision in his will acknowledging the debt of his company, of which he owned 25 percent, there was serious concern that Stanford's estate had more financial obligations than assets and the American people were about to get shortchanged big-time. Consequently, one year after Stanford went to his magnificent tomb, the U.S. Department of Justice filed papers asserting its claim of $15,237,000 from the estate. That was almost exactly how much was locked up in Stanford's Southern Pacific securities. In fact, if the Justice Department were to win its case, the Stanford estate would likely be bankrupt.

The government action caused, as the Associated Press put it, "the greatest excitement."[21] "Under the circumstances, there seemed to Mrs. Stanford's advisors but one thing to be done," a history of Stanford University found. "And that was to close the University." At best, this might be temporary, perhaps a few years.[22] Jennie was apocalyptic. "Only my Father in Heaven knows all I suffered and endured since my husband was called from my side, to keep the doors of the University open."[23]

The case worked its way to the U.S. Supreme Court. Jennie went to Washington, DC, and met with President Grover Cleveland, who leaned on his attorney general, who had a very small staff and a very heavy workload.[24] Mrs. Stanford had a battery of some of the sharpest lawyers in the country to assist her—and one other ally who had been in the service of House Stanford for decades: Supreme Court associate justice Stephen J. Field. Jennie had been "much together," noted Field's biographer, with "society-loving Mrs. Field." And "Field, although he wrote none of the court opinions, gave every possible assistance to Mrs. Stanford in protecting her interests."[25]

Jennie also had enemies, one in particular she had inherited from her husband along with his debt: Collis Huntington, who was then, of course, president of the Southern Pacific. Because the government was preparing, if necessary, to take separate action against him and the heirs of the Hopkins and Crocker estates for money they had contractually promised to pay back with interest, Jennie Stanford and Huntington's goals at that time aligned. Huntington offered to assist her. But the widow could not forget the slights her late husband had suffered by his hand or, no doubt, those that Huntington had cast directly at her. It was, Jennie wrote, "impossible for me to accept assistance from said Companies."[26] At some point, at the urging of her advisors, it became evident to the understandably distraught and ill-prepared widow that financial and legal help from her late husband's partners was just good business. Huntington, at that point feeling scorned, balked. "I am not lying awake nights worrying about this suit," he wrote. "When it is brought against me I will defend it and pay my own expenses of the suit. I have no assistance to offer Mrs. Stanford."[27] Jennie's allies rued her strategic error.

Her lawyers had not been as unprepared as their client. In March of 1896, the Supreme Court ruled unanimously in Mrs. Stanford's favor and against the government: "If the act of 1862, fairly interpreted, excludes the idea that stockholders of the companies receiving subsidy bonds were to be personally liable to the United States for the principal and interest accruing on those bonds, the legislation of 1864, however unwise, did not have the effect of imposing such liability."[28] In other words, although the court noted out of a corner of its mouth that it considered the contracts guarding taxpayers poorly drawn, and the Southern Pacific as a company had to repay the nation for the loan of the 1860s, Stanford, Huntington, Hopkins, and Crocker could not be held personally liable.

Jennie could not let go of her deep resentment of Huntington and his crew. "Although the suit terminated successfully, there yet remains with me the sad memory that my husband's associates gave me no support morally, no sympathy, and no promise of financial aid which the suit would naturally call for," she wrote with more conviction than accuracy. "I sought their helpfulness and their aid but they all positively declined, saying if the case were decided adversely and brought against them they would conduct it at their own expense and not ask my assistance."[29] To Huntington she vowed revenge in the form of her dead son personified in her university students: "When my Stanford boys grow up they will settle with you for your treatment of me."[30] Having demolished Leland Stanford in life, a pitiless Huntington then set about injuring the careworn widow one more time. His "reply was that she would never see the day when one of her boys would ever lift a little finger in her defense," recalled Jennie's favorite "Stanford boy," George Crothers, who would become instrumental in shoring up the shaky school for its spectacular twentieth-century successes and was said to greatly resemble Leland Jr. "In telling this Mrs. Stanford broke into tears."[31]

With the release of the railroad stock and bonds, it seemed as if Leland Stanford Junior University's problems were over. They were not. The economic panic of 1893, triggered largely by the overbuilding of railroads that then could not pay their bills, unsettled not just the nation but the industrialized world, which went into a six-year depression. The panic also devalued Stanford's holdings. Some eulogists had suggested the late Leland Stanford Sr. had been a scryer, foreseeing the economic collapse, but there is no evidence of that. It was rather the opposite—the Southern Pacific was part of the problem not the solution. In fact, David Starr Jordan wrote to the president of Harvard, in a confidential letter, that Stanford "was not expecting" a financial downturn.[32] Moreover, Vina was still in deep trouble. Jennie was still selling off much of her husband's immense, celebrated herd of highbred horses, while clinging to an early university Horses Department, if only out of nostalgia.

Although campus construction resumed, with Jordan carefully suggesting the money should have gone to expanding the faculty, plans to establish everything from kindergartens through postgraduate education were scaled back. The single biggest capital project was the university museum. It is hard to imagine its scale until one looks at photos of the structure taken before the 1906 earthquake destroyed two-thirds of the palatial building. "The Museum, originally planned as an independent institution, was ultimately merged with the university," notes an official history of the campus art collection. "It remained in Mrs. Stanford's mind more intimately identified with memory of her child, whose boyhood collecting it was to continue on a monumental scale." In it were two locked rooms that duplicated the boy's chambers at the Nob Hill mansion, containing his various collections. "They were private spaces to which she often came alone or with her closest friends." The building itself, with more than one million square feet of interior space, was at the time the largest private museum in the world.[33]

Through it all there was never a doubt that the university was first and foremost a memorial to the Stanfords' lost son. When rumors that sexual liaisons were taking place among the undergraduates, Jennie, as the sole, imperial power over the university, dictated an absolute and eternal cap on the number female students: five hundred, emphatically saying that Stanford

University was intended to immortalize the memory of her "darling boy," Leland Jr. "The institution was to be a memorial to her son, and therefore for boys."[34]

What is widely regarded as an authoritative history of the American university system summed up the rocky start for Stanford University: "The financial arrangements for Stanford were sloppy, and they were confounded by Stanford's death, the panic of 1893, his custom of living on money borrowed from one of the subsidiaries of the Southern Pacific Railroad, and a government suit against his estate for fifteen million dollars." The author blamed much of this on interference by the Stanfords themselves: "Leland Stanford referred to 'my university,' and after his death Mrs. Stanford thought of herself as its owner, as in fact she was until she was ready to relinquish her proprietary control."[35]

No single financial maneuver has had a more cash-positive and long-lasting effect for Stanford University—or a costlier one for the taxpayers of California—than what some of Jennie Stanford's agents were able to dispatch at the start of the twentieth century. It dwarfed even the countless millions of dollars Leland Stanford himself engineered out of the public treasury for his privately held railroad corporation.

In short, since 1901 Stanford University has enjoyed a special state constitutional exemption from having to pay property taxes in California.[36] "The Stanford exemption almost exclusively benefited the estate of Leland Stanford, who founded Stanford University," concludes a recent study by a legal journal examining issues before the California Supreme Court. The exemption stands, despite being "contrary to a California constitutional prohibition" against "special privileges," in large measure because after the state controller unsuccessfully challenged the university's special privilege in 1919, "the exemptions were never legally challenged" again. Moreover, "the Stanford exemption is especially problematic because it granted Stanford additional privileges that were not present in the other exemptions," such as sanctioning "Stanford's founding trusts, despite the trusts' questionable validity. The exemption also allowed the university to receive and retain property in any form of conveyance, which was impossible under then-existing trust law. This provision allowed 'several heirless millionaires' to leave Stanford property in their wills." Finally, "Stanford's exemption allowed the legislature to give Stanford corporate status 'by special act,' which the legislature did in 1901."[37] By 1914 the extraordinary situation became a template to extend, and legitimize, the priceless privilege to all legally sanctioned nonprofit schools across the state.

Most notably, the original language of the exemption sheltered much of Stanford University's 8,180 acres across two counties and four cities from having to pay property taxes in return for promising to never charge tuition to California students.[38] That changed in 1921 when the state legislature deleted the proviso, which happened around the same time the university began collecting tuition from Californians as well as out-of-state students, despite the exemption being the key condition for enjoying immunity from property taxes.[39]

Separately, Stanford University has a bank account well in excess of $22 billion and much of the income it accrues is also tax-free because it is a registered nonprofit corporation.

Credit, or blame, for the constitutional property tax escape largely goes to George Crothers, the young Stanford graduate who was said to resemble Leland Jr. and was taken into Jennie's confidence with a handful of others who gave her instrumental assistance in navigating the mess her late husband left her. In his memoirs published thirty years later and when he was a successful lawyer, judge, and then businessman, Crothers recalled that the widow told him in some of the dozens, perhaps hundreds, of conversations they had that taxes would bankrupt the university. Even two years after the extraordinary constitutional exemption Jennie was grumbling about paying her share:

> There is one thing that troubles me very much, this constant comparison of our University with Berkeley, Harvard, Yale, Cornell, etc. These all have behind them the support of states and wealthy citizens and rich students. Every citizen of our state is taxed to support the Berkeley university, as you know, and I do not think there is a citizen in our state who is taxed more heavily than I am to support that institution, as my taxes alone amount to $35,000 a year.[40]

It wasn't as if she was scrimping. Her net worth was then in excess of $15 million. That means that annually she would have paid less than one-quarter of 1 percent of her wealth to the California tax rolls.

Financially secure, Jennie Stanford returned to the railroad, one of her first stops being New York City, to come to terms with her old enemy, Collis Huntington.

CHAPTER 17

Sex and Socialism

Now in her seventies, with so much turbulence behind her, Mrs. Jane Stanford initiated a meeting with the man who had taken her husband's landmark job and his pride. They met on an autumn day at the Southern Pacific building in lower Manhattan, across from the Stock Exchange. She was ashen-colored but poker-faced as she walked into his office. He offered her a comfortable leather chair but she declined and remained on her feet. "Mr. Huntington, I have come to make my peace with you," she stated. Huntington took both her hands and bid her to sit. She did. Wiping his forehead, he simply responded, "Well, I declare." They then spoke for some time about advancing age and the like. Tears appeared is his normally vulpine eyes. They shook hands, and she departed and went to lunch. Jennie Stanford never saw Collis Huntington again.[1]

She once again began to travel extensively. One of the first of her renewed voyages was to England, where she went to Windsor in hopes of seeing Queen Victoria. Managing to get an invitation to a garden party at the castle, she was thrilled to get a glimpse of Her Majesty from a great distance. She also returned to the celebrated spa at Bad Kissingen, where she stayed for six weeks. Jennie was not a healthy woman and did not take medical advice well when it called for cures she did not fancy. Her knees swollen, her sleep irregular, and suffering from chronic cysts, regular indigestion, and frequent headaches, she consulted a physician who told her that staying at a luxurious hotel was not going to help. "It was an unfortunate remark for the doctor to make," Jennie's personal secretary recalled. Jennie dismissed the medical man. While she "considered herself an invalid," Bertha Berner wrote, "it was Mrs. Stanford's fear of being considered sick and unable to bear the responsibility of University cares that prevented her from seeking medical aid which she so greatly needed at times."[2] Regardless, Jennie later traveled adventurously, if in splendor, cruising down the Nile and riding rickshaws in Ceylon.

There was much tidying up to do concerning the outstanding financial and legal chaos that had so roiled the Stanfords, the nation, and the all-important railroad, which by 1900 was arguably the single most powerful industry in the nation. The U.S. economy began to recover, and the Southern Pacific finally agreed to start paying back the debt it had contractually promised in the early 1860s. The original loan to the railroad was almost $28 million. If the financial convention of compound interest had been stipulated, an extra $165 million would have accrued and been due the taxpayers. But the simple interest calculation used reduced that to $50 million. At the end of 1899 the Southern Pacific negotiated terms with the federal government and started paying off the principal and interest.[3]

George Crothers, bringing some discipline to the slapdash legal foundation of Stanford University, provided his patroness, Jennie, even more ease of mind. In spite or because of her reestablished security, the widow Stanford was not yet ready to relinquish her total control over the university, and with that she set off a storm that even today has been called "one of the greatest academic freedom cases in the history of higher education."[4]

The case of sociology professor Edward A. Ross is infamous among academics with an insight into what, especially after the McCarthy era of the early 1950s, remains one of the most important principals of higher education: academic freedom. Less well-known is the prologue to the Ross affair, as it is often called. In the late 1890s Stanford political science professor H. H. Powers had delivered a lecture regarding religion in which he suggested that some critical thinking—very much in keeping with the official tone and tenor of university president David Starr Jordan—might be brought to bear on faith, which tends to eschew independent testing, a method central to science and a top-shelf education. Jennie happened to be in Powers's lecture hall and her Episcopalian, if idiosyncratic, sensibilities offended, she demanded that Jordan fire the young teacher they had just hired from Smith College. He did. Soon afterward, emboldened, Jennie took similar offense and action against Professor Ross, who had transgressed the all-powerful university matriarch on several ideological issues her limited formal education provided her. Jordan had recruited Ross from his former school in Indiana, and the Stanford president was a well-known advocate of rigorous critical thinking, which pleased the faculty, but "unfortunately, the faculty also had, in David Starr Jordan, a president who was compelled by a sense of obligation and by his own sycophantic personality to defer to the wishes of the Founder," observed a landmark history of academic freedom.[5] A Jordan biographer concluded that the Ross affair turned Jordan into a "media Mephistopheles."[6]

Ross was no innocent. Rather, a historian of American universities charitably described him as a "high-spirited agitator."[7] In Ross's 1936 memoirs, wonderfully titled *Seventy Years of It*, he made his eagerness to be a provocateur clear enough. He mightily provoked Jennie in 1900 when, speaking before an Oakland congregation, he expressed sympathy with local governments that took over private utilities such as water and power. Still worse, Ross seemed to be in favor of the public assuming control of privately owned transit systems, such as the Market Street trolley in San Francisco that delivered Jennie a steady if relatively modest additional income. These were decidedly controversial positions for the era and were considered by some partisans to be socialistic. And the Stanfords were always on the lookout for any political philosophy that might imperil rather than augment their fortune. It must be noted that later the same year, Ross also spoke in San Francisco, advocating a limit on the number of Japanese allowed into the United States, arguing that Asians had too many children and would lower what he considered American standards. This was in keeping with the stated if not always practiced Stanfordian political stance and was not far afield from Jordan's pseudoscientific theories about what he deemed the racial superiority of northern Europeans. Ross, somewhat disingenuously, made hay of that talk while downplaying the fact that he had earlier angered Jennie by giving a speech at the Oakland Socialist Club.

Mrs. Stanford, unhappy with Professor Ross, ordered Jordan to fire him. Jordan, no doubt twisting his great mustache in worry as his faculty began to rebel, beseeched her to reconsider, although he also told his patroness he thought Ross "was at bottom just a dime novel villain."[8] Jordan may have also been concerned that Jennie was so upset she would threaten to revoke her inheritance bequest to the university, which would have effectively closed it forever.[9] Ross, relishing the taste of martyrdom, publicly agreed to a deal brokered by Jordan to later resign. History professor George Howard spoke out against the university administration's actions and was shown the door for it. Seven professors quit in protest and in support of their brethren. "Never before had an American faculty demonstrated so great a sense of internal solidarity and so rebellious and courageous a spirit."[10]

As it happens, Ross had earlier made a bit of a splash on the front pages of the San Francisco newspapers when he took a stance on the then national controversy of using a silver or gold standard as a basis for the U.S. dollar. Now it was Jennie's turn to play the guileful one, something she did rarely and not well. She pronounced Ross erratic and dangerous and finally and firmly said that his dismissal was solely because the university should not participate in overtly partisan political activities, which sounded strangely like her old, if equally insincere, nemesis Collis Huntington. In fact, when fifty Stanford professors publicly endorsed William McKinley for U.S. president in 1896, she had no objection. Jordan meekly went along with Mrs. Stanford. "Cowardice never had better reasons," a historian quipped regarding the young university president's lack of starch. "Had Jordan threatened to resign, Mrs. Stanford would no doubt have held her ground; had Jordan carried out his threat and taken the faculty with him, the University might have well expired. In Jordan's scale of judgment, the institution outweighed the individual: the value of the institution's existence was preponderant over other academic values."[11] This behavior, evident earlier during the excitement over alcohol on campus and in town, would present itself far more graphically in just a few years when doctors, attendants, and police rushed to Jennie's hotel room where she had gone into spasms of agony and death.

Sex and socialism may seem incongruous to some, but from Stanford University to San Francisco and beyond the two subjects had quickly become the talk of the town. Before long Jennie had to confront a salacious scandal involving biology professor Charles Henry Gilbert, who was caught in a library alcove with a female library employee, the two in a "peculiar situation," causing "embarrassment and disconcertment."[12] The reporting staff member, Assistant Librarian Alfred Schmidt, wrote to Jennie that when Gilbert realized Schmidt knew about the illicit liaison, the former's cronies looked the other way and implied Schmidt was fabricating a story. Schmidt, trying to save his own skin, told Mrs. Stanford the affair was common knowledge, named others who could corroborate the story, and claimed to have followed procedure by informing the university librarian, who took no action. That would have been Herbert Nash, the same Nash the Stanfords had hired as Leland Jr.'s tutor and who had stayed close to the family after the boy's death.

Then Schmidt looked to Jordan for help, but Gilbert was, like Jordan, an ichthyologist, and one Jordan had persuaded to come with him from Indiana University. Although a top administrator acting on behalf of Jordan wrote letters to the San Francisco papers asking them to "suppress" inflammatory reporting regarding Gilbert, a story about sex in the stacks appeared in the *San Francisco Examiner* and Schmidt was blamed. He swore he had nothing to do with it.[13]

The offended librarian had reason to count on Jennie's attitude regarding sex on campus. Her Victorian sensibilities had long prompted her to severely limit the possibility of what she considered inappropriate behavior at her child's memorial institution. In a letter to Jordan, Mrs. Stanford said she was particularly worried about reports of behavior at what today are called sororities: "As I understand that they are quite lawless and free in their social relations with the young men." Reports of easy virtue at a girls' residence caused her to fume, "They seem to be beyond our control."[14]

German Department chair Julius Goebel, who was said to be a favorite professor of Jennie's—she invited him to dinner parties and asked him on occasion to assess the state of the university—wrote to her in support of Schmidt and his concerns. Goebel said he and others had eyewitness accounts confirming the charges against Gilbert. He contended that Jordan owed Gilbert a great debt for backing the university president in the previous sackings of the other professors. "No greater triumph for Ross and Howard could be imagined," Goebel wrote, "than the downfall of Gilbert under such disgraceful circumstances." Agreeing with Schmidt that a "white-wash" was taking place, he told Mrs. Stanford he had talked to Jordan about Gilbert's conduct. But the university president countered that Schmidt "was a man of sexually perverted character who had been reading in the library books such as Krafft-Ebing's work on sexual perversion and that he had made up his mind to commit him immediately to an insane asylum if he did not leave California at once." Goebel said he went to the library immediately after this conversation and learned the offending book had never even been in the collection. 'I was shocked beyond description at the infamy of the President's charge as well as at his criminal threat to place an innocent, pureminded man of strong moral sense in an insane asylum, because he told the truth."[15] Jordan wrote Mrs. Stanford that the entire episode was a concocted attempt at vengeance and that Schmidt was simply a "tool."[16]

Schmidt was soon pushed out. Just three months after Jennie died a few years later, Jordan fired Goebel, claiming justification in part because Goebel had not properly borrowed library books. Harvard University immediately hired Goebel.[17] Jordan's friend Gilbert remained on the faculty for decades.

Outside the cloistered world of the university, much was afoot.

If history toggles between reaction and overreaction, point and counterpoint, corruption and reform, as most serious students of influence have observed, a natural balance of power sooner or later returns to its duty. The ascendancy of the Stanford group, the consolidation of railroads, and the consequences of the unregulated monopolies of the Gilded Age introduced a powerful new actor on the stage of American politics: the Progressive movement. In the East it was personified by the rise of Theodore Roosevelt, in the Midwest by Robert La Follette, in the West by Hiram Johnson. Some of the ramifications were the Sherman Antitrust Act, bank reform, and what would become the California Public Utilities Commission.

The men known today as the robber barons who followed Stanford could not have avoided seeing the turn of the tide. The wiser among them attempted to do something about it. Could it have been an accident that these men so often emulated Leland Stanford and used education as their vehicle? John D. Rockefeller of Standard Oil, taking a page from the Stanford playbook, endowed the University of Chicago but avoided the foundational missteps that plagued the Palo Alto university in its early years. Andrew Carnegie vowed to give away his steel fortune and largely did so with the establishment of Carnegie Mellon University in Pittsburgh, not to mention creating local libraries coast-to-coast. Joseph Pulitzer, as yellow a journalist as William Randolph Hearst but better able to see past his lurid daily headlines, endowed not just the journalism school at Columbia University but the Pulitzer Prizes, draping his multiple transgressions and unpleasantly peculiar personality with the robe of excellence.

Jennie Stanford was not without her charities. She gave a good deal of money to orphanages and even turned over ownership of the Sacramento mansion, where her son was born, to one run by the Roman Catholic Church. She also gave her childhood home in Albany to a long-standing secular orphanage.[18] In 1892, speaking with a reporter, the subject of regrets arose. "I had lived all my life up to that time entirely for my own pleasure," she reminisced of a time two years before her son died. She and Leland Jr. had gone to visit a kindergarten in a squalid part of San Francisco that she had contributed some money to in 1882. "The experience of that day and the joy expressed by those little children over the insignificant gifts that I had brought them opened my eyes to a phase of life that I did not realize existed," Jennie said. More importantly, "When we came out my boy said 'Mamma, I think that is the best thing you ever did in your life.'" After that Mrs. Stanford began quietly and generously funding kindergartens, at one point fifteen of them. Regardless, she told the reporter reflectively, "I can never live down those wasted years."[19]

Then there was her astonishing collection of jewelry. Several years after unsuccessfully trying to liquidate the lot in London, not much in society anymore, and increasingly finding purpose and pleasure in seeing the university bloom and blossom, Jennie decided to hand over her gems to the school's trustees. She directed them to sell "all my jewels, consisting of diamonds, rubies, emeralds, and other precious stones" and put the money toward the library.[20] This was a testimony to both Mrs. Stanford and President Jordan, as Leland Stanford had much earlier "thought a library 'such as a gentleman would have for his own use, to cost four or five thousand dollars,' would be sufficient," which said a good deal about the elder Leland's limited notions regarding not just the central importance of a library to a university but the purpose of higher education itself.[21]

Jennie, breaking through some of those barriers—in not insignificant measure under the influence of Jordan, who had consistently pushed for a superior library—nevertheless wanted to be able to recall her sentimental if ostentatious collection she would no longer wear, touch, or gaze at. Consequently, just before giving the jewels up, she hired a photographer and then painter to provide a lasting portrait of some of her favorites. Bertha Berner gave a dry account of the artist, barely concealing her dismay:

> The second afternoon he said to me "Do you think Mrs. Stanford will keep on coming in here?" I said "Surely; she is greatly interested in your nice work." Then he rose, turned to the stand with the pitcher of water, made a deep bow with a flourish, drew a flask from his pocket, and took a drink. Then he said, "Now you watch me put a little fire into that sapphire." And surely he did.[22]

He was sent home drunk twice, but he completed the painting.

Jennie, as did her late husband, chronically suffered from one malady or another. Unlike Leland, she regularly and bitterly complained of the stress the scandals caused her, failing to acknowledge her role in much of their creation. She began to divest herself of her responsibilities by selling the unencumbered securities in the railroad company and giving the proceeds to the trustees of the university, as well as ownership of the Nob Hill mansion. But even in that gift of stock, she demonstrated lack of preparedness for the great tasks before her. "Senator Stanford had told her to 'hang onto the Southern Pacific stock, for one day it will soar to par,'" wrote Crothers's biographer, who acknowledged his principal source was the efficient, fair-minded Crothers himself.[23] Instead, Mrs. Stanford found herself, during one of her extended stays in Europe, pressed by an international banking concern to sell her 25 percent interest for what was reported to be $16 million but at the end of the transaction came to $12.5 million.

"Unfortunately, there was no one at hand to advise her. She had invited George [Crothers] to make the trip with her, but he had been too busy to accept, a decision he always regretted as one of the major mistakes of his life." By 1912 the value of the stock had quadrupled, meaning it would have sold for $45 million, "enough to have made [Stanford] the richest university on earth then and for decades to come."[24]

Jennie then relinquished control of the university itself to the board of trustees and prepared to set off for her final, fatal adventure.

CHAPTER 18

"God Forgive Me My Sins.
Am I Prepared to Meet My Dear Ones?"

Jennie Stanford never remarried and there is no hint that she ever had a suitor. She did have, as her late husband had hoped, "something which would interest his wife for the rest of her life and give her solid satisfaction." Stanford University had become the avatar of her boy and the legacy of her man. Just crossing from the sunny side of her seventies, she began to let them go and find their—and her—own peace. It was not an easy transition.

She announced plans to travel for "a year or two," including a visit to Thomas Stanford in Australia, Leland's little brother, who through correspondence had been attentive to his sister-in-law and supportive of the university. "To Mrs. Stanford's astonishment she found him very different from what she expected," personal secretary Bertha Berner recalled. Rather than the healthy young man with a pronounced interest in medicine and the sciences he once was, he had transformed into a middle-aged man "very thin, and extremely nervous" and "not wanting to be diverted from his favorite topic of psychic research."[1]

Although Jennie had clearly never abandoned her interest in séances and what was then called Spiritualism, these leanings had been largely confined to reading about the subjects—though not exclusively so. For example, in the last half of the 1890s, a Stanford student who would go on to a distinguished journalism career was involved in a dispute at what was initially the boy's dormitory of Encina Hall. Getting no satisfaction from the administration, he and a group of other undergraduates went to "the court of last resort"—Mrs. Jane Stanford. After they made their case, she told the boys, "I'm going to talk it over with the Senator and Leland tonight, and get their decision."[2]

Although the late Leland Stanford had been firmly opposed to such superstitions, this kind of thing was a regular practice for his surviving younger
brother, Thomas. During Jennie's visit to him in Australia she quickly learned
that Thomas's Spiritualism was causing anxieties among his associates, which
left her in "a dejected mood" and "frightened her." They parted not on the best
of terms. "She never again attended a séance."[3]

After months of travel, Jennie returned home just in time for Christmas
of 1904. It was her last.

On a Saturday in the middle of January 1905 at the Nob Hill mansion, the
first alarm sounded. Berner recalled twenty-nine years later that Jennie had
been in a morning meeting with her lawyer, Russell Wilson. Then in the
afternoon she met with the university trustees despite her having a respiratory
infection. "Mrs. Stanford frequently had these terrible colds, would be confined to her bed for at least a week, and required another week before she could
get about again," Berner recalled.[4] George Crothers, although writing four
decades after the meeting, said Berner's memory was off: the lawyer named
was paralyzed from a stroke and the trustees met on Fridays. Crothers is not
to be ignored, as his record speaks of a man of integrity and accomplishment
who did honor to himself and Mrs. Stanford while being a great advantage to
the university and its future. On the other hand, Berner may have easily mixed
up Russell Wilson and Mountford Wilson, both of whom were Jennie's lawyers and one of whom had fallen ill.

It is generally agreed that before retiring that night Jennie drank half a
glass of bottled water but ceased because it was unusually bitter, and so she
vomited, stretching a finger down her throat. Jennie called Berner and a maid
named Elizabeth Richmond—there were eight servants at the mansion—and
asked them to taste the bottled water, which had been two-thirds full when
Jennie first poured the glass. Both agreed the water was disagreeably acrid, as
if someone had mixed it with Epsom salts, a mineral compound more properly
known as magnesium sulfate. Richmond took the remaining water to a San
Francisco drugstore for analysis, which forwarded it to another chemist
nearby. He found enough rat poison in it to kill a man.

Although it was Richmond who also drank some of the water, and took
responsibility for bringing it for analysis, Mrs. Stanford sacked her. Rattled,
the widow and Berner fled the city to what was then a comfortable resort hotel
in the warmth of San Jose. After replacing Richmond with a former maid
named Eva May Hunt, Jennie soon returned to San Francisco, this time

staying at the Saint Francis Hotel, being told the Nob Hill home was unsafe. The women did return to the mansion to pack during the day but at night slept at the hotel. That went on for two weeks. "My health somewhat impaired," Jennie wrote, "I am advised by my physician to take a sea voyage to Honolulu."[5] She and her entourage departed in the middle of February and after encountering heavy seas—Jennie was a good sailor but Hunt fared miserably—they went to their rooms at the sort of palatial hotel to which the Stanfords were accustomed, this time the Moana on Waikiki Beach.

In the meantime, Jennie's brother and her lawyer initiated an investigation in the Bay Area, hiring a colorful former sheriff of Alameda County, Harry Morse. He dispatched an operative to follow Richmond, who quickly spotted the tail. Richmond, of English ancestry, contacted Mrs. Stanford's former butler, also English, who incredibly enough, was actually named Alfred.[6] He was sufficiently upset to contact the British consul and complain about the Stanford team's tactics. Then the news from Hawaii exploded.

On the last day of February 1905, Jennie and her entourage went for a picnic on the other side of the Pali lookout about ten miles from their hotel. The small party took a carriage. Aside from being irritated that a gingerbread cake was not fresh from the hotel oven fast enough, Jennie openly enjoyed herself, singing along the route. She sat under the shade of a tree, ate some of the soggy gingerbread, and indulged in several large cream chocolates, ignoring doctor's orders to avoid sweets. Bertha Berner read a story to her, and they sat and ate and talked until about three o'clock, when they prepared to head back to the hotel. Two people had to pull Jennie out of her sitting position, and she had some difficulty walking to the carriage, which was not unusual. She remained, however, in fine fettle, looking forward to getting mail from the mainland in the morning. There is no evidence suggesting Jennie had received any questionable mail containing medicine before then. The party stopped at a clothing store and, with some dark irony, the mausoleum where Hawaiian royalty are interred. They then returned to the hotel.

Jennie rested in her room, donned a light summer dress, and had a dinner of tea and soup, saying she had eaten too much that afternoon. Jennie spent a spell on the lanai chatting with another guest, then she and Berner took a short stroll to a nearby pier. As she prepared to retire for the night, Jennie asked Berner to prepare a glass of water and some bicarbonate of soda, a favorite remedy of hers for indigestion, one she took just about every week. That night she also requested a pill with laxative properties. Berner dipped half a teaspoon of the soda powder out of a bottle and set it on the dressing table along with the capsule. The bicarbonate of soda and the pills had been purchased in the Bay Area and packed for the Hawaii trip. The bottle of soda had been left out during the day at the Nob Hill mansion in a room where packing took place. The doors to that room were locked at night. Moreover, the bicarbonate of soda had not been truly secure during the steamer voyage from San Francisco to Honolulu, which took almost a week. It is unknown whether Jennie used any during the trip.

The women said goodnight, Jennie going to her quarters and Berner to the room she shared next door with the maid they called May. It was about 9:00 P.M. "All was quiet and we were asleep," Berner wrote in her memoirs. Two hours later everyone at her end of the hallway awakened, hearing Jennie "clinging to the frame of her door," trembling and yelling, "Help, I am poisoned!"[7]

Berner rushed to her and led her back into the room. She sat her down in a chair and encouraged Jennie to drink a glass of warm water, but Mrs. Stanford said her jaw was locked. Berner massaged it and held the glass up again, which allowed Jennie to not only finish the drink but ingest another half dozen glasses of water. Berner said the object was to help her vomit and empty her stomach, as she had in San Francisco. Dr. Francis H. Humphries, a local physician with an impressive medical pedigree who lived at the hotel, arrived at the room shortly. Mrs. Stanford told him she had suffered a spasm so severe it had thrown her out of bed. Berner told him about the San Francisco poisoning. Dr. Humphries, first removing Jennie's false teeth, gave her a glass of water with mustard, also to induce vomiting, although only about an ounce of fluid came up. He was making a call to get a stomach pump when another physician arrived, Dr. Harry V. Murray, who saw Jennie sitting in the chair, head thrown back, hands clasped shut with thumbs bent inward. Her knees were apart and her feet arched upward. Her eyes were dilated and bulging, her jaw clenched. Her skin was hot. Berner testified that Jennie seemed to briefly recover but then said she was having another spasm. Both doctors were there.

"Oh God, forgive me my sins," Mrs. Stanford exclaimed, clutching Berner's hands to her neck. "Is my soul prepared to meet my dear ones?" And then her last words: "This is a horrible death to die," just as she experienced another violent spasm lasting about three minutes. Berner wrote that then "I felt her body sink a little in the chair, and her soul had left her body." Jane Lathrop Stanford was seventy-seven years old.[8]

Very shortly after they placed Jennie's dead body on her bed, the man with the stomach pump arrived, Dr. Francis R. Day. Dr. Humphries placed the bottle of bicarbonate of soda and the pills in his pocket. He also took the spoon. Dr. Murray took the small amount of vomit in a container. He also took a flask with some alcohol in it, which Jennie must have brought into her room. Dr. Day accompanied the other two physicians to Humphries's sitting room, where they placed all the possible evidence, keeping it secure. Dr. Humphries went to gather the authorities. Deputy High Sheriff William Rawlins then arrived, sealed the materials, and took them away for analysis. Very early the next morning, Mrs. Stanford's corpse was removed to the morgue at Queen's Hospital and an autopsy was scheduled for the following day. All three physicians had tasted the bicarbonate of soda, each finding it bitter. It should not have been. All three agreed that Jennie Stanford's symptoms replicated those of strychnine poisoning.

Dr. Clifford Wood performed the autopsy, but half a dozen physicians, a chemist, an undertaker, and several assistants were in attendance. A detailed clinical description of the procedure was provided at the official coroner's inquest by Wood and two others, with no material differences. They found that Mrs. Stanford's body position was very much the same as what was noted at the time of death: hands clenched and half closed, feet turned in and arched, toes extended. What few natural teeth she had were shut tight, her jaw set. Much of her body was unusually rigid. Much of her skin was a violet or dark purple. There were no external wounds. The internal organs were unremarkable, with some exceptions. The heart appeared "healthy for an organ of the age of this patient," despite having a good deal of fat on the surface and some small amount of scar tissue near one or two valves.[9] A small amount of blood in the heart was unusually dark and did not clot as it would normally. There was no reason to conclude Jennie died from failure of any internal organ, including the heart. About four fluid ounces were in the stomach but no undigested food. It would not be unusual for someone who ingested a fatal dose of strychnine to have a stomach showing no signs of the dose. However, the unusual rigidity of the body was a classic presentation of strychnine poisoning, or as the doctors spelled the substance, "strichnia" or "strychnia." Moreover, the unusually dark blood in one of the heart chambers and the absence of clotting was clear textbook evidence of one cause of death: strychnine poisoning.

Dr. Wood testified at the inquest that when someone dies of strychnine poisoning there is no "proof of death" from the toxin in the body's organs. Rather, the indication is in the collected evidence such as spasms shortly before death, body rigidity, and dark, clot-free blood in the heart. Noting that a very small amount of strychnine could easily kill an elderly, not terribly fit woman, Wood concluded, as did the other physicians, that "death was due to strichnia."[10] More evidence would be sought in the subsequent procedures.

Many of the internal organs were removed, placed in clean jars, and given to Robert Duncan, a chemist who worked for the then territorial government of Hawaii. He secured the many specimens along with other possible evidence, such as the remaining bottled water and the pills, in a locked laboratory, guarded by a police officer. Duncan was joined by Dr. Edmund Shorey, a chemist who worked for the federal government. They tested the pills and found inconsequentially small traces of strychnine in the capsules. Duncan dismissed this as naturally occurring in the medicine extracted from a plant containing the substance. Three separate tests of the bicarbonate of soda were more alarming, especially the second pair. Each test revealed strychnine, which should not have been in the bottle. And the additive was pharmaceutically pure, not rat poison as in the first attempt in San Francisco.

Then the chemists examined the internal organs and although they were "unable to separate any poisonous substance," Duncan pointed out that could happen if the toxin was distributed throughout the body in quantities too small to isolate. In keeping with the forensic practices of the day, they went so far as to mince the organs and blend them together to see if the aggregate would produce further evidence of strychnine. The result was "a color reaction that is characteristic when performed under proper precautions, of strychnia." Moreover, Dr. Day testified, "that color reaction as far as I know is not given by any other body but strychnia."[11]

The inquest recalled Dr. Humphries, who had arrived in Jennie's room minutes after Berner and Hunt. He had also attended the autopsy and was familiar with the chemical analyses. Humphries was asked, "Do I understand you Doctor, to state here as your opinion that Mrs. Stanford did not die of natural causes?" Humphries answered, "Absolutely." Then: "And what in your opinion was the cause of death?" The answer: "She died of strychnia poisoning." The inquest pushed the answer: "She died of strychnia poisoning." Dr. Humphries responded with one word: "Absolutely."[12]

It was time for the six jurors of the coroner's inquest to render a verdict. It was unanimous:

> Upon their oaths, do say *that said Jane Lathrop Stanford came to her death, at Honolulu, Island of Oahu, Territory of Hawaii, on the twenty-eighth day of February, A.D. 1905, from Strychine poisoning, said strychnine having been introduced into a bottle of bicarbonate of soda with felonious intent by some person or persons to this Jury unknown and the contents of which bottle Jane Lathrop Stanford had partaken.*[13]

She was, in a word, murdered.

The cover-up story began almost immediately. Stanford University president David Starr Jordan was the author.

Accompanied by a member of the university's board of trustees, a San Francisco Police detective, and a private investigator, Jordan sailed to Hawaii four days after Jennie died.[14] They arrived March 4. Jordan quickly contacted a young local physician who had a laudable academic background but had been in practice little more than a year: Dr. Ernest Waterhouse. He had not been at the death scene, nor the autopsy, nor the chemical analysis, nor the coroner's inquest. In fact, he never even saw the body. Jordan paid him to write a report, which he did. The four pages he delivered were not made public.

"I fail to find one characteristic symptom of strychnine poisoning," the doctor wrote to his client. Instead, he found that when Mrs. Stanford experienced the initial spasm reported by Jennie to Berner, it "might have been hysteria, or a mild attack of angina pectoris or sudden start from a dream due to her indigestion, or what not." Dr. Waterhouse reported that "clearly this was hysteria or at least a nervous symptom." Dismissing the following spasms witnessed by the physicians who were present, he added, "The very fact that the patient could remain sitting on an ordinary stiff-backed chair would almost rule out a convulsion from strychnine poisoning." As for the textbook examples cited by the team of analysts, Waterhouse compared experiments with frogs poisoned by strychnine to Mrs. Stanford's situation. Instead of death by poison, he concluded that Jennie may have suffered from angina because she had eaten too much at lunch, not enough at dinner, and had "taken a long ride which was undue exertion for her."

Continuing, Waterhouse wrote that "there was evidently considerable gas in the stomach pressing against the heart and interfering with its action and leading to considerable distress." Waterhouse noted that everyone in the hotel room, convinced that Jennie had been poisoned, added to the mass hysteria that led to her death and their diagnosis. Moreover, the many glasses of water "might readily cause a fatal result from fatty heart." The doctor then cited research evidence that some heart attacks are disguised and "easily overlooked." He called the autopsy report "meager."[15]

Waterhouse simply dismissed or outright disregarded the collected symptoms of strychnine poisoning: the coloration of the internal organs peculiar to the toxin, the spasms that every medical textbook says are indicative of its presence, the unusually dark and clot-free blood of the heart, and the presence of pure strychnine in the bicarbonate of soda that would have had to be added. Moreover, he ignored the empty contents of Jennie's stomach, her delight in the ride to Pali and back, instead suggesting, with no medical evidence whatsoever, that indigestion may have caused the heart to fail, a suggestion that Dr. Humphries openly scoffed. Finally, and emphatically, Waterhouse relied on the hoary shibboleth of female hysteria. He did not even acknowledge the team of notable physicians and scientists who had spent countless hours on the postmortem examinations, not to mention the independent law enforcement officials.

Within a week of receiving Waterhouse's report, Jordan transubstantiated the speculative conclusions into a fish story. "Not a single symptom recognized as occurring in strychnine poisoning was present in her case," Jordan wrote to a university trustee. "The symptoms were those of heart failure." He claimed that "the heart has not been examined." Then he gave a first indication of how he would eventually mutate the medical facts into a narrative so confusing it would effectively conceal the murder for decades: "The carbonate with a trace of strychnine was for some hours in the possession of Dr. Humphries." Further libeling the attending physician, Jordan wrote, "He is man without professional or personal standing and his diagnosis as well as his proposed fee were involved in having strychnine found in Mrs. Stanford's possession." Lastly, Jordan dispensed with the earlier poisoning incident as irrelevant.[16]

David Starr Jordan had traveled from simple sophistry to a reckless disregard for the truth. Jennie Stanford's heart had been closely examined and though found not to be in prime condition, was reasonably normal for an elderly, chronically overweight woman. The bicarbonate of soda had been in

Humphries's possession only long enough to go from Jennie's room to his quarters in the same hotel and was out of view of others, at most, for no more than minutes, if at all. As for the diversionary ad hominem attack on Humphries, his professional and personal standing included being a fellow of the Royal College of Physicians in Edinburgh, licensed by the Royal College of Physicians in London, and a member of the Royal College of Surgeons in England. What's more, he enjoyed so much career-long veneration by the medical community that he was elected by his peers to high position in the Hawaiian medical society before moving back to London, where he earned an international reputation for excellence. Unlike Dr. Waterhouse, who was paid to make an ex post facto report, Dr. Humphries first rushed to assist a dying patient late at night and then appropriately expected compensation for his professional services. Jordan's charges and implications were scandalously unsubstantiated, far beneath even his earlier hypocrisies regarding alcohol, sexual improprieties, and the firing of professors who did not toe his tarnished line.

Jordan, who also wrote and spoke openly about what he regarded as the racial inferiority of Hawaiians—as well as others such as the French and southern Italians—then issued a press release gently smearing the Honolulu authorities and alluding to Waterhouse's conclusions.[17] Ever wily, Jordan released the statement just as he was embarking on a ship back to San Francisco, taking Mrs. Stanford's remains with him. The six-day trip not only would make it difficult for anyone to question his pronouncements but would effectively allow the story to simmer down and fall off the front pages. Before the age of daily transpacific flights between California and Hawaii, email, and instant text messaging, an understandably eager audience of reporters awaited him on the San Francisco Bay docks. There were no representatives from the Hawaiian medical, forensic science, or law enforcement communities. Jordan, consequently, had a good deal of control over the news narrative on the mainland, which he exploited deftly, further confusing the events so much that no one publicly sorted the facts for almost a century.

The Hawaiians did not go quietly. The four physicians involved in the autopsy or inquest issued a joint statement recapping all the documented findings, taking especial umbrage at the implication that the poisoned bottle of bicarbonate of soda had been spiked after Jennie died. "There is a chain of evidence that will hold fast under the fiercest assault," they declared. Warming to the task, the doctors then stated, "It is imbecile to think that a woman of Mrs. Stanford's age and known mental characteristics might have died of an hysterical seizure in half an hour." Finally, they cited leading medical texts of the time that described the classic, if technical, symptoms of strychnine poisoning, which were very much those presented by Mrs. Stanford.[18]

Although many newspaper accounts of the era are best treated with skepticism and sometimes simply skipped when contradictory facts are available, the story that made the national press on the last day of 1905 cannot be so easily dismissed. "The report that Mrs. Stanford was murdered was part of a plot engaged in by several of Mrs. Stanford's servants, who were jealous of the favor with which Mrs. Stanford treated Miss Berner, her private secretary," the *New York Times* as well as many other newspapers across the country reported.

There is no direct proof of the story's source, but it must be noted that at the same time, in a private letter to a colleague, Jordan declared that his patroness had been murdered by her servants.

Nevertheless, the *New York Times* quoted the university president: "'We have established beyond a doubt that Mrs. Stanford died a natural death,' said Dr. Jordan. 'A post-mortem examination showed that the aorta had been ruptured.'"[19] The news story forewent any proof, instead stating that Jordan would present his evidence shortly. Two days later he said he had been misquoted and would have more to say later. Adding some garnish, the private detective Jordan had hired and brought with him to Hawaii jumped in to defend his boss: "I feel sure Dr. Jordan did not come out and make any such statements as those attributed to him," largely because he said Jordan had not seen the detective's report. Moreover, "if we had any such evidence as Dr. Jordan claims is on hand we would have made arrests long ago."[20] Any careful reader would have been baffled.

As difficult as it is to believe that Jordan had not the seen the private detective's report he paid for, it is still more incredible to accept his denial of accusing the help of murder, which he had earlier. But, of course, if he stood by the charge against the household staff, that would contradict his claim that Jennie died of natural causes.

The public story about the ruptured aorta caught the attention of Dr. Humphries. He wrote Jordan asking for an explanation. A week later Jordan replied, writing that he had said Mrs. Stanford died from some manner of heart ailment. That did not placate Humphries, who then requested that Jordan explain his reasoning for suggesting that heart disease caused the death.

Jordan responded again, this time with the tortured rationale he had originally presented.

Jordan next hired a Dr. William Ophüs of Cooper Medical School in San Francisco. That institution was faltering after a scandal involving its top administrator and was searching for a safe harbor, namely, Stanford University. Coincidence or not, Jordan rescued the Cooper Medical School and made it part of Stanford the next year. Dr. Ophüs, coming to Jordan's rescue, and who would be named top man after the tainted Cooper administrator departed, accepted Jordan's request to examine what was left of Mrs. Stanford's remains months after the murder. Most of the internal organs had been reduced to a viscous slurry, which may or may not have included the heart. It was never made clear. Even under the best-case scenario, had the heart been left intact, the outcome of its examination was and remains unclear.

The so-called Ophüs report was never seen in public. Then it completely disappeared.

Jordan just couldn't let his meddling over Jennie's murder languish. Ever. Sixteen years later, at age seventy, he wrote to then Stanford president Ray Lyman Wilbur, stating at the top that there should be some official record at the school about what happened. The letter goes on to recount a revision of the facts, one written by a man uncomfortable about his role in the episode and still trying to spin it. His instinct to falsely fault someone returned to Dr. Humphries, whom he barely condescended to recall, then eagerly libeled again as a "remittance man, if not of good reputation." Among many small and large fictions he manufactured, Jordan wrote that Humphries "seemed dazed as if under the influence of some drug," adding that the doctor "said something to the effect that it contained strychnine enough to kill a dozen men." But that was hardly enough. He also added a snarky line saying that Humphries's "motives can only be inferred from his actions." Jordan then wrote that Dr. Waterhouse had determined Jennie's death was "due, he thought most probably, to a rupture of the coronary artery," which, of course, he never did. Jordan said the heart was "carefully preserved" and sent to the Cooper school, which confirmed Waterman's diagnosis, although that report has never been found. Then Jordan libeled "the chemist" who analyzed the internal organs, saying he was later "dismissed from Government service for fraudulent analyses." He disregarded the fact that there were two notable such men and that neither were ever dismissed or charged with fraud. It is true that a suspect fellow employee of one wrote Jordan a letter making a series of unsubstantiated charges against the principal toxicologist. But that was the end of that.

Finding a way to explain—or further confuse—his earlier contradiction that Jennie died of natural causes and at the same time was poisoned by the physician who rushed to save her, not to mention that he somehow added the strychnine to the bottle *after* she died, Jordan turned again to the servants. He named the almost forgotten English maid, Elizabeth Richmond. He said his private detective had found she was "subject to periodic attacks of mania, that the chief topics of her conversation with her associates turned on her experiences in the houses of the English aristocracy, with numerous anecdotes of those members of high society who had died from poisoning." Such details not only had never surfaced, but the same private detective financed by the Jordan group was the man who had declared Richmond and the other Stanford household servants to be innocent. Moreover, Richmond, fired after the Nob Hill episode, did not travel to Hawaii with Jennie. In his autobiography, published the year after his letter to Wilbur, Jordan called the poisoning a "false rumor" and repeated many of his false assertions.[21]

If one surviving member of this murder mystery cast of characters came to a sordid ending, it was the pivotal figure of Dr. Ernest Waterhouse. Seven years after Jennie died, Waterhouse shut down his medical practice and chased his other interest, rubber tree plantations. In the first years he enjoyed marked commercial success, but by the 1920s this started to dissipate. His personal life also took a turn for the worse, with two divorces. During the subsequent decade, the Great Depression was no friend to Waterhouse. By the late 1930s he was down-and-out in San Francisco's notorious Tenderloin district, living in a flophouse, selling newspapers on the street, and quite ill. History's sometimes grotesque sense of humor found him hospitalized at what was once the Cooper Medical School but had evolved into the Stanford hospital in Palo Alto, where he died at age seventy-five in 1947, leaving an estate of about $125.

Very little of the Jane Lathrop Stanford death story was told with any integrity until 2003, when Stanford University Medical School professor Robert W. P. Cutler inadvertently became curious about the tale. His subsequent expert analysis of the evidence led him to conclude that Jordan's conspiracy theories were "preposterous" and that "President Jordan's efforts to prove that Mrs. Stanford died of some form of heart disease resulted in a cover-up." In Dr. Cutler's finely understated, official medical judgment, "the conclusion that Mrs. Stanford was murdered is difficult to avoid."[22]

Attempting to come to some conclusion about why and who killed Jennie Stanford is a far thornier puzzle. The least likely suspect is Jennie herself.

In trying to make the case for suicide, one can take into consideration that she was one of the few people with access to the bottled water in San Francisco and the bicarbonate of soda in Honolulu. She knew she had been poisoned in both instances. For years she constantly talked and wrote about being reunited with her son and husband. Her correspondence is replete with self-pity and references to enormous stresses, and of course she was chronically ill. However, she not only did not drink the entire first spiked glass of bicarbonate of soda mix in her Nob Hill citadel, she called in two of her most trusted servants and asked them to taste-test the water. The several people who accompanied her on the last day of her life in Hawaii agreed that she was in cheerful spirits and eagerly looking forward to getting mail from home the next day. She also called out as soon as she felt the effects of the strychnine and asked for help. Berner wrote that Mrs. Stanford abhorred suicide and when told or read about it occurring always condemned the practice.

The only other person with direct access to the poisoned bottles in both instances was her long-time personal and confidential secretary Bertha Berner, who was initially the prime suspect and found her name tossed about by investigators and then, naturally, the press. Berner was in Jennie's will and would get $15,000 upon her employer's death, no inconsiderable sum in 1905, when an average working wage was 25 cents an hour, a respectable man's suit cost $15, and a middle-class house sold for $3,000. Jennie's bequest to her secretary had not changed and there was no indication that it would. In addition, Jennie had already given Berner a fine home in Palo Alto and always brought her along on luxurious, first-cabin travel around the world. There is no indication that was about to change either. If Berner was interested in killing the goose that laid the golden egg, she had countless better opportunities during her two decades with her patroness.

There was a good deal of loose talk about Jennie's other servants, such as Elizabeth Richmond, her fellow English subject Alfred Beverly, and the lately hired Eva May Hunt. In addition, a servant of Chinese ancestry was mercilessly interrogated, although no one seemed to be able to fathom why or how he could have been guilty. Richmond had left Jennie's employ before the

Hawaii trip. Beverly had departed the Stanford household service even earlier, albeit under less than cordial circumstances. And Hunt was not employed by Jennie until after the Nob Hill attempt. It is theoretically possible that one or more had dosed the bicarbonate of soda when it was not under lock and key or being watched, but there is no evidence whatsoever of that taking place. There was no apparent motive for any of the help to want Jennie dead. All, including Berner, were emphatically cleared by private and city detectives.

Which brings the mystery to the doorstep of David Starr Jordan. Opportunity, he had none or little. He may have been at the Stanford estate in Palo Alto and perhaps could have salted the bottled water with strychnine, but it's a stretch to imagine how. He might have reached for the bicarbonate of soda bottle shortly before Jennie's party took the steamer to Hawaii, but the same qualification applies. He might have colluded with one of the servants—if so, Berner would have been the most likely—but that scenario implies some level of intimacy of which there is zero evidence. As for motive, some have suggested he may have had one: fear of being the next employee to get fired. Jennie certainly expressed annoyance and even upset with Jordan about many issues, and there is reason to believe she had at least three conversations with some trustees—for example, George Crothers—about replacing Jordan when she was frustrated. But that was her mercurial pattern on and off for years, always ending with warm letters of praise, gratefulness, and more than just polite inquiries about Jordan's wife and children. There is absolutely nothing in Jordan's character indicating he could be capable of murder. It is fairly certain he could have left Stanford University for another, if not commensurate, excellent job in academia, a profession of gypsies to begin with.

"Even the most vivid conjecture resists the notion of Jordan slipping into Mrs. Stanford's San Francisco pantry, bath, or bedroom to spike her mineral water or lace her bicarbonate of soda with strychnine," concluded a scholarly study not disposed to be charitable to Jordan.[23] Finally, it is difficult to suggest a rational motive for his engineering Jennie's demise. Killing her would cause only a huge new crisis, a much bigger problem than he found thrust upon him by her death. The hypothesis makes as much sense as Jordan's own unsupportable, contradictory conspiracy theories.

It is far more likely that Jordan, already dealing with funding crises, scandal, and scorn from some of the most revered people in academia, simply could not accept still another major controversy and fell upon his deep instincts to control at any cost. An intelligent man and a survivor in the serpentine world of politics in the academy, he marshaled his considerable clout to obscure the investigation so seriously that it became essentially impossible to know who killed Jane Lathrop Stanford and why. Which may well have been exactly his intention.

In demanding that the first and famous president of Stanford University answer for his actions, it is apt to recall a skeptical scholar's observation that "Jordan could not afford to admit that the world was a complex place; we cannot afford to deny it."[24]

American Disruptor

Writer Richard Rodriguez, born in San Francisco, raised in Sacramento, and no stranger to Los Angeles, reminisced about his coming-of-age in California, "I cherish our fabulous mythology." "Not the dead California of Spaniards and forty-niners and Joan Didion's grandmother," he wrote in *Days of Obligation*. Instead, he "craved the ALL-NEW and ALL-ELECTRIC" California that today certainly includes the so-called tech campuses and office "parks" of Silicon Valley, the companies and tech celebrities, and even children who affix a dot-com to their names, which are, indeed, their brands.[1]

A father of this progeny is Amasa Leland Stanford. Put another way, he is an anchor asset of the myth, and he continues to deeply inform not just California, the West, and the United States of America, but also the world, if only through the seemingly random course history is likely to take. And yet, the hard, sharp, and glossy stuff of myth also raises questions of depth, scope, and authenticity.

The stock depictions of Stanford as either hero or goat may have tinted the legend but bleached his humanity. Fundamentally, it can be said that Leland Stanford was, in the end, an ordinary man who found himself in extraordinary circumstances. "To measure up to all that is demanded of him," an old adage instructs, "a man must overestimate his capabilities." What Stanford did— what he accomplished—in the state of affairs he found himself in is seldom met in the course of human events. He was certainly guilty of many shabby performances, but given the stage he found himself on, unprepared by upbringing, temperament, and history itself, what else can be fairly expected of a man?

Indeed, Stanford can be justly credited with being instrumental in building modern America under some of the most trying circumstances imaginable, underscoring the American catechistic faith in what a person can accomplish when purpose and perseverance unite. That he as a young man could not possibly have been admitted as a student to the university he created toward the end of his life signifies his ultimate success rather than his penultimate failures.

Churchill wrote of a mysterious ruler of Britain contemporaneous with the far better-celebrated Charlemagne of France, "We are like geologists who instead of finding a fossil find only the hollow shape in which a creature of unusual strength and size undoubtedly resided."[2] Something of the same may be said of Leland Stanford. The world around him molded to his presence, yet he remains enigmatic. Stanford, in an oddly passive-aggressive manner, continues to challenge from afar. Who *was* he? His fidelity to family was irreducible. Beyond that peerless virtue, even eulogist David Starr Jordan privately danced around his patron's checkered integrity in public affairs. In Jordan's copious if superficial memoirs, he described Stanford as a "person of massive build, and rather slow-spoken. Though extremely direct and earnest. He had a considerable fund of dry humor," the afterthought having the faint odor of Jordan cooking his reminiscence to be polite, since it is difficult to find anyone who made a similar observation.[3]

Herbert Nash, who started as Leland Jr.'s tutor but stayed with the Stanfords long after the boy's death and became a family confidant for decades, provides more insight:

> It is doubtful if he has ever given his fullest confidence to any man. . . . [T]here is even to the most intimate relation an unexpressed reserve,—a department of thought and being not wholly disclosed, producing the irresistible conclusion in the minds of his most intimate friends, that the limit of his confidence has been controlled by most judicious measurement.

During their many years together at close quarters, Nash wrote, "I have seen him unmoved by great catastrophies, and by great happiness. Good and evil fortune seem to affect him alike—or rather, alike seem not to affect him." And then, "Senator Stanford is a man I may almost say without any intimate friends," adding "I mean that he has not around him those personal friends which we find most of us have." Certainly, one can catch sight of some emotional depth as early as Stanford's rare letter to his unrequited Hannah when in Wisconsin and his obvious grief following the death of his teenage son, which Nash witnessed. That central loss may have well cauterized Stanford's heartfelt vulnerabilities.[4]

Hubert Howe Bancroft, the often celebrated nineteenth-century historian of the West who fell out with Stanford, did imply the robber baron's tendency to draw back into himself when confronted by his wealth and fame. One day, Bancroft noted, a clerk for a local business directory came to the New York offices of the Southern Pacific to gather some information. Not recognizing the great man, the clerk asked Stanford his occupation. Without any irony, he said to list him as a farmer.[5]

History has had more success catching glimpses of Jane Lathrop Stanford, but not sufficiently so. She is sometimes depicted as a saint, sometimes a battle-ax, but all too frequently as a two-dimensional character. A common public description of Jennie in a newspaper of her day was "lovable for every womanly quality."[6] Bertha Berner, usually laudatory, recalled that 'Mrs. Stanford came to rule people through her wealth, and no crown or title could have made her rule more absolute." Writing with affection and respect, Berner added, "She spoke her mind very freely, and usually people seemed afraid to oppose her in any way."[7]

"Mrs. Stanford remains a particularly enigmatic personality," writer and former Stanford University archivist Roxanne Nilan concluded.

> Her image is remarkably malleable while the reality remains elusive. She seems not quite human. In part, it is because both Leland and Jane Stanford are veiled in the fables of the founding and difficult early years of Stanford University. They are integral to a carefully monitored public image of an institution that personifies itself in such terms as "pioneering," "innovative" and "progressive."[8]

Although many of Jennie's letters are stored and have been scanned, there is reason to believe she had a more intimate and revealing diary she destroyed later in life, as she did much of her husband's correspondence, prompting further questions about what she did not wish known.

More than a few have dismissed Jennie as "emotional," falling into tired female typecasting as did the dubious Dr. Waterhouse, who suggested her death was the result of "hysteria." It may be more appropriate to substitute for "emotional" that she was often sympathetic, usually emphatic, and consistently intense. No one who carefully reads her not inconsiderable surviving correspondence can fail to see that Jennie Stanford was left a mess without much preparation and so understandably lurched from one action to another cleaning it up. But it must be said there is little evidence of outright duplicity. Her sincerity, whether her conduct was even or uneven, hot or cold, right or wrong, was fairly constant. Her last years as a widow took place during a decade of raging seas in big business, in which she created a major university and managed a huge estate in turmoil before she began to feel she had piloted the ships to harbor, very much to her credit.

She did have major help, especially in George Crothers during the latter years, and to some not insignificant extent, David Starr Jordan. But to the latter, the record is compromised. Jennie's murder has been clinically clear since 1905, the year she was fatally poisoned. The subsequent obfuscations by Jordan, who first appeared as the Stanfords' noble vizier, then obsequious courtier, ultimately reveals him as a simple betrayer of the plain justice due to Jennie. Jordan's jumping from one implausible, contradictory, and dishonorable explanation to the next has been so powerfully confusing, yet influential, that it continues to encourage the insufficiently informed, equally sycophantic, and overly timid to retreat to the safer ground of caricature, image—and myth—surrounding the Stanfords.

There is far less risk in coming to terms with the railroad enterprise, which is one good reason there continues to be a surfeit of books, movies, and television shows just about that, however cartoonish or pedantic they can be. It must be said that the rails being central to the history of the nation is without question. "In the view of most historians, whatever the costs, the railroad was *the* key to industrialization," notes a distinguished scholar.[9] One can see the iconography today in our great, and formerly great, cities. It was the train station that was the monument of the late nineteenth- and early twentieth-century metropolis, as were the churches of ancient Europe, and are the corporate headquarters of our age. The restored Ferry Building of San Francisco is the authentic exception proving the rule, being the true terminus of the transcontinental railroad that ran to ground on the opposite side of the bay in Oakland, where the ferry boats gathered passengers for the final leg across the water to the fabled world-class city, now recipient of Stanford-silicon riches and what is commonly considered the second California gold rush.

Leland Stanford as key to the rail enterprise is certain. The "grimly energetic"[10] Stanford group's transcontinental road was, of course, not the only train system, but it was and remains the spine of the iron and steel network that largely achieved the intended tying of the nation together, first because of the Civil War and then for the industrial age. The railroad, as with Stanford's life, was an often sloppy, corrupt, and controversial enterprise. That, also as with Stanford, simply adds boldface type to the importance of knowing and trying to understand its vital role, so often lost to demonization or glorification. This is neatly addressed by eminent historian Robert Fogel, who lamented the celebrated image of the railroad industry, its promoters conceding only an inconsequential blemish or two in an otherwise heroic narrative: "Once formed, myths are sturdy things," Fogel wrote, implicitly remonstrating the mythmakers. 'They can withstand the findings of a dozen documented studies."[11] Stuart Daggett, usually a dry data man, is nonetheless understandably and correctly blunt about the Big Four in his essential 1922 book, *Chapters on the History of the Southern Pacific*, calling the quartet "rough, vigorous and grasping men," describing them as "narrow in vision, uneducated and inexpert in the details of railroad operation."[12]

If one person can personify the epic historic evolution of agrarian, adolescent, America into industrial, world power USA, there is no better avatar than Leland Stanford. Born in a bar along the newborn Erie Canal and first chartered railroad that signified America's entrance to the industrial age; a prime entrepreneur of the mainspring of the nation's emergence as a world power; and taking his last breath on the university campus he created, which a generation later became birthplace and incubator of the silicon age—these facts are enough to tell the Leland Stanford story during an elevator ride. Not to make too fine a point, there is value in reflecting on the almost fateful foreshadowing of the forefather of Silicon Valley: the financial, political, cultural, and environmental havoc caused by the Erie Canal and Mohawk & Hudson railroad of his early youth and the commensurate turmoil created by Stanford's venture; the coincidence of betrayals associated with Stanford's given biblical name of Amasa and his treacherous dramas with Collis Huntington; the lashing together of the nation by Stanford's iron rails and today's internet.

That late-winter 1852 fire in Port Washington, Wisconsin, during the dead of night burned through far more than a square block of an obscure northern village, a country lawyer's office, and all Stanford had pasted together there. It all but incinerated his past and helped lay waste to a way of life America would not see again. That icy, fiery day cleared the board for Leland Stanford's first bold, if anguished, step that changed the way billions of people now live.

In one of those astonishingly prescient testaments given to some, nineteenth-century writer Henry George somehow caught not just the meaning of his time but the future as well, plotting the arc from its brisk curve. Although his article was written the year before the last spike was driven into the desert dirt of Promontory Summit and titled "What the Railroad Will Bring Us," much of it remains a precognition any true Californian will straightaway recognize, as will millions of other Americans now coming under the same spell. Its essence:

> The new era into which our State is about entering—or, perhaps, to speak more correctly, has already entered is without doubt an era of steady, rapid and substantial growth; of great addition to population and immense increase in the totals of the Assessor's lists. Yet we cannot hope to escape the great law of compensation which exacts some loss for every gain.
>
> We imagine that if the genius of California, whom we picture on the shield of our State, were really a sentient being, she would not look forward now entirely without regret. The California of the new era will be greater, richer, more powerful than the California of the past; but will she be still the same California whom her adopted children, gathered from all climes, love better than their own mother lands; from which all who have lived within her bounds are proud to hail; to which all who have known her long to return? She will have more people; but among those people will there be so large a proportion of full, true men? She will have more wealth; but will it be so evenly distributed? She will have more luxury and refinement and culture; but will she have such general comfort, so little squalor and misery; so little of the grinding, hopeless poverty that chills and cramps the souls of men, and converts them into brutes?
>
> No: the potent charm of California, which all feel but few analyze, has been more in the character, habits and modes of thought of her people—called forth by the peculiar conditions of the young State than in anything else. In California there has been a certain cosmopolitanism, a certain freedom and breadth of common thought and feeling, natural to a community made up from so many different sources, to which every man and woman had been transplanted all travelers to some extent, and with native angularities of prejudice and habit more or less worn off. Then there has been a feeling of personal independence and equality, a general hopefulness and self-reliance, and a certain large-heartedness and open-handedness which were born of the comparative evenness with which property was distributed, the high standard of wages and of comfort, and the latent feeling of every one that he might "make a strike," and certainly could not be kept down long.
>
> The characteristics of the principal business—mining—gave a color to all California thought and feeling. It fostered a reckless, generous, independent spirit, with a strong disposition to "take chances" and "trust to luck."[13]

It wasn't that long between the time Leland Stanford took his last breath and Silicon Valley took its first. The two are inextricably entwined.

As early as the 1930s—just a generation after Stanford University's founders had passed—electrical engineers such as Russell Varian, who earned his graduate degree at Stanford in 1927, and his brothers were finding success in aligning the university's heritage of mechanical arts with industry and government, as Leland Stanford would have very much wanted. Immediately after World War II, the university's dean of engineering, Frederick Emmons Terman, steeped in the philosophy of mentors such as Vannevar Bush, brought the concept to a significant new level of play. "The key thing was to turn ideas into technology," a Silicon Valley history notes. And "foremost in Terman's plan was that the university would be the center of the technical community providing innovations, training, and guidance."[14] It was, as two other early Silicon Valley chroniclers put it, a "technological watershed."[15] Stanford's immense land grant, more than eight thousand acres, allowed the university to act on Terman's plans and set property aside for just those industries, where Varian Associates was the first tenant in 1949 and other partnerships took hold during the 1950s.

One of Terman's students, a young man named David Packard, joined by fellow Stanford student and friend William Hewlett, who famously began their work in a Palo Alto garage in 1938, were among the first to house their enterprise in what was called the Stanford Research Park. Others were recruited. Nobel Prize–winner William Shockley, who grew up in Palo Alto and later at Bell Labs in New Jersey was one of the key inventors of the transistor, was lured to Stanford in 1956 but soon started his own semiconductor business in nearby Mountain View, now hometown to Google. Gordon Moore, Robert Noyce, and Eugene Kleiner first came to work for Shockley, then broke off and started their own companies, beginning with Fairchild Semiconductor, which in turn spawned fifty new companies just between 1959 and 1979. By 1971, when Ted Hoff had designed the basic microprocessor architecture, the term *Silicon Valley* came into vogue.

"Stanford is probably the reason the Silicon Valley is here," said James Clark, of Netscape.[16] Clark was one of the valley's first multibillionaires, an event not unnoticed. "More people became richer in Silicon Valley, and became richer faster, than at any time in the history of the western world," noted Shockley's biographer.[17] When Leland Stanford announced that he was starting a university in honor and memory of his fallen son, he famously is reputed to have said, "The children of California will be our children." Those offspring today number Scott McNealy of Sun Microsystems, Steve Ballmer of Microsoft,

Elon Musk of Tesla, and of course, Sergey Brin and Larry Page of Google. The list is very long and growing at a rapid pace. Far more than just a philosopher's stone—the legendary substance said to be capable to turning ordinary metals to gold—Silicon Valley has transformed economies, politics, and cultures across the planet. The internet itself emerged at the Stanford Research Institute in 1969 when the first packet of information arrived from UCLA.[18]

The mythical tool of the alchemist in the nineteenth century might be said to have been the railroad. Some hundred years after the rails connected at Promontory Summit, the internet used silicon microprocessors to bind people across vast differences. As with the transcontinental road, the internet was largely funded by American taxpayers and provided place and purpose, creating worldwide upheaval and fortunes. As with the iron and steel road, the net has passed countless others who are subject to the new world order yet relegated to passenger status, often in third-class compartments and steerage. Its ability to unite—and divide—has little precedent in history and its full consequences are far from understood.

Leland Stanford was no stranger to upheaval and insurrection, hard-featured and even execrable as they often were. He grew up around tumult, embraced it, and finally became known as its engineer and conductor, though so many others actually did the grunt work. He, as with the high-tech stars of today, grew rich and famous, an ambition many have blindly chased for millennia—and paid a steep price for it. Around the time Leland Stanford's ancestor Thomas left England for North America in the mid-1600s, William Penn might have dryly noted No Cross, No Crown. Today it is fair to assert that Leland Stanford was and remains the authentic American disruptor, blessed and damned.

His platinum-plated monument stands today, thousands of acres of patterned tranquility where further chaos is quietly manufactured behind the rough-hewn sandstone walls of handsomely appointed laboratories, classrooms, and offices.

From the start, Stanford University has stirred admiration, envy, curiosity, and contempt. Historian Hubert Howe Bancroft was among the first to spew the latter.

> It is difficult to disgrace a man with 40 millions in his pocket, even though the millions were stolen, and the people enslaved, bound in fetters forged out of their own money, even though the millions were employed in electing governors, buying

legislatures, bribing senators, and insulting and humiliating citizens; or perhaps in erecting churches and hospitals not for the glory of God, but for their own glory, and as a sop to Cerberus; in founding a college wherein young people may forever be taught to honor infamy; in building for vulgar display a Nob Hill palace, which brings neither honor nor comfort and soon to be licked up by charitable flames.

Bancroft added, "In default of an heir he found a university which was to make high crime respectable." Not yet done, Bancroft wrote that when Stanford, as a U.S. senator was accused by a California colleague of stealing the public's money, the railroad baron defended himself by saying his money went to fund a university. Bancroft says the accusing senator responded, "We do not want our children to be educated with stolen money." Putting a still sharper edge on the exchange, Bancroft added, "But from the large attendance at the institution, and the pains taken by the faculty upon all occasions to preach political purity, it would seem that the gentleman from California was mistaken."[19]

Stanford University's robust if appropriately haughty publicity department today simply ignores such historical invectives and does its best to conspicuously ignore modern ones, instead focusing on the university's many notable past and present accomplishments.

Putting it together, it becomes increasingly obvious how and why Silicon Valley is where it is and why it is so difficult to replicate anywhere else. Risk, reward, failure, and then again more risk shared among people of all cultures, complexions, and languages have become as traditional and accepted in California as Bundt cake at a midwestern county fair. This mix hasn't always been—and isn't to this day—always becoming, but surely it has been evolving for centuries. California has long drawn people from around the world with an adventurist, entrepreneurial spirit. That includes the Spanish explorers who conquered much of the Americas. It means the massive wave of forty-niners who came from every nation, swiftly followed by tens of thousands more, including men and women fleeing feudal Chinese villages. And it reckons among them a singular, if struggling, young man born in a frontier bar in upstate New York.

Many different outcomes awaited key participants in Leland Stanford's story.

Leland Stanford's other institution, the Southern Pacific, remained the single most powerful force in the West into the beginning of the twentieth century, but not for very long. In 1911 another state constitutional amendment created what was first known as the Railroad Commission. By the next year this body also gained the power to regulate utilities such as gas, electric, and water as well as marine transport. It was renamed the California Public Utilities Commission in 1946. As the automobile and then truck industries ascended and soon triumphed in California, the trains lost their importance in moving people and cargo. However, when fuel costs soar, so do prospects for rail companies moving freight. Although the Southern Pacific made the Central Pacific a subsidiary in 1885, the two did not fully and legally merge into one company until 1959. At one point the Southern Pacific ran more than thirteen thousand miles of rail covering most of the southwestern United States. In 1996 the Union Pacific bought the Southern Pacific, finally realizing Stanford and Huntington's dream of one railroad company, although it went the opposite way they had imagined and hoped.

Vina remains a village of some 250 people, with Leland Stanford's railroad tracks still running straight through it. Remnants of his ambitious if failed winery also remain and are now the restored and thriving property of the New Clairvaux Trappist order, which makes well-respected wines on a vastly smaller scale and licenses its brand to the Sierra Nevada Brewing Company, which bottles a beer under a similar name. There are no bars in Vina today, but there is a large and vital Catholic church, acres of productive walnut orchards, and a lovely state park popular with campers.

Collis Potter Huntington, his temper never tamed, remained back East as the president of the Southern Pacific while trying to acquire other railroads that he might have connected with the SP terminus in New Orleans. He also invested money in an attempt to build still another rail line to lure the wealthy to an expensive resort in which he had an interest, in the Adirondack Mountains of New York State. On August 13, 1900, the grand old warhorse died of a heart attack at the resort's lodge five minutes before the clock struck midnight. He was seventy-eight years old. No record of Jennie Stanford's reaction has been found.

His nephew and one-third heir, Henry Huntington, subsequently married his uncle's widow, who inherited and consolidated the other two-thirds of his fortune. They sold their interest in the Southern Pacific to E. H. Harriman and moved to Southern California. Henry Huntington invested in Los Angeles trolleys and built a luxurious estate in San Marino. It is today the other originally constitutionally tax-exempt entity in the state: the Huntington

Library and Art Gallery. Collis Huntington is entombed in a palatial mausoleum in the Woodlawn Cemetery in the upper Bronx.

Charles Crocker, who died at his luxurious resort hotel in Monterey, California, rests beneath a sky-high cylindrical sepulcher at Mountain View Cemetery in Oakland. He had three children, one of whom was largely responsible for Crocker Bank, which was acquired by Wells Fargo in 1986. The most colorful of the Crockers was E. B.'s daughter Amy, who "enjoyed an exotic and indulgent lifestyle."[20] Her peculiar 1936 autobiography, *And I'd Do It Again,* breezily discussed her five marriages, once to a Prince Mstislav Galitzine. The Crocker Art Museum in Sacramento is partly in the house built by her father.

Mark Hopkins, who died in Yuma seeking a cure for his multiple illnesses, left his fortune to his widow and adopted son Timothy Hopkins, who worked with Stanford as real estate speculator in Palo Alto. The Nob Hill mansion Mark Hopkins's widow built, burned in the 1906 earthquake and fire and is now the site of the Mark Hopkins Hotel. His final remains are in another magnificent tomb in Sacramento's Old City Cemetery.

David Starr Jordan served as Stanford University president until 1913, when he moved aside to an honorary position and devoted much of his time to eugenics and pacifism. He suffered a severe stroke in 1929 and died two years later from what the coroner determined was what we would call today a brain hemorrhage. He was cremated at the Cypress Lawn Cemetery in Colma, just south of San Francisco. The ashes—or cremains as the funeral industry calls them—were delivered to a now defunct funeral home in Palo Alto, and the records go no further than that. High schools in Long Beach and Los Angeles and a middle school in Burbank are named in his honor. In 2018, Palo Alto renamed what had been David Starr Jordan Middle School because of his advocacy of eugenics.

Bertha Berner, Jennie's longtime private secretary and traveling companion who wrote a reminiscence of her patroness in 1934, died in her Palo Alto home in 1945, age eighty-three. Her remains were cremated, their location unknown. The house given her still stands at 2100 Sand Hill Road, now a four-lane expressway that is the historic financial central roadway of Silicon Valley.

James Harvey Strobridge eventually retired from railroad construction and bought a five-hundred-acre ranch in Castro Valley, California, where he raised fruit and raced horses. It was said he was stern and quiet, but gentlemanly. He and his wife adopted five children. Strobridge died in 1921 and is buried at Lone Tree Cemetery in next-door Hayward. An elementary school and street in Castro Valley are named after him.

George Crothers served Stanford University for the rest of his days. He became a university trustee, a successful lawyer, and judge. He left the law to become a business entrepreneur and made a fortune. Crothers lived in San Francisco and was a well-known figure among the city's bourgeoisie. He was a friend and colleague to Frederick Terman, whom many understandably regard as the true father of Silicon Valley. Crothers's wife died in 1920 and they had no children. He passed away in 1957 at age eighty-six and is buried at Oak Hill Memorial Park in San Jose. Crothers Hall and Memorial on the Stanford campus are named in his honor.

Josiah Stanford, the person most responsible for bringing little brother Leland to California and sustaining him until he found his feet, had a long, successful run as a California businessman and was among the very first in the state's petroleum industry. Leland appointed Josiah to the original Stanford University Board of Trustees, but Jennie removed him shortly after her husband died. Josiah and his wife lived for twenty-three years in a home on the western shore of Oakland's Lake Merritt, where he died in 1890, at age seventy-three, leaving one son. The house, handsomely restored, stands today kitty-corner from the city's aging main library. Josiah Stanford is buried at Mountain View Cemetery in Oakland.

The Stanford mansion on Nob Hill burned to its foundations in the 1906 earthquake and fire. A modern hotel called the Stanford Court now serves a well-heeled clientele at the same location. Adjacent is a venerable restaurant and bar called the Big Four. Jennie's estate was not settled until September 20, 1957. Like so much else involving the Stanfords and their money, the situation was entangled by conflict, uncertainty, and in the end what can be described as not much more than commonplace cupidity. Jennie herself foresaw the situation as early as 1897 when she wrote, "I have learned by very sad experience the greed for gain tempts beyond the ability to resist." Indeed, the California Supreme Court, which made the final ruling on the fracas, quoted as much in its majority opinion.[21]

In 1900, she had given the university her inherited railroad securities with a face value of almost $12.5 million. When she died in 1905, she had left behind almost $3.5 million, with only about $250,000 of that sum designated for the university. The rest Jennie bequeathed largely to nephews and nieces of her family, and their heirs. Stanford University intervened and began a long fight for more. The university's lawyers argued that some of the latter heirs were adopted under circumstances that made them ineligible for inheriting the money from their families. The court finally ruled against the famous university whose symbol is the *sempervirens* redwood and instead in favor of the little-known, mortal family descendants of the American disruptor.

NOTES

PROLOGUE: FELL REDEMPTION

1. Google's famous—or infamous—algorithm is known as PageRank.

2. Battelle, *The Search*, 66–68.

3. Eesley and Miller, *Impact: Stanford University's Economic Impact via Innovation and Entrepreneurship.*

4. The Bull's Head changed hands several times after the Stanfords' proprietorship and it eventually burned to the ground. Situated on what is now Highway 32 (Broadway) in the township of Mendes, New York, today it is the site of the parking lot for the New York State Workers Compensation Fund.

5. Mark Zuckerberg, quoted in the *Telegraph*, May 27, 2016.

CHAPTER I. START-UP

1. *Milwaukee Sentinel*, March 16, 1852.

2. Leland Stanford, outgoing correspondence, April 1, 1852, Leland Stanford Collection, Department of Special Collections and University Archives, Stanford University Libraries.

3. Macaulay, *The History of England*, 18.

4. Leland Stanford's oldest brother, Josiah, in a late-life reminiscence remarked of the family name's provenance: "They say it originated from a stream called Staneyford." Josiah Stanford, "The Dictation of Josiah Stanford," September 19, 1889, p. 1, Bancroft Library, University of California, Berkeley.

5. Churchill, *The Birth of Britain*, 35.

6. The Great Rebellion, headed by Oliver Cromwell, was the best known of England's recurrent civil wars.

7. Vital Records of Massachusetts to 1850 New England Genealogical Society, Charlestown. On August 19, 1688, Thomas Stanford "now entering into Covt" indicated he had not been a member of the church until then.

8. Concord Historical Commission, *Historic Resources Masterplan of Concord, Massachusetts*, 13–22.

9. Josiah Stanford, "The Dictation of Josiah Stanford," 2–6.

10. Ibid.

11. Dillon, *Memoirs of Madame de La Tour du Pin*, 238, 250.

12. Dwight, *Travels in New England and New York: Vol. II*, Letter XVII.

13. Ibid., 54.

14. James Monroe was the last of the founding fathers to occupy the White House.

15. Josiah Stanford, "The Dictation of Josiah Stanford," 4. The manuscript as it stands says "and read a book," but those four words are crossed out in pencil. There is no knowing if this is a corrected version or someone vandalized the manuscript. Nevertheless, there are other indications that young Leland may have sometimes escaped into reading.

16. *San Francisco Chronicle*, June 21, 1893, 1.

17. *California Mail Bag*, June 1871, 1.

18. Hinton, *The History and Topography of the United States*, 356.

19. Bernstein, *Wedding of the Waters*, 26; Sheriff, *The Artificial River*, 36.

20. Marranca, ed., *A Hudson Valley Reader*, 12; Bernstein, *Wedding of the Waters*, 27, 323; Sheriff, *The Artificial River*, 75.

21. Sheriff, *The Artificial River*, 119.

22. Ibid. (variant spellings in original).

23. Reisem and Olenick, *Erie Canal Legacy*, 16.

24. Sheriff, *The Artificial River*, 142 (variant spellings in original).

25. Flannery, *The Story of the Mohawk & Hudson Railroad*, n.p.

26. Ibid., 9A (variant spelling in original).

27. Ibid.

28. Leland Stanford, outgoing correspondence, February 13, 1844.

29. Marranca, *A Hudson Valley Reader*, 13.

30. Sheriff, *The Artificial River*, 57.

31. Wagan, "Shaker Chairs," 171.

32. Sarah Barringer Gordon, in *The Mormon Question*, describes Smith, as have other scholars, as having "a reputation in upstate New York as a counterfeiter, fortune-teller, and treasure hunter" (19). In addition, noting the geographic and temporal proximity to the Oneida movement, Gordon states, "Mormons were not the first to confuse religious freedom with sexual license" (35).

33. Berner, *Mrs. Leland Stanford*, 6.

CHAPTER 2. EVERYTHING VENTURED

1. Leland Stanford, outgoing correspondence, May 21, 1841, Leland Stanford Collection.

2. *United States Magazine and Democratic Review* 17, no. 1 (July–August 1845): 5.

3. Howe, *What Hath God Wrought*, 373.

4. Leland Stanford, outgoing correspondence, October 11, 1844, Leland Stanford Collection.

5. Cassius Marcellus Clay to Salmon Chase, December 21, 1842, in *Annual Report of the AHA*, 1902, Salmon P. Chase Papers, Library of Congress, Washington, DC.

6. Leland Stanford, outgoing correspondence, March 23, 1844, Leland Stanford Collection.

7. Ibid., February 13, 1844.

8. There are no records of Stanford's passing either the New York State or local Albany bar, nor are there other legal records—none in the state archives, none in the Stanford University collections or other likely sources, including a 650-page manuscript by Albany attorney Henry G. Wheaton in the Rare Book Collection, Charles B. Sears Law Library, State University of New York, Buffalo. One writer has cited volume 8 of "The Doolittle Family in America," but an examination of the Doolittle Papers at the FamilySearch Library in Oakland finds no such reference to Stanford.

9. Price, "A History of Port Washington," 1.

10. Sarah Elizabeth Smith, interview with author, June 2016, Port Washington, Wisconsin.

11. Price, "A History of Port Washington," 33–34.

12. *Milwaukee Journal*, May 23, 1896, 10.

13. Leland Stanford, outgoing correspondence, March 25, 1844, Leland Stanford Collection.

14. *Port Washington Democrat*, October 19, 1848.

15. Foner, *Free Soil, Free Labor, Free Men*, 149.

16. Price, "A History of Port Washington," 39–40.

17. Jeanette Barr to Ralph W. Hansen, June 1, 1974, Port Washington Historical Society, Port Washington, Wisconsin.

18. Cigrand, *In Days of Old Ozaukee*, 554.

19. Leland Stanford, outgoing correspondence, June 20, 1850, Leland Stanford Collection. The author is indebted to Melissa Martin and Sharon Goetz of the Mark Twain Papers at UC Berkeley for their expert transcription of this especially challenging-to-read handwritten letter.

20. Jane was born August 25, 1828, in Albany. Eliza may have simply been the clipped spelling for Elizabeth.

21. Herbert C. Nash statement, 1887, in Hubert Howe Bancroft, "Biography of Leland Stanford, 1880–1890," manuscript research, 15 folders, Bancroft Library, University of California, Berkeley.

22. Bancroft, *History of the Life of Leland Stanford*, 10.

CHAPTER 3. CROSSING

1. Crothers, *Outline of the History of the Founding of the Leland Stanford Junior University*, 3.

2. Berner, *Mrs. Leland Stanford*, 10.

3. Ibid., 4.

4. Lamson, *Round Cape Horn*, 64 (emphasis underlined in original).

5. Russell, *Voyage to California Written at Sea*, 81, 86 (emphasis underlined in original).

6. Myers, *Ho for California*, 94.

7. Ingalls, *Journal of a Trip to California*, 15.

8. Myers, *Ho for California*, 61.

9. McKinstry, *California Gold Rush Overland Diary*, 275.

10. Carpenter, *Ho for California*, 103. Americans commonly denigrated the Latter-day Saints during the nineteenth century. Many Christians of established faiths considered the relatively new Mormons apostates if only because of significant objections to the early church practice of polygamy. In 1859 church leader Brigham Young told *New York Herald* editor Horace Greeley of "Go west, young man" fame that he had fifteen wives. What's more, in that year before the outbreak of the Civil War, Greeley had the following exchange with Young. Greeley: "What is the position of your church with respect to slavery?" Young: "We consider it a divine institution, and not to be abolished until the curse pronounced on Ham shall have been removed from his descendants." Greeley, *An Overland Journey from New York to San Francisco*, 179.

11. Myers, *Ho for California*, 103.

12. Ibid., 170–71.

13. Ibid., 59.

14. Ibid., 63, 49.

15. McKinstry, *California Gold Rush Overland Diary*, 194.

16. Ibid., 195, 59.

17. Ibid., 223.

18. Myers, *Ho for California*, 156.

19. *Daily Alta Californian*, April 2, 1853, 2.

20. Wilde, *Picture of Dorian Gray*, 178.

21. Soulé, Gihon, and Nisbet, *The Annals of San Francisco*, 338, 216.

22. De Rutté, *Adventures of a Young Swiss in California*, 10.

23. Soulé, Gihon, and Nisbet, *The Annals of San Francisco*, 250, 248.

24. Sinn, *Pacific Crossing*, 238.

25. Soulé, Gihon, and Nisbet, *The Annals of San Francisco*, 227.

26. Ibid., 316.

27. Ibid., 411.

28. Ibid., 364–65.

29. De Rutté, *Adventures of a Young Swiss in California*, 99–100.

30. Barker, *More San Francisco Memoirs*, 67–68.

31. Soulé, Gihon, and Nisbet, *The Annals of San Francisco*, 245, 420.

32. Ibid., 256.

33. Royce, *California*, 310–11, 313, 312.

34. Kaufman, *Apron Full of Gold*, 106.

35. Heizer, *The Destruction of the California Indians*, 11.

36. *Sacramento Daily Union*, February 3, 1855, 2.

CHAPTER 4. THE GOLD UNDER THE MOUNTAIN

1. Other elements such as silver and platinum are also created in these cosmic phenomena.

2. Christopher Dalbeck, California State Parks senior park aide, telephone interview with the author, January 4, 2013.

3. Henry Bigler diary, 1848, pp. 176–77 (variant spellings in original), Society of California Pioneers, San Francisco.

4. California State Parks, *Leland Stanford Mansion State Historic Park: Historic Structures Report*, 6.

5. Private letter from John Sutter to Mariano Vallejo, February 10, 1848, California Historical Society, San Francisco. Much later Sutter rued the entire gold discovery, blaming it for his failures.

6. Soulé, Gihon, and Nisbet, *The Annals of San Francisco*, 204, 205.

7. Paul, *California Gold*, 21.

8. Knapp, *California in 1851*, 108.

9. Clark, *Leland Stanford*, 65.

10. Crocker, "Facts Gathered from the Lips of Charles Crocker, H. H. Bancroft's *Chronicles of the Builders of the Commonwealth*, 1865–1890," p. 17, Bancroft Library, University of California, Berkeley.

11. Andrew, "Charles Crocker," 3.

12. Ibid., 28.

13. Daggett, *Chapters on the History of the Southern Pacific*, 13.

14. Edward H. Miller, "Notes Regarding Mark Hopkins and Related Material, 1878–1888," pp. 6–10, Bancroft Library, University of California, Berkeley.

15. Ibid., 6.

16. Ibid., 10.

17. David R. Sessions, "The Dictation of Collis P. Huntington," January 14, 1889, Bancroft Library, University of California, Berkeley.

18. Lavender, *The Great Persuader*, 3.

19. Sessions, "The Dictation of Collis P. Huntington," 5.

20. Albert Gallatin, "The Dictation of Albert Gallatin," ca. 1889, p. 2, Bancroft Library, University of California, Berkeley.

21. James Scott, librarian extraordinaire and author of *Sacramento's Gold Rush Saloons: El Dorado in a Shot Glass*, notes that not a few casinos and saloons were pop-up affairs under canvas and whatever boards, branches, or bric-a-brac that could be salvaged.

22. Gallatin, "The Dictation of Albert Gallatin," 38.

23. Hagwood, *The California Debris Commission*, iii.

24. May, *Origins of Hydraulic Mining in California*, 9.

25. Hagwood, *The California Debris Commission*, 19.

26. Faragher, *Eternity Street*, 389.

27. Brewer, *Up and Down California in 1860–1864*, 243 (emphasis in original).

28. A levee project was financed by the Central Pacific Railroad in return for the priceless right-of-way for its tracks to the Bay Area along the city's riverfront. The author is indebted to Sacramento city historian Marcia Eymann for her insights into this period. Hagwood, *The California Debris Commission*, iii.

29. Brewer, *Up and Down California in 1860–1864*, 493.

30. Heizer, *The Destruction of the California Indians*, 219.

31. Ibid., 26. In 1850 the state legislature passed the Act for the Government and Protection of Indians that created a huge locphole: it allowed de facto slaves to be declared "wards" and thereby be made legal.

32. The U.S. Census number is under the category of "free colored." San Francisco's 1850 census records were lost to a fire, meaning those numbers do not show up in the total count. As context, and demonstration of the overwhelming ratio of men to women in the state, the 1850 census also shows a total of 84,708 white males and 6,927 white females. Slaves were not counted separately—only their owners.

33. Lapp, *Blacks in Gold Rush California*, 13.

34. E. B. Crocker was one of Lee's lawyers in the unsuccessful state Supreme Court ruling. Lincoln friend and ally Edward D. Baker, who was also on the defense team, then took the case to a San Francisco court, which ignored the high court ruling and set Lee free.

35. Weber, ed., *Foreigners in Their Native Land*, 170.

36. Stanford bought the bar just before he became justice of the peace, as evidenced by the bill of sale verified by the previous justice of the peace for the township. Placer County Clerk-Recorder, *Index to Deeds*, 4.

37. *Santa Cruz Sentinel*, October 20, 1889, 3.

CHAPTER 5. DITCHING AND HITCHING

1. *New York Press*, July 13, 1890.

2. *The History of Placer County*, 392–94. The mining settlement was rebuilt about a half a mile up to the ridgetop, where a small settlement called Michigan Bluff exists, notable for a California Historic Marker memorializing Leland Stanford's brief stay. The author is indebted to archivist Bryanna Ryan at the Placer County Historical Society for expert assistance with this research.

3. Berner, *Mrs. Leland Stanford*, 12.

4. For a scholarly, and graphic, examination of the serious issue of horse manure in nineteenth-century American cities, see the University of California's Transportation Center publication, *Access* (Spring 2007), www.accessmagazine.org/articles/spring-2007/horse-power-horsepower.

5. Bayard Taylor, *Eldorado*, 177.

6. Leigh Johnson, correspondence with the author, January 2017.

7. Both the Whig and Know-Nothing Parties nominated Mark Hopkins to run for alderman from Sacramento's First Ward. He declined the honor but appeared on the ballot regardless. He barely lost. *Sacramento Daily Union*, April 2, 1855, 2.

8. Anbinder, *Nativism and Slavery*, ix.

9. In "The Rise and Fall of the 'Know Nothings' in California," Peyton Hurt notes that "because of the large numbers of these two elements in the population of California, the Know Nothings of the state could not afford to proscribe them both and expect to win. In fact, the Know Nothings of California were never anti-Catholic and only mildly anti-foreign *in their public expressions of policy*" (38, emphasis added).

10. There were no federal laws regulating immigration before the Civil War. An unprecedented surge of immigrants came to the United States in the 1840s until about 1860, when the Civil War began. Significant immigration began to resume after the war ended.

11. Hurt, "The Rise and Fall of the 'Know Nothings' in California," 109.

12. Ibid., xi.

13. Ibid., 105, 110.

14. Holt, *The Rise and Fall of American Whig Party*, 858.

15. Anbinder, *Nativism and Slavery*, 15.

16. Holt, *The Rise and Fall of American Whig Party*, 485.

17. Ibid., 858.

18. Hurt, "The Rise and Fall of the 'Know Nothings' in California," 44, 110.

19. Engs and Miller, eds., *The Birth of the Grand Old Party*. 34.

20. Gienapp, *The Origins of the Republican Party*, 317.

21. Ibid., 376–77.

22. Republican Party Platform of 1856, the American Presidency Project, https://www.presidency.ucsb.edu/node/273293.

23. Murian, "Booksellers and Libraries in Sacramento, 1849–1862."

24. *Sacramento Daily Union*, April 21, 1856, 2.

25. Ibid., April 30, 1856, 2.

26. The party bosses appointed Stanford to a committee that would chose delegates to the next California state convention. *Sacramento Daily Union*, August 27, 1856, 2.

27. Ibid., April 8, 1857.

28. Ibid., July 10, 1857, 2.

29. Ibid., September 3, 1857, 2, and September 5, 1857, 2.

30. *The Emigrant*, February 8, 1832, 3. Special thanks to Darla Welshons at the Ann Arbor Michigan Public Library for finding this obscure, often incorrectly cited, article.

31. Sobel, *Panic on Wall Street*, 85.

32. William Cooper, *Jefferson Davis, American*, 276.

33. The full report can be found on the Central Pacific Railroad hobbyists' website, http://cprr.org/Museum/PacRRSurvey_Secty_War_1853.html.

34. James Gadsden, of a prosperous South Carolina clan, had run unsuccessfully for political office on several occasions, was a veteran of the War of 1812, a close friend of Andrew Jackson, and a railroad executive very much involved with trying to get a

southern route for a transcontinental track. He was also an active proponent of making Southern California open to slavery.

35. Richards, *The California Gold Rush and the Coming of the Civil War*, 153.

36. Indeed, *Sierra Nevada* means "snow-covered mountain range" in Spanish. *Sierra*, more literally, refers to a saw.

37. Stegner, *Angle of Repose*, 341.

38. Anna Ferona Pierce Judah, correspondence concerning her husband, Theodore D. Judah, 1889, Bancroft Library, University of California, Berkeley.

39. *Themis* magazine, December 14, 1889, 3.

40. The Sierra route used today, including Donner Pass, is very similar to the same one Judah outlined.

CHAPTER 6. "THE ROAD MUST BE BUILT"

1. *Sacramento Daily Union*, June 9, 1859, 1.

2. Ibid.

3. Ibid.

4. The population of the state was a little less than 400,000 at the time. Of the three candidates for governor, two earned more than 90,000 votes, while Stanford won just 10,128. *Sacramento Daily Union*, September 28, 1859, 2.

5. Theodore D. Judah, "Central Pacific Railroad Company of California," 1860, California State Railroad Museum, Library and Archives, Sacramento.

6. That influential Iowa congressman was Rep. Samuel Curtis.

7. Rep. Oak Ames, a member of a Massachusetts family that made a fortune selling shovels to forty-niners, who was also an investor in the scandal-ridden Union Pacific Railroad while a member of Congress, reported this conversation with Lincoln. Ames, *The Ames Family of Easton, Massachusetts*, 145.

8. U.S. Senate, *Testimony Taken by the United States Pacific Railway Commission*, 50th Congress, 1st session (1887) (hereafter PRC), 2964, 2966.

9. Charles Crocker, "Facts Regarding Identification with the Central Pacific Railroad," dictation, Bancroft Library, University of California, Berkeley. Crocker, for one, asserted in these reminiscences that each man had initially invested $15,000.

10. Anna Ferona Pierce Judah, correspondence concerning her husband; Daggett, *Chapters on the History of the Southern Pacific*, 18–25; White, *Railroaded*, 18–19. The *Sacramento Daily Union*, May 1, 1861, implies the $1,500 amount is correct. Fleisig, "The Central Pacific Railroad and the Railroad Land Grant Controversy," 555, concludes the four men "at most" contributed a total of $60,000 by the conclusion of 1863.

11. *Sacramento Daily Union*, January 29, 1862, 2.

12. Clark, *Leland Stanford*, 69.

13. Ibid., 69–70 (quotations); Mason, *History of Amador County*, 153–54 ($300,000 profit).

14. Some years later Stanford was a principal investor in the now tourist ghost town of Bodie, California, which failed while he was involved. He also participated in a

Nevada operation called the South Aurora Silver Mining Company, which also did not succeed, although the extent of his involvement is unclear.

15. Smith, *The History of the Comstock Lode*, 3–10.

16. Hearst would also invest heavily—and wisely—in the Homestake mine of South Dakota, and the copper-rich Anaconda in Montana. He bought the *San Francisco Examiner* in 1880, as people seeking political power were more apt to do before the World Wide Web began to usurp the traditional newspaper business model. His son took over soon afterward.

17. *Sacramento Daily Union*, June 20, 1861, 2.

18. Ibid. Displaying its own outright support of Stanford—and Stanford's support of the paper—the *Sacramento Daily Union* noted that guns were fired off that evening by Republican revelers and "made a great noise, but nothing to compare to the popping of corks from champagne bottles in our office. Thanks to the generous remembrance of the gubernatorial nominee."

19. Dr. Jacob Stillman to his son John, February, 24, 1860, Stillman Folder, California Historical Society, San Francisco.

20. The $600 figure comes from the administration of the state historic park. It is not verified by primary documents, which are largely unavailable due to fire and flood loss as well as insufficient record keeping. California State Parks, which operates the Leland Stanford Mansion State Historic Park today and makes it open and free to the public, in 2002 completed an exhaustive two-hundred-page study of its history, *Leland Stanford Mansion State Historic Park: Historic Structures Report*.

21. Low and Becker, eds., *Reflections of an Early California Governor*, 29–31. Former governor Frederick Low, many years after leaving office, in a pleasantly candid and even-keeled memoir said of J. Neely Johnson that "he became a poor miserable drunkard" (31). Of McDougal, "Well, when you say he was a drunkard, you pretty much state the whole case. There was not much in him outside of whiskey—in those days he would be accounted a sort of whiskey bum. He may have had some talent—but it was drowned in whiskey" (29). Also see Kibby, "Union Loyalty of California's Civil War Governors," 313.

22. *Red Bluff Independent*, September 10, 1861, 2.

23. The full address can be found at the State of California's "Governor's Gallery," http://governors.library.ca.gov/addresses/08-Stanford.html.

24. *Sacramento Daily Union*, August 17, 1859, 1.

25. Bancroft, *History of the Life of Leland Stanford*, 21.

26. Melendy and Gilbert, *The Governors of California*, 133.

27. Josiah Stanford, "The Dictation of Josiah Stanford," 1.

28. Theodore D. Judah, "Pacific Railroad, Report of Theodore D. Judah, Accredited Agent Pacific Railroad Convention upon His Operations in the Atlantic States," August 1860, p. 3, California State Railroad Museum, Library and Archives, Sacramento.

29. Ibid., 8.

30. Sobel, *Panic on Wall Street*, 85.

31. Faragher, *Eternity Street*, 384–94.

32. Rawls and Bean, *California: An Interpretive History*, 127. Stacey L. Smith, in *Freedom's Frontier*, notes that "white Southerners may have been a minority and California masters may have been a miniscule group, but they had clout," adding that "they were vastly overrepresented in the state legislature and judiciary" (8).

33. Walker, Turley, and Leonard, *Massacre at Mountain Meadows*, 37. The cruel and genocidal general was Gen. William S. Harney, of whom the authors make a brief but crisp description. The general prejudice against early LDS adherents is evidenced not only in the widespread attacks they suffered across the country and in many government actions but also in popular literature of the time. In *The Mormon Question*, 29, Sarah Barringer Gordon notes that beginning in the 1850s dozens of anti-LDS novels, magazine, and newspapers stories—most decrying polygamy—attracted wide readership across the United States. This continued into the twentieth century, seen in popular books such as Zane Grey's *Riders of the Purple Sage*.

34. The point has not infrequently been made that E. B. Crocker, older brother of Charles, was as instrumental in the early days of the railroad as the other four and does not get the acclaim he deserves. There is a good deal of truth in that, but also commensurate veracity in his escaping the condemnation that was brewing in his lifetime and matured after his early death. The origin of calling Stanford, Huntington, Hopkins, and Crocker the Big Four remains unclear. There are ample references in the late 1800s to an entertainment act that often played in Sacramento and San Francisco with that name and then a quartet of midwestern railroad companies. However, one of the earliest published references to the entrepreneurs of the Central Pacific Railroad as the Big Four can be found in the *Sacramento Daily Union*, March 28, 1889, 4.

CHAPTER 7. "EGYPTIAN KINGS AND DYNASTIES SHALL BE FORGOTTEN"

1. Mudgett, "The Political Career of Leland Stanford," 26.

2. Chandler, *The Railroads*, 3.

3. Ingalls, *Journal of a Trip to California*, 75.

4. Moody, *The Railroad Builders*, 1–2.

5. Economic historian Leland Jenks points out that the first railways mimicked the routes of waterways and turnpikes, as the Mohawk & Hudson had done with the Erie Canal and Hudson River, taking much of its established traffic. Shortly before the Civil War, railroads began to strike out on their own. This "determination to build railroads in advance of traffic" meant that lines such as the transcontinental sometimes went into territories where there was not only little or no established traffic but hardly any people, which sometimes meant little money. On the other hand, Jenks states, "There is no convincing evidence, however, that railways have ever carried freight at lower costs to either shippers or to society than canals or waterways." Jenks, "Railroads as an Economic Force in American Development," 3, 12.

6. Grodinsky, *Transcontinental Railway Strategy*, 4.

7. Fogel, *The Union Pacific Railroad*, 21.

8. White, *Railroaded*, xxxii.

9. Collis Huntington was reportedly in Washington, DC, for some of this period and may have taken his first baby steps at that time toward his later infamous lobbying work. There is, however, little documented evidence that he was directly involved in fashioning the 1862 railroad bill.

10. Daggett, *Chapters on the History of the Southern Pacific*, 54.

11. England, which is not quite as large as the entire state of Louisiana, is where the locomotive was first developed, and it also had a reasonably comprehensive telegraph system by 1870. In the United States, telegraph lines connected San Francisco and New York as early as 1861, but their reliability was, at best, spotty. The significance of the telegraph is nicely dealt with in Manahem Blondheim's *News over the Wires: The Telegraph and the Flow of Public Information in America, 1844–1897*.

12. There are many excellent explanations for the layperson about how bonds work, such as "Bonds Basics Tutorial," March 27, 2017, https://www.investopedia.com/university/bonds.

13. Crocker, "Facts Regarding Identification with the Central Pacific Railroad." In his reminiscences, Charles Crocker lamented the Big Four's inability to sell the bonds to prospective investors and said they had to start investing substantial sums of their own money, and even borrow some.

14. Haney, *A Congressional History of Railways in the United States*, 66.

15. Ibid., 19.

16. PRC, 3680 (Crocker quotations); Low and Becker, *Reflections of an Early California Governor*, 38–39. Frederick Low, the Republican governor who immediately followed Stanford in office, reminisced twenty years after the scheme that he asked Crocker why they didn't just say the mountains started right in Sacramento itself and that Crocker replied, "For the looks of the thing, I brought it down just as far as Whitney could conscientiously certify." PRC, 3680. Low characterized Whitney as "an eccentric sort of a fellow." At the end of the day, Low concluded, "by it they have made cords of money." Low and Becker, *Reflections of an Early California Governor*, 38–39. The highest peak in the Sierras and the contiguous United States, Mount Whitney, is named in honor of the state geologist. Stanford testified in the Pacific Railway Commission hearings that Arcade Creek was seven miles from Sacramento. Before realizing the implication of what he was stating under oath, he added that laying the rails before the true base of the Sierra commenced "was very light work. Out to 23 miles up from Sacramento the rise is little over 300 feet." Stanford also testified that there was "no difficulty at all" with Theodore Judah on the matter. PRC, 2763–64.

The U.S. Geological Survey (USGS), while noting the exact western commencement of the Sierra Nevada is a "fuzzy line" and open to some discussion, says it most certainly does not begin at Arcade Creek. The consensus is that the mountains begin near the town of Rocklin, where the elevation begins to seriously jump and the first Sierra granite is found. Much of the granite used for the state capitol, which began construction just before Leland Stanford became governor, comes from the well-known quarries of the area and was shipped down to Sacramento on his railroad. James Moore, USGS geologist, telephone interview with the author, April 11, 2017.

17. *Themis* magazine, December 14, 1889, 3.

18. The Panama city was then called Aspinwall, known today as Colón.

19. Anna Ferona Pierce Judah, correspondence concerning her husband.

20. In "A Sketch of the Life of Theodore D. Judah," Carl Wheat wrote, "It seems probable that the future historian, seeking for casual relations, will assign to Judah an important place in the development of California and the transformation of the 'Pacific Railroad' dream into actual rails and rolling stock" (219). Rawls and Bean's *California: An Interpretive History*, among the leading university textbooks surveying the state's history, said of the Big Four after the young engineer's death, "They felt no gratitude toward Judah and did not even name a crossroads station in his honor. When at last something like a suitable monument to Judah was erected at Sacramento in 1930, the initiative came not from the railroad's management but from the American Society of Civil Engineers" (175).

21. Anna Ferona Pierce Judah, correspondence concerning her husband.

22. Collis P. Huntington, "Letters from Collis P. Huntington to Mark Hopkins, Leland Stanford, Charles Crocker, E. B. Crocker, Charles F. Crocker, and D. D. Cotton from August 20, 1867 to August 5, 1869," bound book of handwritten letters, transcribed and printed 1892, p. 188, Collis Potter Huntington Papers, Special Collections Research Center, the Huntington Library, San Marino.

23. Leland Stanford's manuscript editing of "The Biography of Leland Stanford, 1880–1890," by H. H. Bancroft, Bancroft Library, University of California, Berkeley.

24. *Sacramento Daily Union*, July 7, 1862, 8.

25. A full transcript of Stanford's speech can be found in State of California, *Journal of the Senate during the Fourteenth Session of the Legislature, 1863*, 27.

26. *Sacramento Daily Union*, October 30, 1862, 3.

27. Ibid., April 7, 1863, 4.

28. Ibid., March 31, 1863, 4.

29. Ibid.

30. Ibid., November 26 1862, 2.

31. See *The Great Dutch Flat Swindle!!* Asa Philip Stanford was two years older than Leland. He died penniless in New York in 1903.

32. In 1864, the first train connecting San Francisco with San Jose started running but on another railroad company's line. In 1869, a rail connection was made between Sacramento and Oakland, where passengers and freight could ferry across the water to San Francisco. That same year the Central Pacific, in one of many acquisitions and mergers that would soon prompt cries of monopoly and government investigations, acquired the Sacramento–Oakland line.

33. *Sacramento Daily Union*, April 23, 1863, 2.

34. Low and Becker, *Reflections of an Early California Governor*, 35–39.

35. The Great American Desert is today called the Great Basin.

36. *Sacramento Daily Union*, January 31, 1863, 2.

37. Ibid., February 2, 1863, 4.

38. Ibid.

39. Ibid. A very romanticized, very large mural depicting the ceremony has been restored in the recently rehabilitated Sacramento train depot.

CHAPTER 8. DUNGEONS AND DEPREDATIONS

1. The origin of the name is lost, although some have speculated the true phonetic pronunciation was closer to 'kaynteen," and the Spanish-speaking Mexican authorities amended it to a more familiar Quentir.

2. National Park Service, *San Quentin State Prison, Building 22*, 7.

3. Ibid.

4. Office of the Board of State Prison Directors, *Annual Report of the State Prison Directors, for the Year 1862*, 5–6.

5. Historical records of U.S. prison breaks are scant and difficult to verify. Several press accounts pegged the number of escapees at two hundred, while some reported as many as three hundred.

6. *Sacramento Daily Union*, July 7, 1863. 4.

7. Ibid., July 24, 1863, 2.

8. Ibid., July 25, 1863, 4.

9. Office of the Board of State Prison Directors, *Annual Report of the State Prison Directors, for the Year 1862*, 36.

10. Ibid., 23, 26. The statistics in the report are unclear but suggest fifty-six to seventy-eight Native inmates. In addition, State of California, *Appendix to Journals of the Senate and Assembly, Fourteenth Session of the Legislature, 1863*, 95, a report to the state legislature by then attorney general Frank Pixley, estimated sixty Native Californians at San Quentin, most of whom were from the most southern reaches of the state. Pixley also suggested the local sheriffs were bringing up the men in order to get a big mileage allowance.

11. Statutes of California 1863 Cal. Stat., chap. 475 (April 27, 1863).

12. Madley, *An American Genocide*, 303.

13. *Sacramento Daily Union*, June 2, 1363, 2.

14. Ibid., September 19, 1863, 2.

15. Ibid., June 2, 1863, 2.

16. Heizer, *They Were Only Diggers*, 56.

17. *Sacramento Daily Union*, June 2, 1863, 2.

18. Heizer and Whipple, eds., *The California Indians*, 567.

19. *The War of Rebellion: A Compilation of the Official Records of the Union and Confederate Armies*, 360.

20. Madley, *An American Genocide*, 30.

21. Heizer, *They Were Only Diggers*, 55.

22. Madley, *An American Genocide*, 351. "From 1846 to 1873 individuals, vigilantes, California state militiamen, and US soldiers killed at least 9,492 to 16,094 California

Indians, and probably many more," Benjamin Madley estimates in *An American Genocide*, 51. See also Dayton, "The California Militia," 218. In this much earlier and more forgiving though exhaustive doctoral dissertation regarding the history of California's militia, Dello Grimmett Dayton estimated that four thousand Native Californians died "in physical conflict" between 1848 and 1880, most before 1865. Furthermore,

> Certainly the settlers on the frontier preferred volunteers to regular troops. Perhaps this was because the volunteers had the philosophy of the settlers they represented—that the Indians should be exterminated or removed to a remote location where they would not be troublesome. There is no question but that the volunteer companies on occasion aggravated instead of stopped Indian troubles. (218)

23. *Sacramento Daily Union*, April 3, 1862, 4.

24. That Stanford University's team symbol from 1930 to 1972 was a cartoon of an ignoble Indian bears little comment but should not entirely escape notice. An effort to reinstate the Indian as the school mascot in 1975 resulted in a vote along with alternative mascots, some of which were Robber Barons, Railroaders, and Huns. None of the suggestions were accepted. Today the Stanford mascot is the cardinal.

25. Heizer, *They Were Only Diggers*, 99–101.

26. Yen, "Chinese Workers and the First Transcontinental Railroad," 3.

27. Barth, *Bitter Strength*.

28. Yen, "Chinese Workers and the First Transcontinental Railroad," 10.

29. Barth, *Bitter Strength*, 193. Koopmanschap said he had brought more than thirty thousand Chinese before he died in Rio de Janeiro in 1882 while negotiating the passage of Chinese to Brazil. He was well known in San Francisco, belonging to the exclusive Union Club and married to a French hotelier named Desiré.

30. Ibid., 61.

31. Ibid., 91. The Six Companies represented different geographic areas of the Pearl River delta.

32. The word *coolie* was inaccurate. Although it began as a term for indentured workers, by 1850 it referred to outright slave labor.

33. The consul general's April 16, 1863, letter can be found in the Governor Leland Stanford Papers, California State Archives.

34. State of California, *Journal of the Senate during the Fourteenth Session of the Legislature, 1863.*

35. *Sacramento Daily Union*, May 22, 1863, 2.

36. E. B. Crocker wrote an astonishing 238 opinions in his seven months on the bench, none of which dealt with the Central Pacific Railroad or any of the Big Four. Two cases dealt with railroad companies, one in which he ruled for, the other against. It is possible to see a summary using the proprietary LexisNexis database.

37. *Daily Alta California*, May 27, 1862.

38. Lavender, *The Great Persuader*, 135.

39. *Sacramento Daily Union*, May 26, 1863, 2.

40. *Daily Alta California*, June 9, 1863, 2.

41. Senator Conness is recognized by many for sponsoring the first federal legislation protecting Yosemite.

42. *Sacramento Daily Union*, June 4, 1863, 2.

43. Ibid., June 20, 1863, 1.

44. Ibid.

CHAPTER 9. LIVING UP TO THE LANDSCAPE

1. A Howe truss is a box frame made of vertical and diagonal beams of steel or wood that resemble an X. Often used for extra strength to hold up a bridge bed, or road, they have been particularly useful for railroads. A smokebox is a chamber where smoke and hot gases were gathered from flues.

2. Leland Stanford, outgoing correspondence, November 29, 1861, Leland Stanford Collection.

3. Lavender, *The Great Persuader*, 122.

4. Dr. Thomas Durant, the Svengali-like character running the Union Pacific line coming west from Omaha to link with the Central Pacific running east from Sacramento, was very much in Washington, DC, and involved in lobbying Congress at the same time. Klein, *Union Pacific*, 28, asserts there is significant evidence that he spent $250,000 in UP bonds, laundered through a pair of lobbyists, to pay politicians and other influential people in return for the largesse of the 1864 amendments to the Pacific Railway Act. Durant denied the charge in a later federal investigation.

5. Bain, *Empire Express*, 194.

6. A ceaseless debate has carried on regarding repeated assertions that the Chinese workers on Cape Horn used wicker baskets to hold them as they descended the steep cliffs. The baskets would have been held by rope and lowered by men at the top of the hill. But a rail ride going west to east clearly proves the slope is slanted, not vertically sheer.

7. Despite repeated assertions of the legendary eye patch, it is difficult—perhaps impossible—to find a photograph of Strobridge with said patch. It has been suggested that he removed it before standing in front of a camera.

8. Galloway, *The First Continental Railroad*, 89.

9. *Sacramento Daily Union*, January 7, 1864, 2.

10. Leland Stanford, Pres't C.P.R.R. Co., *Central Pacific Railroad: Statement Made to the President of the United States, and Secretary of the Interior of the Progress of the Work*, 7–8. Stanford also told then president Andrew Johnson he was assured by the labor importers that he would be able to get up to fifteen Chinese workers. Chew, *Nameless Builders*, 42, used extant payroll records to calculate that a "minimum" of 23,004 Chinese workers in total worked on Stanford's transcontinental railroad construction. It might be noted that Abraham Lincoln, a couple of years prior to becoming president, declared that "labor is prior to, and independent of, capital; that, in fact, capital is the fruit of labor, and could never have existed if labor had not first existed. . . . Labor is the superior—greatly the superior—of capital." Lincoln's address before the

Wisconsin State Agricultural Society, Milwaukee, September 30, 1859, https://www
.nal.usda.gov/lincolns-milwaukee-speech.

11. Cain, "The Chinese and the Stanfords," 172, 175, 176.

12. Chang and Fishkin, *The Chinese and the Iron Road*, 346. It must be said that the
overall theme of the essay cited is a sort of ambivalence Stanford expressed regarding
the Chinese, something Stanford's brother Josiah characterized as hypocrisy (see
chapter 6). Some others are even more condemnatory: "To this day, there are Chinese
Americans who refuse to set foot on the grounds of the university that carries the
Stanford name" (ibid.).

13. *PRC*, 3107.

14. Another too often contentious debate has been stirred regarding this issue. A
thorough and level-headed examination may be found online at the Chinese Railroad
Workers in North America Project at Stanford University.

15. For a more detailed examination of the Chinese workers' diets, see Spier, "Food
Habits of Nineteenth-Century California Chinese."

16. Galloway, *The First Continental Railroad*, 144.

17. Saxton, *The Indispensable Enemy*, 63–66. *Gandy dancer* was a term used for a
laborer in a railroad section gang.

18. Ibid., 8.

19. The letter, dated 1868, was translated through the courtesy and scholarship of
Professor Charles Egan of San Francisco State University, to whom the author is
indebted. Another full translation can be found in Yung, Chang, and Lai, eds., *Chinese
American Voices*, 23. For a comprehensive treatment of what befell Chinese women in
California, see Tong, *Unsubmissive Women*.

20. Patterson, Ulph, and Goodwin, *Nevada's Northeast Frontier*, 184.

21. For a worthy discussion of this topic, see the Chinese Railroad Workers in North
America Project at Stanford University, especially Miaw, "Three Interpretations of the
Role of Chinese Railroad Workers in the Construction of the Central Pacific Railroad."
It should be noted that industrial accidents went on with little federal government
oversight until 1970, when California Republican Richard Nixon was president.

22. Sinn, *Pacific Crossing*, 266.

23. *Daily Alta California*, June 6, 1867, 1.

24. Didion, *South and West*, xxxi. Sacramento born-and-bred Didion was writing
about more than the Sierra Nevada and referring to all of her native California.

CHAPTER 10. COMMAND AND CONTROL

1. Root, *Personal History and Reminiscences*, 29.

2. Strazdes, "The Millionaire's Palace," 216.

3. On April 29, 1869, the rail workers put down a little more of ten miles of track as
they neared completion, setting some sort of record and causing a good deal of rightful
boasting. The early assembly-line organization and sheer brawn received nationwide
attention.

4. Leland Stanford to Collis Huntington, December 13, 1868, Collis Potter Huntington Papers, Special Collections Research Center, Syracuse University Libraries.

5. Leland Stanford to Collis Huntington, May 15, 1869, ibid.

6. Bain, *Empire Express*, 632.

7. An active free press did buck the established powers in investigating the Union Pacific. In 1868, Charles Francis Adams Jr. authored a piece in the *North American Review* revealing the scandalous Crédit Mobilier, which the UP set up to launder and embezzle money for its executives and shareholders, not a few of whom held key political offices. Adams excused the Central Pacific, writing that as it was "managed by a small clique in California, its internal arrangements are involved in about the same obscurity as are the rites of Freemasonry." Adams, "Railroad Inflation," 147. Fifteen years later Adams became president of the Union Pacific.

8. Collis Huntington to Leland Stanford, October 9, 1868 (emphasis in original), "Letters from Collis P. Huntington to Mark Hopkins et al.," Collis Potter Huntington Papers, Huntington Library.

9. Leland Stanford to Collis Huntington, July 18, 1868, Collis Potter Huntington Papers, Syracuse.

10. Collis Huntington to Leland Stanford, April 3, 1869, "Letters from Collis P. Huntington to Mark Hopkins et al.," Collis Potter Huntington Papers, Huntington Library.

11. Bain, *Empire Express*, 565.

12. Collis Huntington to Leland Stanford, March 23, 1869, "Letters from Collis P. Huntington to Mark Hopkins et al.," Collis Potter Huntington Papers, Huntington Library.

13. DeWitt was the first name of Stanford's little brother who had died in Australia six years before. An exhibit at the Cantor Arts Center at Stanford University—generally referred to as the Stanford museum—about the Stanford family stated the child was born after "likely miscarriages." The museum could not provide a source for this assertion. The boy, following the example of his father who had dropped his first name, later dropped his middle name and became simply Leland Stanford Jr.

14. PRC, 2626; Hayes, *Historical Atlas of California*, 119.

15. It is fair and just to note that Huntington, despite his less attractive characteristics, was an extraordinary man in his own right. As his biographer, David Lavender, writes in *The Great Persuader*, the challenge of the transcontinental railroad "released in him a creative imagination of singular daring" (248).

16. Jane Stanford to Leland Stanford, outgoing correspondence, 1860–69, Jane Lathrop Stanford Papers, Department of Special Collections and University Archives, Stanford University Libraries. One can read a transcribed version in Nagel, *Iron Will*, 21.

17. Cowan, "Steel Rails and the Utah Saints," 183 (variant spellings in original).

18. Dodge, *How We Built the Union Pacific Railway*, 27.

19. Quoted in Clark, *Leland Stanford*, 245.

20. Leland Stanford to Collis Huntington, July 18, 1868, Collis Potter Huntington Papers, Syracuse.

21. Quoted in Clark, *Leland Stanford*, 245.

22. Cowan, "Steel Rails and the Utah Saints," 185.

23. Leland Stanford to Mark Hopkins, outgoing correspondence, March 10, 1869, Leland Stanford Collection.

24. For much of this clarification and detail, the author is especially indebted to David Kilton of the National Park Service.

25. *New York Tribune*, June 26, 1869, 14. Richardson was hardly alone in his sour appraisal of Promontory Summit: "August 14, 1869: Reached Promontory . . . at noon. A fearful place composed almost entirely of open gambling booths and whiskey shops. They tell one someone is killed here nearly every day. One of our passengers fleeced of all he had by the gamblers. Glad to get away after about two hours stay. Weather warm." Henry Carter Austin, "The Diary of Henry Carter Austin," August 1869, courtesy of the National Park Service and grandson David B. Austin.

26. Leland Stanford to Collis Huntington, May 11, 1869, Collis Potter Huntington Papers, Syracuse.

27. The locomotive originally intended to represent the Central Pacific at the Promontory Summit ceremony was the Antelope. The Union Pacific's was the 119.

28. Dodge, "Biography of Major General Grenville M. Dodge," 953–54. The Casement brothers were the rough-and-ready team that ran the Union Pacific's infamous road crew: the men who actually graded the land and laid down the ties and rails. Today's UP company website states about the duo who managed the crew,

> Together, the Casement brothers laid the entire track and undertook some of the grading of the Union Pacific road from just west of Fremont, Nebraska, to Promontory. Though both men were short of stature (Jack was 5'4" and Dan stood at "five feet nothing" according to one wag), they were not men to be crossed. Both hardbitten and fearless, they handled the roughest of Irish crews. The brothers went on to build railroads in Pennsylvania, Ohio, New York, Indiana, Kentucky, West Virginia, Canada and Costa Rica.

29. *New York Tribune*, June 26, 1869, 14.

30. Moreover, much of the detritus from hydraulic mining had washed and continues to do so into San Francisco Bay, adding still more sediment to the floor, filling in marshes and the general shoreline where there is insufficient tidal flow to keep the sediment moving. Today the Port of Oakland, with adequate land to be a modern containerized facility, unlike San Francisco, regularly dredges the bay to create shipping lanes for twentieth-first-century vessels.

31. The official motto of the City and County of San Francisco is "Oro en Paz, Fierro en Guerra" (Gold in Peace, Iron in War).

32. In a June 15, 1869, letter to Huntington, Stanford wrote, "We had better abandon all idea of [G]oat Island." The letter is held in the Collis Potter Huntington Papers.

33. Leland Stanford, outgoing correspondence, January 3, 1869 (emphasis underlined in original), Leland Stanford Collection.

34. *PRC*, 2803, 3614. For a detailed chronology of this lengthy and somewhat complicated—but key—play by the Big Four, see Bain's excellent *Empire Express*.

CHAPTER II. "THE MACHINE OF STEAM ON THE ROAD OF IRON"

1. *History of Alameda County*, 668–70.

2. Daggett, *Chapters on the History of the Southern Pacific*. notes available evidence that Judah had objected to giving the work to Crocker—which meant themselves—and only after the young engineer died did they feel unencumbered "to dominate the situation completely" (71). After Crocker and Hopkins had passed away, Stanford, Huntington and their executive employees would later testify that they had done so for efficiency, speed, and better cost.

3. Collis Huntington to Leland Stanford, May 11, 1870, "Letters from Collis P. Huntington to Mark Hopkins et al.," Collis Potter Huntington Papers, Huntington Library.

4. Collis Huntington to Mark Hopkins, May 8, 1872, ibid., 337.

5. Collis Huntington to Mark Hopkins, December 30, 1873, ibid. Daniel Strong, who helped Theodore Judah find the route over the Sierras, testified in the PRC hearings of 1887 that as early as 1861, when the Central Pacific was being formed, Huntington "intimated" he should be named president of the railroad, not Stanford. *PRC*, 2842.

6. A March 26, 2005, *Los Angeles Times* account of the dispute regarding LA's birth name says,

> Historians cannot agree on the name given to Los Angeles when its Spanish founders formed it Sept. 4, 1781. The early settlers meant to name the town after angels; that much is known. But for more than 75 years, local historians have been quarreling over its actual moniker. Some contend it was El Pueblo de Nuestra Senora de los Angeles. Others assert it was El Pueblo de Nuestra Senora la Reyna de los Angeles. Or perhaps it was El Pueblo de Nuestra Senora de los Angeles de la Porciuncula. Or El Pueblo de Nuestra Senora la Reyna de los Angeles del Rio Porciuncula. Or maybe El Pueblo de la Reina de los Angeles Sobre el Rio de Porciuncula. Or Pueblo del Rio de Nuestra Senora la Reyna de los Angeles de Porciuncula.

At least two other sites are worthy of attention regarding this issue ("A Short History of Los Angeles," http://cogweb.ucla.edu/Chumash/LosAngeles.html; "Los Angeles Almanac," www.laalmanac.com/history/hi03a.php), although neither will likely provide an authoritative account of the origin of LA's name.

7. For a compelling description of 1860s Los Angeles, see Faragher, *Eternity Street*.

8. Hoyt, "The Los Angeles & San Pedro: First Railroad South of the Tehachapis," 327. In 1769, Friar Juan Crespi, chronicler of the Spanish expedition led by Gaspar de Portola, named the river El Rio de Nuestra Señora la Reina de Los Angeles de la Porciúncula, or Rio Porciuncula for short. By 1850, when California became a state, the river was called the Los Angeles River. The author is indebted to Kelly C. Wallace, California subject specialist in the History and Genealogy Department of the Los Angeles Central Library, for assistance with the provenance of the proper nouns.

9. Faragher, *Eternity Street*, 444.

10. Ward McAfee, in *California's Railroad Era*, notes that "in the early days of California's railroad development, railroad companies structured their rate schedules

to discriminate in favor of terminal towns, in order to encourage the long haul and thereby maximize profits" (11).

11. Guinn, "Pioneer Railroads of Southern California," 191.

12. Dinkelspiel, *Towers of Gold*, 80–81.

13. The consequences for Los Angeles are the subject of many books, movies, and articles. As historian James N. Gregory notes in "The Shaping of California History,"

> The railroad turned the state into a second Midwest, encouraging first the production of wheat, then with the spread of irrigation and the invention of refrigerated cars, a shift to fruits and vegetables. While the state remained more urban than rural, by 1870 the fastest growing areas were the inland valleys where the Central Pacific and other promoters were steering immigrants, luring them with a campaign of cornucopia advertising conducted extensively in heartland states like Iowa and Illinois.

When the Santa Fe Railroad finally broke into the LA area later in the nineteenth century, the race was on to bring the rest of America to Southern California. The most spectacular physical monument to that is Los Angeles's handsome Union Station, built in 1939.

14. For detailed discussions regarding this episode, see Daggett, *Chapters on the History of the Southern Pacific*, 271–72, and White, *Railroaded*, 162–67. Lavender, in *The Great Persuader*, points out the Big Four also bought the California Steam Navigation Company, effectively controlling shipments on the San Joaquin and Sacramento Rivers as well as San Francisco Bay (264).

15. Haney, *A Congressional History of Railways*, 19–20.

16. Ramírez, ed., *The Octopus Speaks*, 501.

17. Stanford to Huntington, November 8, 1870, Collis Potter Huntington Papers, Syracuse.

18. McKinney, "The Mussel Slough Episode," 97.

19. Ott, *Manufacturing the Modern Patron in Victorian California*, 37. Also see J. L. Brown, *The Mussel Slough Tragedy*.

20. Massachusetts, Illinois, Michigan, and Pennsylvania began attempts at railroad regulation in 1869–71. Seeman, "California's Constitutional Response to the Railroad," 428; Gerald D. Nash, "The California Railroad Commission," 287.

21. The Virtual Museum of the City of San Francisco, www.sfmuseum.net/hist10 /wralston.html, has a pleasant if not scholarly web page about Bank of California president William Ralston. There was (and remains) widespread belief that he had committed suicide, although an autopsy concluded the forty-nine-year-old had suffered a stroke while swimming off of what today is called San Francisco's North Beach. Huntington biographer David Lavender has also authored a worthy biography of Ralston: *Nothing Seemed Impossible*.

22. Shumsky, *The Evolution of Political Protest*, 4–5.

23. Ibid.

24. Kauer, "The Workingmen's Party of California," 279. The movement lost steam after 1880 and as with the earlier Know-Nothing (or American) Party, dissolved.

25. Leland Stanford to San Francisco's chief of police, outgoing correspondence, 1870–79, Leland Stanford Collection.

26. Crane, ed., *Newton Booth of California*, 160.

27. State of California, *Appendix: Abstract of Evidence Taken before the Assembly Committee on Corporations, Nineteenth Session of the Legislature, January 1872, 3.*

28. McAfee, "Local Interests and Railroad Regulation in California during the Granger Decade," 53, 59.

CHAPTER 12. UNMASKED

1. Ramírez, *The Octopus Speaks*, 448.

2. Charles Crocker to Collis Huntington, October 29, 1877 (punctuation irregularities in original), "Letters from Collis P. Huntington to Mark Hopkins et al.," Collis Potter Huntington Papers, Huntington Library.

3. Leland Stanford, outgoing correspondence, May 1, 1875, Leland Stanford Collection. As early as 1870 Stanford had written to Huntington, "I notice in one of your letters that you were trying to get control of the U.P.," then asking if they did would they have to pay the interest on the U.P. bonds and if so, would it be "profitable." Stanford to Huntington, January 2, 1870, Collis Potter Huntington Papers, Syracuse. Not only was there no law prohibiting such a monopoly, the federal act enabling the transcontinental railroad explicitly stated the two lines "may unite in a consolidated company."

4. She was the mother of the celebrated Madame de Staël.

5. *New York Times*, July 7, 1870, 1.

6. Central Pacific Company vs. Alfred A. Cohen, Argument of Mr. Cohen, Twelfth District Court, City and County of San Francisco, 1876.

7. Ibid., quoting from Edward Robert Bulwer-Lytton, "The Dinner Hour," https://www.bartleby.com/246/705.html.

8. Ibid., quoting from *The Merchant of Venice*.

9. Central Pacific Company vs. Alfred A. Cohen, Argument of Mr. Cohen, Twelfth District Court, City and County of San Francisco, 1876.

10. Collis Huntington to Colton, December 8, 1876, in Ramírez, *The Octopus Speaks*, 325.

11. *San Francisco Chronicle*, June 15, 1876, 3.

12. Ambrose Bierce, in this era, was a writer and then editor of *The Wasp*, sometimes called the *Illustrated Wasp*. At other times, the publication referred to him as "Stealand Standfirm." *The Wasp*, January 31, 1885, 6.

13. According to Jane Stanford's top advisor George Crothers, as told in his biography, "Crothers pointed out that perhaps he was the only living person who knew the inside story of that incident." Leland Stanford had promised to give the Central Pacific Railroad printing contract to the *Union*, no doubt in return for its support, but Crocker, who had another brother in the printing business, gave the lucrative job to his brethren, which was the way the Big Four kept its business in the family. Stanford, although president of the railroad, just shrugged his shoulders. Crothers, by the way, married

the daughter of the eventually railroad-controlled *Union-Record*. Clausen, *Stanford's Judge Crothers*, 137.

14. White, *Railroaded*, 23. For another detailed explanation of the Thurman bill, see Daggett, *Chapters on the History of the Southern Pacific*, 381–94, as well as a brief but pointed rendition in Lavender, *The Great Persuader*, 276.

15. George, "Thomas Hill (1829–1906)," 97.

16. Ball, *The Inventor and the Tycoon*, 316.

17. Leland Stanford, portions of unidentified dictations concerning Leland Stanford, 1890, p. 12, Bancroft Library, University of California, Berkeley.

18. Ott, *Manufacturing the Modern Patron in Victorian California*, 37.

19. Colton to Collis Huntington, September 26, 1877, in Ramírez, *The Octopus Speaks*, 414.

20. Strazdes, "The Millionaire's Palace," 214.

21. Stevenson, *From Scotland to Silverado*, 186.

22. George, "Thomas Hill (1829–1906)," 63–64. George conceded that "it cannot be established with any certainty that the work had been commissioned," as had been widely reported (ibid.).

23. *San Francisco Call*, November 14, 1910, 1, 2.

24. The massive, fanciful portrait hangs inside the California State Railroad Museum, very near the original stores of Stanford, Huntington, Crocker, and Hopkins; near where Stanford had shoveled the first ceremonial scoop of earth for the Central Pacific; and near the Sacramento train station. The painting is highly romanticized and inaccurate. For example, Huntington stands behind Stanford, although he was not there at all. Better yet, Theodore Judah is off to the right side, although at the time of the depicted ceremony he had been dead for almost six years. A pamphlet written by Hill many years later gave his account of the controversy, alleging Stanford had reneged on him. Several newspaper accounts cited the publication.

25. *San Francisco Call*, November 14, 1910, 1.

26. Ayres, *Gold and Sunshine*, 280–81.

27. Orsi, *Sunset Limited*, 115.

28. Conan, "Sidelights on the Investment Policies of Stanford, Huntington, Hopkins, and Crocker," 86.

29. McConnell, "The Stanford Vina Ranch," 19.

30. The *San Francisco Daily Examiner*, in a July 14, 1895, story extensively quoting Jennie Stanford, reported the Vina Ranch as 62,950 acres (p. 9). Every other source consulted says 55,000 acres.

31. McConnell, "The Stanford Vina Ranch," 34.

32. *San Francisco Daily Examiner*, March 26, 1882, 1.

33. McConnell, "The Stanford Vina Ranch," 22.

34. *Sacramento Record-Union*, July 3, 1886, 2.

35. Leland Stanford, portions of unidentified dictations concerning Leland Stanford, p. 10.

36. Maynard A. Amerine foreword in Peninou, *Leland Stanford's Great Vina Ranch*, xi; Peninou, *Leland Stanford's Great Vina Ranch*, 50.

37. Idwal Jones, *Vines of California*, 146.

38. *Daily Alta California*, December 30, 1889, 1.

39. Ibid., April 17, 1885, 5.

40. "Reconciling these two actions caused difficulties" is the droll understatement modern medical historians pronounced in Guly, "Medicinal Brandy."

41. Berner, *Mrs. Leland Stanford*, 64; McConnell, "The Stanford Vina Ranch," 45.

42. Leland Stanford, portions of unidentified dictations concerning Leland Stanford, p. 10.

43. Stanford University's first president, David Starr Jordan, stated in his memoirs that the town's original name was Palo Alto Park. Jordan, *The Days of a Man*, 1:381.

CHAPTER 13. GONE DARK

1. For a summation of the legendary tree's past and condition, see the redundantly named El Palo Alto Redwood Tree—Arborist Report and Appraisal, Attachment A, September 18, 1999, https://trees.stanford.edu/PDF/elpaloalto.pdf.

2. Daggett, *Chapters on the History of the Southern Pacific*. 157. Colton was the same man who replied to Huntington's inquiry about how much cash was taken out of the Central Pacific accounts by the directors (see beginning of chapter 12).

3. Ramírez, *The Octopus Speaks*, 33, 88.

4. Ibid., 63, 67, 123, 202.

5. Ibid., 251.

6. Ibid., 74.

7. Ibid., 372.

8. Ibid., 373.

9. Ibid., 324, 331.

10. Ibid., 51. The "Kar" refers to a private rail coach Jennie made for Leland, but which, of course, she also rode. The asterisks fill places in Huntington's scrawl that were undecipherable.

11. Berner, *Mrs. Leland Stanford*, 92.

12. Shumsky, *The Evolution of Political Protest*, 97.

13. Ibid., 95.

14. Atherton, *Adventures of a Novelist*, 63–64. Gertrude Atherton, née Horn, had married George Atherton, son of Faxon Atherton, who had come to California well before the gold rush and made a fortune during that era in shipping and other businesses. The Atherton estate was originally named Fair Oaks but was later rechristened the town of Atherton, a wealthy enclave now best known as home and destination for Silicon Valley fortunes.

15. *New York Times*, April 8, 1881, 4.

16. State of New York Chamber of Commerce, *Report of the Special Committee on Railroad Transportation on the Reply Made by Hon. Leland Stanford, April 7, 1881*.

17. Ibid.

18. *New York Times*, April 8, 1881, 4.

19. Leland Stanford to Collis Huntington, December 5, 1878, Collis Potter Huntington Papers, Syracuse.

20. Leland Stanford to Collis Huntington, November 13, 1878, "Letters from Collis P. Huntington to Mark Hopkins et al.," Collis Potter Huntington Papers, Huntington Library.

21. McAfee, "A Constitutional History of Railroad Rate Regulation in California," 267–68.

22. State of California, *Report of the Committee on Corporations of the Assembly of California, Twenty-Fifth Session, 1883*, 4–5.

23. Ibid.

24. Ibid. For a somewhat different perspective, see Gerald D. Nash, "The California Railroad Commission."

25. Hendricks, *Albert Bierstadt*, 224.

26. *New York Sun*, October 16, 1887, 7. See also Berner, *Mrs. Leland Stanford*, 188.

27. Purtell, *The Tiffany Touch*, 96, 103. Isabella II officially abdicated in 1870.

28. Berner, *Mrs. Leland Stanford*, 25.

29. Large, *The Grand Spas of Europe*, introduction.

30. Leland Stanford to Jennie Stanford, outgoing correspondence, August 10, 1883, Leland Stanford Collection.

31. Herbert C. Nash, *In Memoriam*, 37.

32. Ibid., 30.

33. Jane Stanford to Timothy and May Hopkins, February 25, 1884, Jane Lathrop Stanford Papers. One can read a transcribed version in Nagel, *Iron Will*, 33.

34. Herbert C. Nash, *In Memoriam*, 59.

35. Leland Stanford to Collis Huntington, March 13, 1884, Collis Potter Huntington Papers, Syracuse.

36. Mark Twain, Notebook, Mark Twain Papers and Project, Bancroft Library, University of California, Berkeley.

37. Berner, *Mrs. Leland Stanford*, 33.

38. Leland Stanford, outgoing correspondence, March 1890, Leland Stanford Collection.

39. Stanford Family Collection, Cantor Arts Center at Stanford University, summer 2017.

40. Grace Church is today Grace Cathedral, a grand Episcopalian assembly at the top of Nob Hill, the former site of Charles Crocker's mansion.

41. Berner, *Mrs. Leland Stanford*, 39.

42. Ibid., 43.

CHAPTER 14. INGENIOUSLY CONTRIVED DEVICES

1. Shumsky, *The Evolution of Political Protest*, 105. The others four were George Hearst, John P. Jones, William Sharon, and James Fair (Nevada). Fair owned the Nob Hill mansion that became the site of the Fairmont Hotel, which is today an international hotel chain.

2. Ibid.

3. In 1995 Congress dismantled the Interstate Commerce Commission and replaced it with the Surface Transportation Board.

4. Swisher, *Stephen J. Field*, 260.

5. Kens, *Justice Stephen Field*, 142–43.

6. Notably for some legal observers, a heading in the printed ruling inferred that a corporation was protected under the Fourteenth Amendment in the same manner as individuals—an opinion Field pushed hard during his long, storied career—although the ruling itself clearly stated it was not making any such decision. Even today some are at odds as to whether the early ruling led to subsequent, still more controversial modern Supreme Court decisions such as *Hobby Lobby* and *Citizens United*.

7. Haney, *A Congressional History of Railways*, 129. In the Pacific Railway Commission hearings, Stanford testified that the trio incorporated in Kentucky "to get a charter that was favorable—that would allow us to lease all the roads in the country." *PRC*, 2809.

8. *PRC*, front cover.

9. Leland Stanford telegram to Collis Huntington, outgoing correspondence, September 23, 1887, Leland Stanford Collection.

10. *PRC*, 9.

11. Ibid., 23.

12. Ibid., 36.

13. Ibid., 26.

14. Ibid., 22, 20. David Nasaw, in his biography of Andrew Carnegie, quotes Huntington telling the steel magnate he had "not read a book for years except my ledger." By the same account, Carnegie did not fully trust Huntington, declining to extend him credit toward buying rails. Nasaw, *Andrew Carnegie*, 194, 484.

15. *PRC*, 4522.

16. Ibid., 2644, 2645, 2634.

17. Ibid., 2630, 2645.

18. Ibid., 2349.

19. Ibid., 2743.

20. Ibid., 2616, 3537.

21. Ibid., 698.

22. Ibid., 2920, 2921. Toward the end of 1870, Huntington had written Stanford, "I would suggest that you get some of our friends to organize (of course, we to own) a railroad company to build from a point on the S.P., viz. Los Angeles to the Colorado

River near Fort Yuma." Collis Huntington to Leland Stanford, "Letters from Collis P. Huntington to Mark Hopkins et al.," 1870, 2:211, Collis Potter Huntington Papers, Huntington Library.

23. *PRC*, 2864.

24. Ibid., 3170, 3172, 3164.

25. Swisher, *Stephen J. Field*, 244. The legal historian also states that "letters show-ing [Field's] close personal relationship with Stanford, Huntington, and others, have been carefully destroyed" (265).

26. *PRC*, 3535, 4525, 4522.

27. *Report of the Commission and of the Minority Commissioner of the United States Pacific Railway Commission*, 84 (hereafter *Rpt. of Comm. PRC*).

28. Ibid., 73, 84, 50.

29. Ibid., 72, 80.

30. The 1886–87 state budget was $5.2 million. For 1887–88 it was $6.6 million. Waterman, *Biennial Message of Governor R. W. Waterman to the Legislature*, 12. National budget numbers are from an author interview with staff from the U.S. Department of Treasury Public Information Office.

31. *Rpt. of Comm. PRC*, 80, 49.

32. Elliott, *Stanford University*, 12.

CHAPTER 15. DEPOSED

1. O'Malley, *Keeping Watch*, 82.

2. Bartky, "The Invention of Railroad Time," 13–22.

3. Kern, *The Culture of Time and Space*, 12.

4. O'Malley, *Keeping Watch*, 123.

5. Bartky, *Selling the True Time*, 144. Ian Barky, as have others over the years, cited an Indianapolis newspaper for this truncated quote. The citation does not stand up under scrutiny—although some have seen the quotation as a spoof, because it rightfully indicates suspicions many had of the railroad it has survived.

6. Chandler, *The Railroads*, 9.

7. Ibid., 8–10. Fogel, in *Railroads and American Economic Growth*, bucked the tide and questioned Chandler's thesis as have some further historians. Other contem-porary scholars, such as Walter Licht, have confirmed and added to the work of Chandler.

8. Trachtenberg, *The Incorporation of America*, preface and p. 4.

9. Stiles, *The First Tycoon*, 434.

10. Farley died early in the next year.

11. *Sacramento Bee*, January 17, 1885, 1.

12. Hart, *In Our Second Century*, 127–28.

13. *Sacramento Record-Union*, February 13, 1886, 1. The same story quotes Stanford as saying he left the governor's office after seeing that the job and the presidency of the railroad were "incompatible" tasks.

14. The Democratic governor was George Stoneman, one of the three California railroad commissioners that state assembly investigators accused of sloth.

15. Hearst died just four years after his appointment.

16. Although this agreement has been cited as a primary source by more than one author, one of whom is highly credible, and is said to be in the Leland Stanford Collection of the Department of Special Collections and University Archives, Stanford University Libraries, archivists there have been unable to find the document.

17. *San Francisco Chronicle*, April 7, 1890, 8. In *The Great Persuader*, Lavender says Huntington wrote out a "fantasy interview" in which he said Stanford's "strong point" was his "vanity" (360). It was one of the kinder expressions in this document, which is held at the Huntington Library.

18. *San Francisco Examiner*, April 10, 1890, 3.

19. Ibid. Huntington condescended, carefully, to add of Stanford, "He has many good points that I like, and it was never my intention to say anything that would give him offense. We get along in business all right, and our personal relations are kept up the same as usual." On a separate but not uninteresting subject, Huntington told the *Examiner* reporter, "I favor the Chinese on the ground that every man born of a woman is deserving of kind consideration until he proves himself a rogue."

20. Berner, *Mrs. Leland Stanford*, 35.

21. *Kern County Californian*, August 23, 1890.

22. Huntington, though he often had no qualms about publicly denigrating his opponents, appears to have been far more discreet in his acts of benevolence. For example, just before Christmas of 1884, Theodore Judah's widow, Anna, wrote to Huntington about being "desperate" for any kind of financial assistance: "You *said* 'you would be my friend' (I believe you are) that you would continue to help me. You would make some money for me." The mortgage payments "*haunt* me like a *nightmare*— keeping sleep from my eyelids." Then, "There are moments when it seemed it would send me to the madhouse!" And, "Remember your promise to me." Four days later, she wrote again to thank him for his charity, saying, "I feel like a 'big sunflower.'" Anna Judah to Collis Huntington, December 12, 1884 and December 16, 1884 (emphasis underlined in original), Collis Potter Huntington Papers, Syracuse.

23. Elliott, *Stanford University*, 261.

24. George C. Perkins was the outgoing Republican governor, who incidentally had vied for the Senate job in 1885 and took Stanford's seat when he passed away.

25. David Starr Jordan to George Hoar, June 20, 1894, p. 1, Jane Lathrop Stanford Papers.

26. Elliott, *Stanford University*, 14.

27. State of California, *Bureau of Labor Statistics, 1887–1888*, 243. MIT, Johns Hopkins, and Cornell, to name just three universities, were already well established and practicing this concept.

28. Butler, *Across the Busy Years*, 149–52.

29. Ibid., 149–52, 16.

30. *Reno Evening Gazette*, February 6, 1890, 2.

31. Jordan, *The Stability of Truth*, 157.

32. Burns, *David Starr Jordan*, 155. Jordan had a master's degree and studied medicine for one year, providing him the nineteenth-century title of medical doctor. He never earned a PhD.

33. Elliott, *Stanford University*, 79.

34. Ibid., 252.

35. Having had the mausoleum built while he was alive, Stanford later revoked that section of his will.

CHAPTER 16. THE FUNDAMENTAL STANDARD

1. Charles Crocker to Collis Huntington, February 15, 1879 (emphasis in original), "Letters from Collis P. Huntington to Mark Hopkins et al.," Collis Potter Huntington Papers, Huntington Library.

2. Clark, *Leland Stanford*, 468. George T. Clark, who was head of the Stanford University library, wrote an early, very generous, but not completely unctuous biography of Stanford. It remains the most readable and credible of the few earlier attempts to chronicle Stanford's life.

3. *New York World*, June 21, 1893, evening edition, 1.

4. *Fort Wayne Sentinel*, June 21, 1893, 1.

5. *Los Angeles Times*, June 21, 1893.

6. *San Francisco Chronicle*, June 21, 1893, 1.

7. Two buxom sphinxes graced each side of the front doors of the mausoleum Stanford had called for. Jennie later had them moved to the far less conspicuous rear of the tomb. She then had sphinxes of indeterminate sex set out front.

8. Berner, *Mrs. Leland Stanford*, 47.

9. *Los Angeles Herald*, October 10, 1893, 4.

10. Elliott, *Stanford University*, 258.

11. Berner, *Mrs. Leland Stanford*, 98.

12. *San Francisco Examiner*, August 29, 1893, 2.

13. The 1906 earthquake and fire destroyed the probate records, compelling the use of secondary sources, such as newspaper accounts, to chronicle this subject.

14. McConnell, "The Stanford Vina Ranch," 56.

15. Jane Stanford to May Hopkins, August 29, 1898, Jane Lathrop Stanford Papers. One can read a transcribed version in Nagel, *Iron Will*, 137–38.

16. Elliott, *Stanford University*, 385.

17. Gullard and Lund, *History of Palo Alto*, 57–58.

18. That covenant remained on the books into the Prohibition era but eventually faded away. Palo Alto city hall officials declined to respond to repeated requests for information.

19. When former U.S. president Benjamin Harrison came to campus to lecture and stayed in a special suite at Encina Hall, then the men's dormitory, the administration provided him with "a quantity of liquors and cigars." After Harrison departed, a pair

of students confiscated some of the leftover contraband and shared it with fellow undergraduates. Elliott, *Stanford University*, 185.

20. This standard remains part of the university's code of conduct to this day: Stanford Office of Community Standards, "Honor Code," https://communitystandards .stanford.edu/student-conduct-process/honor-code-and-fundamental-standard.

21. *Chicago Tribune*, June 7, 1894, 5.

22. Elliott, *Stanford University*, 255.

23. Jane Stanford, outgoing correspondence, March 30, 1895, Jane Lathrop Stanford Papers.

24. Letwin, *Law and Economic Policy in America*, 101–3.

25. Swisher, *Stephen J. Field*, 119, 245.

26. Jane Stanford, outgoing correspondence, April 16, 1895, Jane Lathrop Stanford Papers.

27. Elliott, *Stanford University*, 268.

28. United States v. Stanford, 16 S. Ct. 576 (1896).

29. Jane Stanford, outgoing correspondence, March 16, 1896, Jane Lathrop Stanford Papers.

30. Elliott, *Stanford University*, 312.

31. Crothers, *Outline of the History of the Founding of the Leland Stanford Junior University*, 4.

32. David Starr Jordan to Charles William Eliot, n.d., p. 4, Jane Lathrop Stanford Papers.

33. Osborne, *Museum Builders of the West*, 49, 52, 105.

34. Berner, *Mrs. Leland Stanford*, 45. The limit on female students was dissolved long after Jennie passed away.

35. Rudolph, *The American College and University*, 352–54.

36. Originally enacted in 1901 as Section 10 of Article 9 of the California State Constitution, the exemption was renumbered in 1973 as Article 20, Section 2:

> All property now or hereafter held in trust for the founding, maintenance, or benefit of the Leland Stanford Junior University, or any department thereof, may be exempt by special act from State taxation, and all personal property so held, the Palo Alto Farm as described in the endowment grant to the trustees of the University, and all other real property so held and used by the University for educational purposes exclusively, may be similarly exempted from county and municipal taxation; provided that residents of California shall be charged no fee for tuition unless such fees be authorized by act of the legislature.

The only other institution in the state constitution specifically exempted from property taxes is the spectacular Huntington Library and Art Gallery in San Marino. It was created by Collis Huntington's nephew and heir Henry E. Huntington, who famously married his Uncle Collis's widow, who was the other heir. The property tax exemption was granted to the Huntington, as it is usually known, in 1930, three years after Henry died.

In 1978 Stanford University sued Santa Clara County, protesting the government's contention that taxpayers were entitled to property taxes from the campus golf course, as they are from the commercial properties owned by the university, such as the Stanford Shopping Center (site of the former Stanford hacienda) and the research park that is arguably ground zero of Silicon Valley. The county lost the case. The state tax code later also exempted other private schools such as Santa Clara University and the University of Southern California.

Stanford University officials declined to respond to repeated requests for information about this topic.

37. David Belcher and Michael Belcher, "Constitutionally Suspect Special Property Tax Exemptions," May 9, 2018, http://scocablog.com/constitutionally-suspect-special-property-tax-exemptions. The SCOCA blog is a joint project of Berkeley Law and the *Hastings Law Journal* focused on substantive coverage of the Supreme Court of California.

38. Although Leland Stanford said, "My object is to furnish education to those of small means" (Clark, *Leland Stanford*, 414), tuition as of 2018 was almost $50,000 annually.

39. Statutes of California, 1921 Cal. Stat., chap. 361 § 1, p. 541 (July 29, 1921), added the following language to Education Code Section 94010 (Title 3, Division 10, Part 59, Chapter 1, Article 2): "The trustees of the Leland Stanford Junior University may charge residents and nonresidents of this state such fees for tuition, as are necessary for the administration of the affairs of the university." The author is particularly indebted to Professor Michael Salerno at the University of California's Hastings College of the Law, Professor David Carrillo of Berkeley Law, and most especially David Belcher and Michael Belcher, fellows at Berkeley Law, for vital assistance in researching the tax-exemption topic.

40. Jane Stanford to David Starr Jordan, May 18, 1903, p. 6, Jane Lathrop Stanford Papers.

CHAPTER 17. SEX AND SOCIALISM

1. Berner, *Mrs. Leland Stanford*, 157–58.

2. Ibid., 133, 134, 212–13.

3. Daggett, *Chapters on the History of the Southern Pacific*, 371; White, *Railroaded*, 23.

4. Caruth and Caruth, "Stanford University," 165.

5. Metzger, *Academic Freedom*, 163.

6. Spoehr, "Progress' Pilgrim," 129.

7. Veysey, *The Emergence of the American University*, 400. In his colorful memoir, *Seventy Years of It*, Ross writes, "I came to be regarded as a pest by the Southern Pacific machine and influences were shrewdly brought to bear on Mrs. Stanford to make her distrust me" (63).

8. Jane Lathrop Stanford, ingoing correspondence, David Starr Jordan to Jane Stanford, November 21, 1900, p. 2, Jane Lathrop Stanford Papers.

9. Clausen, *Stanford's Judge Crothers*, 55.

10. Metzger, *Academic Freedom*, 168.

11. Ibid., 165.

12. Jane Lathrop Stanford, ingoing correspondence, Alfred Schmidt to Mrs. Jane Stanford, September 24, 1901, Jane Lathrop Stanford Papers.

13. J. C. Branner to George H. Fitch, May 31, 1901, David Starr Jordan Papers, Department of Special Collections and University Archives, Stanford University Libraries.

14. Jane Stanford to David Starr Jordan, December 1900, p. 2, Jane Lathrop Stanford Papers.

15. Julius Goebel to Jane Stanford, n.d., pp. 1–4, Jane Lathrop Stanford Papers. Richard von Krafft-Ebing was a highly respected German physician and scientist who did pioneering research in sexuality. See Oosterhuis, "Sexual Modernity in the Works of Richard von Krafft-Ebing and Albert Moll."

16. David Starr Jordan to Jane Stanford, November 5, 1902, p. 1, Jane Lathrop Stanford Papers.

17. Carnochan, "The Case of Julius Goebel," 103.

18. For a fairly astonishing portrait of this early twentieth-century orphanage, see *Report of the Albany Orphan Asylum for the Year Ending September Thirtieth 1919*.

19. *Cheyenne Daily Sun*, February 2, 1892, 4.

20. Jane Stanford, outgoing correspondence, May 15, 1905, p. 5, Jane Lathrop Stanford Papers. The "Jewel Fund" was first supposed to go toward building the opulent church in the center of campus. Because that building was completed earlier than expected, she directed the money instead to the library, named after Leland Stanford's brother Thomas. The 1906 earthquake soon destroyed it.

21. Elliott, *Stanford University*, 86.

22. Berner, *Mrs. Leland Stanford*, 105.

23. Clausen, *Stanford's Judge Crothers*, 55–56.

24. Ibid. The par value of a security is the stated value, or face value, because it's the price printed on the face of a bond or stock certificate. Actual market value can be very different.

CHAPTER 18. "GOD FORGIVE ME MY SINS"

1. Berner, *Mrs. Leland Stanford*, 165–66.

2. Irwin, *The Making of a Reporter*, 10–11.

3. Berner, *Mrs. Leland Stanford*, 168.

4. Ibid., 201.

5. Jane Stanford, outgoing correspondence, February 24, 1905, p. 1, Jane Lathrop Stanford Papers.

6. Jennie Stanford's butler was Alfred Beverly; and Alfred Pennyworth, of course, is famously Bruce Wayne's butler.

7. Berner, *Mrs. Leland Stanford*, 206.

8. The final words are taken from Berner's memoirs, *Mrs. Leland Stanford*, 207; they are her sworn testimony at the coroner's inquest into Jennie Stanford's death. Coroner

of Honolulu, *Coroner's Inquest In re Death of Jane Lathrop Stanford*, also includes voluminous testimony from Dr. Humphries and many others directly involved in and informed of the events. In addition to Berner's account, in the Jane Lathrop Stanford Papers at Stanford University Libraries there is a typewritten page among Jennie's preserved correspondence without a date or any other notation. It simply says: "God forgive me my sins. Am I prepared to meet my dear ones?"

9. Testimony of Dr. Francis Day, in Coroner of Honolulu, *Coroner's Inquest In re Death of Jane Lathrop Stanford*, 32.

10. Testimony of Dr. Clifford Wood, ibid., 36.

11. Testimonies of Robert Duncan and Dr. Francis Day, ibid., 44.

12. Testimony of Dr. Francis Humphries, ibid., 60.

13. Coroner of Honolulu, *Coroner's Inquest In re Death of Jane Lathrop Stanford*, 70 (emphasis in original).

14. Timothy Hopkins, Mark Hopkins's adopted son, was the trustee and part of the second generation of the intertwined family business of the Big Four.

15. Testimony of Dr. Waterhouse, prepared for David Starr Jordan, pp. 1–4, Jane Lathrop Stanford Papers, correspondence, Department of Special Collections and University Archives, Stanford University Libraries.

16. David Starr Jordan to Samuel F. Leib, March 22, 1905, David Starr Jordan Papers.

17. In *The Days of a Man*, 2:95, Jordan wrote of the Hawaiians that they were "for the most part supremely and childishly indifferent to work or business." He regarded the French as "dissolute and slovenly" and had still more contempt for southern Italians (Burns, *David Starr Jordan*, 61–62), whose traits he implied were due to drinking wine. Jordan's 1902 screed, *The Blood of the Nation, a Study of the Decay of Races through Survival of the Unfit*, is especially telling of his perversion of scientific methods: "For a race of men or a herd of cattle are governed by the same laws of selection. . . . To select for posterity those individuals which best meet our needs or please our fancy, and to destroy those with unfavorable qualities, is the function of artificial selection. . . . In the world of man similar causes produce similar results" (6–8). And "the feudal nobility of each nation was in the beginning made up of the fair, the brave, and the strong. By their courage and strength their men became the rulers of the people, and by the same token they chose the beauty of the realm to be their own" (22). Finally, "In spite of their lust and cruelty, the victims of the Reign of Terror were literally the best from the standpoint of race development. Their weaknesses were those of training in luxury and irresponsible power" (36).

18. *Pacific Commercial Advertiser*, March 17, 1905, 1.

19. *New York Times*, December 31, 1905, 2.

20. *San Francisco Call*, December 31, 1905, 30.

21. Jordan, *The Days of a Man*, 2:156–57.

22. Cutler, *The Mysterious Death of Jane Stanford*, 88, 103.

23. Carnochan, "The Case of Julius Goebel," 108.

24. Spoehr, "Progress' Pilgrim," viii.

REQUIEM: AMERICAN DISRUPTOR

1. Rodriguez, *Days of Obligation*, 205, 218.

2. Churchill, *The Birth of Britain*, 85, referring to Offa of Mercia.

3. Jordan, *The Days of a Man*, 1:483.

4. Herbert C. Nash, *In Memoriam*, 5–6. See also Leland Starford, portions of unidentified dictations concerning Leland Stanford; and Bancroft, *A History of the Life of Leland Stanford*, 32–33. Jordan said Nash was "practically a member of the household." Jordan, *The Days of a Man*, 1:544.

5. Bancroft, *A History of the Life of Leland Stanford*.

6. *Arizona Republic*, March 3, 1905, 2.

7. Berner, *Mrs. Leland Stanford*, 213.

8. Nilan, "The Life and Times of a Victorian Lady," 3.

9. Perrow, *Organizing America*, 115.

10. Swisher, *Stephen J. Field*, 242.

11. Fogel, *The Union Pacific Railroad*, 110.

12. Daggett, *Chapters on the History of the Southern Pacific*, 454.

13. Henry George, "What the Railroad Will Bring Us," *Overland Monthly*, October 1868.

14. Lenoir, "Inventing the Entrepreneurial University," 93. It bears notice that as early as 1898 Professor A. C. Perrine, who headed Stanford's electrical engineering program, was instrumental in finding a way to bring hydroelectric power from the Sierra Nevada to the Bay Area. For more, see James C. Williams, *The Rise of Silicon Valley* (Cupertino: California History Center Foundation, 1993).

15. Hall and Markusen, eds., *Silicon Landscapes*, 22.

16. Author conversation with John McLaughlin at Silicon Valley Historical Association.

17. Shurkin, *Broken Genius*, 187.

18. The Cold War led to the buildup of nuclear weapons and the missiles to deliver them anywhere on earth. That led to the development of a war-proof communication system: ARPANET, which evolved into the internet. For more, see Kranzberg, "Technology and History."

19. Bancroft, *History of the Life of Leland Stanford*, 235, 238–39.

20. The Crocker Art Museum of Sacramento's website has more on Amy Crocker: https://www.crockerart.org/crockers.

21. Estate of Stanford, 49 Cal.2d 120 (1957).

BIBLIOGRAPHICAL NOTE

The following bibliography does not list every book, journal article, dissertation, newspaper and magazine story, interview, webpage, podcast, tweet, and fortune cookie epigram that have directly or indirectly informed *American Disruptor*. Most sources that are cited directly or otherwise have been primary sources and are listed as such. Sources that have informed the work indirectly—for example, that led me to primary sources—are cited as secondary.

Periodicals of any nature, internet sources including those on the World Wide Web, and interviews and the like that have had a direct effect on *American Disruptor* are also listed, but not those I have considered secondary.

Primary documents take a special meaning in a work of this nature. Correspondence, testimony, interviews, and documents by Leland Stanford fit that category first and foremost. More than five hundred mostly handwritten letters and telegrams by Leland Stanford, scattered through 122 large archival boxes kept at Syracuse University's Special Collections Research Center within the Collis Potter Huntington Papers have proven especially valuable, as it appears only a handful of railroad and Huntington scholars have carefully read and employed only some of these documents in their research. The Leland Stanford papers in the collection have otherwise been largely overlooked, to the peril of U.S. history.

In writing about the Stanfords themselves, and other main subjects of *American Disruptor*, I have consistently either gone directly to the authoritative origin—such as the handwritten totals of the 1859 gubernatorial election held by the California State Archives—or reverse-engineered assertions made by others to get to the provenance of their stated facts. More than a few times I have been bitterly disappointed that the source was misused or not existent at all. In those cases, of course, I either employed the correct information or simply have not used the misinformation. In many instances when a potentially important assertion was made by a previous writer but cannot be independently verified, I have chosen to ignore it, except in rare instances when the credibility of the author and context of the assertion reach a high standard.

Internet sources warrant some bibliographical comment: it bears repeating that great care must be taken in the ever-expanding online universe. Much of what is asserted there, especially on the web, is questionable at best and far too frequently flatly inaccurate. Other hazards of online research: URLs change, servers go down, and content alterations take place often without notice. This can be especially frustrating for scholars, journalists, and other researchers who seek primary sources, but it is the hard reality we face in the internet age. Fortunately for the historian, old—analog—media such as books, periodicals, and primary source documents are usually still available with a little extra sleuthing. Much of that used here can be found at Stanford University's excellent Special Collections and University Archives housed at the Cecil H. Green Library.

A quick sidebar regarding some particular primary documents held by the wonderful Bancroft Library at the University of California, Berkeley: The Bancroft holds many published and unpublished manuscripts that are simple, lightly edited dictations from people whom nineteenth-century historian, book collector, and bookseller Hubert Howe Bancroft considered significant figures in the history of California and the West. These are largely unquestioning documents that allowed people such as Josiah Stanford and Collis Huntington, as well as Leland Stanford, to recount their history the way they wanted to remember—and wanted us to remember—it. Bancroft hired people to take many of these reminiscences, although Bancroft himself and his wife, Matilda, also did some of the work. Bancroft accepted payment from his subjects in return for their published dictations. The collection was printed in luxurious leather-bound, marble-edged editions and sold as a set called *Chronicles of the Builders of the Commonwealth*.

This led to a specific conflict with Leland Stanford. Both men have taken their versions of the events to the grave, but it is largely agreed that Stanford agreed to pay a set amount for his book, but when presented with the bill, balked, accusing Bancroft of double-dealing and duplicitously trying to sell him the entire set of the hagiographic *Chronicles*. (If this seems reminiscent of Stanford's quarrel with painter Thomas Hill, it is.) Bancroft considered this an unforgivable retrenchment and refused to print the volume about Stanford as he had for the others. It sat in unfinished manuscript form for decades in the Bancroft Library until an Oakland publisher printed a run in 1952, although he missed some crucial pages, recovered here for *American Disruptor*. John Caughey, a distinguished UCLA historian, discusses much of this in his biography of Bancroft, *Hubert Howe Bancroft, Historian of the West* (Berkeley: University of California Press, 1946).

Having spent most of my adult life as a news reporter concentrating on investigative projects prompts me to add a special note regarding the necessarily orthodox practice of using news stories for historical information: The *Washington Post*'s Philip Graham famously called news stories "the first rough draft of history," as indeed they are. It is prudent to let the eye linger on "rough draft." More than two hundred years before the *Post* publisher, Voltaire wisely noted that "in the case of news, we should always wait for the sacrament of confirmation." The French philosopher and wit's goals remain excellent if sometimes elusive.

In the sources in the following bibliography I have been constantly surprised and delighted to discover significant and interesting untold facts and insights about American and California history, the formation of Silicon Valley, and of course, Leland and Jennie Stanford. Yet, as I sometimes stand before the suitably imposing family tomb in a copse of woods near the posh shopping center on their university campus, I am always sorrowful that Mr. and Mrs. Stanford could not be better primary sources in their own story. It was a choice Leland and Jennie made and one the living must live with.

BIBLIOGRAPHY

BOOKS: PRIMARY SOURCES

Ames, Winthrop. *The Ames Family of Easton, Massachusetts*. Privately printed, 1938.

Anbinder, Tyler. *Nativism and Slavery: The Northern Know Nothings and the Politics of 1850*. New York: Oxford University Press, 1992.

Atherton, Gertrude. *Adventures of a Novelist*. New York: Blue Ribbon Books, 1932.

Ayres, James J. *Gold and Sunshine: Reminiscences of Early California*. Boston: Richard G. Badger, the Gorham Press, 1922.

Bain, David Haward. *Empire Express: Building the First Transcontinental Railroad*. New York: Penguin, 2000.

Bancroft, Hubert Howe. *History of the Life of Leland Stanford: A Character Study*. Oakland: Biobooks, 1952.

Barker, Malcolm E. Barker, ed. *More San Francisco Memoirs, 1852–1899; The Ripening Years*. San Francisco: Londonborn Publications, 1996.

Barth, Gunther. *Bitter Strength: A History of the Chinese in the United States, 1850–1870*. Cambridge, MA: Harvard University Press, 1964.

Bartky, Ian R. *Selling the True Time: Nineteenth-Century Timekeeping in America*. Stanford: Stanford University Press, 2000.

Battelle, John. *The Search: How Google and Its Rivals Rewrote the Rules of Business and Transformed Our Culture*. New York: Penguin Group, 2005.

Berner, Bertha. *Mrs. Leland Stanford: An Intimate Account*. Stanford: Stanford University Press, 1934.

Bernstein, Peter L. *Wedding of the Waters: The Erie Canal and the Making of a Great Nation*. New York: W. W. Norton, 2005.

Brewer, William H. *Up and Down California in 1860–1864: The Journal of William H. Brewer*. Berkeley: University of California Press, 2003.

Brown, J. L. *The Mussel Slough Tragedy*. N.p.: J. L. Brown, 1958.

Burns, Edward McNall. *David Starr Jordan: Prophet of Freedom.* Stanford: Stanford University Press, 1953.

Butler, Nicholas Murray. *Across the Busy Years: Recollections and Reflections.* New York: Scriber's Sons, 1939.

Chandler, Alfred D., Jr., ed. *The Railroads: The Nation's First Big Business, Sources and Readings.* New York: Harcourt, Brace and World, 1965.

———. *The Visible Hand: The Managerial Revolution in American Business.* Cambridge, MA: Harvard University Press, 1977.

Churchill, Winston. *The Birth of Britain.* New York: Dodd, Mead, 1956.

Cigrand, Dr. B. J. *In Days of Old Ozaukee.* Chicago: Western Historical, 1881.

Clausen, Henry C. *Stanford's Judge Crothers: The Life Story of George E. Crothers.* San Francisco: E. Crothers Trust, 1967.

Cooper, William J., Jr. *Jefferson Davis, American.* New York: Vintage, 2000.

Crane, Lauren E., ed. *Newton Booth of California, His Speeches and Addresses.* New York: G. P. Putnam's Sons, the Knickerbocker Press, 1894.

Cutler, Robert W. P., *The Mysterious Death of Jane Stanford.* Stanford: Stanford University Press, 2003.

Daggett, Stuart. *Chapters on the History of the Southern Pacific.* New York: Augustus M. Kelley, 1966.

Daniels, Roger, ed. *Anti-Chinese Violence in North America.* New York: Arno Press, 1978.

de Cordova, Don A. *A Voyage of Discovery to the Strait of Magellan: With an Account of the Manners and Customs of the Inhabitants and of the Natural Productions of Patagonia, Undertaken by Order of the King of Spain Admiral Don A. de Cordova, of the Royal Spanish Marine.* London: Printed for Sir Richard Phillips and Company, 1820.

Delgado, James P. *To California by Sea: A Maritime History of the California Gold Rush.* Columbia: University of South Carolina Press, 1990.

de Rutté, Théophile. *Adventures of a Young Swiss in California: The Gold Rush Account of Théophile de Rutté.* Translated by Mary Grace Paquette. Sacramento: Sacramento Book Collectors Club, 1992.

Didion, Joan. *South and West: From a Notebook.* New York: Alfred A. Knopf, 2017.

Dillon, Henriette Lucie, Marquise de La Tour du Pin Gouvernet. *Memoirs of Madame de La Tour du Pin.* Edited and translated by Felice Harcourt. New York: McCall, 1971.

Dinkelspiel, Frances. *Towers of Gold: How One Jewish Immigrant Named Isaias Hellman Created California.* New York: St. Martin's Press, 2008.

Dodge, Grenville M. *How We Built the Union Pacific Railway.* Ann Arbor: University Microfilms, 1966.

Dwight, Timothy. *Travels in New England and New York: Vol. II, Journey to Vergennes, Letter XVII; Vol. IV, Journey to Niagara, Letter I.* London: William Baynes and Son, 1823.

Eesley, Charles E., and William F. Miller. *Impact: Stanford University's Economic Impact via Innovation and Entrepreneurship.* Stanford: Stanford University, 2012. https://

engineering.stanford.edu/sites/default/files/stanford_alumni_innovation_survey_report_3–2-13.pdf.

Elliott, Orrin Leslie. *Stanford University: The First Twenty-Five Years.* Stanford: Stanford University Press, 1937.

Engs, Robert F., and Randall M. Miller, eds. *The Birth of the Grand Old Party: The Republicans' First Generation.* Philadelphia: University of Pennsylvania Press, 2002.

Faragher, John Mack. *Eternity Street: Violence and Justice in Frontier Los Angeles.* New York: W. W. Norton, 2016.

Flannery, Thomas V. *The Story of the Mohawk & Hudson Railroad, Albany–Schenectady; August 9, 1831: The Pioneer Unit of the New York Central System.* [Albany, NY]: Prepared as a contribution to early American Americana on behalf of the Railroadians of America, 1944.

Fogel, Robert W. *The Union Pacific Railroad: A Case of Premature Enterprise.* Baltimore: Johns Hopkins Press, 1960.

Folkman, David I. Folkman, Jr. *The Nicaragua Route.* Salt Lake City: University of Utah Press, 1972.

Foner, Eric. *Free Soil, Free Labor, Free Men: The Ideology of the Republican Party before the Civil War.* New York: Oxford University Press, 1995.

Freiberger, Paul, and Michael Swaine. *Fire in the Valley: The Making of the Personal Computer.* New York: McGraw-Hill, 1984.

Fulton, Robert Lardin. *The Epic of the Overland.* San Francisco: A. M. Robertson, 1924.

Galloway, John Debo. *The First Continental Railroad.* New York: Simmons-Boardman, 1950.

Gates, Paul W. *The Illinois Central Railroad and Its Colonization Work.* New York: Johnson Reprint Corporation, 1968.

Gay, Theressa. *James W. Marshall: The Discoverer of California Gold; A Biography.* Georgetown, CA: Talisman Press, 1967.

Gibbs, Mifflin Wistar. *Shadow and Light: An Autobiography With Reminiscences of the Last and Present Century.* Lincoln: University of Nebraska Press, 1995.

Gienapp, William E. *The Origins of the Republican Party, 1852–1856.* New York: Oxford University Press, 1987.

Grodin, Joseph R., Darien Shanske, and Michael B. Salerno. *The California State Constitution.* New York: Oxford University Press, 2016.

Grodinsky, Julius. *Transcontinental Railway Strategy, 1869–1893: A Study of Businessmen.* Philadelphia: University of Pennsylvania Press, 1962.

Gullard, Pamela, and Nancy Lund. *History of Palo Alto: The Early Years.* San Francisco: Scottwall Associates, 1989.

Hagwood, Joseph J., Jr. *The California Debris Commission: A History of the Hydraulic Mining Industry in the Western Sierra Nevada of California, and of the Government Agency Charged with Its Regulation.* Sacramento: U.S. Army Corps of Engineers, 1981.

Hall, Peter, and Ann Markusen, eds. *Silicon Landscapes.* London: Allen and Unwin, 1985.

Haney, Lewis H. *A Congressional History of Railways in the United States.* New York: Augustus M. Kelley, 1968.

Hanks, Patrick, and Flavia Hodges, eds. *A Dictionary of Surnames*. London: Oxford University Press, 1988.

Hart, Jerome A. *In Our Second Century: From an Editor's Note-Book*. San Francisco: Pioneer Press, 1931.

Heizer, Robert F., ed. *The Destruction of the California Indians*. Lincoln: University of Nebraska Press, 1993.

———. *They Were Only Diggers: A Collection of Articles from California Newspapers, 1851–1866, on Indian and White Relations*. Ramona, CA: Bellena Press, 1974.

Heizer, Robert F., and M. A. Whipple, eds. *The California Indians: A Source Book*. Berkeley: University of California Press, 1971.

Hendricks, Gordon. *Albert Bierstadt: Painter of the American West*. New York: Harrison House, 1988.

Hey, David. *Family Names and Family History*. London: Hambledon, 2000.

Hinton, John Howard, assisted by several literary gentlemen in England and America. *The History and Topography of the United States of North America from the Earliest Period to the Present Time*. Vol. 2. Boston: Samuel Walker, 1834.

History of Alameda County: Geography, Topography, Soil and Townships. Oakland: M. W. Wood Publishers, 1883.

The History of Placer County, California, with Illustrations and Biographical Sketches of Its Prominent Men and Pioneers. Oakland: Thompson and West, 1882.

Hittell, Theodore H., and Charles H. Parker. *General Laws of California, 1850 to 1864*. San Francisco: H. H. Bancroft, 1871.

Hochfelder, David. *The Telegraph in America, 1832–1920*. Baltimore: Johns Hopkins University Press, 2012.

Holt, Michael F. *The Rise and Fall of American Whig Party: Jacksonian Politics and the Onset of the Civil War*. New York: Oxford University Press, 1999.

Howe, Daniel Walker. *What Hath God Wrought: The Transformation of America, 1815–1848*. New York: Oxford University Press, 2007.

Ingalls, Eleazar Stillman. *Journal of a Trip to California by the Overland Route across the Plains in 1850–51*. Fairfield, WA: Ye Galleon Press, 1979.

Irwin, Will. *The Making of a Reporter*. New York: G. P. Putnam's Sons, 1942.

Jones, Idwal. *Vines of California*. New York: William Morrow, 1949.

Jordan, David Starr. *The Days of a Man: Being the Memoirs of a Naturalist, Teacher, and Minor Prophet of Democracy*. Vols. 1 and 2. Yonkers-on-Hudson: World Book Company, 1922.

———. *The Stability of Truth: A Discussion of Reality as Related to Thought and Action*. New York: H. Holt, 1911.

Kaufman, Polly Welts, ed. *Apron Full of Gold: The Letters of Mary Jane Megquier from San Francisco, 1849–1856*. Albuquerque: University of New Mexico Press, 1994.

Kemble, John Haskell. *The Panama Route, 1848–1869*. Berkeley: University of California Press, 1943.

Kens, Paul. *Justice Stephen Field: Shaping Liberty from the Gold Rush to the Gilded Age*, Lawrence: University of Kansas Press, 1997.

Kern, Stephen. *The Culture of Time and Space, 1880–1918*. Cambridge. MA: Harvard University Press, 2003.

Klein, Maury. *Union Pacific: Birth of a Railroad, 1862–1893*. Garden City, NY: Doubleday, 1987.

Knapp, Louise Amelia, writing as Dame Shirley Clappe. *California in 1851: The Letters of Dame Shirley*. Vols. 1 and 2. San Francisco: Grabhorn Press, 1931.

Lamson, J. *Round Cape Horn: Voyage of the Passenger-Ship* James W. Paige, *from Maine to California in the Year 1852*. Bangor, ME: Press of O. F. and W. H. Knowles, 1878.

Lapp, Rudolph M. *Blacks in Gold Rush California*. New Haven, CT: Yale University Press, 1977.

Large, David Clay. *The Grand Spas of Europe: A History of Intrigue, Politics, Art, and Healing*. New York: Rowman and Littlefield, 2015.

Lavender, David. *The Great Persuader*. New York: Doubleday, 1970.

Lécuyer, Christophe. *Making Silicon Valley: Innovation and Growth of High Tech, 1930–1970*. Cambridge, MA: MIT Press, 2006.

Lenoir, Timothy. "Inventing the Entrepreneurial University: Stanford and the Coevolution of Silicon Valley." In *Building Technology Transfer within Research Universities: An Entrepreneurial Approach*, edited by Thomas J. Allen & Rory P. O'Shea, 88–128. Cambridge: Cambridge University Press, 2014.

Letwin, William. *Law and Economic Policy in America: The Evolution of the Sherman Anti-trust Act*. Chicago: University of Chicago Press, 1965.

Low, Frederick F., and Robert Becker, eds. *Some Reflections of an Early California Governor in a Short Dictated Memoir by Frederick F. Low, Ninth Governor of California, and Notes from an Interview between Governor Low and Hubert Howe Bancroft in 1883*. Sacramento: Sacramento Book Collector's Club, 1959.

Macaulay, Thomas Babington. *The History of England from the Accession of James II*. Vol. 1. London: Folio Press, 1985.

Madley, Benjamin. *An American Genocide: The United States and the California Indian Catastrophe*. New Haven, CT: Yale University Press, 2016.

Marranca, Bonnie, ed. *A Hudson Valley Reader*. New York: Overlook Press, 1991.

Mason, Jesse. *History of Amador County, California, with Illustrations and Biographical Sketches of Its Prominent Men and Pioneers*. Oakland: Thompson and West, Pacific Press Publishing House, 1881.

Mattes, Merrill J. *The Great Platte River Road: The Covered Wagon Mainline via Fort Kearny to Fort Laramie*. Lincoln: University of Nebraska Press, 1969.

May, Philip Ross. *Origins of Hydraulic Mining in California*. Oakland: Holmes, 1970.

McAfee, Ward. *California's Railroad Era, 1850–1911*. San Marino, CA: Golden West Books, 1973.

McKinstry, Bruce L., ed. *The California Gold Rush Overland Diary of Byron N. McKinstry, 1850–1852*. Glendale, CA: Arthur H. Clark, 1975.

Metzger, Walter P. *Academic Freedom in the Age of the University*. New York: Columbia University Press, 1955.

Moody, John. *The Railroad Builders: A Chronicle of the Welding of the States.* New Haven, CT: Yale University Press, 1919.

Myers, Sandra L., ed. *Ho for California: Women's Overland Diaries from the Huntington Library.* San Marino, CA: Huntington Library, 1991.

Nagel, Gunther W. *Iron Will: The Life and Letters of Jane Stanford.* Stanford: Stanford Alumni Association, 1975.

Nasaw, David. *Andrew Carnegie.* New York: Penguin, 2006.

———. *The Chief: The Life of William Randolph Hearst.* Boston: Houghton Mifflin, 2001.

O'Malley, Michael. *Keeping Watch: A History of American Time.* Washington, DC: Smithsonian Institution Press, 1990.

Orsi, Richard J. *Sunset Limited: The Southern Pacific Railroad and the Development of the American West, 1850–1930.* Berkeley: University of California Press, 2005.

Osborne, Carol M. *Museum Builders of the West.* Stanford: Stanford University Museum of Art, 1986.

Ott, John. *Manufacturing the Modern Patron in Victorian California: Cultural Philanthropy, Industrial Capital, and Social Authority.* Farnham, England: Ashgate, 2014.

Patterson, Edna, Louise Ulph, and Victor Goodwin. *Nevada's Northeast Frontier.* Reno: University of Nevada Press, 1991.

Paul, Rodman W. *California Gold: The Beginning of Mining in the West.* Lincoln: University of Nebraska Press, 1947.

Peninou, Ernest P. *Leland Stanford's Great Vina Ranch, 1881–1919: A Research Paper; The History of Senator Leland Stanford's Vina Vineyard and the World's Largest Winery Formerly the Site of Peter Lassen's Bosquejo and Henry Gerke's Ranch.* San Francisco: Yolo Hills Viticulture Society, 1991.

Perrow, Charles. *Organizing America: Wealth, Power, and the Origins of Corporate Capitalism.* Princeton, NJ: Princeton University Press, 2002.

Purtell, Joseph. *The Tiffany Touch.* Kingsport, TN: Kingsport Press, 1971.

Ramírez, Salvador A., ed. *The Octopus Speaks: The Colton Letters.* Carlsbad, CA: Tentacled Press, 1982.

Rawls, James J., and Walton Bean. *California: An Interpretive History.* 8th ed. New York: McGraw Hill, 2002.

Read, Georgia Willis, and Ruth Gaines, eds. *Gold Rush: The Journals, Drawings, and Other Papers of J. Goldsborough Bruff.* Vols. 1 and 2. New York: Columbia University Press, 1944.

Reisem, Richard O., and Andy Olenick. *Erie Canal Legacy: Architectural Treasures of the Empire State.* Rochester: Landmark Society of Western New York, 2000.

Report of the Albany Orphan Asylum for the Year Ending September Thirtieth 1919. Albany: Brandow Printing Co., 1920. https://babel.hathitrust.org/cgi/pt?id=uiu g.30112105275702;view=1up;seq=35.

Richards, Leonard L. *The California Gold Rush and the Coming of the Civil War.* New York: Alfred A. Knopf, 2007.

Roberts, Warren. *A Place in History: Albany in the Age of Revolution, 1775–1825*. Albany: State University of New York Press, 2010.

Rodriguez, Richard. *Days of Obligation: An Argument with My Mexican Father*. New York: Penguin, 1992.

Root, Henry. *Personal History and Reminiscences with Personal Opinions on Contemporary Events, 1845–1921*. San Francisco: Printed for private circulation, 1921.

Ross, Edward Alsworth. *Seventy Years of It*. New York: Arno Press, 1977.

Royce, Josiah. *California: A Study of American Character*. Berkeley: Heyday Books, 2002.

Rudolph, Frederick. *The American College and University: A History*. Athens: University of Georgia Press, 1990.

Russell, Amy Requa, ed. *Voyage to California Written at Sea, 1852: The Journal of Lucy Kendall Herrick*. San Marino, CA: Huntington Library, 1998.

Saxton, Alexander. *The Indispensable Enemy: Labor and the Anti-Chinese Movement in California*. Berkeley: University of California Press, 1975.

Sheriff, Carol. *The Artificial River: The Erie Canal and the Paradox of Progress, 1817–1862*. New York: Hill and Wang, 1996.

Shumsky, Neil Larry. *The Evolution of Political Protest and the Workingman's Party of California*. Columbus: Ohio University Press, 1991.

Shurkin, Joel N. *Broken Genius: The Rise and Fall of William Shockley*. New York: Macmillan, 2006.

Sinn, Elizabeth. *Pacific Crossing: California Gold, Chinese Migration, and the Making of Hong Kong*. Hong Kong: Hong Kong University Press, 2013.

Smith, Grant H. *The History of the Comstock Lode, 1850–1997*. Reno: Nevada Bureau of Mines and Geology in association with the University of Nevada Press, 1998.

Sobel, Robert. *Panic on Wall Street: A Classic History of America's Financial Disasters*. New York: Truman Talley Books / E. P. Dutton, 1988.

Soulé, Frank, John H. Gihon, and James Nisbet. *The Annals of San Francisco*. Berkeley: Berkeley Hills Books, 1999.

Stegner, Wallace. *Angle of Repose*. New York: Fawcett Crest, 1971.

Stevenson, Robert Louis. *From Scotland to Silverado*. Cambridge: Belknap Press of Harvard University Press, 1966.

Swanberg, W. A. *Citizen Hearst*. New York: Bantam, 1963.

Swisher, Carl Brent. *Stephen J. Field: Craftsman of the Law*. Washington, DC: Brookings Institution, 1930.

Taylor, Bayard. *Eldorado: Adventures in the Path of Empire*. Berkeley: Heyday Books / Santa Clara University, 2000.

Trachtenberg, Alan. *The Incorporation of America: Culture and Society in the Gilded Age*. New York: Hill and Wang, 2007.

Veysey, Laurence R. *The Emergence of the American University*. Chicago: University of Chicago Press, 1965.

Wagan, Robert M. "Shaker Chairs." In *A Hudson Valley Reader*, edited by Bonnie Marranca, 171–74. Woodstock, NY: Overlook Press, 1991.

Walker, Ronald W., Richard E. Turley Jr., and Glen M. Leonard. *Massacre at Mountain Meadows*. New York: Oxford University Press, 2011.

Weber, David J., ed. *Foreigners in Their Native Land: Historical Roots of the Mexican Americans*. Albuquerque: University of New Mexico Press, 1973.

White, Richard. *Railroaded: The Transcontinentals and the Making of Modern America*. New York: W. W. Norton, 2011.

Wilde, Oscar. *The Picture of Dorian Gray*. New York: Oxford University Press, 2008.

Williams, R. Hal. *The Democratic Party and California Politics, 1880–1896*. Stanford: Stanford University Press, 1973.

Yung, Judy, Gordon H. Chang, and Him Mark Lai, eds. *Chinese American Voices: From the Gold Rush to the Present*. Berkeley: University of California Press, 2006.

BOOKS: SECONDARY SOURCES

Ambrose, Stephen. *Nothing Like It in the World: The Men Who Built the Transcontinental Railroad, 1863–1869*. New York: Simon and Schuster, 2001.

Arrington, Leonard J. *Brigham Young: American Moses*. Urbana: University of Illinois Press, 1986.

Ball, Edward. *The Inventor and the Tycoon: A Gilded Age Murder and the Birth of Motion Pictures*. New York: Doubleday, 2013.

Bancroft, Hubert Howe. *Retrospection: Political and Personal*. New York: Bancroft Company, 1915.

Beatty, Jack. *Age of Betrayal: The Triumph of Money in America, 1865–1900*. New York: Vintage, 2008.

Blackhawk, Ned. *Violence over the Land: Indians and Empires in the Early American West*. Cambridge, MA: Harvard University Press, 2006.

Blondheim, Manahem. *News over the Wires: The Telegraph and the Flow of Public Information in America, 1844–1897*. Cambridge, MA: Harvard University Press, 1994.

Brodie, Fawn. *No Man Knows My History: The Life of Joseph Smith*. New York: Vintage, 1973.

Brown, James S. *California Gold: An Authentic History of the First Find with the Names of Those Interested in the Discovery*. Oakland: Pacific Press Publishing, 1894.

Burgess, Sherwood D. *The Water King: Anthony Chabot, His Life and Times*. Davis, CA: Panorama West Publishing, 1992.

Cain, Ella M. *The Story of Bodie*. San Francisco: Fearon Publishers, 1956.

Caughey, John Walton. *Hubert Howe Bancroft: Historian of the West*. New York: Russell and Russell, 1970.

Chaffin, Tom. *Pathfinder: John Charles Frémont and the Course of American Empire*. New York: Hill and Wang, 2002.

Chang, Gordon H., and Shelley Fisher Fishkin. *The Chinese and the Iron Road: Building the Transcontinental Railroad*. Stanford: Stanford University Press, 2019.

Chew, William F. *Nameless Builders of the Transcontinental Railroad*. Victoria, BC: Trafford Publishers, 2004.

Clark, George T. *Leland Stanford: War Governor of California, Railroad Builder and Founder of Stanford University.* Stanford: Stanford University Press, 1931.

Cole, Cornelius. *Memoirs of Cornelius Cole: Ex–senator of the United States from California.* New York: McLoughlin Brothers, 1908.

Cooper, Bruce C., ed. *Riding the Transcontinental Rails: Overland Travel on the Pacific Railroad, 1865–1881.* Philadelphia: Polyglot Press, 2005.

Crocker, Aimee. *And I'd Do It Again.* Mansfield Centre, CT: Martino Publishing, 2010.

Curtis, Edward. *Two California Sketches: William Watt, Representative Miner, a Tribute to His Memory; Leland Stanford, Ex-governor of California and President of the Central Pacific Railroad, a Biography.* San Francisco: Thomas' Steam Printing House, 1880.

Dana, Richard Henry. *Two Years before the Mast: A Personal Narrative.* New York: Signet, 1964.

Deverell, William. *Railroad Crossing: Californian and the Railroad, 1850–1910.* Berkeley: University of California Press, 1994.

Duffus, R. L. *The Innocents at Cedro: A Memoir of Thorstein Veblen and Some Others.* New York: Macmillan, 1944.

Eckman, Anne M. "The Transcontinental and Utah Central Railroads." In *Museum Memories,* vol. 1, edited by Daughters of Utah Pioneers Lesson Committee, 393–444. Salt Lake City: International Society, Daughters of Utah Pioneers, Talon Printing, 2009.

Emmons, Terrance, ed. *Around California in 1891.* Stanford: Stanford Alumni Association, 1991.

Evans, Cerinda W. *Collis Potter Huntington.* Newport News, VA: Mariners' Museum, 1954.

Fogel, Robert William. *Railroads and American Economic Growth: Essay in Econometric History.* Baltimore: Johns Hopkins Press, 1964.

Gordon, Sarah Barringer. *The Mormon Question: Polygamy and Constitutional Conflict in Nineteenth-Century America.* Chapel Hill: University of North Carolina Press, 2002.

Graham, Howard Jay. *Everyman's Constitution.* Madison: State Historical Society of Wisconsin, 1968.

Greeley, Horace. *An Overland Journey from New York to San Francisco in the Summer of 1859.* New York: Alfred A. Knopf, 1964.

Greever, William S. *The Bonanza West: The Story of the Western Mining Rushes, 1848–1900.* Norman: University of Oklahoma Press, 1963.

Gregory, James N. "The Shaping of California History." In *Encyclopedia of American Social History.* New York: Scribner, 1993.

Griffin, Helen S., ed. *The Diaries of Peter Decker: Overland to California in 1849 and Life in the Mines, 1850–51.* Georgetown, CA: Talisman Press, 1966.

Hayes, Derek. *Historical Atlas of California.* Berkeley: University of California Press, 2007.

Heizer, Robert F., ed. *Federal Concern about Conditions of California Indians, 1853 to 1913: Eight Documents.* Socorro, NM: Ballena Press, 1979.

Hill, Mary. *Geology of the Sierra Nevada*. Berkeley: University of California Press, 2006.

Hoexter, Corinne K. *From Canton to California: The Epic of Chinese Immigration*. New York: Four Winds Press, 1976.

Holliday, J. S. *The World Rushed In: California Gold Rush Experience*. New York: Simon and Schuster, 1981.

Hoyt, Edwin P. *Leland Stanford: A Biography of the Governor of California Who Built a Controversial Railroad and Founded a Great University*. London: Abelard-Schuman, 1967.

Hurtado, Albert L. *Indian Survival on the California Frontier*. New Haven, CT: Yale University Press, 1988.

Johnson, J. Edward. *History of the Supreme Court Justices of California*. Vols. 1 and 2. San Francisco: Bender-Moss, 1963.

Jordan, David Starr. *The Blood of the Nation, a Study of the Decay of Races through Survival of the Unfit*. Boston: American Unitarian Association, 1902.

Josephson, Matthe. *The Robber Barons: The Great American Capitalists, 1861–1901*. New York: Harcourt, Brace, 1934.

Kneiss, Gilbert H. *Bonanza Railroads*. Stanford: Stanford University Press, 1954.

Kraus, George. *High Road to Promontory: Building the Central Pacific across the High Sierra*. Palo Alto: American West Publishing, 1969.

Kurutz, Gary F. *The California Gold Rush: A Descriptive Bibliography*. San Francisco: Book Club of California, 1997.

Lantis, David, Rodney Steiner, and Arthur Karinen. *California: Land of Contrast*. Dubuque, IA: Kendall / Hunt Publishing, 1977.

Larkin, F. Daniel. *Pioneer American Railroads: The Mohawk and Hudson and the Saratoga and Schenectady*. Fleischmanns, NY: Purple Mountain Press, 1995.

Latta, Estelle. *Controversial Mark Hopkins*. Sacramento: Cothran Historical and Research Foundation, 1963.

Lavender, David. *Nothing Seemed Impossible: William C. Ralston and Early San Francisco*. Sanger, CA: American West Publishing, 1975.

Lewis, Oscar. *The Big Four*. New York: Alfred A. Knopf, 1938.

———. *Sea Routes to the Gold Fields: The Migration by Water to California in 1849–1852*. New York: Alfred A. Knopf, 1949.

Licht, Walter. *Working for the Railroad: The Organization of Work in the Nineteenth Century*. Princeton, NJ: Princeton University Press, 1983.

Matthews, Glenna. *The Golden State in the Civil War: Thomas Starr King, the Republican Party, and the Birth of Modern California*. New York: Cambridge University Press, 2012.

McCague, James. *Moguls and Iron Men: The Story of the First Transcontinental Railroad*. New York: Harper and Row, 1964.

McClellan, Robert. *The Heathen Chinese: A Study of American Attitudes Towards China, 1890–1905*. Columbus: Ohio State University Press, 1971.

Melendy, H. Brett, and Benjamin F. Gilbert. *The Governors of California: Peter H. Burnett to Edmund G. Brown*. Georgetown, CA: Talisman Press, 1965.

Morgan, Dale, ed. *Overland in 1846: Diaries and Letters of the California-Oregon Trail.* Vols. 1 and 2. Lincoln: University of Nebraska Press, 1993.

Nagel, Gunther W. *Jane Stanford: Her Life and Letters.* Stanford: Stanford Alumni Association, 1975.

Norris, Frank. *The Octopus: A Story of California.* New York: Penguin, 1986.

O'Connor, Richard. *Iron Wheels and Broken Men: Railroad Barons and the Plunder of the West.* New York: G. P. Putnam's Sons, 1973.

Petry, Bonnie L., and Michael Burgess, eds. *San Quentin: The Evolution of a Californian State Prison.* Richmond, TX: Ergodebooks, 2005.

Platt, Anthony M., with Cecilia E. O'Leary. *Bloodlines: Rediscovering Hitler's Nuremberg Laws, from Patton's Trophy to Public Memorial.* Boulder: Paradigm Publishers, 2006.

Rayner, Richard. *The Associates.* New York: W. W. Norton, 2008.

Reaney, P. H. *A Dictionary of British Surnames.* Abingdon, England: Routledge and Kegan Paul, 1958.

———. *The Origin of English Surnames.* Abingdon, England: Routledge and Kegan Paul, 1980.

Redding, Benjamin Bernard. *A Sketch of the Life of Mark Hopkins of California.* San Francisco: A. L. Bancroft and Company, 1881.

Rich, Paul J. *Stanford Patriarchs: Preliminary Notes on the Prosopographical Significance of the Beards, Dundrearies, and Muttonchops of the First (Rather Anonymous) Trustees of Stanford University, with the Rare Bancroft Company Edition of the Founding Documents.* Cambridge: Enneit, 1993.

Riesenberg, Felix. *Cape Horn.* New York: Dodd, Mead, 1939.

Robinson, John W. *Southern California's First Railroad.* Los Angeles: Dawson's Book Shop, 1978.

Sabin, Edwin L. *Building the Pacific Railway.* Philadelphia: J. B. Lippincott, 1919.

Scott, James. *Sacramento's Gold Rush Saloons: El Dorado in a Shot Glass.* Charleston, SC: Arcadia Publishing, 2014.

Secret, William B. *Behind San Quentin's Walls.* Fresno: Craven Street Books, 2015.

Shutes, Milton H. *Lincoln and California.* Stanford: Stanford University Press, 1943.

Smith, Stacey L. *Freedom's Frontier: California and the Struggle over Unfree Labor, Emancipation, and Reconstruction.* Chapel Hill: University of North Carolina Press, 2013.

Starr, Kevin. *Americans and the California Dream, 1850–1915.* New York: Oxford University Press, 1973.

Stiles, T. J. *The First Tycoon: The Epic Life of Cornelius Vanderbilt.* New York: Alfred A. Knopf, 2009.

Stillman, J. D. B. *The Horse in Motion: As Shown by Instantaneous Photography, with a Study on Animal Mechanics Founded on Anatomy and the Revelations of the Camera, in Which Is Demonstrated the Theory of the Quadrupedal Locomotion.* Executed and published under the auspices of Leland Stanford. Boston: James R. Osgood and Company, 1881.

Stoddard, William O. *Men of Business.* New York: Charles Scribner's Sons, 1893.

Sung, Betty Lee. *Mountain of Gold: The Story of the Chinese in America.* New York: Macmillan, 1967.

Swisher, Carl Brent. *Motivation and Political Technique in the California Constitutional Convention, 1878–79.* New York: Da Capo, 1969.

Taylor, George Rogers. *The Transportation Revolution, 1815–1860.* North Castle, NY: M. E. Sharpe, 1951.

Tong, Benson. *Unsubmissive Women: Chinese Prostitutes in Nineteenth-Century San Francisco.* Norman: University of Oklahoma Press, 1994.

Tutorow, Norman E. *The Governor: The Life and Legacy of Leland Stanford a California Colossus.* Vols. 1 and 2. Spokane, WA: Arthur H. Clark, 2004.

———. *Leland Stanford: Man of Many Careers.* Tacoma, WA: Pacific Coast Publishers, 1971.

Usselman, Steven W. *Regulating Railroad Innovation.* Cambridge: Cambridge University Press, 2002.

Wilkins, James H. "The Evolution of a State Prison: Historical Narrative of the Ten Years from 1851 to 1861, during the Period When the Care and Employment of Convicts Was Turned Over to Lessees. Typed manuscript prepared by Clinton T. Duffy, Warden, California State Prison, San Quentin, California, 1918." In *San Quentin: The Evolution of a Californian State Prison.* Richmond, TX: Ergodebooks, 2005.

Wilson, Neill C., and Frank J. Taylor. *Southern Pacific: The Roaring Story of a Fighting Railroad.* New York: McGraw-Hill, 1952.

Young, Alida E. *Land of the Iron Dragon.* Garden City, NY: Doubleday, 1978.

JOURNALS

Adams, Charles F., Jr. "Railroad Inflation." *North American Review* 108, no. 222 (January 1869): 130–64.

Altenberg, Lee. "An End to Capitalism: Leland Stanford's Forgotten Vision." *Sandstone and Tile* (Stanford Historical Society) 14, no. 1 (Winter 1990): 8–20.

Anderson, David L. "Between Two Cultures: Frederick F. Low in China." *California History* 59, no. 3 (Fall 1980): 240–54.

Bartky, Ian R. "The Invention of Railroad Time." *Railroad History,* no. 148 (Spring 1983): 13–22.

Boswell, Terry E. "A Split Labor Analysis of Discrimination against Chinese Immigrants, 1850–1882." *American Sociological Review* 51, no. 3 (June 1986): 352–71.

Brown, Charles Leroy. "Abraham Lincoln and the Illinois Central Railroad, 1857–1860." *Journal of the Illinois State Historical Society* 36, no. 2 (1943): 121–63.

Carnochan, W. B. "The Case of Julius Goebel: Stanford, 1905." *American Scholar* 72, no. 3 (Summer 2003): 95–108.

Caruth, Donald L., and Gail D. Caruth. "Stanford University: A Case Study in Commitment." *Journal of Business Studies Quarterly* 4, no. 2 (2012): 159–69.

Clark, George T. "Leland Stanford and H. H. Bancroft's 'History': A Bibliographical Curiosity." *Papers of the Bibliographical Society of America* 27, no. 1 (1933): 12–23.

Cole, Donald B. Review of *The Age of Jackson after Forty Years*, by Arthur M. Schlesinger Jr. *Reviews in American History* 14, no. 1 (March 1986): 149–59.

Collins, Wayne D. "Trusts and the Origins of Antitrust Legislation." *Fordham Law Review* 81, no. 5 (April 2013): 2279–348.

Conan, Edwin T., Jr. "Sidelights on the Investment Policies of Stanford, Huntington, Hopkins, and Crocker." *Bulletin of the Business Historical Society* 16, no. 5 (November 1942): 85–89.

Cowan, Richard O. "Steel Rails and the Utah Saints." *Journal of Mormon History* 27, no. 2 (Fall 2001): 177–96.

Fleisig, Heywood. "The Central Pacific Railroad and the Railroad Land Grant Controversy." *Journal of Economic History* 35, no. 3 (September 1975): 552–66.

Guinn, J. M. "Pioneer Railroads of Southern California." *Annual Publication of the Historical Society of Southern California* 8, no. 3 (1911): 188–92.

Guly, Henry. "Medicinal Brandy." *Resuscitation* 82, no. 7 (2011): 951–54.

Helmich, Mary A. "The Railroad King's Party." *Sacramento County Historical Society* 35, no. 4 (Winter 1989).

Hoyt, Franklyn. "The Los Angeles & San Pedro: First Railroad South of the Tehachapis." *California Historical Society Quarterly* 32, no. 4 (December 1953): 327–48.

Hurt, Peyton. "The Rise and Fall of the 'Know Nothings' in California." *California Historical Society Quarterly* 9, no. 1 (March 1930): 16–49.

Jenks, Leland H. "Railroads as an Economic Force in American Development." *Journal of Economic History* 4, no. 1 (May 1944): 1–20.

Kauer, Ralph. "The Workingmen's Party of California." *Pacific Historical Review* 13, no. 3 (September 1944): 278–91.

Kibby, Leo P. "Union Loyalty of California's Civil War Governors." *California Historical Society Quarterly* 44 (1965): 311–22.

Kotchemidova, Christina. "Why We Say 'Cheese': Producing the Smile in Snapshot Photography." *Critical Studies in Media Communication* 22, no. 1 (March 2005): 2–25.

Kranzberg, Melvin. "Technology and History: 'Kranzberg's Laws.'" *Technology and Culture* 27, no. 3 (July 1986): 544–60.

Kraus, George. "Chinese Laborers and the Construction of the Central Pacific." *Utah Historical Quarterly* 37, no. 1 (1969): 41–57.

McAfee, Ward M. "A Constitutional History of Railroad Rate Regulation in California, 1879–1911." *Pacific Historical Review* 37, no. 3 (August 1968): 265–79.

———. "Local Interests and Railroad Regulation in California during the Granger Decade." *Pacific Historical Review* 37, no. 1 (February 1968): 51–66.

McClure, Maggie, and Boutwell Dunlap. "Some Facts concerning Leland Stanford and His Contemporaries in Placer County." *Quarterly of the California Historical Society* 2, no. 3 (October 1923): 203–10.

Morris, Eric. "From Horse Power to Horsepower." *Access*, no. 30 (Spring 2007): 2–9.

Nash, Gerald D. "The California Railroad Commission, 1876–1911." *Southern California Quarterly* 44, no. 4 (December 1962): 287–305.

Nilan, Roxanne. "The Life and Times of a Victorian Lady: Jane Lathrop Stanford." *Sandstone and Tile* (Stanford Historical Society) 21, no. 3 (Summer 1997).

Oosterhuis, Harry. "Sexual Modernity in the Works of Richard von Krafft-Ebing and Albert Moll." *Cambridge Journals Medical History* 56, no. 2 (April 2012): 133–55.

Seeman, Carolyn. "California's Constitutional Response to the Railroad: The Commission of 1880–1882." *Southern Californic Quarterly* 81, no. 4 (Winter 1999): 423–48.

Spier, Robert F.G. "Food Habits of Nineteenth-Century California Chinese." *California Historical Society Quarterly* 37, no. 1 (March 1958): 79–84.

Stanley, Gerald. "Slavery and the Origins of the Republican Party in California." *Southern California Quarterly* 60, no. 1 (Spring 1978): 1–16.

Strazdes, Diana. "The Millionaire's Palace: Leland Stanford's Commission for Pottier & Stymus in San Francisco." *Winterthur Portfolio* 36, no. 4 (Winter 2001): 213–43.

———. "The Visual Rhetoric of the Leland Stanford Mansion in Sacramento." *Stanford University Museum of Art Journal* 14–15 (1994–95): 13–24.

Wheat, Carl I. "A Sketch of the Life of Theodore D. Judah." *California Historical Society Quarterly* 4, no. 3 (September 1925): 219–71.

White, Richard. "Information, Markets, and Corruption: Transcontinental Railroads in the Gilded Age." *Journal of American History* 90, no. 1 (June 2003): 19–43.

DISSERTATIONS AND THESES

Andrew, Bunyan Hadley. "Charles Crocker." MA thesis, University of California, Berkeley, 1931.

Bristow, Barbara M. "Mussel Slough Tragedy: Railroad Struggle or Land Gamble?" MA thesis, Fresno State College, 1971.

Cain, Julie A. "The Chinese and the Stanfords: Immigration Rhetoric in Nineteenth-Century California." MA thesis, California State University, East Bay, 2011.

Cioffi, Ralph Walter. "Mark Hopkins, Inside Man of the Big Four." MS thesis, University of California, Berkeley, 1950.

Dayton, Dello Grimmett. "The California Militia." PhD dissertation, University of California, Berkeley, 1951.

Fahey, Frank Michael. "Denis Kearney, a Study in Demagoguery." PhD dissertation, Stanford University, 1956.

Garber, Paul Neff. "The Gadsden Treaty." PhD dissertation, University of Pennsylvania, 1923.

George, Hardy Sloan. "Thomas Hill (1829–1906)." MA thesis, University of California, Los Angeles, 1963.

McConnell, Joseph A., Jr. "The Stanford Vina Ranch." MA thesis, Stanford University, 1961.

McKinney, William Clyde. "The Mussel Slough Episode: A Chapter in the Settlement of the San Joaquin Valley, 1865–1880." MA thesis, University of California, 1948.

Mudgett, Margaret H. "The Political Career of Leland Stanford." MS thesis, University of Southern California, 1933.

Murian, Richard Miller. "Booksellers and Libraries in Sacramento, 1849–1862." MA thesis, California State University, 1975.

Price, Sister M. Jane. "A History of Port Washington, Ozaukee County, Wisconsin." MA thesis, DePaul University, 1943.

Spoehr, Luther William. "Progress' Pilgrim: David Starr Jordan and the Circle of Reform, 1891–1931." PhD dissertation, Stanford University, July 1975.

Yen, Tzu-kuei. "Chinese Workers and the First Transcontinental Railroad of the United States of America." PhD dissertation, St. John's University, 1977.

GOVERNMENT AND LEGAL DOCUMENTS

California Department of Parks and Recreation. *Interpretive Plan.* Sacramento: California Department of Parks and Recreation, December 2002.

———. *Leland Stanford Mansion State Historic Park: Historic Structures Report.* Sacramento: State of California, the Resources Agency, California State Parks, April 1996.

Central Pacific Company vs. Alfred A. Cohen. Argument of Mr. Cohen, the Defendant, in Person, before the Honorable W. P. Daingerfield, Presiding Judge, without a Jury. Twelfth District Court, City and County of San Francisco, 1876.

Concord Historical Commission. *Historic Resources Masterplan of Concord, Massachusetts.* Concord: Concord Historical Commission, 2001.

Coroner of Honolulu. *Coroner's Inquest in re Death of Jane Lathrop Stanford, District of Honolulu, Island of Oahu, February 28, 1905.* Honolulu: Coroner's Office, 1905.

———. *Coroner's Inquest in re Jane L. Stanford, District of Honolulu, Island of Oahu, March 6, 1905.* Honolulu: Coroner's Office, 1905.

Estate of Stanford, 49 Cal.2d 120 (1957). https://scocal.stanford.edu/opinion/estate-stanford-29728.

Hay, Duncan. *Statement of Significance; Erie Canalway National Heritage Corridor Preservation and Management Plan.* Waterford, NY: National Park Service, 2006.

International Conference Held at Washington for the Purpose of Fixing a Prime Meridian and a Universal Day: Protocols of the Proceedings. Washington, D.C. Gibson Brothers, Printers and Bookbinders, 1884.

Johnston-Dodds, Kimberly. *Early California Laws and Policies Related to California Indians.* Prepared at the request of Senator John L. Burton, President Pro Tempore. Sacramento: California Research Bureau, September 2002.

National Park Service. *San Quentin State Prison, Building 22.* Washington, DC: Historic American Buildings Survey, National Park Service, U.S. Department of the Interior, 1933–. Library of Congress, https://www.loc.gov/item/ca3606.

Office of the Board of State Prison Directors. *Annual Report of the State Prison Directors, for the Year 1862.* Sacramento: Benj. P. Avery, State Printer, 1863. https://babel.hathitrust.org/cgi/pt?id=uc1.31175004160258;view=1up;seq=11;size=125.

Placer County Clerk-Recorder. *Index to Deeds.* Vol. 1, *1851–1872, S–Z, Placer County.* Auburn, CA: Placer County Clerk-Recorder, 1851–72.

Report of the Commission and of the Minority Commissioner of the United States Pacific Railway Commission. Washington, DC: Government Printing Office, 1887. (Abbreviated *Rpt. of Comm. PRC* in notes.)

Stanford, Leland, Pres't C.P.R.R. Co. *Central Pacific Railroad: Statement Made to the President of the United States, and Secretary of the Interior of the Progress of the Work.* Sacramento: H. S. Crocker & Co., Printers, October 10, 1865.

State of California. *Appendices to the Journal of the Senate and Assembly of the State of California, 1862–64.* Sacramento: O.–M. Clayes, State Printer, 1864.

———. *Appendix: Abstract of Evidence Taken before the Assembly Committee on Corporations, Nineteenth Session of the Legislature of the State of California, January 1872.* Sacramento: T. A. Springer, 1872.

———. *Appendix to Journals of the Senate and Assembly, Fourteenth Session of the Legislature of the State of California, 1863.* Sacramento: Benj. P. Avery, State Printer, 1863.

———. *Bureau of Labor Statistics, 1887–1888.* John J. Tobin, Commissioner. Sacramento: J. D. Young, Supt. State Printing, 1388.

———. *Journal of the Senate during the Fourteenth Session of the Legislature of the State of California, 1863.* Sacramento: Benj. P. Avery, State Printer, 1863.

———. *Journals of the Senate and Assembly of the State of California, 1862–64.* Sacramento: O. M. Clayes, State Printer, 1864.

———. *Report of the Committee on Corporations of the Assembly of California Twenty-Fifth Session, 1883.* Sacramento: James J. Ayers, Supt. State Printing, 1883.

U.S. Senate. *Testimony Taken by the United States Pacific Railway Commission.* 50th Congress, 1st session (1887). (Abbreviated *PRC* in notes.)

The War of Rebellion: A Compilation of the Official Records of the Union and Confederate Armies. Published under the direction of Daniel S. Lamont, Secretary of War. Series I, vol. L in two parts. Part II, correspondence, etc. Washington, DC: Government Printing Office, 1897.

Waterman, R. W. *Biennial Message of Governor R. W. Waterman to the Legislature of the State of California.* Sacramento: J. D. Young, Supt. State Printing, 1888.

MANUSCRIPTS, CORRESPONDENCE, AND COLLECTIONS

Austin, Henry Carter. "The Diary of Henry Carter Austin." August 1869. Courtesy of the National Park Service and grandson David B. Austin.

Bancroft, Hubert Howe. "Biography of Leland Stanford, 1880–1890." Manuscript research, 15 folders. Bancroft Library, University of California, Berkeley.

Barr, Jeanette, Historical Society historian, to Ralph W. Hansen, Stanford University archivist. June 1, 1974. Port Washington Historical Society, Port Washington, Wisconsin.

Bigler, Henry. Henry Bigler diary. 1848. Society of California Pioneers, San Francisco.

Brown, Arthur. Arthur Brown Collection. California State Railroad Museum Library, Sacramento.

Clay, Cassius Marcellus, to Salmon Chase. December 21, 1842. In *Annual Report of the AHA*, 1902. Salmon P. Chase Papers. Library of Congress, Washington, DC.

Crocker, Charles. "Facts Gathered from the Lips of Charles Crocker, H. H. Bancroft's *Chronicles of the Builders of the Commonwealth*, 1865–1890." Bancroft Library, University of California, Berkeley.

Dodge, Grenville M. "Biography of Major General Grenville M. Dodge from 1831 to 1871." Vol. 4 (of 5 typewritten by Dodge). 1914. Council Bluffs Public Library Special Collections, Council Bluffs, Iowa.

"The Doolittle Family in America." Vol. 8. N.d. Doolittle Papers. FamilySearch Library, Oakland LDS temple, Oakland.

Gallatin, Albert. "The Dictation of Albert Gallatin." Ca. 1889. Bancroft Library, University of California, Berkeley.

Historic Resources Masterplan of Concord, Massachusetts. 2001. Concord Historical Commission, Concord, Massachusetts.

Huntington, Collis P. Collis Potter Huntington Papers. Special Collections Research Center, Syracuse University Libraries.

———. "Letters from Collis P. Huntington to Mark Hopkins, Leland Stanford, Charles Crocker, E. B. Crocker, Charles F. Crocker, and D. D. Cotton from August 20, 1867 to August 5, 1869." Bound book of handwritten letters, transcribed and printed 1892. Collis Potter Huntington Papers, Special Collections Research Center, Huntington Library, San Marino.

Jordan, David Starr. David Starr Jordan Papers. Department of Special Collections and University Archives, Stanford University Libraries.

Judah, Anna Ferona Pierce. Correspondence concerning her husband, Theodore D. Judah. 1889. Bancroft Library, University of California, Berkeley.

Judah, Theodore D. "Central Pacific Railroad Company of California." Towne and Bacon Excelsior Book and Job Office, San Francisco, 1860. California State Railroad Museum, Library and Archives, Sacramento.

———. "Pacific Railroad, Report of Theodore D. Judah, Accredited Agent Pacific Railroad Convention upon His Operations in the Atlantic States." August 1860. California State Railroad Museum, Library and Archives, Sacramento.

Miller, Edward H. "Notes Regarding Mark Hopkins and Related Material, 1878–1883." Bancroft Library, University of California, Berkeley.

"Report of the Chief Engineer of the Central Pacific Railroad Company of California on His Operations in the Atlantic States." H. S. Crocker & Co., Sacramento, 1862. California State Railroad Museum, Library and Archives, Sacramento.

"Report of the Chief Engineer on the Preliminary Survey, Cost of Construction, and Estimated Revenue of the Central Pacific Railroad of California, across the Sierra Nevada Mountains, from Sacramento to the Eastern Boundary of California." H. S. Crocker & Co., Sacramento, October 22, 1862. California State Railroad Museum, Library and Archives, Sacramento.

"Report of the Chief Engineer upon Recent Surveys, Progress of Construction, and an Approximate Estimate of Cost of the First Division of Fifty Miles of the Central Pacific Railroad of Cal." James Anthony and Co., Sacramento, July 1, 1863. California State Railroad Museum, Library and Archives, Sacramento.

Sessions, David R. "The Dictation of Collis P. Huntington." January 14, 1889. Bancroft Library, University of California, Berkeley.

Stanford, Jane. Jane Lathrop Stanford Papers. Department of Special Collections and University Archives, Stanford University Libraries.

Stanford, Josiah. "The Dictation of Josiah Stanford." September 19, 1889. Bancroft Library, University of California, Berkeley.

Stanford, Leland. Governor Leland Stanford Papers. California State Archives, Sacramento.

———. Leland Stanford's manuscript editing of "The Biography of Leland Stanford, 1880–1890," by Hubert Howe Bancroft. Bancroft Library, University of California, Berkeley.

———. Outgoing correspondence. Leland Stanford Collection (SC0512). Department of Special Collections and University Archives, Stanford University Libraries.

———. Portions of unidentified dictations concerning Leland Stanford. 1890. Bancroft Library, University of California, Berkeley.

Stillman, Dr. Jacob, to his son, John. Februry 24, 1860. Stillman Folder. California Historical Society, San Francisco.

Sutter, John. Private letter from John Sutter to Mariano Vallejo. February 10, 1848. California Historical Society, San Francisco.

Twain, Mark. Notebook. July 1885. Mark Twain Papers and Project. Bancroft Library, University of California, Berkeley.

Vital Records of Massachusetts to 1850. New England Genealogical Society, Charlestown, Massachusetts.

Wheaton, Henry. "Day Book of Henry Wheaton." Vols. 2 and 3. Handwritten manuscript. Ca. 1840. Rare Book Collection. Charles B. Sears Law Library, State University of New York, Buffalo.

PAMPHLETS

The California King: His Conquests, Crimes, Confederates, Counselors, Courtiers and Vassals; Stanford's Post-prandial New-Year's Day Soliloquy. San Francisco: San Francisco News Company, 1876.

Crothers, George E. *Outline of the History of the Founding of the Leland Stanford Junior University.* Reprint from the Fortieth Anniversary number of the *Stanford Illustrated Review* (Stanford Alumni Association) 33, no. 1 (1931).

The Great Dutch Flat Swindle!! The City of San Francisco Demands Justice!! The Matter in Controversy, and the Present State of the Question: An Address to the Board of Supervisors, Officers and People of San Francisco. [San Francisco, 1864.]

Jones, J. Roy. *The Old Central Pacific Hospital.* N.p.: Western Association of Railway Surgeons, 1961.

Nash, Herbert C. *In Memoriam: Leland Stanford, Jr.* N.p.: Privately printed, 1884.

Stanford: A Man, a Woman and a University. Stanford: Publications Service, Encina Hall, Stanford University, 1962.

State of New York Chamber of Commerce. *Report of the Special Committee on Railroad Transportation on the Reply Made by Hon. Leland Stanford, April 7, 1881.* New York: Press of the Chamber of Commerce, 1881.

Widney, R. M. *Los Angeles County Subsidy: Which Subsidy Shall I Vote For, or Shall I Vote against Both? Discussed from a Business Standpoint for the Business Community.* Los Angeles: Los Angeles Star Print, 1872.

MAGAZINES AND NEWSPAPERS

Arizona RepublicCalifornia Mail Bag
California Spirit of the Times
Cheyenne Daily Sun
Chicago Tribune
Daily Alta California
The Emigrant
Fort Wayne Sentinel
Kern County Californian
Los Angeles Herald
Los Angeles Times
Milwaukee Journal
New Ulm Review
New York Press
New York Sun
New York Times
New York Tribune
New York World
Pacific Commercial Advertiser
Port Washington Democrat
Red Bluff Independent
Reno Evening Gazette
Sacramento Bee
Sacramento Daily Union
Sacramento Record-Union
San Francisco Call
San Francisco Chronicle
San Francisco (Daily) Examiner
Santa Cruz Sentinel

Themis
United States Magazine and Democratic Review
The Wasp

CURATED WEBSITES

Chinese Railroad Workers in North America Project at Stanford University. http://
    web.stanford.edu/group/chineserailroad/cgi-bin/wordpress.
"A Fragile Machine: California Senator John Conness." 2008. *The Free Library.* https://
    www.thefreelibrary.com/A+fragile+machine%3a+California+senator+John+Co
    nness.-a0189159887.
Lincoln, Abraham. "First Annual Message." December 3, 1861. The American Presi-
    dency Project. https://www.presidency.ucsb.edu/node/202175.
Miaw, Calvin. "Three Interpretations of the Role of Chinese Railroad Workers in the
    Construction of the Central Pacific Railroad." Chinese Railroad Workers in North
    America Project at Stanford University. http://web.stanford.edu/group/chinese-
    railroad/cgi-bin/wordpress/three-interpretations-of-the-role-of-chinese-railroad-
    workers-in-the-construction-of-the-central-pacific-railroad-2.
Polk, James K. "Fourth Annual Message." December 5, 1848. The American Presidency
    Project https://www.presidency.ucsb.edu/node/200618.
Sacramento City election totals. *Sacramento Daily Union,* April 1857. California
    Digital Newspaper Collection. https://cdnc.ucr.edu/cgi-bin/cdnc?a=d&d=
    SDU18570408.2.8&e=-------en--20--1--txt-txIN--------1.

OTHER

Stanford Family Collections. Cantor Arts Center at Stanford University.

INDEX

ABOUT THE AUTHOR

Journalist and historian Roland De Wolk is a graduate of the History Department at the University of California, Berkeley. A distinguished investigative reporter, he has been honored by most professional citations in his field. Among many international, national, and regional stories, he has covered Stanford University, Silicon Valley, and the growth of tech for decades. De Wolk has been an adjunct professor at San Francisco State University for twenty-five years, an online journalism pioneer, and author. He grew up in the San Francisco Bay Area, where he, his wife, and children still live. More can be learned at RolandDeWolk.com.

Founded in 1893,
UNIVERSITY OF CALIFORNIA PRESS
publishes bold, progressive books and journals
on topics in the arts, humanities, social sciences,
and natural sciences—with a focus on social
justice issues—that inspire thought and action
among readers worldwide.

The UC PRESS FOUNDATION
raises funds to uphold the press's vital role
as an independent, nonprofit publisher, and
receives philanthropic support from a wide
range of individuals and institutions—and from
committed readers like you. To learn more, visit
ucpress.edu/supportus.